st. Pete -

1|4

Victy
Sve Rd Ramp
onto x PSwy
to Glen Exit

1 way
to Bach of NGE

Pg. 298 Course of Crisis
ambiguous language of VII
was deliberate w/ agenda
forward looking twd VIII which
would complete VII which
progressives saw as merely
a pt. of departure -
Congar, 7
Kung

To Marianne Mastropolo, with my best regards. In Jesu et Maria, [handwritten inscription] *March 9, 2012*

COLLECTION

ELI, ELI, LAMMA SABACTHANI? [1]

Volume I

IN THE MURKY WATERS
OF VATICAN II

3ʳᵈ EDITION

Foreword by Fr. Malachi Martin, S.J.

Atila Sinke Guimarães

---

1. See explanation for the choice of this title in § 14 of the General Introduction.

ISBN-13: 978-0-9726516-7-7
Library of the Congress Number: 2007908238

Tradition in Action, Inc.
P.O. Box 23135
Los Angeles, CA 90023
www.TraditionInAction.org

"The Council is like a spring that becomes a river. The river's current follows us even though its spring may be far away. One may say that the Council leaves itself as a legacy to the Church that held it. The Council does not oblige us so much to look back at the act of its convening, but it does oblige us to take into account the inheritance we have received, which is present and will remain present in the future. What is this inheritance?" [2]

Paul VI

---

2 Paul VI, General Audience of January 12, 1966 *Insegnamenti di Paolo VI,* Tipografia Poliglotta Vaticana, vol. IV, p. 698.

TABLE OF CONTENTS

*   *   *

SPECIAL FOREWORD

Fr. Malachi Martin, S.J.

This first volume of the Collection *Eli, Eli, Lamma Sabacthani?* establishes the author Atila Sinke Guimarães as one of the best informed latter-day students of that epochal event, the Second Vatican Council. Up to this moment, the most encyclopedic and detailedly informed examination of the Council was provided by Professor Amerio in his *Iota Unum.* Guimarães' Collection bids fair to replace *Iota Unum* as the best all-purpose source-book about the Council; and it is not hazardous or rash to predict that this work of Guimarães will be a standard reference work on the subject – and well into the 21st century.

The title of this first volume, *In the Murky Waters of Vatican II,* tells exactly what the contents are. All of us who lived through the years of Vatican II (1962-1965) and have had to deal with the consequences can recognize immediately the pinpoint accuracy of this first volume: The ambiguity, cultivated and, as it were, perfected in the composition of the sixteen main documents of the Council, is now seen as the most skillful means devised to undo the essential Roman-ness and Catholicism of the Roman Catholic Church, and to deliver that entire one-billion member institutional organization into the ready and eager hands of those for whom the existence of the traditional Papacy and hierarchical organization has long been anathema.

One reads in this volume with a certain sickening feeling of the unified way in which the Church's own theologians and Prelates conspired willingly to bring about the present trend to the de-Romanization and de-Catholicizing of the once monolithic institution.

New York, September 25, 1997

FOREWORD

To shed light where before there was obscurity, to bring order to mayhem is a great charity that can be done by one man for another not only in the realm of things, but also in that of events and ideas. For the last three decades, a controversy regarding Vatican Council II has engaged "conservatives" and "liberals" inside the Catholic Church, with the former group performing every form of intellectual gymnastics in order to comprehensively fit the "spirit" and the "letter" of the Council into the traditional Magisterium of the Church. At the same time, the progressivistss and neo-modernists have pushed increasingly radical reforms based on this "spirit" and "letter" of the Council. The debate has been further confused by certain ecclesiastics, who show amazing tolerance toward heresies, yet lose their ecumenical spirit of tolerance when dealing with those who stand for Tradition.

It is a great intellectual *tour de force* of Atila Sinke Guimarães to have prepared this eleven-volume Collection with unprecedented documentation entitled *Eli, Eli, Lamma Sabacthani?* in order to clarify and analyze with a scholarly and objective study the letter, spirit, thinking and fruits of the Second Vatican Council. Doing so, he provides us with a most important tool for the defense of the Holy Catholic Church against progressivist currents, such as the *We Are Church* movement, which is now calling for a Third Vatican Council "to finish the work begun at Vatican Council II." For years, faithful Catholics have struggled with the avowed ambiguities present in the conciliar documents. Using an inductive method, Atila S. Guimarães has delimited and documented these ambiguities, their historical roots and their consequences in the impressive analysis entitled *In the Murky Waters of Vatican II.*

The polemics over the letter and spirit of Vatican Council II have been at the center of Church life over the last three decades and raise great passion on all sides of the religious/ideological spectrum. It takes great care, as well as rare courage, to stand up and speak frankly about what the Council mentors intended when hitherto there have been veiled allusions or undocumented accusations. As we reach the threshold of the new millenium with all the events and promises it portends in the ecclesiastical sphere, the work of Atila Sinke Guimarães takes on a new urgency and importance.

These last thirty years the Church has been afflicted by a particularly strange phenomenon – the fear of any comprehensive, objective critique of a controversial Council. Fear of being labeled "integrist," "narrow-minded," "close-minded" or out of synch with the Vatican has set unwritten, but predetermined, limits to this debate. This one-sided fear – for there is no fear on the side of the progressivists to draw ever more radical consequences from Conciliar ambiguities – has only proven its protagonists to have a profound lack of objectivity.

"And refrain not to speak in the time of salvation." (Eccles. 4:28). Failure to define, clarify and then arrest doctrinal and spiritual ambiguity ultimately has been the vehicle used by the progressivists to neutralize opponents and to give free reign to dissent and heterodoxy – with all the multiform evils that this represents for the Church and, consequently, temporal society. Silence and submissiveness in the name of respect for authority and obedience does not take into account that all disciplinary authority and all obedience presupposes the clear and unequivocal doctrinal teaching of the Holy Church.

It is significant that the spirit of the author of *In the Murky Waters of Vatican II* is not that of a dissident, hostile to Papacy or authority, but one of humility, love, obedience, and fidelity to the Holy Catholic Church, the Successor of Peter, and the ordinary and extraordinary teachings of the Magisterium, in whose defense he undertook this great effort. For this reason, this work deserves the careful reading and reflection of Bishops, priests, scholars, historians and the faithful.

Atila S. Guimarães undertook this endeavor at the request of Prof. Plinio Corrêa de Oliveira, a great Catholic thinker and man of action who commissioned and directed the study, desired this work to be published, and never feared public opinion more than God. Prof. Plinio viewed the Council not as an isolated event that ignited a great crisis, but placed it within its historical perspective. Already in 1943, Prof. Corrêa de Oliveira perceived the re-emergence of the Modernist errors in his prophetic work *In Defense of Catholic Action* and denounced these trends that would contend for control of the Second Vatican Council.

Time has only confirmed these early perceptions, making more opportune than ever this important analysis by Atila S.

Guimarães. Already in 1991, Prof. Corrêa de Oliveira sent these words of encouragement to the author:

"An enormous effort of both intelligence and will enabled the author to achieve this work for the glory of Our Lady, the Holy Church and Christian Civilization. When published, it will constitute an irreparable blow to the forces of the Revolution that have infiltrated the Holy Church in this phase of self-demolition and the internal expansion of the smoke of Satan."

Thus, it seems an opportune moment to bring this unique study before the American public. It is in tribute to Prof. Plinio Corrêa de Oliveira and his spirit of obedience to and love for the Holy Catholic Church that *Tradition in Action* promotes this study.

Marian T. Horvat, Ph.D.
President, *Tradition in Action*

HOMAGE AND GRATITUDE

I wish the first lines of the Collection *Eli, Eli, Lamma Sabacthani?* to be of homage and gratitude to the outstanding paladin of the Holy Catholic Church and Christian Civilization, Professor Plinio Corrêa de Oliveira. To him I owe the spiritual and intellectual formation which, since 1964, I was honored to receive in daily contact with him, his words and works, in the ranks of the Brazilian Society for the Defense of Tradition, Family and Property (TFP).[1] By him I was given the task – kindly presented as an invitation but respectfully accepted as a duty – to analyze Ecumenical Council Vatican II.

His example of dedication and courage gave me strength to undertake this work. His unshakable faith, untiring hope and edifying charity were the mainstays that supported me at a crucial moment when these virtues vacillate all over the world. To his penetrating discernment, unique global view and great learning I had recourse in every difficulty. To him, therefore, as Author of the idea of this Collection and my mentor, I want to offer a most respectful and filial homage of gratitude.

> "Through your will my heart was encouraged,
> Upon only hearing your words,
> So that I have returned to my first purpose.
> Now then, if both of us have only one will
> You are my guide, you are my lord and master." [2]

To this homage, after his death on October 3, 1995, I add my profound sadness at his absence and growing nostalgia for the noble bonds that increasingly united us during the 31 years I was privileged to share with him.

---

1. About the TFP, see Notes 12 and 16 in the General Introduction.

2. *"Tu m'hai con disiderio il cor disposto / si al venir con le parole tue, / ch'i' son tornato nel primo proposto. / Or va, ch'un sol volere è d'ambedue: / tu duca, tu segnore e tu maestro."* (Dante, *La Divina Commedia, Inferno* II, 136-140).

I should also express my sincere gratitude to the competent team of editors of TFP who, upon the request of Prof. Plinio, assisted me with great dedication and disinterest in the realization of the works of the present Collection.

I also want to make a special acknowledgement of Mr. Paulo Hideo Moriyama, who for 20 years has been my secretary in these studies and who discharged the various functions of typist and computer technician in regard to this Collection.

With regard to the English edition of this work, I thank the following counter-revolutionary friends:

Marian T. Horvat, Ph.D., the articulate and dynamic president of Tradition in Action, Inc. (TIA). To her selfless dedication to the Catholic Cause, I owe a thorough and accurate revision of the English text. Because of this extended, careful and enriching revision, I consider her to be the final translator of the present volume.

Remi E. Amelunxen, Ph.D., a scholarly and responsible editor both from the doctrinal and linguistic standpoints. Along with Dr. Horvat, he made the necessary contacts to facilitate the publication.

*   *   *

GENERAL INFORMATION

§ 1   The Collection *Eli, Eli, Lamma Sabacthani?* contains, at the time of the publication of Volume I, approximately 14,000 quotations from around 900 authors.

§ 2   Various quotations appear in more than one place in the 11 Volumes of this Collection. If it is a merely informative quotation, it will simply be repeated for the Reader's convenience. If it is a doctrinal quotation, it may be repeated for an analysis from a different viewpoint or to give the subject the emphasis that we deem necessary. Repetitions, however, are not frequent.

§ 3   The Church publications that were regularly followed as this study was written are: *L'Osservatore Romano, La Civiltà Cattolica, Concilium, II Regno, 30 Giorni, Adista.* Religious sections of lay periodicals routinely monitored were those from *Corriere della Sera, Avvenire, La Repubblica, Time, Newsweek, Folha de S. Paulo, 0 Estado de S. Paulo.* Other news items were taken from publications we receive occasionally or were drawn from the well-organized documentation service of the Brazilian TFP's Readers Commission.

§ 4   Seeking to delve deeply into conciliar thought and the tactics used at the Council, as well as to assemble a more select bibliography to grasp the spirit of the Council, the Author of this Collection traveled to seven European countries in the beginning of 1983 to interview personages, some of them major ones, who participated in the Council, wrote about it or helped to implement it. Such interviews will be cited as required. Tapes of the interviews can be found in the Author's file.

§ 5   For Portuguese-language quotations of conciliar documents in this book, we have used the work, *Documentos do Vaticano II – Constituições, decretos e declarações,* introduction and analytical index by Fr. Boaventura Kloppenburg, O.F.M., general coordination by Fr. Frederico Vier, O.F.M. (Vozes, Petrópolis, 1966); bilingual edition with the Portuguese text reviewed by sub-secretaries of the National Conference of Brazilian Bishops. For English-language quotations, we have used *Vatican Council II – The Conciliar and Post-Conciliar Documents,* ed. Austin Flannery, O.P. (Collegeville, MN: Liturgical Press, 1975).

§ 6   Following the reforms by John XXIII and Paul VI in the Roman Curia, John Paul II carried out yet more reforms with the apostolic Constitution *Pastor Bonus* (June 28, 1988). The latter caused name changes in various Dicasteries, for example, in the three main ecumenical Secretariats: The Secretariat for the Union of Christians, established by John XXIII on July 5, 1960, came to be called the Pontifical Council for the Union of Christians; the Secretariat for Non-Christians, founded by Paul VI on May 19, 1964, was changed to the

Pontifical Council for Inter-Religious Dialogue; the Secretariat for Non-Believers, established by Paul VI on April 9, 1965, is now called the Pontifical Council for Dialogue with Non-Believers.

Such changes caused a minor problem to our work regarding references. Should we replace the names of the old Secretariats with their current designations each time they appear? We thought it better to keep their names as they appear in the documentation. Warned about the name changes, our Reader will know what we are referring to as they appear.

§ 7   Since this Collection cites documents from about 900 authors, it became quite difficult to accompany – for the entire time span during which this study was put together – the itinerary of the ecclesiastical and intellectual careers of contemporary authors in order to update their titles. Thus, although we have made an effort to update such data, it is unlikely that it has been carried out to the extent we would have liked.

§ 8   The Collection was written in Portuguese and has been translated into English. The English edition of Volume I is the first of the Books in the Collection to be published.

§ 9   The Author clarifies that while he has been a member of the Brazilian TFP since 1964, the publication of this Collection is not intended as an official or unofficial position taken by the Brazilian, American or any other TFP. The Author, therefore, assumes full and exclusive responsibility for what he wrote.

The references to the TFP contained in Volume I were revised by Prof. Plinio Corrêa de Oliveira, who is unfortunately no longer with us. The Author publishes them as a homage to that great Catholic knight and as a token of admiration for the organization to which he dedicated his life.[3]

---

3. Since the death of Prof. Plinio in 1995 the new leadership of TFP abandonned its glorious fight against Progressivism. To this date, 2008, no significant action against this force has been developed by any of the 26 TFPs then existing: a practical surrender to the enemy.

In this spirit, it came as no surprise that, when the first American edition of *In the Murky Waters* was published in 1997, the Directors of the Brazilian TFP, afraid of possible progressivist counter-attacks for having a TFP member publicly analyzing Vatican II, sent an ultimatum to the Author to suspend its dissemination, or he would be expelled from TFP. The Author did not suspend it. He was expelled from the organization in 1998, and moved to the US. Ironically, some time later, the TFP split over internal issues causing it more harm than any external attack. Today both sides compete for the favors of the progressivist high and low clergy, which they used to combat.

In this edition, the Author did not make any essential changes to the original text as a homage to the ideals TFP represented, which he continues to defend.

ABBREVIATIONS

1. The Books of the Bible:

Abd	Abdias	**Jude**	Jude
Acts	The Acts of the Apostle	**1 Kgs**	1 Kings
Agg	Aggeus	**2 Kgs**	2 Kings
Amos	Amos	**3 Kgs**	3 Kings
Apoc	Apocalypse	**4 Kgs**	4 Kings
Bar	Baruch	**Lam**	Lamentations
Cant	Canticle of Canticles	**Lev**	Leviticus
1 Cor	1 Corinthians	**Luke**	Luke
2 Cor	2 Corinthians	**1 Mach**	1 Machabees
Col	Colossians	**2 Mach**	2 Machabees
Dan	Daniel	**Mal**	Malachias
Deut	Deuteronomy	**Mich**	Micheas
Eccles	Ecclesiastes	**Mark**	Mark
Ecclus	Ecclesiasticus	**Matt**	Matthew
Eph	Ephesians	**Nahum**	Nahum
1 Esd	1 Esdras	**Num**	Numbers
2 Esd	2 Esdras, alias Nehemias	**Osee**	Osee (Hosea)
Esther	Esther	**1 Par**	1 Paralipomenon
Ex	Exodus	**2 Par**	2 Paralipomenon
Ezech	Ezechiel	**1 Peter**	1 Peter
Gal	Galatians	**2 Peter**	2 Peter
Gen	Genesis	**Philem**	Philemon
Hab	Habacuc	**Phil**	Philippians
Heb	Hebrews	**Prov**	Proverbs
Is	Isaias	**Ps**	Psalms
Jas	James	**Rom**	Romans
Jdth	Judith	**Ruth**	Ruth
Jer	Jeremias	**Soph**	Sophonias
Jgs	Judges	**1 Thess**	1 Thessalonians
Joel	Joel	**2 Thess**	2 Thessalonians
John	John (Gospel)	**1 Tim**	1 Timothy
1 John	1 John (Epistle)	**2 Tim**	2 Timothy
2 John	2 John (Epistle)	**Titus**	Titus
3 John	3 John (Epistle)	**Tob**	Tobias
Job	Job	**Wis**	Wisdom
Jon	Jonas	**Zach**	Zacharias
Jos	Josue		

We do not adopt the abbreviations 1 Sam (1 Samuel) and 2 Sam to refer to the 1st and 2nd Book of Kings; 1 Chron (1 Chronicles) and 2 Chron to designate the 1st and 2nd Book of Paralipomenon; Sir (Sirach) to replace reference to Ecclesiasticus. When such abbreviations appear in the documents used in this Collection, they are replaced with their traditional designations.

2. The Conciliar Documents:

LG *Lumen gentium:* The Dogmatic Constitution on the Church

DV *Dei Verbum:* The Dogmatic Constitution on Divine Revelation

GS *Gaudium et spes:* The Pastoral Constitution on the Church in the Modern World

SC *Sacrosanctum Concilium:* The Constitution on the Sacred Liturgy

UR *Unitatis redintegratio:* The Decree on Ecumenism

OE *Orientalium Ecclesiarum:* The Decree on the Catholic Churches of the Eastern rites

AG *Ad gentes:* The Decree on the Church's Missionary Activity

CD *Christus Dominus:* The Decree on Bishops

PO *Presbyterorum Ordinis:* The Decree on Priests

PC *Perfectae caritatis:* The Decree on Religious Life

OT *Optatam totius:* The Decree on the Training of Priests

AA *Apostolicam actuositatem:* The Decree on the Apostolate of the Laity

IM *Inter mirifica:* The Decree on the Media of Social Communication

GE *Gravissimum educationis:* The Declaration on Christian Education

DH *Dignitatis humanae:* The Declaration on Religious Liberty

NA *Nostra aetate:* The Declaration on the Church's Relations with non-Christian Religions

3. Abbreviation of References:

a., aa.	article(s)		lect.	*lectura*
bk., bks.	book(s)		n., nn.	number(s)
chap(s).,	chapter(s)		op. cit.	*opus citatus* (in
can., cans.	canon(s)			aforecited work)
cf.	confer		P.	Part
col., cols.	column(s)		p., pp.	page(s)
d., dd.	distinction(s)		q., qq.	question(s)
disp.	*disputatio*		sec.	section
f., ff.	and following page(s)		ses.	session
ibid.	in the same place		sol.	solution
	(as previous ref.)		t., tt.	tome(s)
idem	the same		th.	thesis
i.e.	*id est* (that is)		V.A.	various authors
lec.	*lectio*		vol.,vols.	volume(s)

3. Bibliographic Abbreviations:

CSEO Monthly review of *Centro Studi per 1'Europa Orientale*

D Henricus Denzinger, *Enchiridion Symbolorum* – a collection of the most important excerpts of the Magisterium, put together by the German priest Heinrik Joseph Denzinger (1819-1883), first published in 1854

DB Henricus Denzinger and Clemens Bannwart. Denzinger's collection updated by Banwart between 1908 and 1921

DR Henricus Denzinger and Karl Rahner. *Idem,* updated by Rahner between 1946 and 1954

DS Henricus Denzinger and Adolphus Schönmetzer. *Idem,* updated by Schonmetzer between 1955 and 1965

DTC *Dictionnaire de Théologie Catholique,* published under the responsibility of Alfred Vacant and Eugene Mangenot between 1923 and 1972

ICI *Informations Catholiques Internationales*

LThK *Lexikon für Theologie and Kirche*

NRTh *Nouvelle Revue Théologique*

MüThZ *Münchener Theologische Zeitschrift*

PG *Patrologie Grecque – Latine* (PG), 217 vols., more than 3 indexes, published by Paul Migne.

PL	*Patrologie Latine* (PL), 161 vols., more than 1 index, *idem.*
REB	*Revista Eclesiástica Brasileira*
Rev.Th. Louv.	*Revue Théologique de Louvain*
SEDOC	*Serviço de Documentação*
TS	*Theological Studies*

5. Abbreviations of Names of Religious Orders and Congregations:

C.M.F	*Cordis Mariae Filii* (Sons of the Heart of Mary).
C.SS.R.	*Congregatio Sanctissimi Redemptoris* (Redemptorists).
M.M.	U.S. Society for Foreign Missions (Maryknoll).
O.C.	*Ordo Carmelitarum* (Carmelites).
O.C.D.	*Ordo Carmelitarum Descalciatorum* (Discalced Carmelites).
O.F.M.	*Ordo Fratrum Minorum* (Franciscans).
O.P.	*Ordo Praedicatorum* (Dominicans).
O.S.B.	*Ordo Sancti Benedicti* (Benedictines).
S.I. or S.J.	*Societas Iesu* (Jesuits).
S.V.D.	*Societas Verbi Divini* (Divine Word Missionaries).

* * *

NOTES ON STYLE

§ 1   Due to the large number of authors and works quoted and commented upon in this Collection, as well as to the frequent references to other Volumes of the Collection, when we refer to books, works or volumes by other authors, we use lower case. When referring to this Collection, we capitalize the first letter: Collection, Work, Study, Volume, Chapter, Author, etc. Likewise, we capitalize the first letter when referring to our Reader to distinguish him from readers of other authors.

§ 2   For the sake of uniformity in our presentation, we take the following liberties in relation to the transcribed texts:

• When the author being quoted puts any word, expression or phrase in bold, we put it in italics.

• All foreign words used by the authors are not translated but simply italicized by us, regardless of the criterion used by the author.

• Book, newspaper and magazine titles are italicized, thus rendering uniform the various criteria used by the authors quoted.

• When an author places a bibliographical reference in parentheses in his own text, we place it into a footnote that stands out from the others by adding an asterisk; for example, if in the text you have [4]*, in the footnote you find also 4*.

§ 3   Bold emphasis is always our responsibility.

§ 4   In the texts cited, comments between parentheses are by their authors, and those between brackets are ours.

*   *   *

GENERAL INTRODUCTION
TO THE COLLECTION
ELI, ELI, LAMMA SABACTHANI?

§ 1   The **primary goal** of this Collection is to analyze Vatican Council II. This analysis will include the conciliar documents as such, the spirit of the Council, its underlying thought and the fruits it has generated. Its **secondary goal** is to study the unity that these elements present among themselves.

§ 2   The **criterion of analysis** is twofold. *First,* it is traditional Catholic doctrine as known by a layman endowed with a general culture and who studies sociological, historical, philosophical and theological matters related directly to Christian Civilization and indirectly to the Holy Catholic Church. *Second,* it is the *sensus fidelium,*[1] that is, common sense in matters of Faith and Morals.

---

1. a. The expression *sensus fidelium* is used here according to the doctrine of St. Vincent of Lerins in his *Commonitorium* (PL 50, 670), in the sense that a faith that was believed *semper, ubique, ab omnibus* [always, everywhere, by everbody] in the Holy Church is the true Faith, thanks to a special protection the Holy Spirit gives the ensemble of the faithful along the centuries.

b. Even before St. Vincent of Lerins, Tertullian wrote about this characteristic of the faith of all faithful: "Will the Spirit of truth let the churches believe something other than that which Christ preached?" *(De praescriptionibus adversus haereticos 28,* in PL 2, 40). St. Gregory Nazianzen also appealed to the faith of the martyrs and Bishops: "If this is not true, our faith is vain; in vain have the martyrs died, in vain have the Bishops governed the peoples" *(Epistula 102, 2 ad Cledon,* in PG 37, 200). But perhaps no one was more conscious of this fact than St. Augustine as he invoked the Church's faith in the non-repetition of Baptism for heretics *(De baptismo contra Donatistas,* lib. 2, chap. 9, n. 14, in PL 43, 135); on the necessity of grace, indicated by the meaning that the faithful give to prayer *(De dono perseverantiae,* chap. 23, n. 63, in PL 45, 1031); on the need for, and efficacy of baptism for the salvation of all, especially of children *(Sermo 294,* chap. 17, in PL 38, 1346, in Vicente Proaño Gil, "Infalibilidad," in *Gran Enciclopedia,* Madrid: Ed Rialp S/A, 1971-1976, vol XII, p. 683).

c. The *sensus fidelium* (sense of the faithful) comes from the *sensus Fidei* (sense of Faith) and is the universal adherence of the faithful to the teachings in matters of Faith and Morals. "What does the expression *[sensus Fidei]* mean? In the opinion of theologians, it is a gift of God that has to do with the subjective reality of the Faith and gives the whole Church the assurance of an indefectible Faith. It is a strength, an almost instinctive power to know the truth revealed by God, adhere to it, discern it and penetrate it in all of its amplitude. It certainly is not a religious sentiment of a modernist type; it is a knowledge by assimilation, adaptation, conformity or co-naturalness" *(ibid.,* pp. 683-684). To this definition we would add, in the spirit of St. Vincent of Lerins, that it also is a special affinity with everything that Holy Church has taught over the centuries in a uniform and consistent manner and which has always stirred up enthusiasm in the best that could be found among the faithful.

d. Based on the well-known work by Melchior Cano, *De locis theologicis,* Fr. Claudio Garcia Extremeño, O.P., professor of Dogmatics at the Dominican Faculty of Theology in Madrid, studied the field in which the *sensus fidelium* is applied and its limitations: "Naturally, the sense of the faithful will be exerted upon matters of Faith and Morals, but not the subtleties and explanations proper to theologians. 'Demanding an opinion of the people [about such matters] is so absurd that it would not occur to the wise, nor even the fool'" (M. Cano, *De locis theologicis,* lib. IV, chaps. IV, VI, Rome, 1890, in C. Garcia Extremeño, "El sentido de la Fe, criterio de la Tradición," in *La Ciencia Tomista,* Salamanca, July-December, 1960, p. 576).

Cano adds: "There are two kinds of things that, as we said, are believed by the Church. One, the things that equally regard everyone ... and in this case it is not very difficult to know the faith and the sense of everyone. ... Another kind regards those matters whose knowledge is not of interest to the simple and unscholarly, but to the experienced and learned. Asking the people to pronounce themselves about matters of this second type would be tantamount to calling upon a blind man to distinguish between colors" *(ibid.,* note 25).

e. Garcia Extremeño studies the *sensus fidei* and enumerates related expressions used to designate the faith of the faithful as a whole, namely: *sensus Ecclesiae, sensus Catholicus, sensus* or *consensus fidelium, sensus socialis Ecclesiae, Christiani populi fides* and *communis Ecclesiae fides.* He also studies the nature of the *sensus Fidei,* its subjective principles – the virtue of Faith, the gift of knowledge, science and wisdom, its objective principles and the relation between the *sensus Fidei* and the teaching of the Ecclesiastical Magisterium *(ibid.,* pp. 569-605).

f. According to the Spanish Dominican, "The Holy Ghost watches over the twofold reality of the faith, objective and subjective, in order to keep the former always intact and give the faithful Christian a nearly instinctive power of faith to adhere to its object in order to perceive it and discern it" *(ibid.,* p. 572). This assistance of the Holy Ghost to the *sensus fidelium* gives it an authority that often contributed decisively to guarantee orthodoxy and advance the progress of Dogmatics. "Thus, for example, take the definition of the real presence of the Body and Blood of Christ under the sacramental species of bread and wine, against Berengario; the truth of the immediate vision of God by the souls without need to wait for the Last Judgment; the introduction of the *Filioque* in the Creed of the Mass and, finally, the mysteries of Mary" *(ibid.,* p. 585).

g. Of the innumerable cases of accurate judgment by the *sensus fidelium* in the course of History, we would like to point out two of the most expressive.

The *first one* is related to the generalized defection of the Episcopate during the Arian crisis in the 4th century. John Henry Cardinal Newman spoke strongly on this subject: "What I sustain is that, at that time of great confusion, the sublime dogma of the divinity of Our Lord was pro-claimed, strengthened, defended and (humanly speaking) guaranteed far more by the Church *discens* than by the Church *docens;* that in general, the Episcopate as a body were unfaithful to their office, while the laity as a body remained faithful to their baptismal grace" (J. H. Newman, "On consulting the faithful in matters of doctrine," in *The Rambler,* 1859, p. 217, in C. Garcia Extremeño, *El sentido de la fe,* p. 602).

Writing about this topic, theologian Joseph Ratzinger also refers to the example of the Arian crisis: "In the universal Church there is something like an infallibility of faith by virtue of which this universal Church can never let herself fall into error as a Church in its totality. This is the laity's share in infallibility. That this share can at times take on an extremely active meaning can be seen in the Arian crisis, during which at times it appeared as though the whole Hierarchy had fallen prey to the Arianizing tendencies of mediation and only the firm position of the faithful ensured the victory of faith in Nicea ... for truth is not a privilege of the hierarchs, but a gift made to the Spouse of Christ as a whole" (J. Ratzinger, *Il nuovo popolo di Dio,* Brescia: Queriniana, 1971, pp. 164-165, in J. M. Gonzalez Ruiz, "Lettera aperta al Cardinale Ratzinger - Le 'verità' del Cardinale prima e dopo it S. Ufficio," *in Adista,* Rome, January 19-21, 1987, pp. 4-5.).

h. In some way the *second case* is even more grave than the first, since it entailed "resistance" to the doctrine taught by a Sovereign Pontiff: "In 1332, Pope John XXII, in Avignon preached with his private authority that the souls of the just would not enjoy beatific vision until after the resurrection of the dead and the Last Judgment. Gerard Eudes, Superior General of the Franciscans, made this opinion his own and spread it, preaching it publicly in Paris. Upon hearing it, *magnum murmur inter scholas auditum est* [A great murmuring was heard among the colleges].

As the matter was examined, professors of the University of Paris and the King, impelled by the common feeling of the people, asked the Pope to define the truth 'in the sense it was always defended by the piety of the Christian people.' It was solemnly defined by Benedict XII on January 29, 1336 (DS 530-531: Xavier-Marie Le Bachelet. *Benoit XII,* in V.A., *Dictionnaire de Théologie Catholique,* eds. A. Vacant & E. Mangenot, vol. II, Paris: Letouzey & Ané, 1923-1972, cols. 657-696; Denifle-Chatelain, *Chartularium Universitatis Parisiensis,* Paris, 1851. II, nn. 970-987, in C. Garcia Extremeño, *El sentido de la Fe,* pp. 599-600).

i. Among the famous people who wrote about the *sensus fidelium,* its premises and consequences, several others, in addition to those already mentioned, stand out: St. Basil, *Adversus Eunomium,* 3, 1 in PG 29, 654; St. Jerome, *Contra Vigilantium,* 5 in PL 23. 343; St. Augustine, *Contra Julianum,* 1, 7, 31 in PL 44, 662; *De duabus animabus contra Manichaeos,* chap. 11 in PL 42, 105; Cassianus, *De Incarnatione Christi contra Nestorium haericutum,* 1, 6 in PL 50, 30, in C. Garcia Extremeño, *El Sentido de la Fe,* p. 573, note 14. According to the same author, in various places St. Thomas Aquinas dealt with knowledge through co-naturality, a premise of the *sensus fidelium,* notably in the *Summa Theologiae,* I, q.1, a.6, ad 3; *III Sententiarum,* d.24, q.1, a.2, sol.2; d.23, q.3, sol.2, ad 2. The Angelic Doctor also considers the gifts of the Holy Spirit as characterizing an "instinct" and a "motion" that should complete the contribution of reason (*Summa Theologiae,* I-II, q.68, a.8 *sed contra;* a.2). St. Thomas deals with the gift of understanding, which according to the scholars is present in the *sensus fidelium,* in *III Sententiarum,* d.25, q.2, a.2, sol.1; *Summa Theologiae,* II-II, q.8, aa.1 ad 3; 2, 4 ad 2, 6, 7; q.49, a.2 ad 2; q. 9, a.1. As for the gift of knowledge, in connection with this subject, see *idem,* q.9, a.1; ad 2; q.8, a.6; q.9, a.3. In relation to the gift of wisdom, see *idem,* q.45; q.9, a.2 ad 1; ad 2; q.45, a.2; q.8, a.5.

j. On the importance of the *sensus fidelium* as a testimony to the indefectible Faith of the Church, G. Extremeño, cites, among others: F. Suarez, *De Christo,* q.27, d.3, s.6, n.4; J. M. de Ripalda, *De Fide,* d.8, s.2, n.24; J. de Lugo, *De Fide,* d.1, s.13, n. 277, St. Robert Bellarmine, *De Verbo Dei,* 1.1, chap. 10, ad 2 (Garcia Extremeño, *El sentido de la Fe,* p. 596).

k. Some contemporary authors - whose theories should be viewed with reservations - attribute to the *sensus fidelium* an even greater amplitude. They designate it with expressions such as "inerrancy *in credendo*" (Herbert Vorgrimler, "Dal *sensus fidei* al *consensus fidelium,*" in *Concilium,* April 1986, p. 17), "infallibility *in credendo*" (A. Grillmeier, LThK, K I, 189, in Hans Waldenfels, "Autorità e conoscenza," in *Concilium,* April 1984, p. 62) or the "passive infallibility" of the faithful (Heinrich Fries, *C'è un magistero dei fedeli?, ibid.,* p. 115, based on F. van der Horst, E. J. de Smedt, B. van Leeuwen); or when they attribute to the "experience" of the *sensus fidei* a profundity that could approach

§ 3   The **prism of the analysis** adopted here is an overall view of the Council. Having studied the conciliar documents, the Author noticed they were dissonant in a certain number of points with the ordinary and universal teaching of the Magisterium of the Church. They also clashed at other points with the *sensus fidelium*. Asking himself what could be the underlying unity that would explain such points, as well as the post-conciliar fruits they bore, the Author put together an over-all picture that sheds some light on so much confusion. Thus, in addition to analyzing each part in itself, the Work strives to discern in each one its most profound foundation and the relationships of the various parts among themselves in order to arrive at a unitary conception of Vatican Council II and its fruits.

§ 4   The **method** used is inductive. Aware of his small authority, the Author will let the facts speak for themselves as much as possible. When dealing with doctrine rather than fact, he will cite the opinions of renowned specialists in the matter.

In the face of certain groups of facts or opinions, the Author will ask himself whether there are enough proofs or clues to present a plan of conduct or to describe a current of opinion in the case of doctrinal matters. He will present conclusions on a level of either cer-

---

the experience of an interior "revelation" of a Modernist bent (Zoltán Alszeghy, *Sens de la Foi,* in V.A., *Vatican II: Bilan et perspectives, vingt-cinq après,* ed. R. Latourelle, Montreal/Paris: Belarmin-Cerf, 1988, vol. 1, pp. 162-163).

Others, founded on *Lumen gentium* (n. 12), go as far as to uphold a generic infallibility of the believers, "overturning the fatal distinction between the passive and active infallibility of the Magisterium" (H. Vorgrimler, "Dai *sensus fidei* al *consensus fidelium,*" p. 18).

The goal pursued by the most advanced progressivists is well-defined by the commentary of French Dominican Christian Duquoc, professor at the Faculty of Theology of Lyon and member of the boards of directors of the magazines *Lumière et Vie* and *Concilium:* "The Constitution *Lumen gentium,* subverting the relationship between the hierarchy and the people, bears good witness to this need for a rupture with the model born out of the Counter-Reformation, in which the people were practically nothing and the hierarchy made decisions unsupervised" (C. Duquoc, "Il popolo di Dio, soggetto attivo della fede nella chiesa," in *Concilium,* 1985/4, pp. 102-103).

I. Obviously, we will not consider the *sensus fidelium* from this progressivist perspective. Quite on the contrary, this Work is intended to reflect it in harmonious and submissive consonance with the perennial teachings of the hierarchical Magisterium through whose voice the Holy Spirit has directed the Church along the centuries.

tainty or hypothesis, according to the usual rules of the inductive method. Exceptionally, when the matter dealt with is clearly opposed to Catholic doctrine or gravely offends against the *sensus fidelium,* he will use the deductive method, beginning by examining the truths that were transgressed.

The use of the inductive method will be conditioned by this factor: Since the authors who deal with the Council often use hermetic language or refer only fragmentarily to concepts not expressed in their works, it will be necessary at times to present views that explain the thinking implicit in their language and the unexpressed unity of the fragments so that the analysis may be accessible to Readers presumably not specialized in the subject. Such explanatory overall views, presented as hypotheses, always refer to the places in the Collection where the matter is proved by induction. They are, therefore, necessary anticipations to overcome obstacles rather than preconceptions contrary to the method adopted.

§ 5   This Collection's **plan** is designed to analyze the Council by stages. An ideal plan for the Work was made on the basis of the documents chosen prior to the writing.

In practice, however, the ideal plan underwent some changes that turned into the actual completed Work. Let us say an explanatory word about each part of this Collection so as to clarify how the parts relate to one another.

The **ideal plan** called for analyzing first the letter of the conciliar documents, and then the spirit according to which the doubtful points of its letter should be understood; next, the concrete fruits produced by the Council in the institutional and doctrinal spheres by virtue of its principles and dynamism; and finally, the underlying thought that would provide a unity to the letter, spirit and fruits.

Since the writing started, however, the plan was adapted according to the probative value of the documents used. In fact, the latter very often inductively proved more than the specific point we wanted to make. For example, as we analyze the spirit of Vatican II, we will collaterally point out to the Reader innumerable fruits of the Council, as well as several facets of its thought. Thus, when the analysis of the spirit is over, the Reader will already have an approximate notion of the fruits of the Council and a sketch of its thought. Likewise, as the fruits are analyzed later in the Work, the great panoramas of conciliar thought collaterally become evident.

For this reason, that is, the cumulative character of the proofs, the actual plan of the Collection is an imperfect rendition of the ideal plan, albeit as close to it as possible.

Concretely, the **actual plan** of the present Collection is:

- analysis of the letter of the conciliar documents (Volume I);
- analysis of the spirit of the Council (Volumes II, III, IV, V);
- analysis of the fruits of Vatican II (in addition to those treated in previous Volumes, especially Vols. VI, VII, IX, X, XI);
- analysis of conciliar thought in conjunction with the study of its fruits (Volume VIII and parts of Volumes VI, VII, IX, X XI).

§ 6   The **limits** of the Work are inherent to the multiple topics dealt with, the method adopted and the probative character to which it aspires.

In view of the multiplicity of topics covered and the inductive method adopted, this Collection could go on indefinitely piling up proofs and arguments about each topic. The Author selected only those that he found more expressive of each subject and conducive to an overall view of the Council as a whole.

The probative character of the Collection is made up of unequal parts. Many times the proofs presented will lead to certainty, at other times to a mere hypothesis. This nuance can be apprehended in the course of the expositions and, more characteristically, in the conclusions.

Even the unitary conception that comes across in the analysis as a whole does not have the character of an absolute certainty. It is a consistent, explanatory, comprehensive hypothesis that takes on, for *humility* the Author, the characteristics of a moral certainty. Nevertheless, he does not lay aside the possibility that some aspects of the general architecture unifying the letter, spirit and thought of the Council may have escaped his perception. Nor does he exclude that there may exist a more profound and complete conception to explain the Council and what has followed it. If that should be the case, he would be grateful for any correction enabling him to know the unitary reality he so earnestly sought.

§ 7   The **credentials** permitting the Author to make such an analysis do not go beyond those of a Catholic layman.

Indeed, Natural Law entitles a Catholic to speak about his Faith as long as he is moved by love of the Church and does so according to the dogmatic and moral precepts taught by her, with due respect for the members of the Hierarchy and, above all, the Sovereign Pontiff. However, when one takes into account that Pope Paul VI characterized the present situation in the Church as a process of

✗"auto-demolition,"² and that such a process cannot take place without the participation of many Prelates, that which for a Catholic was only a right becomes a duty. This duty is not only to talk about points of the Faith, but also to question those responsible for deviations regarding those points of the Faith.³ This duty is all the more cogent

---

2. In his Allocution to the Students of the Lombard Seminary on December 7, 1968, the Pontiff said: "Today the Church is going through a moment of disquiet. **Some practice self-criticism, one would even say auto-demolition. It is like an inner, acute and complex disturbance such as no one would have expected after the Council.** People thought of a flourishing, a serene expansion of the concepts that matured in the great conciliar assembly. This one aspect, of flourishing, does still exist in the Church. But since *bonum ex integra causa, malum ex quocumque defectu,* attention falls especially on the painful aspect. **The Church is struck also by those who are part of her**" (*Insegnamenti di Paolo VI,* vol. VI, p. 1092).

3. a. The doctrine on the right of the faithful, even the most simple ones, to resist decisions by the ecclesiastical authority that are dangerous to the Faith and objectively erroneous, was expounded by Fathers and Doctors of the Church as well as by theologians and canonists, some of whom were elevated to the altars.

b. St. Thomas Aquinas, in many passages of his works, upholds the principle that the faithful can question and admonish prelates. For example: "There being an imminent danger for the Faith, Prelates must be questioned, even publicly, by their subjects. Thus, St. Paul, who was a subject of St. Peter, questioned him publicly on account of an imminent danger of scandal in a matter of Faith. And, as the *Glosa* of St. Augustine puts it (*Ad Galatas* 2,14), 'St. Peter himself gave the example to those who govern so that if sometime they stray from the right way, they will not reject a correction as unworthy even if it comes from their subjects'" (*Summa Theologiae,* Turin/Rome: Marietti, 1948, II-II, q.33, a.4).

Referring to the same episode, in which St. Paul resisted St. Peter "to his face," St. Thomas teaches: "The reprehension was just and useful, and the reason for it was not light: there was a danger for the preservation of evangelical truth. ... The way it took place was appropriate, since it was public and manifest. For this reason, St. Paul writes: 'I spoke to Cephas,' that is, Peter, 'before everyone,' since the simulation practiced by St. Peter was fraught with danger to everyone. In 1 Tim. 5:20, we read: 'Admonish those who sin before everyone.' This should be understood to refer to manifest sins, not hidden ones, since in these cases one should proceed according to the rules proper to fraternal correction" *(Super Epistulas S. Pauli, Ad Galatas,* 2, 11-14, lec. III, Turin/Rome: Marietti, 1953, nn. 83-84).

The Angelic Doctor also shows how this passage of the Scriptures contains teachings not only for Hierarchs but for the faithful as well: "To the

Prelates [was given an example] of humility so that they do not refuse to accept reprehensions from their inferiors and subjects; and to the subjects, an example of zeal and liberty so they will not fear to correct their Prelates, above all when the crime is public and entails a danger for many" *(ibid., n. 77).*

In his *Comments on the Sentences of Peter Lombard,* St. Thomas teaches how respectfully correcting a Prelate who sins is a work of mercy all the greater as the Hierarch's position is higher: "Fraternal correction, being a spiritual alms, is a work of mercy. But mercy is due mainly to the Prelate since he runs the greatest danger. Hence St. Augustine says in *Regula* (n. 11, PL 32, 1384): 'Have pity not only on yourselves, but on them as well,' that is, on the Prelates 'among you who run a danger as high as the position they occupy.' Therefore, fraternal correction extends also to the Prelates.

"Furthermore, Ecclus. 17:12, says that God 'gave to every one of them commandment concerning his neighbor.' Now, a Prelate is our neighbor. Therefore, we must correct him when he sins. ... Some say that fraternal correction does not extend to the Prelates either because man should not raise his voice against Heaven, or because the Prelates are easily scandalized if corrected by their subjects. However, this does not happen, since when they sin, the Prelates do not represent Heaven and, therefore, must be corrected. And those who correct them charitably do not raise their voices against them, but in their favor, since the admonishment is for their own sake. ... For this reason, according to other [authors], the precept of fraternal correction extends also to the Prelates, so that they may be corrected by their subjects" *(IV Sententiarum,* d. 19, q. 2, a. 2).

In addition to St. Thomas Aquinas, other prominent Saints and Doctors have also pronounced on the right of the faithful to resist in grave circumstances. For example:

c. St. Augustine thus comments on the episode of St. Paul's public resistance to St. Peter: "Peter accepted with holy and pious humility the useful observation St. Paul had made, inspired by the freedom of love, thus leaving for posterity a rare example for them not to despise being corrected by their inferiors whenever they have strayed from the right way" *(Epistula 82,* n. 22, in PL 33, 285-286).

d. Fr. Francisco de Vitoria, OP: "Caietano, in the same work defending the superiority of the Pope over the Council, says in chap. 27: 'Therefore, a Pope must be resisted who publicly destroys the Church, for example, by refusing to give ecclesiastical benefits except for money or in exchange for services; and with all obedience and respect, the possession of such benefits must be denied to those who bought them.' And Silvestre (Prierias), in the entry *Pope,* § 4, asks: 'What should be done when the Pope, because of his bad customs, destroys the Church?' And in § 15: 'What should be done if the Pope wanted, without reason, to abrogate Positive Law?' To which he answers: 'He would certainly sin; he should neither be permitted to act in such fashion nor should he be obeyed in what was evil; but he should be resisted with a courteous reprehension.'

"Consequently, if he wished to give away the whole treasure of the Church or the patrimony of St. Peter to his relatives, if he wanted to destroy the Church or the like, he should not be permitted to act in that fashion, but one would be obliged to resist him. The reason for this is that he does not have the power to destroy; therefore, if there is evidence that he is doing it, it is licit to resist him. The result of all this is that if the Pope destroys the Church by his orders and acts, he can be resisted and the execution of his mandates prevented. ...

"Second proof of the thesis: By Natural Law it is licit to repel violence with violence. Now then, with such orders and dispensations the Pope exerts violence, since he acts against the Law, as we have proven. Therefore, it is licit to resist him. As Caietano observes, we do not affirm all this in the sense that someone could have competence to judge the Pope or have authority over him, but meaning that it is licit to defend oneself. Indeed, anyone has the right to resist an unjust act, to try to prevent it and to defend himself" (Obras de Francisco de Vitoria, Madrid: BAC, 1960, pp. 486-487).

e. Fr. Francisco Suarez, SJ: "If [the Pope] gives an order contrary to good customs, he should not be obeyed; if he attempts to do something manifestly opposed to justice and the common good, it will be licit to resist him; if he attacks by force, by force he can be repelled, with a moderation appropriate to a just defense" (De Fide, disp. X, sec. VI, n. 16, in Opera omnia, Paris: Vivès, 1958, vol. XII, in A. V. Xavier da Silveira, La nouvelle Messe de Paul VI: Qu'en penser?, Chiré-en-Montreuil: Diffusion de la Pensée Française, 1975, pp. 323-333.).

f. St. Robert Bellarmine, the great paladin of the Counter-Reformation, maintains: "Just as it is licit to resist the Pontiff who aggresses the body, it is also licit to resist the one who aggresses the souls or who disturbs civil order, or, above all, who attempts to destroy the Church. I say that it is licit to resist him by not doing what he orders and preventing his will from being executed; it is not licit, however, to judge, punish or depose him, since these are acts proper to a superior" (De Romano Pontifice, lib. II, chap. 29, in Opera omnia, Neapoli/Panormi/Paris: Pedone Lauriel, 1871, vol. I, p. 418).

g. Fr. Cornelius a Lapide, SJ, shows that St. Augustine, St. Ambrose, St. Bede, St. Anselm and other Fathers teach that St. Paul resisted St. Peter publicly "so that the public scandal given by St. Peter was amended by a likewise public reprehension" (Commentaria in Scripturam Sacram, Ad Galatas 2:11, Paris: Ludovicus Vivès, 1876, vol. XVIII, p. 528).

Later on, a Lapide argues that "superiors can be, with humble charity, reprehended by their inferiors in the defense of truth; that is what St. Augustine (Epistula 19), St. Cyprian, St. Gregory, St. Thomas and others cited above declare about this passage (Gal 2:11). They clearly teach that St. Peter, being a superior, was reprehended by St. Paul. ... With good reason, therefore, St. Gregory said: 'Peter kept quiet so that, being first in the Apostolic Hierarchy, he would also be first in humility' (*Homilia 18 in Ezechielem*). And St. Augustine wrote: 'By teaching that superiors should not refuse to be reprehended by inferiors, St. Peter gave posterity an example more rare and holier than that of St. Paul as he taught that, in the defense of truth and with charity, inferiors may have the audacity to resist superiors without fear' (*Epistula 19 ad Hieronymum*)."

h. Dom Prosper Guéranger, Abbot of Solesmes, notes: "When the shepherd turns into a wolf, it falls to the flock first to defend itself. Doctrine normally flows from the Bishops down to the faithful people, and subjects should not judge their chiefs. But, in the treasure of Revelation, there are certain points that every Christian necessarily knows and must obligatorily defend" (*L'année liturgique - Le temps de la septuagesime,* Tours: Maison Mame, 1932, pp. 340-341).

i. Frs. Francisco Xavier Wernz and Pedro Vidal, theologians at the beginning of the 20th century, citing Suarez, admit the licitness of resisting a bad Pope: "The just means to be employed against a bad Pope are, according to Suarez *(Defensio Fidei Catholicae,* lib. IV, cap. 6, nn. 17-18), a more abundant help from the grace of God, the special protection of one's Guardian Angel, the prayer of the Universal Church, admonishment or fraternal correction in private or even in public, as well as the legitimate self-defense against aggression, whether physical or moral" *(Ius canonicum,* Rome: Aedes Universitatis Gregorianae, 1927, vol. II. p. 436).

j. Antonio Peinador, C.M.F., a contemporary Spanish theologian, adopts the sentences of those who preceded him: "'Also a subject may be obliged to fraternally correct his superior' (*Summa Theologiae,* II-II, q.33, a.4). For also a superior can be spiritually indigent, and nothing prevents him from being liberated from such indigence by his subjects. Nevertheless, 'in the correction in which subjects reprehend their Prelates, they must act in a proper manner, that is, without insolence and harshness but with meekness and reverence' (ad 2)" *(Cursus brevior Theologiae Moralis,* Madrid: Coculsa, 1946, vol. I, p. 287).

k. More details about the circumstances in which it is licit for the faithful to resist their Prelates can be found in F. Suarez, *De legibus,* lib. IX, chap. XX, nn. 19-29; *Defensio Fidei Catholicae,* lib. IV, chap. VI, nn. 14-18; Anacletus Reiffenstuel, *Theologia Moralis,* Venice: Bortoli, 1704, tract. IV, d. VI, q.5, nn. 51-54, pp. 162-163; Joannes Petrus Gury and Antonius Ballerini, *Compendium Theologiae Moralis,* vol. I, pp. 222-227; Camillus Mazella, *De Religione et Ecclesia,* pp. 747-748; Teofilo Urdanoz, *Commentaire sur les "Relecciones Teologicas de Francisco Vitoria,"* Rome: Tip. Polygl., 1880, pp. 426-429, in A. V. Xavier da Silveira, *La nouvelle Messe).*

since failure to fulfill it would amount to a sin known as *peccatum taciturnitatis* [the sin of being silent].[4] For these reasons, the Author believes he has the right and the duty to analyze the Council. His *first*

---

4. Dealing with the *peccatum taciturnitatis* (sin of being silent) in general, Vincent de Beauvais thus explains this grave moral fault: "Next we should consider taciturnity. For one must know that just as an excess of loquacity is vicious, so also is, at times, excessive taciturnity. Indeed, 'There is a time to keep silence and a time to speak' (Eccles. 3:7); St. Isidore: 'The tongue must be watched, but not inflexibly arrested.' For it is a vice, by keeping quiet, to allow someone unworthy or unfit to be chosen for promotions and honors, or permit someone worthy to lose his dignity, goods or honor.

"The same can be said if, in meetings of the council, you keep quiet out of ignorance or malice and thus withhold the truth from the other advisers. Likewise, during a court hearing, if you see someone make a fraudulent accusation or be unjustly condemned, you will sin. And if you fail to reprehend the detractors in conversations defaming others, by neither excusing nor praising the person defamed, if you keep quiet, you will sin. Likewise, when you perceive that a word to edify, instruct, exhort or correct someone is necessary, you commit a sin if you withhold that wholesome advice. Hence Isaiah exclaimed: 'Woe is me, because I have held my peace' (6:5). The same is said in Ecclesiasticus: 'And refrain not to speak in the time of salvation' (4:28)" (*Speculum quadruplex sive speculum maius,* Graz, Akademische Druck-Verlagsanstalt, 1964, col. 1228).

This command is directed primarily to the Hierarchs and clerks who keep quiet. Nevertheless, their defection obliges all laymen to speak up, since Vincent de Beauvais, cited below, uses the adverb **especially** when referring to the Prelates, which means that those who are not vested with priestly dignity have an analogous duty.

"This is obligatory **especially** for Prelates and all those who direct or take care of souls. This is clearly stated in Exodus: 28, whose precept called for placing little bells alternating with pomegranates hanging from the priestly chasubles so that the priest would be heard as he entered or left the sanctuary and thus would not die. St. Gregory explains this by saying: 'The priest who enters will die if the sound is not heard, for he will attract for himself the wrath of the Eternal Judge if the sound of preaching does not come from him.' Likewise, Ezekiel, 33:6: 'And if the watchman sees the sword coming, and sounds not the trumpet: and the people look not to themselves, and the sword comes, and cuts off a soul from among them: he indeed is taken away in his iniquity, but I will require his blood at the hand of the watchman'" (*ibid.*).

Furthermore, failure to exercise this duty of the laymen to speak up when Prelates defect also implies a sin. The Church's ancient Codes of

credential is, therefore, the fact that he is a Catholic.

§ 8   The Author's *second credential is* his condition as a layman. Vatican Council II itself so exalted the mission of the laity [5] that its documents of themselves would suffice to place the Author entirely at

---

Law defined the *peccatum taciturnitatis* incurred by the faithful who failed to warn Prelates who deviated from their mission (B. Kloppenburg, A *Eclesiologia do Vaticano II,* Petrópolis: Vozes, 1971, p. 53).

5. a. On the mission of the laity stemming from the Council it is opportune to see the synthesis presented by Fr. Boaventura Kloppenburg, a conciliar expert, chronicler of Vatican II, member of the International Theological Commission and Bishop of Novo Hamburgo, Brazil, in which he consistently enumerates the various conciliar documents exalting the laity to such a point that he states:

"The theology of the laity appears to have placed the theology of the priest into a crisis. Having been abundantly instructed by Vatican Council II about the lay people, we now know that a true equality reigns among all the baptized in regard to the dignity and action common to all faithful in building the Body of Christ (LG 32c); that everyone participates in the mission of the whole Christian people in the Church and the world (LG 31a); that all play an active role in the life and action of the Church (AA l0a); that the lay people are now 'brothers' of their Shepherds (LG 32c, 37a); that absolutely everyone *(quicumque sum)* is called by the Lord to the fostering and perennial sanctification of the Church (LG 33a; AA 2a); that everyone *(omnes omnino Christifideles)* is destined by the Lord himself to the apostolate (LG 33c); that all laymen have the noble burden of working to make the divine plan of salvation reach increasingly all men at all times and in all places (LG 33d); that all who have been baptized participate in the priestly, prophetic and royal mission of Christ (LG 31a; AA 2b, 10a); that the Supreme and Eternal Priest wants to continue his testimony and his service also through the lay people (LG 34a), by granting them, in part, his priestly charge (LG 34b); that the Great Prophet exerts his prophetic mission not only through the Hierarchy but through the laity as well (LG 35a), having, for this reason, made them into witnesses and embellished them with the sense of faith and the grace of the word (*ibid.*); that also the lay people play an active role in the Eucharistic action, during which they should also offer up themselves and 'not only through the hands of the priest' (SC 48).

"All this generous conciliar doctrine on the nature of lay people and their place and action in the Church has caused many to ask themselves about the meaning and reason for being of ministers in the Church, and precisely to what degree they are distinct from those who hold the common priesthood" (B. Kloppenburg, A *ecclesiologia do Vaticano II,* pp. 203-204).

b. Should laymen, in this great participation opened by the Council, passively accept everything their Shepherds propose to them, or would it be possible for them to disagree when faced with serious and well-weighed reasons? It would seem that the orientation of Vatican II gives lay people a freedom of analysis that few would dare to advocate some years ago. This can be deduced from the comments of the above cited Franciscan theologian, whose notion of contestation would deserve, it seems to us, certain reservations:

"In principle, an attitude of contestation in the Church is possible and can be legitimate and necessary. It is perfectly possible to love the Church, be identified with her, live in her and for her, and at the same time to want her to become more consistent with herself, holier and more immaculate, without stains or wrinkles. For, according to the Council, in fact the Church is 'at the same time holy and always in need of purifying herself' (LG 8d); and as a human and earthly institution she is 'in need of constant reform' (UR 6a). For this reason, as Mother, 'she exhorts her children to purification and renewal so that the sign of Christ may shine brighter on the face of the Church' (LG 15). These words, 'renewal' and 'purification' frequently reappear in the documents of Vatican II and invite us to take an attitude of criticism and contestation. ...

"The Council goes so far as to invite the faithful to 'examine with a sincere and attentive mind that which must be renewed and accomplished inside the Catholic family itself, so as to give a more faithful and luminous testimony of the doctrine and teachings received from Christ through the Apostles' (UR 4e). It is an authentic invitation to contestation, especially if the word is understood in its etymological and positive meaning, which includes the idea of bearing witness to.

"The Council asks laymen to 'manifest to Shepherds their needs and wishes with the freedom and trust becoming children of God and brethren in Christ. According to their knowledge, competence, and ability, they have a right and at times even a duty to express their opinion about things related to the good of the Church' (LG 37a). And the Council asks that the just freedom of investigation and of thought of the faithful, clergy, or laity, be recognized, as well as their just freedom to express their ideas with humility and firmness in matters of their competence' (GS 62g).

"The old collection of ecclesiastical law spoke of *peccatum taciturnitatis,* the sin of those who failed to freely warn Prelates when they were harming the Church. A good contester exerts the function of a prophet. But a prophet is not always pleasant. In the history of the Church there have been powerful contesters, some of whom have even been canonized; but before being canonized, they were burned..." (B. Kloppenburg, *A ecclesiologia do Vaticano II, pp.* 52-53).

ease to analyze the Council.

§ 9   Furthermore, in the post-Council period there has been no lack of exhortations in this same sense, which can be found, for example, in the *Code of Canon Law* [6] and in the conclusions of the Extraordinary Synod convened by the Holy Father John Paul II in 1985 to review Vatican Council II, analyze its consequences and relive its spirit.

In the *Message to the People of God,* the final document of the meeting, the Synod's Bishops recommended that everyone strive to study Vatican II in depth: "We invite you to know Vatican Council II in a better and more complete way, intensify and deepen your study of it, and better understand the unity and riches of all its Constitutions, Decrees and Declarations." [7] John Paul II gave a homily endorsing the message of this Synod. [8]

§ 10   In October 1987, a Synod of Bishops was held in Rome to study the role of the laity in the Church and temporal society. In the

---

6. See canons 224-231. On the emphasis given in the new *Code* to the role of the laity in the Church, Fr. Jesus S. Hortal, commentator, writes: "One of the complaints about the 1917 *Code* was that it paid little attention to the laity, dedicating only one canon to them (can. 682), since the others found in Part II of Book II spoke about associations of *the faithful,* which also included the clergy. Now, in addition to the canons of Title I, common to all faithful, are also laid down the obligations and rights of those who make up the immense majority in the Church: the lay people" (*Comments,* in John Paul II, *Código de Direito Canônico,* pp. 98-99).

7. Extraordinary Synod of Bishops, "Mensagem ao povo de Deus," in *L'Osservatore Romano,* Portuguese edition, December 15, 1985, p. 1.

8. "The Synod has attained the goals for which it has been convened: to celebrate, evaluate and promote the Council. As we leave this Synod, it is our desire to intensify pastoral efforts to make Vatican Council II more widely and profoundly known; so that the orientation and guidelines it has given us may be assimilated in the depth of hearts and translated into the lives and behavior of all members of the people of God, with consistency and love. ...

"At the end of this Eucharistic celebration, the *Message* the Synod Fathers want to direct to the Church and the world will be proclaimed in various languages. Would that it touches [people's] hearts, reinforcing the commitment of everyone to generously and consistently put in practice the teachings and guidelines of Vatican Council II" (John Paul II, Homily at the Mass closing the Synod, in *L'Osservatore Romano,* "Solene encerramento do Sinodo extraordinário dos Bispos - O Sínodo projeta Concílio para o terceiro milênio," December 15, 1985, n. 7).

homily closing the Synod, John Paul II expressed his satisfaction not only with the participation of lay people in the works of the Synod but also with the more profound understanding of the importance of the laity in the present day:

> "Today, the last day of the Synod's assembly, we wish to thank the Good Shepherd for bringing us together from all peoples in order to give us a new heart and bring upon us a new spirit (Ezech. 36: 24-26). This 'Spirit' ... manifested itself with new clarity and strength in the teaching of Vatican Council II about the life and vocation of the laity in the Church and in the world. ... We are thankful for the fact that during the Synod we were able to rejoice not only in the participation of laymen (male and female attendants), but also because the development of the Synod's discussions enabled us to listen to the voices of those invited, representatives of the laity coming from all around the world from various countries, who allowed us to take advantage of their experience, advice and suggestions springing from their love of the common cause. In a certain sense, this Synod experience is unprecedented, and we hope it may become a 'model,' a point of reference for the future. ... The Synod endeavored to deepen [the understanding of] the figure of the faithful lay person, bringing to light his extraordinary importance in today's world. The starting point was the teaching of the Council on the Church in her reality as a 'Mystery' of 'communion' and 'mission.'" [9]

§ 11   Since this Synod, there has been no lack of exhortations in every ecclesiastical echelon about the mission of laymen in the Church and today's world. This stimulates us to speak out publicly.

§ 12   *Tempora mutantur!* In the past, the great St. Ignatius of Loyola – when still a mere layman – confronted the tribunals of the Inquisition several times. He was accused by Church personalities who claimed he had no right to speak about the great problems of the Church and highest concerns of the Faith since he had no titles or courses that permitted him to do so. [10] Admonished eight times in

---

9. John Paul II, "Homilia na concelebração final da Assembléia sinodal," in *L'Osservatore Romano,* Portuguese edition, October 30,1987.

10. St. Ignatius of Loyola himself explains this to the King of Portugal, Dom João III, in a letter sent from Rome on March 15, 1545: "And if Your Highness wishes to be informed why there was so much indignation and inquisition against me, know that it was not for something having to do with schismatics, Lutherans or the illuminated, since I have never met them or talked with them; but it was because people were surprised, mainly in Spain, that I, not a graduate in letters, would speak and converse at such great length about spiritual matters" *(Obras Completas,* Madrid: BAC, 1952, p. 701).

juridical proceedings by the Inquisition and imprisoned twice (one time for 42 days and the other for 22), the indomitable Saint did not lose heart. He was honored to be able to wear "the mantle of Our Lord Jesus Christ, which is that of opprobrium, false testimonies and all other insults."[11] What an heroic, fiery example! It should be imitated by those faithful who feel they have a duty to raise their voices in defense of the Catholic Faith and Christian Civilization.

Would St. Ignatius, the outstanding paladin of the fight against Protestants, encounter similar problems today? Consistent with the pattern of behavior of innumerable Church authorities, the Saint should be able to speak freely about all the problems of the Faith and the world without any constraint from some new Inquisition.

§ 13   The *third credential of* the Author is that, since 1964, he has had the honor of being a disciple of Plinio Corrêa de Oliveira and a member of the Brazilian Society for the Defense of Tradition, Family and Property – TFP. [12]

Indeed, the struggle that Plinio Corrêa de Oliveira – a Crusader of the 20th Century [13] – has waged for more than half a century

---

11. *Ibid.,* p. 702.

12. Working in the temporal sphere in defense of the perennial values of Christian Civilization — tradition, family and property — against the wily infiltration of socialism and the brutal attacks of Communism, the TFPs base their civic action on the social doctrine of the Church and undertake it according to the principles of Catholic morality. The TFPs also combated Progressivism in the Church as a main enemy.

The Brazilian Society for the Defense of Tradition, Family and Property was founded in São Paulo in 1960 by Prof. Plinio Corrêa de Oliveira. It was the starting point for the formation of 26 other autonomous and kindred organizations that exist on four continents.

In 1998 after the death of Prof. Plinio (1995), the Author was expelled from TFP for having published the present Work, an action hardly proper to the glorious militant past of the entity (see also note 3 in the *General Information* section).

13. Prof. Corrêa de Oliveira indisputably stood out among the most outstanding Catholic personalities in contemporary Brazil. His thinking has become ever more known and appreciated. His renown as an intellectual and a man of action has made him the subject of dissertation studies.

The writings of the founder of the Brazilian TFP number over 2,300 published titles, including books and articles, and were the object of a graduation thesis (1984) at the University of São Paulo by Prof. Lizânias de Souza Lima, titled *Plinio Corrêa de Oliveira, a Crusader of the 20th*

as a Catholic layman [14] is an example of how fidelity to the traditional teaching of the Magisterium and the *sensus fidelium* can be employed by a layman to analyze questions related to the Church and Christian Civilization.

To speak of books alone, leaving aside the inestimable public action that he carried out since 1928 in this struggle, the following works are especially noteworthy:

Works related to the Church:

- *In Defense of Catholic Action* (1943);
- *Agreement with the Communist Regime – For the Church, Hope or Self-Destruction?*, originally published under the title *The Freedom of the Church in the Communist State* (1963);
- *Unperceived Ideological Transshipment and Dialogue* (1965);
- *The Church Faced with the Escalation of the Communist Threat Appeal to the Silent Bishops* (1976);
- *Indigenous Tribalism: A "Communist-Missionary" Ideal for Brazil in the 21ˢᵗ Century* (1977);
- *At the "Sandinista Night," "Christian" Sandinistas Incite the Catholic Left in Brazil and Hispanic America to Wage Guerilla Warfare* (1980);

Century (about this thesis, see the article by Gregório Lopes under the same title in *Catolicismo,* September 1985).

Two quite controversial Ph.D. papers also dealt with notable episodes of the public action of Plinio Corrêa de Oliveira. The *first,* presented in 1971 at the Columbia University College of Political Sciences by Prof. Margaret Patrice Todaro, was titled *Pastors, Prophets and Politicians: A Study of the Brazilian Catholic Church, 1916-1945,* University of Columbia, 1971, pp. 180, 192, 225, 238, 318-319., 321, 449-450, 503-506; the *second,* presented in 1981 by Fr. José Ariovaldo da Silva, OFM, at the Anselmianum's Liturgical Institute in Rome: *0 movimento litúrgico no Brasil – Estudo histórico* (Petrópolis: Editora Vozes, 1983).

14. About the action of Plinio Corrêa de Oliveira for over more than 50 years, the Reader may consult *A Half Century of Epic Anti-communism* (New York: The Foundation for a Christian Civilization, Inc., 1980); *Um homem, uma obra, uma gesta - Homenagem das TFPs a Plinio Corrêa de Oliveira,* (São Paulo: Edições Brasil de Amanhã, 1989); Comisión de Estudios de las TFPs, *Tradición, Familia, Propiedad – Un ideal, un lema, una gesta – La Cruzada del siglo XX* (São Paulo: Artpress, 1990).

- *The BCCs ... Much Talked About but Little Known –
  The TFP Describes Them as They Are;* in collaboration
  with Gustavo A. Solimeo and Luís S. Solimeo (1982).

**Works related to Christian Civilization and indirectly to the
Church:**

- *Revolution and Counter-Revolution* (1959, updated in
  1977 and 1992);
- *Agrarian Reform, a Question of Conscience;* in collabo-
  ration with Bishop A. Castro Mayer, Archbishop G. de
  Proença Sigaud and L. Mendonça de Freitas (1961);
- *The Morro Alto Declaration;* in collaboration with Bishop
  A. Castro Mayer, Archbishop G. de Proença Sigaud and
  L. Mendonça de Freitas (1964);
- *Self-Managing Socialism: In Regard to Communism, a
  Barrier? Or a Bridgehead?* (1981);
- *As a Catholic, May I Oppose Land Reform?,* in collabo-
  ration with Carlos del Campo (1981);
- *Private Property and Free Enterprise in the Hurricane
  of Land Reform,* in collaboration with Carlos del Campo
  (1985);
- *Warriors of the Virgin: The Response of Authenticity –
  The TFP without Secrets* (1985);
- *In Brazil, Land Reform Takes Misery to Countryside and
  City - The TFP Informs, Analyzes, Alerts* (1986);
- *Projected New Constitution Anguishes the Country*
  (1987);
- *Is Communism Dead? And Anti-communism as Well?*
  (1989);
- *Communism and Anti-communism in the Fringe of
  the Last Decade of the Millenium* (1990);
- *Nobility and Traditional Elites in the Allocutions of
  Pius XII to the Roman Patriciate and Nobility* (1993).

In these works the author analyzes delicate contemporary
problems of the Church, especially from the standpoint of their repercussions in civil society. Along with a remarkably penetrating analysis
of today's problems and the vigorous logic of his thinking, his language reflects a deep-rooted *sensus fidelium* or *sensus Fidei.*[15]

---

15. The qualities of Prof. Plinio Corrêa de Oliveira were described by the
Holy See itself in two honorable letters of praise that it sent him.

To the same effect, much could be said about the civic action of the TFPs, established in 26 countries, inspired by principles of the traditional doctrine of the Church and in the *sensus fidelium*. But this would unduly prolong the present Introduction.

Having been a TFP member, therefore, is the Author's *third credential.*

§ 14   Having thus dealt with the credentials that allow the Author to analyze the Council, a word should be said about the **supplementary nature** of this Study. Indeed, since the holding of Vatican II, Prof. Plinio has requested several Prelates and ecclesiastics of a high intellectual caliber to analyze it in depth from the standpoint of perennial Catholic doctrine. Prof. Plinio proposed to make great sacrifices in order to facilitate such a study. But for various reasons that do not need to be pursued here, these initiatives proved to have been in vain. Thus, facing the imperative of conscience to analyze Vatican Council II, Prof. Plinio decided vicariously to take up the task that others refused. And so he invited the Author to carry out that task. Ecclesiastical preparation and theological erudition, therefore, should not be required of him, but only a level of competence normal to a layman not specialized in theological studies.

The *first,* written in the name of Pius XII by the then Substitute of the Secretary of State, Archbishop Giovanni Baptista Montini, later Paul VI, conveys the applause of that Pontiff to the Brazilian thinker for his book *In Defense of Catholic Action,* with a preface by the Apostolic Nuncio in Brazil, Archbishop Bento Aloisio Masella, later Cardinal. Dated February 26, 1949, the letter is published in the second edition of the book, celebrating the 40th anniversary of its publication (São Paulo: Artpress, 1983, p. 3).

The *second* refers to the essay, *The Freedom of the Church in the Communist State,* which Prof. Corrêa de Oliveira wrote during the first session of the Second Vatican Council and had distributed to the Conciliar Fathers. In this letter, signed by Cardinal Giuseppe Pizzardo and Archbishop Dino Staffa, Prefect and Secretary of the Dicastery respectively, the Sacred Congregation of Seminaries and Universities congratulates the "scholarly author, deservedly celebrated for his philosophical, historical and sociological science," and deems his work "a most faithful echo of the documents of the supreme Magisterium of the Church."

This letter is dated December 2, 1964 and appears in the essay's several editions. In it, these high Prelates augur "the widest possible distribution of the significant booklet." The book had ten editions in Portuguese, eleven in Spanish, five in French, four in English, three in Italian, two in Polish, one in German, one in Hungarian, one in Ukrainian and one in Vietnamese, for a total of 171,000 copies. It was also transcribed by 39 newspapers or magazines in 13 countries.

§ 15

The **words of the title of this Collection,** *"Eli, Eli, Lamma Sabacthani?"* [My God, My God, why hast Thou forsaken Me?], were the words Our Lord Jesus Christ pronounced on the height of the Cross. These words seem to signify the supreme affliction and perplexity in which Catholics, including the Author of these lines, find themselves *vis-à-vis* the enigmatic silence and the surprising "unconcern" of the Sovereign Pontiffs and the Catholic Hierarchy in regard to the disarray, unprecedented in History, that has become installed in the bosom of Holy Church and in the treasure of Catholic doctrine since the conciliar winds began to blow.

The TFP (founded in 1960) and, prior to that, the group gathered around the monthly *Catolicismo* (founded in 1951), as well as the staff of the weekly *Legionário* (1933-1947), under the leadership of Plinio Corrêa de Oliveira, have had recourse innumerable times to the Holy See. Curiously, however, after the elevation of John XXIII to the pontifical throne, he and the conciliar Popes who followed appeared to be deaf to the clamors of these Catholics.[16]

---

16. a. It is not within the goals of this Collection to enumerate the several instances in which this lay family of souls had recourse to the Apostolic See and the Sovereign Pontiffs. We mention only two initiatives of the TFPs, of gigantic proportions, addressed to Paul VI and which received complete silence for an answer:

In 1968, denouncing leftist infiltration in Catholic circles, the Brazilian TFP organized a petition drive in support of a message that it sent Paul VI, asking that efficacious measures be taken against such an infiltration. The campaign to collect signatures was held in 229 cities and towns all over the country. In only 58 days, 1,600,368 Brazilians had signed. A similar campaign was carried out in Argentina, Chile and Uruguay on the initiative of the local TFPs. The number of signatures in the four countries reached the impressive grand total of 2,038,112. Microfilms of the petition – the largest in Latin America's history – were delivered to the Vatican on November 7, 1969. Nevertheless, this appeal to the Supreme Shepherd from millions of children of Holy Mother Church only drew from Paul VI an inexplicable silence.

Greater details about this document can be found in *Catolicismo* (August-October 1968) and in the articles by Plinio Corrêa de Oliveira, "Das páginas da imprensa para as da História -1," and "SOS de Milhões - A mala pequena - Tudo normal," in *Folha de S. Paulo,* August 17, 1968 and November 31, 1969 respectively.

b. In 1974, the TFPs published in papers world-over a manifesto of resistance to the Vatican *Ostpolitik* initiated during the Council and continued by Paul VI. The policy of *Ostpolitik* consisted of a gradual "relaxation of tensions" between the Holy See and the Communist regimes.

Significant milestones in this policy included the audience John XXIII granted Alexis Adjubei, chief-editor of *Izvestia* and Nikita Kruschev's son-in-law, and the audience that Paul VI granted Nicolai Podgorny, president of Soviet Russia. Nevertheless, this new road to *rapprochement* was impassable without removing certain obstacles. One of these was Cardinal Mindszenty, the hero of Hungary's Catholic anti-communist struggle. As the policy of Paul VI required, the Prelate was demoted from his Primate Seat of Esztergom and obliged to leave his exile in the American Embassy in Budapest. In his Memoirs, the Cardinal himself describes the episodes of this tragedy, involving a whole nation with a venerable history (József Mindszenty, *Erinnerungen,* Frankfurt: Ullstein, 1974, pp. 410-413).

Another event profoundly troubling for Catholics was the visit to Russia by Cardinal Willebrands, president of the Secretariat for the Union of Christians, to attend the installation ceremony of Pimen, a notorious puppet of the Kremlin's bosses, as new "patriarch" of the Russian Schismatic Church. During the Bishop's Synod of 1971, statements by Cardinal Josyf Slipyj, Archbishop of the Ukrainians, revealed details hitherto unknown about the negotiations of the Holy See with Communist regimes. Furthermore, the frequent travels of Cardinal Casaroli – then Secretary of the Vatican Council for Public Affairs – to Iron Curtain countries were disquieting because of his cordiality toward Communist leaders. Most disconcerting were his words after a visit to the island-prison of the Caribbean: "Catholics living in Cuba are happy with the Communist regime" (*O Estado de São Paulo,* April 7, 1974).

Such attitudes could only cause perplexity among faithful followers of the true social teaching of the Church. Indeed, especially in the Encyclicals of Leo XIII, Pius XI and Pius XII, she had condemned Communism as a complete subversion of the natural order (see Chap. I, Note 14c). At the same time, such attitudes placed anti-communist Catholics in a disturbing situation, since their position became inexplicable to public opinion.

Thus, pressed by the successive advances of Vatican *detente,* the TFP declared itself in a **state of resistance** to the *Ostpolitik* of Paul VI. It made known its stand in the manifesto, *The Vatican Policy of Detente with Communist Governments. For the TFP: To Do Nothing? Or to Resist?*

In Brazil, the document was published in its entirety in 37 newspapers around the country, namely: *Catolicismo,* April 1974; *Folha de S. Paulo,* 4/10/1974: *Folha da Tarde,* São Paulo, 4/10/1974; *Diário da Noite,* São Paulo (SP), 4/10/1974; *Correio do Ceará,* Fortaleza (CE), 4/11/1974; *Estado de Minas,* Belo Horizonte (MG), 4/16/1974; *Novo Jornal,* Londrina (PR), 4/21/1974; *A Tribuna,* Santos (SP), 4/21/1974; *O Globo,* Rio de Janeiro (RJ), 4/23/1974; *Folha de Londrina,* Londrina (PR), 4/23/1974; *Correio do Povo,* Porto Alegre (RS), 4/23/1974; *A Tribuna,* São Carlos (SP), 4/23/1974; *Jornal de Santa Catarina,* Blumenau (SC), 4/27/1974;

Jornal da Manhã, Ponta Grossa (PR), 4/27/1974; *Diário de Natal,* Natal (RN), 4/27/1974; *Jornal de Hoje,* Maceio (AL), 4/28/1974; *Díario da Região,* São José do Rio Preto (SP), 4/28/1974; *A Cidade,* Ribeirão Preto (SP), 4/28/1974; *Diario da Manhã,* Recife (PE), 4/29/1974; 0 *Estado do Paraná,* Curitiba (PR), 4/30/1974; *Jornal dos Municípios Brasileiros,* Rio de Janeiro (RJ), April 1974, *Diário de Aracaju,* Aracaju (SE), 5/3/6/ 1974; *A Tarde,* Salvador (BA), 5/4/1974; *Diário de Pernambuco,* Recife (PE), 5/5/1974; *O Popular,* Goîania (GO), 5/8/10/1974; *Jornal da Cidade,* Olimpia (SP), 5/11/1974; *A União,* João Pessoa (PB), 5/12/1974; *A Província do Pará,* Belem (PA), 5/12/1974; *Comércio de Franca,* Franca (SP), 5/28/1974; *Diario de Borborema,* Campina Grande (PB), 5/28/ 1974; *O Jornal,* Manaus (AM), 5/30, 6/1/2/5/1974; *Centro Sul,* Barra do Pirai (RJ), 6/1/1974; *Jornal da Paraíba,* Campina Grande (PB), 6/2/ 1974; *O Estado do Maranhão,* Sao Luis (MA), 6/19/1974; *Jornal Pequeno,* São Luís (MA), 6/22/1974; *A Gazeta,* Vitória (ES), 8/7/1974; *Correio Braziliense,* Brasília (DF), 9/10/1974.

Summaries were published in *Folha do Comércio ,* Campos (RJ), 4/14/ 1974; *Correio do Povo,* Porto Alegre (RS), 4/16/1974; *A Cidade,* Campos (RJ), 4/16/1974; *Tribuna do Ceará ,* Fortaleza (CE), 4/17/1974; *Unitá rio,* Fortaleza (CE), 4/18/1974; *A Nação,* Blumenau (SC), 4/21/1974; *Correio do Sul,* Cachoeira do Itapemirim (ES), 4/26/1974; *O Social Democrata,* Cuiabá (MT), 5/1/1974.

It was also published by 21 periodicals in ten countries. In Argentina, *La Nacion,* of Buenos Aires and *Voz del Interior,* of Córdoba; in Bolívia, *El Diario* of La Paz; in Canada, *Speak Up* of Toronto; in Chile, *La Tercera,* of Santiago, *El Sur* of Concepcion, *El Diario Austral* of Temuco and *La Prensa* of Osorno; in Colombia, *El Tiempo* and *El Espectador* of Bogotá; in Ecuador, *El Comercio* of Quito; in Spain, *Hoja del Lunes* and *Fuerza Nueva* of Madrid, and *Región* of Oviedo; in the United States, *The National Educator* of Fullerton, California; in Uruguay, *El País* of Montevideo; and in Venezuela, *El Universal, El Nacional, Ultimas Notícias, El Mundo* and *2001* of Caracas.

The Declaration of Resistance was also published by the following organs of the TFPs: *Tradición, Familia, Propiedad* of the Argentine TFP; *Fiducia* of the Chilean TFP; *Cristiandad* of the Young Bolivians for a Christian Civilization; *Reconquista* of the Ecuadorian TFP; *Cruzada* of the Colombian TFP; *Covadonga* of the Venezuelan TFP; and *Crusade for a Christian Civilization* of the American TFP. In Spain, the Covadonga Cultural Society distributed 300,000 copies of the manifesto in the streets of Madrid and other cities. The Bureau Tradition, Famille, Propriété distributed it in France and also among German Catholic circles in a booklet titled *TFP – der Kreuzzug des 20. Jahrhunderts.*

To this gigantic initiative the Holy See did not deign to give any answer whatsoever.

Thus, the cry of Our Lord Jesus Christ on the Cross, *"Eli, Eli, Lamma Sabacthani?,"* forsaken by His own Eternal Father, seems to express well the situation of the innumerable faithful who, though loving and obedient children of Holy Church and of the Vicar of Christ, see themselves abandoned and with no avenue of recourse.

The title of this Collection is also and above all a prayer to Almighty God, through the intercession of Mary Most Holy, to protect and restore the Holy Catholic Church.

We beseech Him to shorten the days of agony His Church is going through and to make her rise again from the present crisis even stronger, more beautiful and perfect than ever. This is also a plea that He may bring to completion in history the full implantation of His Kingdom through the triumph of the Immaculate Heart of Mary, so that as many souls as possible will be saved according to the initial design of Divine Wisdom for the Church Militant and the Church Triumphant.

§ 16

To whom is this Collection addressed?

First of all, to the Shepherd of Shepherds, so that he may receive our analysis as an homage to the only one true Church, the Holy Roman Catholic and Apostolic Church, Mystical Body of Christ, against whom the gates of Hell shall never prevail, and of which he, as Sovereign Pontiff, is the visible Head. May he deign to consider what we expound here as an expression of our love and obedience to the perennial teaching of the Ecclesiastical Magisterium and orient us in this regard. If we are wrong, let him offer us the charity of pointing out where we have strayed from the infallible path of truth. His correction will be considered an honor and a gift and will be received with an open heart. If we are right, let him save the Bark of Peter from the storm in which it appears to be going asunder and thus acquire, in the eyes of God and of History, the angelic stature of a St. Gregory VII that would be reserved for him.

It is also addressed to the ensemble of Hierarchs, successors of the Apostles, Princes of the Church, guardians of Faith and Morals and to theologians as a whole. To all of these, we renew our above request to the Sovereign Pontiff.

Finally, it is addressed to the faithful so that they may consider this ensemble of events and give us their opinions and suggestions on what should be corrected or perfected.

We hope that the present Collection will serve to enlighten

those who do not see the whole picture of what is happening and act as a cry of alert to those who see and do nothing.

§ 17   Therefore, the **state of mind** of the Author is one of love, obedience and fidelity to the Holy Catholic Church, to the Successor of Peter, to the ordinary and extraordinary teaching of the Ecclesiastical Magisterium, to the *sensus fidelium.*

From first line to last, this Collection has been written with the most sincere dispositions of faith, hope and charity. Our dispositions have not been altered even by the profound perplexity that took hold in our mind as we noted in the documents, spirit and fruits of the Council an apparent or real installation of a new conception different from the Catholic one.

§ 18   As we present our dispositions of veneration and obedience to the Sovereign Pontiff, it is well to say a word advising the Reader about the **style** we will use in this Collection when referring to the Popes.

In a study of an analytical type such as this, it did not seem feasible for us to combine the reverence we would like to display with the coldness proper to this method of exposition. If renewed at every mention, the reverential manifestations of our obedience would even further increase the size of this Work, which, due to the method adopted, is already quite large. We had to choose a style. And although lamenting that it prevents us from always paying the homages we would like, we chose brevity.

As a general rule, references to the Holy Pontiffs will be simple and bereft of adjectives. Our analyses of their words will seek to get to the bottom of the matters raised. And if, at one time or another, the thinking of one of the recent Popes apparently disagrees with the perennial teaching of the Magisterium of the Church, we will say so in the hope that, if we are wrong, we will be paternally corrected. And for this, as we have said, we are disposed *toto corde.*

No arrogance dwells in our hearts as a son. And if we analyze, among several excerpts from other authors, the thinking and action of the conciliar Pontiffs, it is out of duty of conscience and following venerable examples from Saints who acted likewise without the least prejudice to their zeal for the Papacy or their love of the Church. Even in extreme cases, no one was ever branded as arrogant for having analyzed the attitude of a Pope in an upright manner to fulfill an imperative of conscience.

This is what one learns from the life of St. Augustine. Faced with the attitude of Pope Zozimus, "praising as true and Catholic the faith of Pelagius and his accomplice Celestius," [17] he did not fear to raise his voice in a vigorous *obtestatio* [18] addressed to Rome. [19] In it the great Bishop of Hippo, along with St. Aurelius, Bishop of Carthage, and other African Bishops, stated that the previous judgment of the Church, opposed to Zozimus' opinion, remained in force. [20]

　　　　Later, the future St. Zozimus, realizing that he had been deceived by Pelagius and his accomplice, agreed with St. Augustine and the African Bishops. [21] In a long document titled *Tractoria,* he demonstrated the Pelagian errors and expressed his gratitude for the service rendered by his African sons. [22]

---

17. Facundus Hermianensis: "They will find blessed Zozimus, Bishop of the Apostolic See, praising as true and Catholic the faith of the same Pelagius and of his accomplice Celestius, against the sentence of St. Innocent, his predecessor, who had condemned the Pelagian heresy ... and also censuring the African Bishops for considering the two of them as heretics" *(Liber VII,* chap. 3, in PL 45, 1723; *Pro defensione trium capitulorum,* in PL 67, 687).

Among the works of Pope Zozimus, see the letter *Postquam nobis,* of September 21, 417; Joannes Dominicus Mansi, *Sacrorum Conciliorum nova et amplissima collectio,* Venice, 1759, vol. VI, col. 353; Jaffe-Wattembach, *Regesta Pontificum Romanorum,* Leipzig, 1885, 330; cited by G. de Plinval, *Les luttes pelagiennes,* in V.A., *Histoire de l'Eglise depuis les origines* jusqu'à *nos jours,* ed. A. Fliche and V. Martin (Paris: Bloud & Gay, 1945), vol. IV, p. 108.

See also, by the same Pontiff, Letter *Magnus pondus;* J. D. Mansi, *Sacrorum Conciliorum,* vol. IV, col. 350; Jaffe-Wattembach, *Regesta Pontificum Romanorum,* vol. IV, 329, in G. de Plinval, *Les luttes pelagiennes.*

18. *Obtestatio* = an oath that takes God as witness.

19. G. de Plinval, *Les luttes pelagiennes.*

20. Here is the text of the *obtestatio* referred to by St. Prosper of Aquitaine: "We declare before God that the sentence pronounced from the See of most blessed Peter by the venerable Bishop Innocent, against Pelagius and Celestius, stands until they profess, most clearly, that we are helped by the grace of God, coming from Our Lord Jesus Christ, not only to know justice but also to put it into practice in each of our actions, for without such a grace we can have, think and do nothing with a true and holy piety" *(Liber contra Collatorem,* in PL 45, 1808).

21. G. de Plinval, *Les luttes pelagiennes,* p. 109.

22. St. Augustine, *De gratia Christi et peccato originali,* II.XXIV, in G. de Plinval, *ibid.*

This Collection's particular aim, however, is not to analyze the position of this or that conciliar or post-conciliar Pontiff. Their thoughts will come into the analysis of Vatican II in conditions analogous to those of the other authors cited.

Having thus explained our position of veneration for the Papacy and the methodological necessity of using a cold, almost scientific language, we close this part of the General Introduction that sets out the premises of the Collection *Eli, Eli, Lamma Sabacthani?*

*

§ 19   The Author finds it opportune to add to these introductory remarks a **brief history** of how this Collection took shape. This will certainly help the Reader understand the actual plan that we presented above.

Having received from Prof. Plinio Corrêa de Oliveira an invitation to do this work, we dedicated ourselves to studying the texts of the official documents of Vatican II.

After some time of analysis and reflection, we reached the conclusion that it would be difficult to harmonize the conciliar texts among themselves. They present a fundamental dichotomy of language in which one can perceive, behind the most important concepts, a clash between two currents of thought. For the most part, this conciliar language appeared to us to have been written so that it could be interpreted either from the standpoint of sound and traditional Catholic doctrine or, surprisingly enough, from that of the doctrines of the neo-Modernist current, which has billeted itself into so many key positions of the contemporary Church. Such language appears to be a masterpiece of a linguistic wordsmith. Woven like precious Flemish lace, with the inestimable threads of the traditional doctrine's vocabulary, it nevertheless seems to reveal the specter of another mentality. Thus, Progressivism [23] entered the official documents of the Magisterium with its head covered by the laced veil of the old traditional language.

---

23. Asked by the Author in a Paris interview on February 16, 1983 how he would define the current of thought to which he belongs and that prevailed in Vatican II (Vol. I, *In the Murky Waters of Vatican II*, Chap. VI), Fr. Yves Congar stated that it can be defined as *progressiste* or better, *progressante.*

In our view, this current took on the name "progressivist" in order to avoid the label "modernist," since Modernism had been vigorously condemned

As we advanced in our present study, we verified that analysts of great standing and renown had reached the same conclusions that we had, even though their position was quite opposed to ours. So we dedicated the first Volume of this Collection to expound this initial difficulty we faced: the ambiguities in the documents of Vatican II.

An immediate consequence of such ambiguities is to make an analysis of the conciliar texts sterile and fruitless. Indeed, since they

---

by St. Pius X in the Encyclical *Pascendi Dominici gregis*. But Progressivism is essentially the same as Modernism, as we will see during this Collection. Incidentally, even though this is not so well-known, the very modernists at times called themselves progressivists (Antonio Fogazzaro, *Il Santo,* Milan: no publisher mentioned, 1907, pp. 121, 124, 223; Th. Delmont, *Modernisme et modernistes,* Paris: P. Lethielleux, 1909, pp. 24-25., 103; Emmanuel Barbier, *Histoire du Catholicisme liberal et du Catholisme social en France – Du Concile du Vatican à l'avénement de S.S. Benoît XV,* Bordeaux: Imp. Y. Cadoret, 1924, vol. III, p. 191). That makes sense, since both modernists and progressivists profess an unlimited adherence to modern progress under its various facets: historical, sociological, psychological, technical, etc. They also profess the same desire of reforming the institution and doctrine of the Church in order to adapt them to modern progress.

After the Encyclical *Humani generis* by Pius XII cautioning against certain errors of that current, the word "progressivism" (which soon became widely used to designate that set of errors, even though it was not used in the Encyclical) took on a suspect connotation. With the advent of John XXIII, that connotation disappeared from official Vatican circles and was kept only in traditionalist milieus.

Nevertheless, in the post-conciliar period, due to a muted but considerable reaction that sprung up in the Catholic "silent majority" in regard to the Council's innovations (Vol. I, *In the Murky Waters of Vatican II,* Chap. X.1-4), the term was taken up by some theologians representing the Holy See's official line in order to distinguish their own moderate positions from those of theologians eager to draw every last consequence from the Council. These people the moderates call "progressivists," but using the expression in such a way that it has lost the heterodox connotation that *Humani generis* had given it. Now it is taken more like a synonym of "advanced" or, at worst, "imprudent."

In this Collection the expressions "progressivism" and "progressivist current" will be used with the suspect connotations, from the standpoint of orthodoxy, which stemmed from *Humani generis.* The French expression *progressante* undoubtedly conveys with greater cogency the ongoing evolutionism professed by this current. But even though Congar used it during our conversation, it is not habitually employed, so we will not use it to designate this more advanced current.

If Bing taught thomistic theo/philo how is it you/they can't see the discontinuity of Vat II w/TRADITION.

If Bing professes Fatima lifestyle, how is it he doesn't promote full msg. 3rd Secret of consecration

are ambiguous, they can be used to a greater or lesser degree by any of the currents – conservative or progressivist – in order to draw as much advantage for its respective camp as possible. And any discussion based on the letter of the conciliar documents will be doomed to futility for lack of unity among doctrinal points of reference.

*

§ 20   Since there are difficulties with the letter, one must seek in the spirit of the Council the elements required to interpret it correctly. What is the spirit of the Council?

Usually one has recourse to the spirit of a Code or a Constitution as an element to elucidate the letter of a law or norm that can lend itself to confusion. This is done by searching for the general line of thinking that oriented the legislator as he wrote the ensemble of laws in question. The thinking of an author is normally supposed to have a unity, hence the possibility of using this method to clarify points in doubt.

Therefore, in its current expression, spirit is synonymous with an unexpressed unity of thinking.

As we prepared to apply this criterion to Vatican II, we ran into yet another difficulty. Since the letter of the conciliar documents is ambiguous because of the clash between the thinking of two currents, the documents as a whole cannot be understood as having a unity of thought. It is difficult, therefore, to define what is the spirit of the Council in the current meaning of the word. Logic dictates that since the writing of the documents obeyed two opposed conceptions, the only fitting definition would be that the spirit of Vatican II is a spirit of conflict. This definition, however, helps little to clarify the equivocal points in the conciliar documents.

Having thus eliminated the usual meaning of "spirit" to determine the spirit of Vatican II, we strove to define other meanings in which the expression could be understood.

§ 21   As one considers the ambiguity of conciliar texts, it becomes clear that it was due mainly to the introduction of new concepts of a progressivist substratum. In fact, everyone knows that the perennial thinking of the Church, as well as her spirit, is habitually crystalline, most holy and upright. If there is ambiguity in the documents of Vatican II, it was not due to the current of conciliar Fathers who adhered to the clarity and uprightness traditionally found in the documents of the Church. Therefore, it can only have resulted from the action of individuals who desired ambiguity and perhaps were co-

Spirit = unity of thought

2 Currents Traditional vs. Modernist

Vat. II is a Spirit of conflict

Reason for conflict introduced Modernist substratum

natural with it. Such action is fraught with harmful results, since it soils the pure waters of the Church documents and gives the progressivists a convenient "right of citizenship." When one wants to delve into the composition of murky waters, one does not argue about its composition when the water was crystalline – that has already been established. What is necessary is to determine the nature and makeup of the new element that has soiled it.

So, it becomes indispensable to determine the thinking of the progressivist current of the conciliar Fathers in order to analyze if it has filtered – and to what degree – into conciliar ambiguity.

During our writing, we found that the expression "the spirit of the Council" can be legitimately understood as the spirit of the progressivist current. In this case one really can find an unexpressed unity of thought that explains many ambiguities contained in the texts. It is, therefore, a valid and consistent meaning for the "spirit of the Council."

In this sense, the search for the spirit of Vatican II coincides with the search for the unity of the progressivist thinking. It is from this standpoint that the letter of the conciliar documents should be understood.

Another meaning of the "spirit of the Council" that we frequently encountered is one whereby the spirit of the Council coincides with the dispositions of soul and the purposes of those who convened it. Therefore, the "spirit of the Council" would be the effusive manifestation of goodness on the part of John XXIII, who gave the Council an impulse and a direction to which Vatican II was meticulously faithful to the end. [24] Thus, the underlying intention of the Council would be a particularly broad mercy toward the world and the false religions so that the resulting thaw would cause the militant character of the Church to deteriorate as much as possible. Therefore, such a spirit would be characterized by tolerance toward the

---

[24] These are the words of John XXIII at the Council's solemn *Opening Speech* on October 11, 1962: "As the Ecumenical Vatican Council II begins, it becomes more evident than ever that the truth of the Lord remains eternally. Indeed, as one epoch succeeds another, we see that men's opinions also succeed each other, excluding one another. ... The Church has always opposed these errors; many times she has even condemned them with the greatest severity. In our days, however, **the Spouse of Christ prefers to use the remedy of mercy more than that of severity;** she deems to better satisfy today's needs by showing the validity of her doctrine than by condemning errors. ... **The Catholic Church**, raising by means of this Ecumenical Council the torch of religious truth, **wishes to show herself as the loving mother of all,**

less ✓   *v̄* *↗ Ecumenism*
Religion
world and the false religions and opposition to Catholic militancy. And   *Tolerance*
every writing interpreted under this prism would reveal the underlying
unity of the conciliar documents.

§ 23   In our view these are the two most widely employed meanings for the expression the "spirit of the Council," they are seldom   *#1 Plot*
clearly identified. The second meaning – the spirit of tolerance – usu-   *to Modernity*
ally takes precedence over the first, the unity of the progressivist thinking. The reason for this precedence is that the second appears less   *#2 Tolerance*
threatening and more attractive to many people, whereas the first,
when confronted with traditional Catholic thinking, has the drawback
of suggesting that there must have been some progressivist plot to
dominate the Council and the Church.

          After making this analysis of the meanings of the spirit of the
Council, we found that the first meaning is so comprehensive that
studying it would be tantamount to expounding the whole matter contained in this Collection. In other words, there would be no real distinction between the spirit of the Council and the thinking of the progressivist current that inspired it. We believe that to do this would
introduce an element of confusion in a Work whose goal is to clarify.

          For this reason, we adopted the second meaning to analyze
the spirit of the Council.[25]   *(Tolerance)*

§ 24   As we endeavored to delve deeply into the much-trumpeted
kindness and mercy toward the world and the false religions, we found
in innumerable authors a veritable apologia for tolerance and an utter
aversion for the militant, sacral and hierarchical character of Holy
Church. Their attitudes were so categorical and laden with hatred   *whose?*
that, in our view, far from reflecting a "constructive" and disinterested
mercy, they constitute a real *animus injuriandi* (desire to injure) toward the Catholic Church and Religion. As a matter of fact, their
hostility goes so far as to characterize an *animus delendi* (desire to
destroy). Thus, the *animus injuriandi* and *animus delendi* shown

---

benign, patient, full of mercy and kindness. ... **The Church** ...
through her children, also **extends everywhere the amplitude of
Christian charity,** which is the best aid to eliminate the seeds of dis-
cord; and nothing is more efficacious to foment concord, a just peace
and the fraternal union of all" (John XXIII, *Opening Speech,* in B.
Kloppenburg, *Concílio Vaticano II,* Petrópolis: Vozes, 1963, vol. II, pp.
310-311).

25. The Reader can find a more detailed examination of the expression
the "spirit of the Council" and the reasons why we have adopted the
second meaning in Vol. II, *Animus Injuriandi I,* Introduction, which for
practical purposes was repeated in Vol. IV, *Animus Delendi I,* Introduction.

by innumerable and important exponents of conciliar theology would reveal the other side of the coin of the conciliar spirit, whose sugary side is usually presented.

It is to expound the impressive roll of such offenses and self-destructive designs, inasmuch as they express the spirit of the Council, that we dedicated Volumes II to V of this Collection.

§ 25   What is the underlying thinking of the Council? How can it be determined?

Two possible ways came to our mind to determine the thinking of Vatican II.

The *first* consists in examining the key concepts of the conciliar documents – the Church as Mystery, as Spouse, as People of God, as Sinning Church; the concept of pastoral, world, man, history, evolution, etc. – trying to analyze them and draw from each concept all that is implicit in it both in the field of ideas and of tendencies, as did Prof. Plinio Corrêa de Oliveira with the word "dialogue." In his work *Unperceived Ideological Transshipment and Dialogue,* [26] he draws from the "talisman-word" dialogue all the consequences it carries in its bosom. He shows how it presents the peculiar characteristic of luring those who hear or use it into a dialectical game and of eliciting a series of psychological reactions, first sympathy and then connivance, which turn the one who dialogues into the victim of a subtle process of psy war.[27] Without perceiving it, the victim who goes through the various stages of this process will end up by tendentially adhering to Hegelian dialectics and will even acquire a propensity to accept the Socialist and Communist ideas that he once fought.

---

26. Plinio Corrêa de Oliveira, *Unperceived Ideological Transshipment and Dialogue*, in *Crusade for a Christian Civilization*, New York, vol. 12, n. 4, Oct.-Dec. 1982.

27. a. The expression *psychological warfare,* or *psy war* for short, is being used more and more frequently. We believe it can be applied not to military battles specifically, even though its primary analogical sense is that of a confrontation between armies. Thus, the Communist offensive to conquer the West is to a large extent a *psy war*. By analogy, we apply the expression to the progressivist expansion in the Church. Here are some testimonies by specialists corroborating the broader concept of warfare contained in the expression, *psy war*.

b. Russian Marshall Nikolay Bulganin states: "Modern war is a psychological war, requering the Armed Forces only to stave off an armed attack or, occasionally, to occupy territory conquered through a psychological action" (in Hermes de Araujo Oliveira, *Guerra revolucionária,* Rio de Janeiro: Bibliex, 1965, p. 60).

§ 26   As for the progressivist offensive, there are many proofs and indications that *psy war* has been used in its development, based on certain concepts. For example, "Church as Mystery" favors conceptions of modernist pneumatology; "Spouse Church" induces a new theology with certain erotic connotations of a Freudian kind; "People of God" paves the way for democracy in Church government, common ownership of property and a structuralist tribalism; "Sinning Church" pays tribute to Protestant *kenosis*, which in turn ends up in the theology of the "death of God," a remote daughter of Nietzsche; "pastoral" leads to existentialism, etc.

A demonstration of this matter would lead us to describe a method of the progressivist current of thought and how it determines the goals it has in mind. If it were proven that the accomplishment of this project were the intention of the progressivist wing in Vatican II, we would have gone a long way toward determining what their thinking was.

§ 27   The *second* way would consist in studying the thinking of the principal theologians who idealized and applied the Council, and in trying to determine their system of thinking: its substratum, methods

---

Terence H. Qualter, from the University of Waterloo (Iowa, USA), observes: "Originally psychological warfare was designed as a preliminary to military action, demoralizing the enemy soldiers before the attack was launched, or as an aid to military action, hastening and cutting the cost of victory. Today it has become a substitute for military action. ... A defeat in the Cold War could be as real and as final as a military defeat and, certainly, it would be followed by military defeat" (*Propaganda and Psychological Warfare,* New York: Random House, 1962, pp. XII-XIII).

French specialist Maurice Megret explains that "from Clausewitz to Lenin, technological evolution and the progress in the psychological sciences have conspired to give psychological warfare the quasi magical powers of an 'art of subversion'" (*La guerra psicologica,* Buenos Aires: Paidos, 1959, p. 31).

Another well-known French scholar, Roger Mucchieli, notes with special lucidity: "The classic conception [of warfare] viewed subversion and psychological warfare as one war tool among others, employed during hostilities only. Modern day States, immobilized by this archaic distinction, have failed to understand that psychological warfare explodes the classic distinction between war and peace. It is a non-conventional war unknown to the norms of International Law and the usual rules of war; it is a total war that disconcerts jurists and pursues its goals under the protection of their [law] codes ... Modern warfare is above all psychological, and its relation with classic arms has been inverted" (*La subversión,* Paris: Bordas, 1972, pp. 26-27).

and goals.

After a symposium in which we expounded to Prof. Corrêa de Oliveira the advantages we found in each of the two ways, it was decided to opt for the second.

So we set ourselves to it.

§ 28   A trip to Europe, during which we were kindly received by prominent theologians who inspired or wrote various of the Council's documents, and by other personalities highly placed in the theological world, enabled us to clarify various points of their thinking, learn some details about the history of their action in the Council and collect a select bibliography. This also saved us years of study, giving us the advantage of a navigator who possesses a precise map as opposed to one who sails at random.

Upon our return, we carefully organized the knowledge thus gathered and, following the compass of Catholic sense that assists one of the common faithful, set out to read and study.

Progressivist thought as a whole, with its foundations and ultimate goals, as well as the fruits of the Council, will be presented beginning in Volume VI; Volume VIII will be especially dedicated to it. Incidentally, several characteristics of this thought are outlined in Volumes II to V as we analyze the spirit of the Council.

*

§ 29   Among progressivist authors, especially the most prominent ones, we found a vigorous unity of thought and habitual coordination in action.

Nevertheless, the yet unachieved part of their ideological yearnings and practical goals explicably casts, to a certain degree, a shadow of uncertainty upon their very followers. Such uncertainty generates differences in methods and even, at times, in the understanding of final goals.

For minds less inclined to grand overall visions and more prone to advancing safely in a reasoned fashion from stage to stage, it could seem that small differences in methods or disagreement over ultimate goals among progressivists would generate profound and irreconcilable differences. This is as absurd as if the various army corps assaulting a given fortress could not have different methods of attack and varying intentions on how to maintain the citadel and take the most strategic advantage from it once it was conquered. These minds perceive neither clearly nor immediately the whole ensemble that unites the progressivists and the miniscule points that divide them. They would begin by classifying them in schools, and then divide these into sub-schools. Very quickly, the risk rises of fragmenting the unitary vision of the progressivist thinking. As a consequence, such people would be led to doubt the accuracy of the underlying unity in the progressivist current that this Work presents.

In order to save Readers who have this legitimate way of reasoning from embarrassment, we suggest they read the Volumes of this Collection in which we analyze the unity of thought taking into account the diversities among the schools of conciliar Progressivism.[28]

Normally, however, we will address the progressivist current as a whole, without excessive concern about real or fictitious differences that many of its components present among themselves.[29] While paying concious tribute to a certain imprecision, such generalization appears to us the only way to analyze the current's unity of thought. We thus follow the example of St. Pius X, who, in the Encyclical *Pascendi,* did not delve into accidental distinctions between schools and authors, but instead presented a synthesis of modernist thought in that which was most essential and general.

---

28. Vol. IV, *Animus Delendi I,* Chap. III.1.A, C-E; Vol. V, *Animus Delendi II,* Part II, Chap. V.B; Vol. VI, *Inveniet Fidem?,* Chaps. III.2,5, V.6; Vol. VII, *Destructio Dei,* Chaps. II, III; Vol. VIII, *Fumus Satanae, passim*; Vol. IX, *Creatio,* Chaps. I.1, IV.3; Vol. X, *Peccatum-Redemptio,* Chaps. V, VI.2, VII.

29. About the harmonization between an overall view of a historic phenomenon – whether it be social, political or religious – and its nuances, one can certainly apply to the conciliar reform carried out by progressivists the principles made explicit by Prof. Plinio Correa de Oliveira in this brilliant page commenting on the *Allocution* of Pius VI of June 17, 1793 about the French Revolution and the beheading of Louis XVI: "**The revolutionary phenomenon is seen here in its ensemble: ideology, impulse, countless multitudes filling streets and squares, impious and unseen plotters, the radical goals that attracted the revolutionaries from the outset to the outcome. In this terrible outcome could be seen, behind the initial and at times mild formulas, the radical goals toward which, more and more openly, the Revolution marched as a whole.**

"**This way of seeing the Revolution does not ignore the existence of nuances in the revolutionary phenomenon.**

"Thus, one cannot equate the *Feuillants* of the early stage of the Revolution with the Girondins. The first were liberal monarchists who, compared with the unconditional enthusiasts of the *Ancien Regime*, were to a certain extent revolutionary figures; the latter were for the most part republicans hostile to the clergy and nobility but favorable to the conservation of a liberal socio-economic regime that spared free enterprise, private property and the like from the revolutionary hurricane. The Girondin position had all the elements to appear radically revolutionary not only to the manifest counter-revolutionaries *(Emigrés, chouans* and other royalist guerrillas) but also to the *Feuillants.* Yet it enraged the ultra-radicals of *La Montagne*, who besides demanding the abolition of royalty and the radical and bloody persecution of the clergy and nobility, frequently cast threatening glances upon the great fortunes of the bourgeois class.

"**Having observed this succession of nuances from the *Feuillants* to the members of the Committee of Public Safety** and their throngs of admirers, **one perceives that each nuance or stage of the revolutionary march seems markedly leftist when compared to the preceding nuance or stage, and ultra-conservative in relation to the subsequent one.** This continues until the **Revolution's last breath, exhaled as it was dying in 1795. This gasp was the Communist revolution of Babeuf,** to whose left one can conceive nothing except chaos and vacuity, and to whose right a Babeufist would consign everything that preceded it.

"**A way of considering the Revolution that distinguishes its nuances,** implicitly or explicitly, **presupposes the need to take into account that even the most moderate analysts of the Revolution manifested, along with their moderate intentions, an inexplicable and contradictory indulgence toward and at times outright sympathy for the crimes and criminals of the Revolution.**

"**The simultaneous presence of moderate inclinations and revolutionary connivances** in the minds of 'moderates' throughout the Revolution's stages **led one of the most fervent defenders of the revolutionary phenomenon – Clemenceau – to parry the accusation of contradiction by the summary assertion that 'la Revolution est un bloc'** [the Revolution is a whole] (in Francois Furet and Mona Ozouf, *Dictionnaire critique de la Révolution Française,* Paris: Flammarion, 1988, p. 980), **in which cracks and contradictions are only apparent.**

"In other words, the Revolution – the consequence of a miscellanea of propensities, doctrines and agendas – cannot be praised or censured when identified with only one of its nuances or stages. It must be considered in the light of all of this evident miscellanea.

"**Clemenceau's expression** may appear attractive to many minds; nevertheless, it **is still an insufficient description of the historical reality.**

"In fact, **in this apparent miscellanea, one notices an ordering**

§ 30   The research we carried out to determine the thinking of the Council also enabled us to discover many of its fruits.

To us such fruits appear indisputable, since they are consequences of Vatican II that are found in the realm of actual facts and are thus susceptible to an easy comprehension.

§ 31   At first we planned to analyze the fruits of the Council in dogmatics, morals and liturgy, and to dedicate a minutely detailed study to ecumenism and secularization (understood as the desacralization of the Church and the abolition of Christendom). [30] Finally, we intended to present the various models of "Church" that are outlined for the future. [31] Although we had the necessary material to do this, in order to save time we thought it better to deal for the time being only with the fruits in dogmatics (Volumes VI to XI). So the possibility of continuing the analysis of the fruits of the Council, if need be, remains open.

§ 32   Having analyzed the letter, spirit, thought and fruits of the Second Ecumenical Vatican Council, we hope to have fulfilled our duty as *miles Christi* by providing elements for the defense of Holy Church. In other words, such analysis resulted in an exposition of the situation that the Catholic Church and her doctrine find themselves before the onslaught of the progressivist current, so that those who have eyes may see and those who have power may judge.

This is the history of the present Study.

---

principle of primary importance. From the outset, almost until Babeuf, each stage of the Revolution sought to destroy something and, at the same time, retain something of the old socio-politico-economic edifice. This may and must be admitted, but without ignoring that at each stage the destructive ferment acted with more efficacy, self-assurance and victorious impetus than the conservative tendency did. In fact, the latter always appeared intimidated, insecure and minimalist in what it wished to preserve and readily compliant in what it consented to sacrifice.

'In other words, from beginning to end, the same ferment was active in each of these nuances or stages, making each stage a fleeting marker in the march toward a full surrender. Consequently, the Revolution was already entirely present in its ferment, just as a tree is entirely present in its seed" (*Nobility and Analogous Traditional Elites in the Allocutions of Pius XII*, York, PA: TFP, 1993, pp. 411-412).

30. Ecumenism and secularization are analyzed in summary fashion in Vol. *V, Animus Delendi II* in light of the spirit of the Council.

31. A rather brief summary of this matter is found in Chap. VII of Vol. IV, *Animus Delendi-I.*

COLLECTIOM
ELI, ELI, LAMMA SABACTHANI?

VOLUME I

IN THE MURKY WATERS OF VATICAN II

Letter of the Conciliar Documents

*

CLARIFICATION

§ 1   The title of this Volume, *In the Murky Waters of Vatican II,* could appear as a disrespectful accusation hurled at the Council right at the beginning of a Collection that seeks to analyze it impartially.

However, the "murky waters" image that refers to Vatican II is not ours. It was used by Msgr. Philippe Delhaye, professor emeritus at the University of Louvain-la-Neuve and secretary general of the International Theological Commission (1973 to 1988). Indeed, Msgr. Delhaye says: "Vatican II was an apex in Church life to which contributed movements of ideas such as the liturgical movement; an apex from which flow and will continue to flow torrents of living water for the Church. **At the moment these waters are** at times **murky;** certain deviations occur; but what will occur with this Council is what has happened with others: It will take years for its effects to be seen."[1]

§ 2   Cardinal Leo Józef Suenens, the late retired Archbishop of Malines, one of the four moderators who directed the Council and certainly one of the most influential personages at the conciliar assembly, also employs the metaphor of turbulent waters. He says: "In a few words, a work remains to be done: that of harmonizing two viewpoints and leading them back into a perfect synthesis. There is in Ireland a place well-known to tourists, called the meeting of the waters. It is **a valley in which two rivers impetuously clash against each other to form, downstream, only one river of calm waters.** I offer you this metaphor as an invitation to carry out, in a fraternal dialogue, the marvelous symphony – unfortunately incomplete, like all human creation – of *Lumen gentium.*"[2]

§ 3   Referring to the same conflict of tendencies, this time in the post-conciliar phase of the pontificate of Paul VI, Card. Suenens also employs the "murky waters" metaphor: "**Paul VI had to steer the**

---

1. Philippe Delhaye, *In caritate non ficta,* Louvain-la-Neuve: Centre Cerfaux-Lefort, p. 108, in Eliodoro Mariani, "La morale cristiana di fronte ai problemi degli uomini d'oggi," in *L'Osservatore Romano,* 1/5/1984.

2. Leo Józef Suenens, "Discorso ufficiale d'apertura - Alcuni compite della teologia oggi," in V.A., *L'avvenire della Chiesa - Il libro del Congresso,* Brescia: Queriniana. 1970, p. 48 (Congress of *Concilium* magazine in Brussels. September 1970).

§ 4

bark of Peter between opposing currents that made the waters murky. For some, in Rome itself, he too strongly welcomed the majority [progressivist] tendencies, and the reforms carried out met strong local opposition. Meanwhile, outside of Rome, sluggishness and hesitation [toward reform] became accentuated."[3]

One thus sees that the image of murky and turbulent waters did not come originally from us. The reason we used the "murky waters" metaphor employed by Msgr. Delhaye and Card. Suenens as the title to this Volume is that we believe it expresses the actual reality.

Any disrespectful intent, therefore, is far removed from our motives.

*   *   *

---

3. L. J. Suenens, *Souvenirs et espérances,* Paris: Fayard, 1991, p. 253

INTRODUCTION TO VOLUME I

§ 1   In this Volume we endeavor to show the ambiguity of the Council's documents. We say *show,* rather than *demonstrate,* because the number of authors who take the uncertainty of such documents as a premise of their analyses is so large as to make any demonstration practically superfluous.

Nevertheless, the Volume follows the logical order of a demonstration.

§ 2   Before asking any question, we give the Reader, as a few samples of many that could be cited, some of the Council's ambiguous or contradictory texts (Chapter I). We then bring to the fore a whole array of questions so as to help him orient himself amidst the several hypotheses that could explain the use of ambiguity, whether it be fortuitous or not (Chapter II). Next we assemble the testimony of well-respected authors who affirm that there is ambiguity in the texts of Vatican Council II (Chapter III). Could not the elusiveness of Vatican II have been the result of a strategy? In Chapter IV we bring to the Reader several famous authors who state that this was indeed the case. Consistent with that strategy, once the Council was over, the progressivist current began to draw from that ambiguity a new stimulus for its adherents (Chapter V). In addition, the Council's ambiguity reflects a temporary equilibrium of forces between the two opposing currents of thought, the conservative and the progressivist, which we demonstrate in Chapter VI. Now then, if two opposing currents clash over basic concepts, would there be, latent in the ambiguity, a new doctrine different from Catholic doctrine? This is what we strive to answer in Chapter VII. In Chapter VIII we point out how, in addition to clear ambiguities, there are also omissions that favor progressivist concepts.

At that point it will have become clear to a Reader endowed with simple Catholic sense, or even mere common sense, without the need for an elaborate theological formation, that the lack of clarity in the Council's documents is an indisputable reality.

§ 3   Having attained this level of certainty about the ambiguity of the Council – which is what we try to demonstrate in this first Volume – we begin to draw the chief consequences from that conclusion. The first consequence, of a doctrinal order, is that the very ambiguity of the conciliar documents entails grave concessions to other religions

false Ecumenism

and to the modern world, implying a virtual destruction of the Faith and a modification of the concept of the Catholic Church. To this we dedicate Chapter IX. Other consequences are the crises of Faith and discipline among the faithful. We show how the Council's ambiguity brought about a crisis in Church unity. Progressivist and conservative currents interpret the ambiguous texts each in its own way and with its own criteria, tearing apart the unity that bound them together. In addition to this ominous consequence, the authority of the Bishops and even that of the Pope began to be brought into question in view of such ambiguous positions. Finally, we deal with the crisis that affected the secular clergy and religious orders as a result of the Council. Chapter X studies this consequence.

§ 4   Although much could be concluded from the exposition contained in the ten Chapters of this Volume, we will restrict ourselves to saying the undeniable: The Council's texts are ambiguous. Some scholar or Reader may understandably wish to draw from this Volume conclusions other than those stated herein. We have no objections provided that they are guided by the same spirit of faith and love of the Church that inspires these lines.

*

§ 5   The first Chapters of this Volume will be very brief.

Someone might imagine that we found only a few quotations to prove the theses of these Chapters. That would be an error. Practically all the texts that corroborate the theses expounded throughout the Work could also be cited in the first few Chapters. It was difficult to find a criterion of selection to put in proper order a number of texts that were both eloquent and proved several things at the same time. Further on we will say a word about this criterion. In later Chapters, as we repeat some quotations that show ambiguity in language, ambiguity as a method, and so on, the theses expounded in the first Chapters will become stronger in the Reader's mind.

The method of exposition, which we chose from among several, is of a psychological type, born of our own experience. It is aimed at a Catholic reader who, like ourselves before carrying out this study, would be inclined not to admit that there could be the slightest shadow of ambiguity in documents of the Catholic Church such as those of Vatican Council II, whether the ambiguity arose from contradiction or any factor of the sort. We first endeavor to open the

Reader's eyes to the possibility of ambiguity to exist, then to its probability, then to its certainty and once this certainty has been established, we draw various conclusions that flow naturally from the analyzed documents. It is a criterion aimed at showing the painful situation of the Church in our days in a gradual and objective manner.

§ 6

Another objection that could be raised, and to which we would like to answer *avant la lettre,* is that we fail to expound our thinking with the elegant concision that has come to be increasingly appreciated in certain intellectual circles, and that we quote a large number of long texts, making the exposition heavy.

We were actually not especially concerned with elegance. In this Volume, as in the whole Collection *Eli, Eli, Lamma Sabacthani?,* we follow the inductive method, which requires that a sufficient number of texts be cited before each conclusion is drawn. In truth, this method might not be elegant.

However, who in his right mind would criticize a sailor for failing to act elegantly as he attempts to plug a gaping hole in a sinking ship's hull?

Is Holy Mother Church not immersed in a "mysterious process of auto-demolition"? Does the Bark of Peter not seem to be sinking? Is the "smoke of Satan" not penetrating everywhere? The hour, therefore, is not one calling especially for elegance, but rather for dedication and courage. [1]

*   *   *

---

1. To corroborate the need for courage facing the present crisis in the Church, we could cite the words of Paul VI in the audience for the participants of the International Thomistic Congress (September 12, 1970): "Do we not see an excess of crazy Christian ideas drag in their unrestrained tumult the more well-founded certainties and the more secure beliefs? What an admirable work you can and must carry out, in this hour that calls, more than ever for the 'courage of truth!'" *(Insegnamenti di Paolo VI,* vol. VIII, p. 865; Allocution to the Sacred College of May 18, 1970, *ibid.,* pp. 585-586).

Chapter I

AMBIGUITY IN THE TEXTS OF
VATICAN II'S OFFICIAL DOCUMENTS

§ 1   If someone gifted with an average Catholic culture and moved by his love for the Church were to study the documents of Vatican Council II, his mind would gradually be filled with questions as he progressed in his reading.

Right in the first Chapter of the Dogmatic Constitution *Lumen gentium,* he would be in for a surprise: "This ... sole Church of Christ which in the Creed we profess to be One, Holy, Catholic, and Apostolic ... constituted and organized as a society in the present world, **subsists in** the Catholic Church, which is governed by the successor of Peter ... Nevertheless, many elements of sanctification and of truth are found outside its visible confines [sic]. Since these are gifts belonging to the Church of Christ, they are forces impelling towards Catholic unity" (LG 8b).

This passage would have been clear if it had stated that the Church of Christ is the Catholic Church or that the Church of Christ **exists exclusively in** the Catholic Church. As written, it implicitly affirms that there are two distinct realities – the Church of Christ and the Catholic Church – and that the latter, which would be more restricted, would receive its life from the former, more universal and more noble.[1]

What "Church of Christ" would this be, different from and nobler than the Catholic Church, which would receive its very life from it? Would it be a "church" containing the "elements of sanctification and truth" that are found "outside" the visible Catholic structure? As he searches for an explanation, the Reader ends up in an even greater confusion: Could there be, then, habitually, "sanctification and truth" outside the sacred bosom of the Catholic Church?

This statement implying the existence of two different churches clashes both with the perennial teaching of the Magisterium and the

---

1. The progressivists base themselves on the supposed distinction between the Catholic Church and the "Church of Christ" to promote ecumenism with heretical and schismatic confessions. The Reader can find more about this matter in Vol. *V, Animus Delendi II,* Part II.

Catholic sense of the faithful, who have always nourished themselves, as children with their mother's milk, on the idea that the Catholic Church is the sole Church of Christ. [2] Desirous of finding a respectful solution to such an awkward statement, the faithful Catholic is led to ask himself whether the expression *subsistit in* was used inadequately.

---

2. a. In his Allocution *Ubi primum,* of December 17, 1848, Pius IX recalls the traditional doctrine that the Church of Christ is the Catholic Church: "Let those, therefore, who wish to be saved, come to this column, this foundation of the truth which is the Church." **Let them come to the true Church of Christ which, in her Bishops and in the Roman Pontiff, supreme chief of all, possesses the uninterrupted succession of apostolic authority,** which has desired more than anything to preach, preserve and defend the doctrine announced by the Apostles, fulfilling the command of Jesus Christ. [**The Church**] which, since the times of the Apostles, grew amid all kinds of difficulties and, radiant with the luster of miracles, multiplied by the blood of Martyrs, ennobled by the virtues of the Confessors and Virgins, fortified by the testimonies and sage writings of the Fathers, **laid roots and flourished in all countries of the earth, and shines through the perfect unity of faith in the same Sacraments and the same spiritual regime.**

"**We who,** in spite of Our indignity, occupy the supreme Chair of the Apostle Peter, upon which Our Lord Jesus Christ established the foundation of His Church, **have never spared effort nor work to bring back to this sole way of truth and salvation,** by the grace of the same Jesus Christ, **those who are in ignorance in error. And let all those who are our adversaries remember** that though heaven and earth shall pass, none of the words of Christ can pass; **that nothing can be changed in the doctrine that the Catholic Church received from Jesus Christ to preserve, defend and preach**" (in V.A., *Recueil des Allocutions Consistoriales, Encycliques et autres Lettres Apostoliques des Souverains Pontifes Clement XII, Benoît XIV, Pie VI, Pie VII, Léon XII, Gregoire XVI et Pie IX. Citées dans l'Encyclique et le Syllabus du 8 décembre 1864, suivi du Concordat de 1801 et de divers autres documents,* Paris: Adrien le Clere, 1865, p. 207).

b. Thus says Leo XIII in the Encyclical *Parvenu, of* March 19, 1902: "Returning to Christianity will not be a real and efficacious medicine if it does not mean returning to and loving the One, Holy, Catholic and Apostolic Church. Indeed, **Christianity acts through and identifies with the Catholic Church,** a sovereignly spiritual and perfect society **that is the Mystical Body of Jesus Christ** and whose visible chief is the Roman Pontiff, the Successor of the Prince of Apostles. It is she who continues the mission of the Savior, daughter and heiress of His Redemption; she it was who propagated the Gospel all over the earth, spreading it at the cost of her blood; and it is she who, according to the promise of divine assistance and immortality, never compromising with error, carries out the mission of preserving in its fullness the doctrine of Christ till the end of time" (Petrópolis: Vozes, 1960, n. 26).

c. In the Encyclical *Satis cognitum,* of June 29, 1896, the same Pontiff teaches: "**We say,** therefore, **that the Catholic Church is unique** in its essence, in its origin and in its excellence ... Furthermore, **the eminence of the Church arises from its unity,** as the principle of its constitution – 'a unity surpassing all else, and **having nothing like unto it or equal to it'** (St. Clemens Alexandrinus, *Stromatum,* lib. VIII, chap. 17). For this reason **Christ, speaking of the mystical edifice, mentions only one Church, which He calls His own:** 'I will build My Church.' **Any other church except this one,** since it has not been founded by Christ, **cannot be the true Church**" (Petrópolis: Vozes, 1960, n. 7).

And later on, Leo XIII quotes St. Optatus de Milevis: "Explaining this passage, Optatus de Milevis says: 'It is written in the Prophet Isaiah: 'From Sion the law shall go forth and the word of the Lord from Jerusalem.' For it is not from the concrete mount Sion that Isaiah sees the valley, but from the [symbolic] holy mountain, that is, the Church, which has grown over the entire Roman world and raises its summit to the heavens. ... **The Church is, therefore, the spiritual Sion in which Christ has been constituted King by God the Father, and which exists throughout the entire earth, on which there is but one Catholic Church'** *(Libri septem de schismate Donatistarum,* lib. III, n. 2)" (n. 9; nn. 10, 18).

d. In his Encyclical *Mortalium animos,* of January 6, 1928, Pius XI equally identifies the Church of Christ with the Catholic Church: "**In this sole Church of Christ, no one is found nor does anyone remain unless he recognizes and accepts, in obedience, the authority and power of Peter and of his legitimate successors**. ... Unfortunately there have been children who deserted the paternal home ... **Let them hear the voice of Lactancius** exclaiming: '**Only** ... **the Catholic Church** preserves the true worship. She **is the source of truth, the dwelling place of faith, the temple of God. He who does not enter her, or he who leaves her, loses all hope of life and salvation.** Let no one allow himself to be carried away by recalcitrant contestations. This is a matter of life and salvation. If one is not attentively and prudently vigilant, it is perdition and death' *(Lactantii divinarum institutionum libri septem IV,* 30, 11-12" (*Actes de S.S. Pie XI,* Paris: Bonne Presse, vol. IV, p. 80).

e. In the beginning of the Encyclical *Mystici Corporis Christi,* of June 29, 1943, Pius XII is also peremptory: "**In order to define and describe this true Church of Christ – which is the Holy, Catholic and Apostolic Roman Church** (Council Vatican I, *Constitutio dogmatica de Fide catholica, c.* 1), **there is nothing more noble, excellent or more divine than the concept expressed in the designation 'Mystical Body of Jesus Christ'**"(Petrópolis: Vozes, 1960, nn. 9, 103).

The impression of ambiguity becomes even more striking when, after the consideration above, one returns to the text to see whether it could be interpreted in a benign but consistent manner.

? "The sole Church of Christ which in the Creed we profess to be ... Catholic ...**subsists in** the Catholic Church governed by the successor of Peter."

If the intention was to state that the Catholic Church is the Church of Christ, as it has always been taught, why cast a doubt in the mind of the faithful? Why this ambiguity of the *subsistit in?* [3]

---

3. a. Here is an astonishing statement by Cardinal Yves Congar, O.P., one of the most authoritative theologians on Vatican II: "It is said [in LG 8b] that the Church of Christ and of the Apostles *subsistit in,* is found in the Catholic Church 'even though many elements of sanctification and truth are found outside its structure.' Therefore, there is not a strict identification, *that is, an exclusive identification,* between the Church Body of Christ and the Catholic Church. Deep down, Vatican II admits that non-Catholic Christians are members of the Mystical Body and not merely *ordinati ad* [ordered to it]. The categories used in the Decree on Ecumenism and also in a number of documents and speeches of H. H. Paul VI are: fully belonging to the sole Church through baptism [but having] an imperfect subsequent communion" (Yves M. J. Congar, *Le Condit du Vatican II – Son Eglise, people de Dieu et Corps du Christ,* Paris: Beauchesne, 1984. pp. 160-161).

b. For his part, Christopher Basil Butler, General Abbot of the Benedictines in England and later Auxiliary Bishop of Westminster, a member of the Congregation for the Doctrine of the Faith and Customs during the Council who participated in the writing of *Lumen gentium,* believes that the *subsistit in* marks an "advance": "Here we can gauge the advance of the Constitution *(Lumen gentiiun)* over *Mystici Corporis,* [and we have] the basis for the Decree on Ecumenism and other elements of the Council's teaching and proposals. An exclusive material identification of the Church with Roman Catholic communion is carefully avoided" (C. B. Butler, *The Theology of Vatican II,* London, 1967, p. 70, in Y. Congar, *Le Condit du Vatican II, p.* 160).

c. Fr. Avery Dulles, SJ, a well-known American theologian, draws some consequences from this general principle: "The Church of Jesus Christ does not exclusively identify with the Roman Catholic Church. It certainly subsists in Roman Catholicism, but is also present, in various ways and in diverse degrees, in other Christian communities inasmuch as they are faithful to that which God started with Jesus and obey the inspirations of the Spirit of Christ.

"As a result of their common participation in the reality of the only Church, the various Christian communities already have among themselves a

§ 2   Taking a brief look at the beginning of chapter II of the same dogmatic Constitution, a Catholic mind could not fail to raise, with concern, several questions about whether it would be opportune to replace the notion of a hierarchical and sacral Church with the notion of the "people of God." We would like to say a word about its context, leaving the analysis of the text for later.[4]

Even though the expression, "people of God," of itself can be legitimately applied to the Holy Church, a Catholic could ask whether, in a world devastated by a tendency to abolish all superiority,

---

real, though imperfect, communion. Relations among churches, therefore, are not simply 'external relations' that can exist between distinct sovereign States, but 'domestic relations' analogous to those that exist between groups inside an individual political society. Under certain aspects the relationship is also a more intimate one, because all Christians are incorporated into the single body of Christ, animated by His Spirit. Intimacy among all Christian groups, which is a divine gift, makes more imperative the restoration of full communion among all" ("Ecumenismo: problemi e possibilité per il futuro," in V.A., *Verso In Chiesa del terzo millennio,* Brescia: Queriniana, 1979, pp. 108-109).

d. Other renowned theologians around the world, in addition to the three cited above, comment that the *subsist in* represents an important opening toward recognizing the existence of an ecclesial reality that extends beyond the borders of the Catholic Church. They are pointed out by Francis A. Sullivan, S.J. in his article "Le sens et l'importance de la décision de Vatican II de dire, à propos de l'Eglise du Christ, non pas qu'elle 'est' mais qu'elle 'subsiste dans' l'Eglise Catholique Romaine," in V.A., *Vatican II - Bilan et perspectives,* vol. II, p. 302: G. Philips, *L'Eglise et son mystêre an deuxiême Concile du Vatican,* vol. I, p. 119; J. Feiner, untitled, in V.A., *Commentary on the Documents of Vatican II,* Herder, vol. II. p. 69; A. Grillmeier, untitled, *ibid.,* vol. I, p. 150; E. Fischer, *Kirche and Kirchen each dent Vatikanum II,* München, 1967. pp. 79-80; H. Fries, *Eglise et Eglises,* in V.A., *Problèmes et perspectives de théologie fondamentale,* ed. R. Latourelle, Paris-Turin-Montreal: G. O'Collins, 1982, p. 418; A. Dulles, *The Church, the churches and the Catholic Church,* in T.S., 33, 1972, p. 211; A. de Halleux, "Les principes catholiques de l'oecumenisme," *Revue Théologique Louvain,* 16, 1985, pp. 320-322.

e. Quite different from the interpretation these authors present to explain this controversial passage of *Lumen gentium* is the teaching of the traditional Magisterium, which has always identified the Church of Christ exclusively with the Catholic Church.

4. The progressivist notion of the "people of God" is analyzed in Vol. IV, *Animus Delendi I,* Chap. IV. §§ 1-7; Vol. XI. *Ecclesia,* Chap. II.

contaminated by the errors of the Enlightenment and the French Revolution and profoundly undermined by the virulent germs of Communism,[5] it was opportune to present the structure of the Church predominantly as a people and no longer as a hierarchy.[6] Is this not
opening a door to that egalitarian tendency?[7]

---

5. Plinio Corrêa de Oliveira, *Revolution and Counter-Revolution,* York,
PA: The American Society for the Defense of Tradition, Family and Property, 1993, Part I, chap. III, 5.C, D.

6. Within the context of the conciliar document, we refer especially to
these excerpts:

• "Christ the Lord ... made the new people 'a kingdom of priests to God,
His Father' (Apoc 1:6; cf. 5:9-10). The baptized, by regeneration and
the anointing of the Holy Spirit, are consecrated to be a spiritual house
and a holy priesthood, that through all the works of Christian men they
may offer spiritual sacrifices and proclaim the perfection of him who has
called them out of darkness into his marvelous light (1 Ptr 2:4-10)" (LG
l0a).

• "All men are called to belong to the new People of God. This People
therefore, whilst remaining one and only one, is to be spread throughout
the whole world and to all ages in order that the design of God's will may
be fulfilled" (LG 13a).

• "The one People of God is accordingly present in all the nations of the
earth, since its citizens, who are taken from all nations, are of a kingdom whose nature is not earthly but heavenly" (LG 13b).

• "This character of universality which adorns the People of God is a gift
from the Lord himself whereby the Catholic ceaselessly and efficaciously
seeks for the return of all humanity and all its goods under Christ the
Head in the unity of his Spirit" (LG 13b).

• "Hence it is that the People of God is not only an assembly of various
peoples, but in itself is made up of different ranks" (LG 13c).

7. a. This egalitarian tendency inspires movements such as the Basic
Christian Communities (BCCs) and "small groups" struggling to insti-
tutionalize a type of participatory democracy in the Church. Such a tendency has found support, for example, in the expression "communion"
or *koinonia,* that should exist in the "people of God," used in several
documents of the Council (LG 4, 7b, 9b, 13a, 15; GS 32d; UR 2d). This
enabled one of the conciliar *periti* [experts], Bishop Boaventura Kloppenburg, to state that "strictly speaking there are no 'superiors' and
'inferiors' or 'subjects' in the Church. One must read this and take it
seriously (Matt 23:8-11; Lk 22:25-27): 'All you are brethren' (Matt 23:8)
– brethren in only one large family which has no special 'dignitaries.'
The Church is and must be a fraternity, *a koinonia,* a communion. It is
certain that even though all are brethren and equal in dignity, there must

be diversity in *services* or ministries so that the people of God may believe ... That is why the Church is *a communio hierarchica.* But the word 'hierarchical' is an adjective and should not be turned into a noun so as to identify with the Church" *(A eclesiologia do Vaticano II,* p. 127).

Further on, comparing the Church with democracy, the theologian writes: "Drawing from the non-democratic nature of the Church an argument against the people's active participation in designating candidates for ecclesiastical posts would be a simple fallacy. That which is most praised in democracy – liberty, fraternity, equality, co-responsibility – will perfectly have its place in *koinonia.* By means of a government of love *(per gubernationem in dilectione),* the fraternal concord of the family of God will be attained (UR 2d). Neither democracy nor, even less, monarchy, but rather *koinonia,* through which 'there reigns a true equality between all with regard to the dignity and to the activity which is common to all the faithful in the building up of the Body of Christ' (LG 32c). This concept must be taken seriously and put into practice" *(ibid.,* p. 128).

b. For his part, Spanish theologian Joaquim Losada, commenting on the fundamental lines of the Council's conception of the Church, writes: "The doctrinal assertion that *all* members of the people of God, each in his own way, participate in the threefold function of Christ, implies recognizing the ministerial character of the whole Church. ... This recognition opens the way for a real participation of everyone in the life of the Church, which can find concrete forms in the models offered by modern democratic society. From here onward, based on the Council's ecclesiology, it is necessary to speak of the urgency of a process of *democratization of the Church*" (Joaquim Losada, *El posconcilio: El problema de la transformación de la Iglesia,* in V.A., *Desafios cristianos,* Madrid: Loguez Ediciones, 1990, p. 89).

c. One can see that as B. Kloppenburg and J. Losada understand it, when the Council's documents speak of communion, of *koinonia* in the "people of God," they are speaking for the immediate establishment of a representative democracy in the Church, to be later replaced by the kind of participatory democracy so fiercely proposed by BCCs leaders.

d. In this regard, Leonardo Boff's explanation of the Basic Christian Communities as a new "manner of being Church" is quite meaningful: "The principal characteristic of this new manner of being Church is community and fraternity. All are effectively brethren, everyone participates, everyone takes up his own task. This is the first commandment. Afterward comes the incipient structure of leadership and coordination. Though all are essentially equal, not everyone does the same job. Thus there are the coordinators, who are often times women responsible for maintaining order, for presiding over celebrations and for the sacramental aspect of the community. We know that in the first centuries the Church was known mainly as *communitas fidelium,* a community of the faithful, with a great participation of the people in everything. After the year 1000 there was a greater and greater imposition of a hierarchical Church. The

[handwritten margin notes: "Catholic Action errors? What are they", "Not necessarily!", "Not merely", "it helps us / understand", "§ 3", "more our", "true", "nature as", "will be later revealed."]

In this context, doesn't the affirmation of the common priesthood of the faithful [8] act to stimulate Rousseau's myth of the people's sovereignty? Is this not a revival of the old errors of Catholic Action,[9] which called for the laity to participate in the hierarchical *munus*?

After the Council approved such singular notions, apparently to the detriment of the Church's hierarchical constitution, how could one avoid excesses such as those of Leonardo Boff [10] and Fr. Edward Schillebeeckx,[11] who call for an egalitarian Church? In the long run, what can be the efficacy of the laudable admonishments that

---

sacred power came to be considered the structuring element, and not so much the community *(koinonia)*. This way of organizing the Church certainly was due to an historical necessity, but it did not facilitate the responsible participation of everyone. The Basic [Christian] Community opens up the possibility of a greater participation and equilibrium among the various Church functions" *(Igreja – Carisma e poder – Ensaio de eclesiologia militante,* Petrópolis: Vozes, 1982, p. 200).

8. The excerpts of *Lumen gentium* especially in question are:

• "Though they differ essentially and not only in degree, the common priesthood of the faithful and the ministerial or hierarchical priesthood are nonetheless ordered one to another; each in its own proper way shares in the one priesthood of Christ. The ministerial priest, by the sacred power that he has, forms and rules the priestly people; in the person of Christ he effects the eucharistic sacrifice and offers it to God in the name of all the people. The faithful indeed, by virtue of their royal priesthood, participate in the offering of the Eucharist. They exercise that priesthood too, by the reception of the sacraments, prayer and thanksgiving, the witness of a holy life, abnegation, and active charity" (LG 10b).

• "The sacred nature and organic structure of the priestly community is brought into operation through the sacraments and the exercise of virtues" (LG 11a).

• "The holy People of God shares also in Christ's prophetic office *[munus]*: it spreads abroad a living witness to him, especially by a life of faith and love and by offering to God a sacrifice of praise, the fruit of lips praising his name *(*Heb 13:15)" (LG 12a).

9. Plinio Corrêa de Oliveira, *Em Defesa da Ação Católica,* São Paulo: Ave-Maria. 1943, especially Part I pp. 54-106.

10. Especially in *Igreja: Carisma e poder,* pp. 204-219.

11. See for example, E. Schillebeeckx, *Le Ministère dans l'Eglise,* Cerf, Paris, 1981, pp. 108-116. See also his contribution "Funcionamento da autoridade na Igreja," in V.A., *Cinco problemas que desafiam a Igreja de hoje,* São Paulo: Herder, pp. 39-54.

Cardinal Ratzinger has made to those authors, [12] who actually feel protected by the ambiguity in the text and context of *Lumen gentium?* NCBB bucked the Cong. for Doct. of Faith /Rome,

§ 4

Regarding the ecclesiological notion of the "people of God," ⟶ Errors of ambiguity is found not only in incidental passages. It pervades the whole context in which the Church appears to adapt herself to the errors of the Enlightenment, the French Revolution and, indirectly, of Communism, [13]

{ Enlightenment
Fr. Revolt.
Communism

---

12. "Notification de la Congrégation pour la Doctrine de la Foi à propos du livre de L. Boff: 'Eglise: Charisme et pouvoir,'" in *La Documentation Catholique*, 5/5/1985, pp. 484-486; see also the "Lettera della Congregazione per la Dottrina della Fede a P. Schillebeeckx" of June 13, 1984, published in *L'Osservatore Romano*, 1/11/1985.

In spite of the censure by the Congregation for the Doctrine of the Faith, the former Franciscan from Brazil was offered the solidarity of 115 Capitulary priests of his Order, including its Superior General, and of 108 European theologians, in different petitions. He was clearly supported by the leadership of the National Conference of Brazilian Bishops (NCBB). In addition, about 20 Bishops publicly came out in his support against the Roman Congregation *(Roma locuta – Documentário sobre o livro "Igreja: Carisma e poder – Ensaios de eclesiologia militante" de Frei Leonardo Boff, O.F.M.,* Petrópolis: Vozes, 1985, pp. 58-59, 61, 71-73).

13. a. We are not the only ones to consider the ecclesiology of the people of God under this prism. Henri Fesquet, a well-known French journalist and chronicler of Vatican II, concludes his work about the Council with the expressive subtitle: *Liberté, Egalité, Fraternité.* He explains: "This liberation of Catholic thinking, for so long a prisoner of the negative current of the Counter-Reformation, makes it possible somehow to merge with the trilogy of the French Revolution. ...'Liberty, Equality, Fraternity': this glorious motto that was, in short, that of Vatican II, as Hans Küng has recently suggested" *(Le journal du Concile,* Folcalquier: Robert Morel, 1966, p. 1127).

Fesquet,
Fr. Revolt =
Liberty,
Equality
Fraternity
Motto
Hans küng

↓

Indeed, Fr. Hans Küng, a conciliar *perito* (expert), defends the idea that the Church must become more democratic in accordance with the revolutionary trilogy, which, in his view, is a Christian motto. Thus, the first chapter of his book *Prêtre, pour quoi faire?* (Paris: Cerf, 1971, pp. 19-32) is titled: *The Church, Communion in Liberty, Equality and Fraternity.*

his motto too!

b. On the support of conciliar Popes, Bishops and famed theologians for the ideals of the French Revolution, see Vol. IV, *Animus Delendi I*, Chap. IV.1.

c. Also in regard to the affinity between the ecclesiological ideas of the Council and Communist yearnings, it is opportune to transcribe here the euphoric finding of the Italian Communist Party (ICP) referred to by

all of which she had fought up until then. [14]

§ 5　　　A person who analyzes the ensemble of the Council's documents beginning with *Lumen gentium* enjoys a moment of calm as he reaches Chapter II. Indeed, it reads: "Hence they cannot be saved who, knowing that the Catholic Church was founded by God through Christ as a necessary institution, would nonetheless refuse either to enter it, or to persevere in it" (LG 14a).

Bishop Rudolf Graber of Regensburg. During its 1964 congress, the ICP published a special issue of the magazine *Propaganda,* dedicated to "dialogue with Catholics," in which it states:

"The extraordinary eruption of the Council, justly compared to the General Assemblies of 1789, has demonstrated to the whole world that the old political-religious Bastille has been shaken in its foundations. A new situation has thus been produced which we must face with proportionate means. Thus, there appears an unheard-of opportunity for us to draw closer to the final victory by means of a suitable maneuver" ("Statements on Dialogue with Catholics," in *Propaganda,* in R. Graber, *Athanasius and die Kirche unserer Zeit,* Arensburg: Josef Kral, 1973, p. 69).

Another paragraph in the same Communist magazine, subtitled *Arguments,* quoted by the Bishop of Regensburg, concludes: "Thus, the Council itself gratuitously places at our disposal the best resources to reach the Catholic public" *(ibid.,* p. 70).

This part of the ICP magazine's commentary on the matter closes with the words: "Never has the situation been so favorable to us."

14. The Popes have been fighting the nefarious errors of the Enlightenment, the French Revolution, Liberalism, Religious Indifferentism, as well as Socialism and Communism, since the end of the 18th century. Here is a list of the main pontifical documents condemning those errors:

a. Against the Principles of the French Revolution:

Pius VI: Letter-Decree to the Cardinal de La Rochefoucauld and the Archbishop of Aix-en-Provence, of March 10, 1791, in *Pii VI Pontificis Maximi acta* (Rome: Typis S. Congreg. de Propaganda Fide, 1871), vol. II, pp. 70-71; Allocution in the Secret Consistory, of June 17, 1793 confirming the words of the Encyclical *Inscrutabile Divinae Sapientiae,* of December 25, 1775, *ibid.,* vol. I, pp. 26-27; Bull *Auctorem fidei,* of August 28, 1794.

b. Against Liberalism, Naturalism, and Religious Indifferentism:

Gregory XVI: Encyclical *Mirari vos,* of August 15, 1832, in V.A. *Les enseignements pontificaux - La paix interieure des nations,* ed. Monks of Solesmes (Tournai: Desclée & Cie., *1952),* nn. 24-25.

Pius IX: Encyclical *Qui pluribus, of* November 9, 1846; in DS 2785;

(Petrópolis: Vozes, 1960), n. 8; Allocution *Ubi primum,* of December 17,1847, in V.A. *Recueil des allocutions,* pp. 205, 207; Encyclical *Nostis et nobiscum,* of December 8, 1849, *ibid.,* p. 243; Letter *Multiplices inter,* of June 10, 1851, *ibid.,* p. 287; Allocution *Acerbissimuni,* of September 27, 1852, *ibid.,* p. 325; Allocution *Singulari quadam,* of December 9, 1852, in D 1642; Allocution *Nemo vestrum,* of July 26, 1855, *ibid.,* pp. 351-355; Encyclical *Singulari quidem,* of March 17, 1856, *ibid.,* pp. 365, 367, 369; Allocution *Nunquam fore,* of December 15, 1856, *ibid.,* p. 387; Allocution *Iamdudum cernimus,* of March 1861, *ibid.,* pp. 435, 437, 439; Allocution *Maxima quidem,* of June 9, 1862, *ibid.,* pp. 455, 457, 459; Letter *Gravissimas inter* to the Archbishop of Munich-Freising, of December 22, 1862, in DS 2850-2861; Encyclical *Quanto conficiamur,* of August 10, 1863, in DS 2865f-2867; V.A., *Recueil des allocutions,* p. 477; Letter *Tuas libenter* to the Archbishop of Munich-Freising, of December 21, 1863, in DS 2875.

St. Pius X: Apostolic Letter *Notre charge apostolique, of* August 25, 1910 (Petrópolis: Vozes, 1953), nn. 12, 20.

c. Against Socialism and Communism:

Pius IX: Encyclical *Nostis et nobiscum,* of December 8, 1849, in V.A., *Les enseignements pontificaux,* n. 36; Encyclical *Quanta cura,* in DS 2890; (Petrópolis: Vozes, 1951), nn. 5, 7; *Syllabus,* of December 8, 1864, in DS 2902, 2915-2918, 2977-2980, § 4.

Leo XIII: Encyclicals *Quod apostolici muneris,* of December 28, 1878, in DS 3133; V.A., *Les enseignements pontificaux,* nn. 62-64, 71, 77, 81, 83-84.; *Diuturnum illud,* of June 28, 1881, *ibid,* n. 105; *Auspicatum concessum,* of September 17, 1882 (Petrópolis: Vozes, 1953), n. 24; *Humanum genus,* of April 20, 1884 (Petrópolis: Vozes, 1960), n. 23; *Immortale Dei,* of November 1, 1885 (Petrópolis: Vozes, 1953), nn. 32, 38; *Libertas praestantissimum,* of June 20, 1888, in V.A., *Les enseignements pontificaux,* n. 195; *Rerum novarum,* of May 15, 1891 (Petrópolis: Vozes, 1954), nn. 7, 9, 22; *Laetitiae sanctae,* of September 8, 1893 (Petrópolis: Vozes, 1953), n. 5; *Graves de communi,* of January 18, 1901 (Petrópolis: Vozes, 1956), nn. 2, 6, 27; *Parvenu,* of March 19, 1902 (Petrópolis: Vozes, 1960), n. 19.

St. Pius X: *Motu proprio* about the Catholic Popular Action, of December 18, 1903, in *Lettres Apostoliques de S. Pie X* (Paris: Bonne Presse, 1926), pp. 109-111.

Benedict XV: Encyclical *Ad Beatissime*, of November 1, 1914, in V.A., *Les enseignements pontificaux,* nn. 479-481; Encyclical *Soliti nos,* of March 11, 1920, *ibid.,* n. 496.

Pius XI: Encyclical *Quadragesimo anno,* of March 15, 1931, in DS 3742-3744; (Paris: Ed. Spes, 1954), nn. 2, 11, 16, 34, 51, 61-63, 105, 119-139; Encyclical *Divini Redemptoris,* of March 19, 1937, in DS 3773; (Buenos Aires: Ed. Roma, n.d.), nn. 8-24, 57-58.

In fact, we are facing here the perennial axiom of dogmatic teaching: *Extra ecclesiam nulla salus* (outside the Church there is no salvation).

In this passage, the consistency of the thinking of Vatican II with the whole Tradition of the Church gives the person studying it a feeling of security, confidence and hope that the ambiguities cited previously can be resolved by a crystal clear explanation.

Nevertheless, such hopeful and filial sentiments are shattered like a wave dashing against a rock when the person reaches the text of the Decree on Ecumenism, *Unitatis redintegratio;* and further on, the Declaration on Religious Liberty, *Dignitatis humanae;* and finally, the Declaration on Relations with Non-Christian Religions, *Nostra aetate.*

Let us consider, for example, the Decree *Unitatis redintegratio,* which reads: "Large communities became separated from full communion with the Catholic Church. ... However, **one cannot charge with the sin of separation** those who at present are born into these communities and in them are brought up in the faith of Christ, and the Catholic Church accepts them with respect and affection as brothers. ... Moreover, some, even **very many of the most significant elements** and endowments **which go together to build up and give life to the Church itself, can exist outside the visible boundaries of the Catholic Church:** the written Word of God; **the life of grace; faith, hope, and charity** with the other interior gifts of the Holy Spirit, as well as visible elements. ... The brethren divided from us also carry out many liturgical actions of the Christian religion. ... These **can aptly give access to the communion of salvation**" (UR 3a,b,c).

[handwritten margin note: old. true because it's all the know. It is Grace that draws 'em to full communion]

Pius XII: Christmas Radio Message 1944 (Petrópolis: Vozes, 1951), n. 28; Speech at the 9th International Conference of Catholic Associ-ations, May 7, 1949, in *Discorsi e radiomessaggi,* vol. XI, pp. 63-64; Decree of the Sacred Congregation of the Holy Office Against Communism, June 1, 1949, in AAS, vol. XLI, p. 334; Speech to the International Congress of Social Studies and the International Christian Association, June 3, 1950, in *Discorsi e radiomessaggi,* vol. XII, pp. 100-101.; Speech to the First International Congress on the Problems of Rural Life, July 2, 1951, *ibid.,* vol. XIII, pp. 199-200; Radiomessage to the *Katholikentag* of Vienna, September 14, 1952, *ibid.,* vol. XIV, p. 314; Letter to the 41st Social Week of France, July 14, 1954, *ibid.,* vol. XVI, pp. 465-466; Speech to the 7th Congress of Italy's Christian Union of Corporate Leaders and Managers, March 7, 1957, *ibid.,* vol. XIX, p. 30

In this case we no longer appear to be dealing with ambiguities; one would say that we are faced with inconsistency and contradiction. How could one not see a contradiction between what has been said here and the above quotation from *Lumen gentium*?

I don't think the 2 are mutually exclusive! Its the way the world went "secular! God loves us & finds or makes a way

§ 6   We have presented three examples of ambiguity and contradiction taken from only two of the sixteen final documents of Vatican Council II.

How much would have to be written in order to make a complete analysis only of the ambiguous, contradictory and incomplete points in the documents of Vatican II …

when it seems to us there is no way! w/ The Heart [The pt. is of one lives Love & Salvation! holy the law written on his heart What more does God look @ in the end? Its the fault of Church To be vague, abandon the faithful!

*   *   *

Chapter II

WHY THE AMBIGUITY?

§ 1   The ambiguous is defined as that which has more than one meaning, that which is equivocal, uncertain, hesitant.

As a means of expression, the deliberate use of ambiguity can be seen today in several instances:

§ 2   In a political strategy, it can be used to persuade people to accept that which they would reject if it were stated clearly. For example, ambiguity can be used by some politicians to deceive legislators in order to approve a bill, or later it can be used to confuse public opinion, so that it will accept that used-approved bill.

§ 3   Ambiguity can also be conceived in a formula resulting from the fight of two opposing currents of equal strength. Each side, desiring a truce that provides some temporary respite, accepts an ambiguous formula that gives victory to neither current.

§ 4   One can also imagine someone with debatable sanity who sees ambiguity as the expression of an ideal doctrine. He believes nothing should be expounded clearly because everything is mysterious. There should not be distinct manifestations of good and evil, truth and error, light and darkness. Such unequivocal expressions, if stated conciously, should be condemned as manifestations of "Manichaeanism;" if spoken spontaneously, they should be condemned as an outburst of sinful pride.

§ 5   Finally, ambiguity can be understood merely as a transitional phase of an ascending or descending process. Thus, an adolescent - in the case of an ascending organic process - has certain ambiguous characteristics, which at times show him as an adult and, at other times, reveal the child who is still there. In a process of decay, something analogous takes place, as in the case of a man who is leaving maturity and entering old age.

Contrary to what it might seem, listing such possibilities for the use of ambiguity is not superfluous. In the following Chapters we will see how a large number of celebrated and widely read authors have recourse to one or more of the types of ambiguity we have mentioned as they attempt to explain and justify ambiguities in the documents of Vatican II.

§ 6   We know from History that the Modernist movement largely employed indefinition and ambiguity on the pretext that its inspiration in ecclesiastical matters is so profound that only with difficulty could it be made explicit. When Modernism took a powerful blow with the publication of the Encyclical *Pascendi,* its defense was to take refuge in the shadows of a pretended "intermediary phase" between the universal tendencies it fancied to possess and the still embryonic tenets it had managed to make explicit. After the most acute phase of the Holy See's official anti-Modernist reaction had passed, the Modernists continued to resort to indefinition and confusion to carry on their work.

Let us consider some excerpts by Fr. Ernesto Buonaiuti, perhaps the main exponent of Modernism in Italy, which attest to this fact.

In the first excerpt, the author is very clear about the doctrinal fluidity in which his movement deliberately placed itself:

"The distinctive character of Modernism is the indefinition of its first program. In it, Modernism does not stick to a given point of official dogmatics; it does not rise up against a disciplinary rule ... Actually, Modernism is something other than taking a position on one single problem of Catholic dogmatics. In the process of the development of modern spirituality, it is essentially a new and original orientation tending to draw, from the different tendencies of speculation, a more powerful and objective representation of religious experience, and to obtain, from the moral crisis of our time, a clearer and purer adhesion to the innovative message of the New Testament's preaching"[1]

Seeking to defend the movement from the condemnations of the Decree *Lamentabili,* Buonaiuti again presents theological fluidity and a confused yearning for change as the characteristic traits of Modernism. Indeed, he says:

"Being a vast, collective and multiform movement of believing consciences, Modernism was, especially in its beginning, like an incandescent matter that could not be poured into the narrow molds of theological speculation without completely changing its nature. A confused aspiration to a full rebirth of the evangelical spirit beyond all dry formulas and conventional disciplines, it could represent a force whose direction and development should have been followed by men of faith, instead of barred without pity."[2]

---

1. Ernesto Buonaiuti, *Le modernisme catholique* (Paris: Ed. Rieder, 1927), pp. 28-29.

2. *Ibid.,* p. 46.

Further on, the author boasts that Modernism escaped the condemnations of *Pascendi* precisely because of its undefined nature, which derived from an ardent and vague affinity with the achievements of modern times. Buonaiuti writes:

"At the Holy Office one must have had the impression that the Encyclical *Pascendi,* in spite of the solemn and severe controls that it demanded, in spite of its relentless application in the dioceses of the Catholic world, had still been unable to extirpate the 'poison' of modernist tendencies from the hearts and minds of the young clergy. Not being a defined system, representing above all a disposition of spirit ready to complacently regard and to ardently desire all the conquests of modern times in the realm of culture and social progress, the movement, struck by the brutal measures of the Curia, could not be stamped out by an incorrect doctrinal exposition and a series of police measures. It kept resurfacing in the minds of young churchmen who were necessarily in contact with the procedures of modern critique and speculation. It continued to permeate the enthusiasm of their vocations and, imperceptibly, to gain proselytes. Two years of arduous persecution ... should have shown that the roots of Modernism and its capacities for conquest were more solid than the theologians of the opposed party had imagined."[3]

We can thus see that Modernism deliberately employed indefinition, confusion and, consequently, ambiguity, as an efficient strategy to introduce the movement and to defend it against the attacks of St. Pius X, or as a means to survive all the condemnations of which it was the object.

§ 7

Therefore, it does not appear inopportune to focus our attention on certain aspects of ambiguity in the progressivist movement, the heir and perpetuator of Modernism. We might also ask ourselves whether or not ambiguity, to the degree that its influence was present in conciliar documents, was also employed for strategic purposes.

By pointing out this historic precedent, we do not intend to pre-judge the Council. By reading the following chapters the Reader will have elements to gauge, with equity, to what point the progressivist movement was present in Vatican II.

Let us now go on to study testimonies on ambiguity in conciliar documents.

* * *

---

3. *Ibid.,* p. 62.

Chapter III

AUTHORITATIVE TESTIMONIES THAT THE LANGUAGE OF VATICAN II IS AMBIGUOUS

§ 1   A person analyzing the documents of Vatican II will be able to see, without much difficulty, that the Council deliberately abandoned the rigor of Thomistic language. Incidentally, this fact is clearly avowed by several theologians cited in this Collection, [1] who express their satisfaction with the end of what they call the "era of theological cloistering," a fruit of Scholasticism.

§ 2   Scholasticism, of which Thomism is the supreme expression, represents the apex of a long process of perfecting theological and philosophical language, a process unleashed by the polemics of the Fathers and Catholic doctors against the heresies and errors that had sprung up during the first twelve centuries of the Christian era. Indeed, in the battles waged in favor of orthodoxy, nothing was more indispensable than a systemization of theology and philosophy and the elaboration of a highly precise technical language placed at their service. This prevented the infiltration of ambiguous expressions that could favor the promoters of error. So great was the effort made to clearly express theological and philosophical concepts that finding precise terms and formulas which left no shadow of doubt about a controversial doctrinal point was like discovering a treasure.

   Thus, in 1588, explaining the origin, nature and excellence of Scholastic doctrine, Pope Sixtus V stated: "By the divine generosity of Him who alone imparts the spirit of wisdom and, along the ages and according to necessity, ceases not to enrich His Church with new benefits and endow her with new defenses, our forefathers, men of profound science, invented Scholastic Theology. Above all, however, it was the two glorious Doctors, the angelic St. Thomas and the seraphic St. Bonaventure, both illustrious professors ... who, with their incomparable talent, assiduous zeal, great works and vigils, cultivated this science, enriched it and gave it as a legacy to future generations, organized in perfect order, amply and admirably developed.

   "Undoubtedly the knowledge and habit of such a wholesome science, which emanates from the most fecund sources of the Sacred

---

1. In addition to the testimonies contained in this Chapter, the Reader will find this subject dealt with in more detail and with sufficient proofs in Vol. VI, *Inveniet Fidem*?, Chap. IV.2,3.

Scriptures, the holy Fathers and the Councils, has been an invaluable help to the Church at all times, whether to facilitate a wholesome comprehension and true interpretation of the Scriptures, or to read and explain the Fathers with greater assurance and usefulness, or to unmask and refute the several errors and heresies. But these latter days, which have already brought us the critical times predicted by the Apostle, in which blasphemous, proud and seductive men make progress in evil, erring and leading others into error, the science of which we speak is more than ever necessary to confirm the dogmas of the Catholic Faith and refute heresies." [2]

Thus, Scholastic Theology and Philosophy gradually built over the centuries an invulnerable wall protecting Revelation and the Magisterium from the insidious attacks of adversaries. That is why they deserved such high praise from Sixtus V, who saw in them "this tight and perfect cohesion between cause and effect, this symmetry and order resembling those of an army in battle array, these luminous definitions and distinctions, this solidity of argumentation and subtlety in controversy by means of which light is separated from darkness, truth distinguished from error, and the lies of heresy, deprived of the prestige and fictions enveloping them, are unveiled and laid bare." [3]

§ 3   Nevertheless, the language adopted by Vatican II despised that "tight and perfect cohesion between cause and effect," those "luminous definitions and distinctions," that "solidity in argumentation" typical of Scholastic language. Vatican II preferred texts that were "patched up," "worked over," "incoherent," "promiscuous," more appropriate to a "Babel" and its "confusion of languages." [4] That which the Thomists of old feared was thus achieved: the entrance of ambiguity into the expression of theological thinking.

*

§ 4   In this Chapter we will bring to the Reader's attention a selection of texts by famed theologians who acknowledge the existence of ambiguity in conciliar documents.

First we will present texts regarding the Council's documents as a whole; later, some texts relating to the most important documents.

---

2. Sixtus V, Bull *Triumphantis,* 1588, in Leo XIII, Encyclical *Aeterni Patris,* August 4, 1879 (Petrópolis: Vozes, 1960), n. 28.

3. *Ibid.,* n. 23.

4. These various expressions are used by renowned theologians, as the Reader will see in the following texts.

§ 5   Msgr. Luigi Sartori, President of the Italian Theological Association (ITA), professor of theology and a consultant to the Secretariat for Non-Christians, comments on the texts of the Council in general: **"Different, not to say opposed interpretations, are given of the Council; everyone pulls toward his own side. Worse, not a small part of responsibility for the mixups and confusions arising today out of the Council, is attributed to the Council itself. Some go as far as to speak, with irritation, of 'Babel' and the 'confusion of languages.' "** [5]

Msgr. Sartori goes on to say: **"With Vatican II comes an end to the era of 'cloistering,' of the defensive belt, of the** internal **(esoteric)** [sic] **technical language, of uniformity.** The foundations have been laid for the catholicity of Church language. **In order to attain that,** Vatican II committed itself to the arduous work of achieving a synthesis that seemed impossible. In a large number of cases **it was necessary to resort to compromise, as always happens with texts prepared in collegiality.**

"The difficulty in reading, the obstacle created by the evident promiscuity of language, find a clear **explanation** in the three reasons mentioned above [6] ... Nonetheless, all of the Council Fathers and all the experts worked with the conviction that they were preparing a synthesis that only at the end would be revealed clearly. This synthesis, or fundamental structure of Vatican II, was therefore sought in spite of the **strong impressions of disequilibrium, discontinuity, excessive variety of languages. Therefore, in the language of** Vatican II one should expect a **desired, intentional and conscious plurality."** [7]

---

5. L. Sartori, "Il linguaggio del Vaticano II," in V.A., *Il linguaggio teologico oggi,* ed. Associazione Teológica Italiana (Milan: Áncora, 1970), p. 236.

6. The three reasons for this mentioned by Sartori are: 1) The clash of the "Scholastic" mentality with the so-called "open" mentality; 2) The specialized literature and language of the "cultural movements" formed in the pre-conciliar period, such as the biblical movement, the liturgical movement, the apostolate of the laity; 3) The role played by the different "cultural regions" from where the Council Fathers had come. The latter were further influenced by the presence of Protestants and Schismatics, by representatives of the laity and women, and by the constant reference to the "voice of public opinion" *(ibid.,* pp. 244-246).

7. *Ibid.,* pp. 246-247.

Sartori also says: "Here is the new fact. **The Council has preferred the imperfection of patched-up, worked over, incoherent, promiscuous texts** in spite of initiating this attempt at achieving a superior synthesis of diverse perspectives." [8]

§ 6   Fr. Alfredo Marranzini, SJ, was professor of Dogmatic Theology and Rector of the Regional Seminary of Reggio Calabria from 1951 to 1961. From there he went on to teach at the San Luigi Faculty of Theology; he wrote for *L'Osservatore Romano, La Civiltà Cattolica, Concilium* and other theological journals and was secretary of the Italian Theological Association and a consultant to the Secretariat for the Unity of Christians. In the introduction to a work about current theological language, Fr. Marranzini remarks:

> **"A Council that,** in living contact with tradition and the thinking of the past, **wished to lead the whole Church toward a greater communication with all men today, should necessarily use a polyvalent language"** [9]

§ 7   4   Fr. René Laurentin, a conciliar *perito,* one of the best known chroniclers of Vatican II and a journalist of *La Croix,* dedicates a special item of his work *L'Enjeu et le Bilan du Concile* [the bet and the balance of the Council] to the various ambiguities of Vatican II and gives some examples:

> **"Another ambiguity went through the whole Council itself: the one involving the word 'pastoral.' This adjective, launched by John XXIII, was a success. . . . Its usage remained vague and pragmatic during the first session. But, beginning in the second session, some fell into the trap of understanding 'pastoral' as unrelated to 'doctrinal,'** as if, for instance, collegiality in matters of hierarchy and love in matters of marriage had to do with 'pastoral' and not 'doctrinal.' **The wish was to find a solution for opposing tendencies: That which was 'pastoral' escaped the requirement for rigor that is posed by doctrine.** . . . Right from the beginning of the fourth session Cardinal Silva was surprised that such a principle had found its way even into the official explanation for the amendments to the *Schema XIII*." [10]

§ 8   Writing on conciliar production as a whole, Fr. Angel Antón, SJ, notes: "On essential points **this Council attained a compromise**

---

8. *Ibid.,* p. 252.

9. Alfredo Marranzini, Introduzione, in V.A., *Il linguaggio teologico oggi,* p. 24.

10. René Laurentin, *L'enjeu et le bilan du Concile – Bilan de la quatrième session* (Paris: Seuil, 1966), pp. 359-360.

not **related** to contents but **only to formal enunciations. Hence such divergent positions adopted to interpret the texts of the Council,** absent a compromise on contents, **remained necessarily ambiguous."** [11]

§ 9

Further on, writing on the dispute over papal primacy versus episcopal collegiality, Anton reaffirms: "Once again **one must recognize that Vatican II reached nothing but a compromise on the formulas about this theme, whereas in relation to its content, a tendency to equivocation prevailed among the majority and the minority** at the conciliar assembly. [12]

§ 10

Fr. Brian Harrison, of Rome's Nepomucene College, draws a conclusion worthy of attention as he writes about ambiguity in the Council's language and its relation with the current crisis in the clergy:

"In the crisis of the contemporary Church we are faced with an extraordinary fact: the two contending parties [conservatives and progressivists] claim to be the authentic interpreters of Vatican II. We find nothing like this in the History of the Church and in the Councils of Florence, Trent and Vatican I. The teaching of these Councils did not lend itself to different and opposing interpretations. He who did not accept these teachings knew he was placing himself outside [the Church]. The unity and vitality of the Church were not threatened.

"**It seems to me essential for the leaders of the Church to honestly recognize the *ambiguities* we have inherited from the Council. It frequently happened, in the Council, that a traditional,** orthodox **proposal would be approved with modified language** or placed in the footnotes **because of the strong resistance from the liberals.** With this, **the conciliar Church issued an uncertain call** about practical matters, **achieving the result predicted by the Apostle Paul: 'For if the trumpet give an uncertain sound, who shall prepare himself to the battle?'** (1 Cor 14:8)"[13]

§ 11

Bishop Gérard Philips of Louvain, who acted in the Council under several titles, stood out as the main writer of *Lumen gentium*.[14]

---

11. Angel Antón, "L'ecclésiologie postconciliaire – Les attentes, les résultats et les perspectives pour l'avenir," in V.A., *Vatican II: Bilan et perspectives,* vol. I, p. 428.

12. *Ibid.,* p. 432.

13. Brian Harrison, "Se a trompa emite um som confuso... ," in *30 Giorni* (Portuguese edition), July 1989, p. 82.

14. Y. Congar, "À guisa de conclusão," in V.A., *A Igreja do Vaticano II,* ed. G. Barauna (Petrópolis: Vozes, 1965), p. 1289.

He is, therefore, highly qualified to assess the degree of precision to be found in the language of the conciliar documents. Speaking generally, Msgr. Philips makes this apology: "**No one is trying to say that the texts promulgated are perfect.** But the perspective of time will help discover what was the openness of mind and heart that Vatican Council II has inaugurated in History." [15]

*

§ 12   Let us see some comments on the most important documents.

About *Lumen gentium,* Msgr. Philips states: "The first phrase [LG 37a], which begins, 'Like all Christians, the laity,' **is an example of a declaration that can be read with very different sentiments and interpreted in contradictory ways**" [16]

§ 13   Fr. René Laurentin also comments on *Lumen gentium:* "**In some difficult cases, solutions went only half-way, or even less. Formulas were wisely calculated to leave the road open to opposing opinions. Hence a certain fluctuation [in the texts].** Thus, a theologian who is well-known for his preoccupation with doctrinal integrity was able to deem himself authorized to publish, several months after the promulgation of the Constitution on the Church, a thesis claiming that 'the doctrine of collegiality is false.'" [17]

§ 14   In a critique of *Lumen gentium,* Fr. Antón says: "**If the post-conciliar Church does not show considerable progress in this participation of the laity in respective directive organs in the Church, one must also look for the cause of this in the *doctrinal ambiguity* of the Council's decrees on important points** of the theology on the laity.

"**a. We find this ambiguity in the purely descriptive notion of lay person that *Lumen gentium* left us** after having refused to present an *ontological definition,* taking a position on points already discussed about ecclesiology and Canon Law. ...

"**b. Vatican II showed the same lack of precision when called upon to decide whether to classify, as part of the Hierarchy, a lay person who takes part in certain ecclesiastical offices** *(munera),* **or who replaces ministers in certain sacred func-**

---

15. Gerard Philips, *La Chiesa e il suo mistero nel Concilio Vaticano II Storia, testo e commento della Costituzione Lumen Gentium* (Milan: Jaca Book, 1975), pp. 13-14.

16. *Ibid.,* p. 380.

17. R. Laurentin, *L'enjeu et le bilan du Concile,* p. 357.

tions *(officia sacra)* **or,** finally, **who is called by the Bishop to consecrate himself entirely to apostolic tasks.**" [18]

§ 15   Testimonies by highly authoritative Fathers of the Council can be cited about the deliberate risk of assuming ambiguities in *Gaudium et spes.* Such testimonies were drawn from the discussions held during the 132nd and 133rd general congregations of the Council. [19]

Therefore, the following testimonies by five Cardinals do not deal with the definitive text of *Gaudium et spes.* We cite them mainly to demonstrate that the Council's Fathers already had a clear awareness of the risk that ambiguity would bring. Furthermore, some of the objections were manifestly not heeded, such as those about the title, *Pastoral Constitution,* and the methodology adopted. At least in these cases, criticisms of the project can be applied to the definitive text.

§ 16   Cardinal Bea, of the Secretariat for the Union of Christians, admits that **"it is necessary to perfect the text afterwards."** He criticizes the **presence of "improper terms joined with rather obscure expressions." "The ambiguity,"** he adds, **"derives from the effort to use classic Latin," and "in some points it was necessary to resort to French in order to understand the Latin."** [20]

§ 17   Speaking on behalf of 91 German-language Fathers, including some from Scandinavian countries, Cardinal Döpfner implicitly recognizes flaws in the text of *Schema XIII* and proposes that its final writing be postponed until "after the Council." The then-Archbishop of Munich states:

"Finally, **since it seems impossible,** in such a new subject, **to arrive at a perfect text, it will be good to recognize it with simplicity and consider the text as the beginning of a dialogue that shall be prolonged after the Council** and allow the Church to progressively cast, upon the problems of a world in evolution, the treasures of her own doctrine... " [21]

---

18. A. Antón, "L'ecclésiologie postconciliaire," pp. 433-434.

19. *Schema XIII,* which later became *Gaudium et spes,* was debated up until the 153rd session, when the text was delivered to the commission in charge of presenting the definitive writing. This final text was voted upon in the 161st, 162nd and 163rd sessions, with some amendments (B. Kloppenburg, *Concílio Vaticano II,* vol. V, p. 324).

20. Augustin Bea, "Comments on the 13th Schema in the Conciliar Assembly," in Giovanni Caprile, *Il Concilio Vaticano II* (Rome: *La Civiltá Cattolica,* 1969), vol. V, p. 70.

21. Julius Döpfner, "Comments on the 13th Schema in the Conciliar Assembly," *ibid.,* p. 74.

§ 18   The Archbishop of Palermo at the time, Cardinal Ruffini, says that **the language employed in the schema "is such that it cannot even be called Latin and is unworthy of a conciliar document. It contains several expressions so obscure and confusing as to become unintelligible and presents, furthermore, some rather inexact, not to say false, statements!"** [22]

§ 19   Cardinal Silva Henríquez of Santiago, Chile, notes: **"It is necessary to make precise the meaning** and the value **of the schema, beginning with its title. The expression, 'Pastoral Constitution,' should be suppressed because it is ambiguous."**[23]

§ 20   Cardinal Landázuri Ricketts, then Archbishop of Lima, Peru, warns: **"By adopting the two methods** [philosophical and humanist] **at the same time, the schema runs the risk of satisfying neither the expectations of the faithful nor those of the non-Christians."** [24]

§ 21   The celebrated Fr. Henri de Lubac, SJ, a conciliar expert honored in 1983 by John Paul II with the Cardinal's purple, referring not to the schema of *Gaudium et spes* but to its definitive text, points out the ambiguity:

"The title of the first part, even more so in French than in Latin, **is somehow ambiguous, and undoubtedly this ambiguity was necessary** in order to enable it to cover the whole field of the exposition. 'Human vocation' here is the vocation of man *(vocatio hominis).* Now, this vocation of man – everything that follows shows it – is not only human, but divine." [25]

§ 22   Fr. Giuseppe Dossetti, who during the Council had been secretary to the four Moderators and in some way a spokesman for them, tries to reflect a general opinion about the Pastoral Constitution. He says: "All of these fathers spoke in the sense of finishing up the schema and tying it nicely together; to the point that **one may now**

---

22. Ernesto Ruffini, "Comments on the 13th Schema in the Conciliar Assembly," *ibid.,* p. 71.

23. Raul Silva Henriquez, "Comments on the 13th Schema in the Conciliar Assembly," *ibid.,* p. 69.

24. Juan Landázuri Ricketts, "Comments on the 13th Schema in the Conciliar Assembly," *ibid.*

25. Henri de Lubac, *Athéisme et sens de l'homme – Une double requête de "Gaudium et spes"* (Paris: Cerf, 1968), p. 92.

say, as is almost unanimously recognized, that the doctrine expressed in *Gaudium et spes* is a doctrine *in fieri* [being made], requiring further development."[26]

§ 23   Fr. Laurentin provides a few more examples of ambiguity in the text of *Gaudium et spes* as he examines the following formulation in the chapter on Matrimony: "'Love is profaned by illicit customs against conception.' Should it be understood that all the customs against conception are illicit (something that would settle the case of certain 'pills' still under discussion) or that the Council condemns only those that are illicit but admits the lawfulness of some others? One can say the same about the wording of note 14 of the same chapter about the doctrine of Pius XI and Pius XII: '*Sic stante doctrina Magisterii.*' Should it be understood as: 'The doctrine of the Magisterium remains stable, unshakable'?"

"Here and there," Laurentin continues, "ambiguity was cultivated as an escape from inextricable oppositions. One could lengthen the list of such wordings encompassing opposing tendencies, because they could be looked at from both sides just like those photographic tricks whereby you see two different people in the same picture depending on the angle you look at it. For this reason, Vatican II already has given, and will continue to give rise to many controversies."[27]

§ 24   Commenting on one of the Council's most important documents, the Constitution *Dei Verbum,* in his *dissertatio ad lauream* in Theology at the Gregorian University - recommended to the Author of this work by Cardinal Alfons Stickler, at the time the offcial Vatican Librarian - Fr. Alberto Franzini, SJ, notes:

"The concept of Tradition in the Constitution [*Dei Verbum*] is understood with different meanings not always clearly specified or even intelligible, thus giving rise to confusions that theological reflection, based on good textual hermeneutics, should attempt to eliminate. ... Regarding the first criticism, *Dei Verbum* can hardly escape the accusation that a certain 'semantic sleight-of-hand' has taken place. Until the various meanings of the term 'Tradition' are clarified, it will be difficult even to agree upon the precise meanings that, at times, it may take on. ...

---

26. Giuseppe Dossetti, "Vaticano II: Quale recezione," in *Il Regno,* 12/1/1991, p. 706.

27. R. Laurentin, *L'enjeu et le bilan du Concile,* p. 357.

"In n. 8 of *Dei Verbum* are seen fundamentally two concepts of Tradition which are constantly interchanged: a concept which is broader in some contexts and more restricted in others." [28]

A little further, Franzini concludes: **"The semantic uncertainty found in *Dei Verbum* is perhaps the sign of a more profound uncertainty** regarding the complexity of the reality of Tradition." [29]

§ 25   The various texts cited in this Chapter speak for themselves.

The general opinion about the existence of ambiguities in the language of the final documents of Vatican II is, therefore, indisputable.

*

Once the pervasive lack of clarity in the texts of Vatican II has been verified, a question naturally arises: Why this ambiguity? Is it for tactical reasons? Because of an evolutionary method? A clash between currents? Ideological dictates?

The following Chapters strive to help the Reader see this ambiguous panorama more clearly.

*   *   *

---

28. Alberto Franzini, *Tradizione e Scrittura – Il contributo del Concilio Vaticano II* (Brescia: Morcelliana, 1978), pp. 241-243.

29. *Ibid.,* p. 243.

Chapter IV

STRATEGIES THAT LED TO AMBIGUITY
DURING THE COUNCIL

§ 1

Two currents of thought confronted each other in Vatican II. [1]

§ 2

The *first* current, called conservative, was based mainly on the perennial teachings of the Councils of Trent (1545-1563) and Vatican I (1869-1870). Pius IX (1846-1878) and St. Pius X (1903-1914) were the two Pontiffs who best represented this thinking in the the last two centuries of the Tridentine era for their overt action against the errors of the modem world, their fearless proclamation of the anti-egalitarian, monarchic and sacral character of the Church, and their struggle against Liberalism and Modernism. For this reason, they have become symbols of the conservative thinking and movement. At the time of Pius XII (1939-1958), the echoes of Trent and Vatican I and the reflections of these two great Pontiffs' personalities still held strong sway over the conservatives who, in large numbers, took part in the Council's Preparatory Commissions. So, this current had a significant influence on the preparation of the projects that were to be presented at Vatican II (1962-1965). It can be said without any doubt that, as a whole, the schemata presented by the Preparatory Commissions were an indication of the orientation the conservatives wanted to impart at the August Assembly.

That program, nevertheless, was condemned by the progressivist current right at the beginning of the Council and eliminated by the authority of Pope John XXIII. [2]

---

1. We deal with this confrontation in more detail, though not exhaustively, in Chap. VI.1.

2. On November 22, 1962, John XXIII rejected the schema *De fontibus Revelationis* and with it nearly all the schemata of the pre-conciliar Theological Commission. In his chronicle, B. Kloppenburg comments: "Thus came to a close, in a melancholy way, the discussion on the text prepared by the Pre-Conciliar Theological Commission: *rejected.* Yesterday's vote still gave its proponents a glimmer of hope. The absolute majority, however, clearly had already given its *non placet.* Indeed, it would have been useless to go on discussing a text practically already rejected, since it would never be approved by two-thirds [of the Assembly] as required by the rules. Thus the Pope decided to give it the *coup de grace.* And it died" *(Concilio Vaticano II,* vol. II, p. 193). It was perhaps

§ 3

The *second* current, called progressivist, is a direct heir to the old romanticist school of Tübingen – particularly in regard to ecclesiology – whose main proponent was Fr. Johann Adam Möhler (1796-1838). In the philosophical field it is an indirect heir to German Idealism, notably of Kant, Schelling, Hegel, above all Schleiermacher and, more recently, of Husserl, Scheler and Heidegger.[3]

Möhler's followers were the defeated wing during Vatican Council I.[4] Later, St. Pius X condemned many of their ideas as part of Modernist thought.[5]

---

due to this fact that Henri Fesquet called the first conciliar session the "demolition session" *(Le journal du Concile,* p. 1031).

For more about the role of John XXIII in the rejection of the pre-conciliar schemata, see Chap. VI §§ 49-56 and in § 83 the comment Fr. Chenu made to the Author of this work.

3. a. For the sake of brevity, this view is necessarily simplified. Let us point out some other sources of the progressivist current: the religious influence of the movements for biblical, patristic and liturgical renewal of the missionary and lay apostolate. An editorial in *La Civiltà Cattolica* notes: "Indeed, Vatican II is not interpreted as an episode which erupted abruptly, but as a terminal point that completes a prior evolution and maturation of an ecclesial conscience that inherited and perfected those movements which, since the middle of our century, had prepared biblical, patristic, liturgical and pastoral renewal through study and experiences." *(La Civiltà Cattolica:* "Concilio, post-Concilio, para-Concilio," 1/5/1985). Such movements were fruits of the work of the Dominicans from Le Saulchoir, the Jesuits from Innsbruck, the Faculties of Theology of Louvain, Paris, Lyon, and the Biblical School of Jerusalem (Joseph Comblin, "La théologie catholique depuis la fin du pontificat de Pie XII," in V.A., *Bilan de la théologie au XXe. siècle,* eds. R. Vander Gucht and H. Vorgrimler, Tournai-Paris: Casterman, 1970, vol. I, pp. 479-495).

b. We also emphasize the philosophical influence of the Danish philosopher Sören Kierkegaard and the French philosophers Maurice Blondel and Henri Bergson, among various thinkers worthy of note (On the philosophical origin of the progressivist current, see Vol. VI, *Inveniet Fidem?,* Chap. III, *passim).*

Therefore, when this Work refers mainly to Möhler and German Idealism as the basis for the progressivist current's ecclesiology and philosophy, it defines the picture by its key note, rather than its entire composition.

4. The confirmation of this assertion is found in Chap. VI, §§ 4-15.

5. a. On the influence of Möhler's ideas in French Modernism (Loisy and Le Roy) and English Modernism (Newman and Tyrrel), see Edmond Vermeil, *Jean-Adam Moehler et l'Ecole Catholique de Tubingue* (Paris: Armand Colin, 1913), pp. 451-473.

b. Independent of its historical genesis, it is worthwhile to highlight some basic ideas of the professor from Tübingen that later became the patrimony of Modernism, and today are adopted by Progressivism. Here are some excerpts from and comments on the works of Möhler found in the entry *Moehler* by A. Nicolas Fonck, in DTC, vol. X:

c. **Concept of faith:** " 'According to the doctrine of the primitive Church, the true faith, the true knowledge of religion could not exist without the Holy Spirit, who could not be received if the person was not linked to the Church. But if we attentively examine how this doctrine was understood, we will obtain the following result: Each individual should, through an immediate impression, gather in himself the holy life diffused in the Church; he should, through an immediate contemplation, transform the experience of the Church into his own experience; he should rouse in himself pious sentiments and a holy conduct, and from the depths of his sanctified soul he should develop the knowledge of religion' (*Unity in the Church,* p. 8). Every Christian should, therefore, be a mystic. This is full-blown Schleiermacherism: faith begins with sentiment, with religious experience" (col. 2057).

"Love engenders faith: 'Love is the source of truth; the faith of a Christian is formed by the rays of his holy love which rise from his soul, are captured by his spirit, are reflected and transformed into ideas' (*Unity,* p. 18)" (*ibid.*). "Who does not see the relationship between the origins of the faith and that which the Encyclical *Pascendi* finds in the Modernists?" (*ibid.*).

d. **Concept of dogmatic teaching:** " 'Just as each one in particular receives the principle of life and the interior faith only from the community ... so also the true expression of the interior faith and the true doctrine cannot be determined and preserved except by the community' (*Unity,* p. 26)" (col. 2058).

" 'The same Holy Spirit who animated the Church while these holy men were alive (the preceding Fathers), animating it always, in like manner manifests himself in him (the Catholic man of these times) as He had in them; for this reason, he [the Catholic] believes that which Christians had always believed before him: his faith is **not** a faith of authority ... his concordance with the faith of all time is a necessary sequence of the special character of Christianity' (*Unity,* pp. 36-37.)" (col. 2058).

e. **Concept of Tradition:** "Definitively, and to speak clearly, Tradition would be nothing else but interior faith, still not formulated as doctrine, which the Holy Spirit constantly preserves and renews in the Church; it is an 'intimate sense, 'a conscience' (*Symbolik,* vol. I, pp. 36-39) that enables the Church to discern Christian truth intuitively and infallibly, or better, that contains this truth in such a way that the Church need only fall into herself to know true Christianity ... Vermeil warns us that this Möhlerian conception of Tradition is none other than Schleiermacher's (*ibid.,* p. 139) and his disciple Neander's (*ibid.,* p. 152, note 5)" (col. 2059).

We do not intend to deal here with the genesis of this school and its appearance in Vatican II. References made to it in this Work are general and, therefore, relatively superficial.[6]

---

f. **Evolution from natural to supernatural:** "Möhler arrives at 'a kind of *sui generis* transformism which takes pleasure in seeing religious conscience as a living being and making it evolve under the action and with the help of divine grace' (Vermeil, p. 46). *Likeness of God,* that is, the supernatural, is nothing but a 'development' of the *image of God,* that is, of our natural 'spiritual faculties' (*Symbolik,* vol. I, p. 15)" (col. 2061).

g. **Concept of Church:** "For Möhler, the spiritual powers of the Church have a 'charismatic' origin. 'Ordination, as it presents itself exteriorly, is a recognition by the whole Church that her spirit is found in a certain faithful, enabling him to represent the love of a certain number of faithful and unite them with the whole Church: thus, the Holy Spirit is not communicated only in the ordination, but one recognizes that He had *already* communicated *in advance* a certain gift to the one being ordained' (*Unity,* p. 217). Read in annex XIII *(ibid.,* pp. 283-295) the curious theories of Möhler on 'the participation of all Christians in the vocation of churchmen,' particularly in the power of forgiving sins" (col. 2062).

6. In addition to the previously cited book by Edmond Vermeil, here are some bibliographical data on where to find more information about the genesis of this school:

V.A., *Bilan de la théologie du XXe. Siècle,* eds. R. Vander Gucht–H. Vorgrimler, (Tournai/Paris: Casterman, 1970); the collaborations of R. Aubert, *La théologie catholique au milieu du XXe. siècle,* vol. I, pp. 437, 444; J. Comblin, *La théologie catholique depuis la fin du pontificat de Pie XII,* vol. I, pp. 479, 484; R. Marie, *Méthodes historiques et problemes theologiques,* vol. II, p. 53; Werner-Kummel, *Les recherches exégetiques sur le Nouveau Testament,* vol. II, pp. 190, 193; G. Colombo, *La création,* vol. II, p. 272; J. Frisque, *L'ecclésiologie au XXe. siècle,* vol. II, pp. 415-416, 440; J. Beumer, *Histoire de la theologie et des dogmes,* vol. II, pp. 654, 657; V.A., *L'ecclésiologie au XIXe. siècle* (Paris: Cerf, 1960), especially the writings by R. Aubert, *La géographie ecclésiologique au XIXe. siècle,* pp. 25-35; W. Bartz, *Le Magistère de l'Eglise d'après Scheeben,* pp. 309-327; A. Chavasse. *L'ecclésiologie au Concile du Vatican - L'infallibilité de l 'Eglise,* pp. 233-245; Y. Congar, *L'ecclésiologie, de la Révolution Française au Concile du Vatican, sous le signe de l'affrmation de l'autorité,* pp. 100-114; H. F. Davis, *Le rôle et l'apostolat de la Hiérarchie et du laïcat clans la théologie de l'Eglise chez Newman,* pp. 329-349; B. D. Dupuy, *Schisme et primauté chez J. A. Moehler,* pp. 197-231; J. R. Geiselmann, *Les variations de la definition de l'Eglise chez J. A. Moehler,* pp. 141-195; O. Rousseau, *Les attitudes de pensée concernant l'unité chrétienne au XIXe. siècle,* pp.

§ 4

The pontificates of John XXIII and Paul VI and Vatican II
crowned the great counter-offensive launched by this wing.[7]

351-373; V.A., *Nouvelle Histoire de l'Eglise*, eds. R. Aubert–M. D.
Knowles–L. J. Rogier (Paris: Seuil, 1975), vol. V, pp. 581-689; A. Acerbi,
*Due ecclesiologie - Ecclesiologia giuridica et ecclesiologia di communione
nella "Lumen Gentium"* (Bologna: Dehoniane, 1975), pp. 9, 19, 330,
361, 406, 422; K. Adam, Die *Katholische Tübingen Schule,* in
Gesammelte Aufsätze (Augsburg, 1936), pp. 389-412; H. U. von
Balthasar, *El complejo antirromano – Integración del papado en la Igle-
sia universal* (Madrid: BAC. 1981), chaps. II, IV, *passim*; *Love Alone:
The Way of Revelation* (London/Dublin: Sheed & Ward, 1982), pp. 25-
42. Y. Congar, *Le Concile de Vatican II,* pp. 124, 148-152; J. R. Geiselmann, Introduction to the critical edition of *Die Einheit* (Kohl-Olten, 1956);
*Der Wandel des Kirchenbewusstseins und der Kirchlichkeit in der
Theologie J. A. Möhler* (Freiburg, 1961), pp. 531-675; S. Jaki, *Les
tendances nouvelles de ['ecclésiologie* (Rome: Herder, 1957), pp. 24-
35, 57-58, 61-62, 84, 148-149, 156. 174, 202; J. Pinsk, "La situation
actuelle de la théologie catholique en Allemagne," in V.A., *Catholicisme
allemand* (Paris: Cerf, 1956), pp. 343-345; O. Rousseau, "A Constituicão
no quadro dos movimentos renovadores de teologia e de pastoral das
últimas décadas." in V.A., *A Igreja do Vaticano II,* pp. 115-134.

See also the following note.

7. a. An editorial in *La Civiltà Cattolica* (Rome) entitled "Dalla 'società
perfetta' alla Chiesa 'mistero,'" 1/19/1985, p. 111, describing the genesis and history of the new ecclesiology, says: "Thus, just as the movement started by Bellarmine led to the definition of papal primacy and
infallibility in Vatican I, so also the movement begun by Möhler culminated in the Encyclical *Mystici corporis* (June 29, 1943) of Pius XII
and in Vatican II."

b. Fr. Angel Antón concurs with this summary statement: "That which
in Vatican I was the ecclesiology of a minority became [the ecclesiology of] a majority in Vatican II, whereas the minority in Vatican II was
the majority in Vatican I" (*L'ecclésiologie postconciliaire,* p. 427).

c. To prove what we just said, no words could be more explicit than
these of Fr. Hans Küng: **"How could we have arrived, with regard
to Vatican II, to this turnaround ... if there had not been a long
preparation before the Council, a sort of hibernation? John XXIII,
a charismatic in the Seat of Peter, was the wick ... How could he
have unleashed this process unless, long before the Council, there
had not been people both known and anonymous who gathered
the material that made the spark become a flame? ... We have
every reason to bow with respect and gratitude before the Christian commitment of these silent heroes of the struggle for a**

renewed truthfulness. ... **Suspected, impeached, discredited, branded as heretics, persecuted and exiled by their brethren, shepherds and theologians in the Church, they carried on their work** as best they could! **Singled out as dangerous, extremists, ultra-radicals, heretics, revolutionaries, they always advanced** as far as they were allowed to and, at times, even beyond. ...

"Many times only after decades, other times only after death, was there a gesture of gratitude shown toward them; some of them were rehabilitated only by Vatican Council II. ... That which a few started with modesty and insignificance, **that which only slowly succeeded in taking hold amidst great efforts, has now developed and multiplied many times over: in the renewal of liturgy, of Church life in general. ... It has been proven that those harbingers were not** people on the fringe, **lonely outsiders, but rather the vanguard of an army which, though undoubtedly slow, had strongly determined to forge ahead, an army to which some official representatives of theology and the heads of the Church have shown themselves to be the rearguard"** (H. Küng, *Veracidade – O futuro da Igreja,* São Paulo: Herder, 1969, pp. 161-162).

d. Already at the inception of the Modernist crisis, Italian senator Antonio Fogazzaro, in his novel *Il Santo,* placed on the *Index* by order of St. Pius X, mentioned the existence of modernist groups – apparently the "slow army" to which Küng refers – that wanted reforms in the Church like those carried out during and after the Council: **"We are a good number of Catholics,"** says Giovanni Selva, a personage in the cited novel, "in Italy and outside of Italy, **ecclesiastics and laity, who desire a reform in the Church. We want it without rebellion, carried out by the legitimate authority. We want reforms in the religious teaching, reforms in the Liturgy, reforms in the discipline of the clergy and reforms also in the supreme government of the Church. In order to achieve that, we need to create a public opinion that will lead the authorities to act according to our opinions, even if this takes 20, 30 or 50 years.** We do not know each other, except for the few who publish books. Very likely, **there is in the Catholic world an enormous number of religious and cultured people who think as we do."** *(Il santo,* Milan: s.p., 1907, p. 38).

Fogazzaro makes the tenor of such reforms more explicit in the advice that Benedetto, *"il santo"* in the novel, offers the Pope: "Holy Father ... the Church is ill. Four evil spirits have entered her body to wage war against the Holy Spirit. One is the spirit of the lie. ... Today, few Christians know that religion is not mainly an adhesion of the intelligence to formulas of truth, but it is principally to act and live according to this truth. ... And **those who know this are fiercely combated, defamed as heretics, reduced to silence, all through the work of the spirit of the lie which for centuries has installed in the Church a tradition of deceit.** ... Holy Father! **Honor before the whole Church some of these men, some of these priests combated by the spirit of the lie. Elevate**

some of them to the Episcopate, to the Sacred College! And also this, Holy Father! Advise exegetes and theologians, if necessary, to advance with prudence, ... but **do not permit the *Index* and the Holy Office, on account of some excessive audacity, to remove men who are the honor of the Church.**

"[The second evil spirit] is the spirit of domination by the clergy. The priests imbued with the spirit of domination are not pleased that souls communicate directly and normally with God to ask Him advice and orientation. ... He [the evil one] has suppressed the ancient and holy Catholic liberty. He attempts to make obedience, even when not required by law, into the first of virtues; he would want to impose non-obligatory submissions, retractions of one's conscience ... Do not give in, Holy Father! ... Take on public advisers, let the Bishops gather frequently in national councils, and **allow the people to participate in electing the Bishops ... and let the Bishops mix with the people** ...

"The third evil spirit ... is the spirit of greed ... The spirit of poverty is not taught there [in the Church] as Christ taught it. ... Enjoying pomp and the honors of riches, adhering with their whole souls to the comforts of wealth appears licit to many preachers of Christ's word and example. ... It is not one day's work, but **let the day be prepared for when the priests of Christ may give the example of real poverty**. ...

"The fourth evil spirit ... is the spirit of immobility. All **clergymen,** Your Holiness, **above all those who are today adversaries of progressivist Catholicism, would have crucified Christ,** in good faith, in the name of Moses. **They are idolaters of the past, they would want to keep everything in the Church immutable, from the forms of pontifical language all the way to the *flabelli*"** *(ibid.,* pp. 219-223).

e. In the 1920s, Ernesto Buonaiuti, an expressive figure of Italian Modernism, made the following assessment of his movement, apparently foreseeing Vatican II: "In fact, one finds that **if the repression meticulously commanded by the Encyclical *Pascendi* stopped Modernism as an organized *movement,* nevertheless something of the methodological and intellectual tendencies that it defended remained**. ... After a long and tiresome clandestine circulation, the problems of critique and exegesis that Modernism timidly raised are reappearing in the conscience of the Catholic clergy ... **However little may be known about the secret tendencies of a part of the Italian clergy, one may say that, despite this cold disciplinary uniformity** imposed by the Encyclical *Pascendi,* **latent forces lie dormant, ready to provoke a new explosion. The day they become active, Modernism will be able to look back and contemplate without repentance its long wait and anxious suffering"** *(Le modernisme catholique,* pp. 176-177).

f. Regarding this phase of "disciplinary uniformity," the modernists were fully aware that they were the forerunners of a change in the Church. Such a premonition is clear in the words with which the anonymous editors of a Modernist Roman magazine, *Nova et Vetera,* responded to a polemic: "And who knows if, even as we are writing, in some seminary in Italy, deep in some faraway monastery, the soul predestined to accomplish all this that we have merely prepared is already throbbing and praying? May God permit it! Each one of us is ready to say with joy: *Me oportet minui, ilium autem crescere* [I must diminish, that he may grow]" *(ibid.,* p. 125).

g. The Modernist dream of changing the ecclesiastical institution and possibly obtaining a Pope favorable to it coincides with Masonic aspirations in relation to the Church. Indeed, the well-known anti-Modernist and anti-Masonic author, Fr. Barbier, transcribes authoritative documents originally published by Copin Albancelli, Crétineau-Joly and Delassus. In one of these documents dated April 3, 1844, a high-ranking leader of the Italian secret forces, called Nubius, commented in a letter to another highly-placed Mason:

"Now then, in order to ensure a Pope in the required proportions, we must first of all prepare a generation worthy of the kingdom of which we dream. Cast aside the old and mature age men; go to the youth, and if possible, even to children ... It is to the youth that we must go, it is the youth that we must lead, unperceived by them, under the banner of the secret societies. In order to advance with prudent steps on this dangerous but sure way, two things are absolutely necessary. You must have the simplicity of doves and the prudence of the serpent ... Never pronounce before them a word of impiety or impurity: *Maxima debetur puero reverentia* [The greatest reverence is owed to the child] ... Once your reputation has been established in colleges, high schools, universities and seminaries, once you have gained the confidence of professors and students, make sure that especially those who enter the ranks of the clergy are pleased with your meetings ...

"**Such reputation will give your doctrine access to the young clergy and to convents. In a few years, this clergy will naturally have invaded all functions: they will govern, administer, judge, form the Sovereign's council, be called to choose the Pontiff who must reign; and this Pontiff, like most of his contemporaries, will be more or less imbued with Italian and humanitarian principles** that we will start placing in circulation ...

"**Let the clergy move forward under your standard always believing they are advancing under the banner of the apostolic Keys. Cast your net like Simon Bar Jonah; spread it to the bottom of sacristies, seminaries and convents,** rather than casting it to the bottom of the sea; **if you do not precipitate anything, we promise you a catch [even] more miraculous than his ... You will have fished a revolution dressed in [the Pope's] triple crown and cape, carrying the cross and the flag, a revolution that will need only a small stimulus to set fire to the four corners of the earth**" (Nubius. *Secret Instructions on the Conquest of the Church,* in Emmanuel Barbier,

§ 5   Among the thinkers of this current who were active in Vatican II stand out Frs. Karl Rahner, SJ, Yves Congar, OP, Henri de Lubac, SJ, Marie-Dominique Chenu, OP, Edward Schillebeeckx, OP, and Hans Küng. Influential even without having participated in the Council were Frs. Hans Urs von Balthasar and Pierre Teilhard de Chardin, SJ.[8]

§ 6   At the Council's assembly this current had spokesmen of great prestige such as Cardinals Giovanni Battista Montini, Archbishop of Milan and later Paul VI; Leo Józef Suenens, Archbishop of Malines and Brussels, Primate of Belgium; Julius Döpfner, Archbishop of Munich; Giacomo Lercaro, Archbishop of Bologna; Augustin Bea, president of the Secretariat for the Union of Christians, former confessor of Pius XII and a close friend of John XXIII; Joseph Frings, Archbishop of Cologne and leader of the German Episcopate; Achille Liénart, Bishop of Lille and president of the French Bishops Conference; Bernard Alfrink, Archbishop of Utrecht.[9] Beginning in the second session, Cardinals Suenens, Döpfner and Lercaro directed the Council as Moderators.

§ 7   The situation between the two wings was one of confrontation. However, the enthusiasm of the conservatives was soon dampened as the schemata drawn up by the Council's Preparatory Commission were withdrawn and the opposition of John XXIII became manifest, while the progressivists became triumphant, especially after Cardinal Montini ascended to the papal throne.

Les infiltrations maçoniques dans l'Eglise, Paris/Brussels: Desclée de Brouwer, 1901, p. 5).

8. These names are among the ten greatest ones of Catholic theology in our time. according to Fr. Battista Mondin *(Os grandes teólogos do século XX,* São Paulo: Paulinas, 1979. vol. I). Although the name of Hans Küng does not appear in this study, in a more recent work Mondin placed him among the greatest theologians of the day *(Introduzione alla teologia,* Milan: Massimo, 1983, pp. 372, 375-376).

Küng, for his part, already enjoyed great notoriety in his capacity as official expert at the Council on account of the "frankness" with which he expounded his bold doctrinal positions. As Henri Fesquet puts it, "his writings acquire considerable importance and exert considerable influence" *(Le journal du Concile,* pp. 548-549).

9. This list includes the progressivist *aile marchante* of what Fr. Ralph Wiltgen called the "European Alliance," made up of Bishops from ten nations but also widely supported by non-Europeans. About the "European Alliance" and the Fulda Conference, interesting details are to be found in R. Wiltgen, *The Rhine Flows into the Tiber* (Devon, England: Augustine, 1978), pp. 15-17, 78-80.

The conservatives counted on an enormous latent force made up mainly of the consistency of their thinking with the past of the Church, the peaceful support of that thinking by a majority of Catholic public opinion and by the implicit adherence of a large part of the Council's Fathers. In addition, the conservatives could easily have brandished against the progressivists the weapon of innumerable condemnations by previous Pontiffs against the liberal-modernist-progressivist current. This enormous force could have been used at any moment during the Council.

The progressivists enjoyed the considerable advantage of surprise, intelligent and shrewd organization and the great force represented by the support of John XXIII and later of Paul VI, as will be shown in this Collection.

That precarious balance of forces imposed a delicate strategy on the progressivists as they gained ground. Above all, they had to prevent the conservatives from waking from their lethargy and consequently making use of the tactical potential at their disposal, as explained above.

The concern of the progressivist current was, therefore, understandable: avoid dissension and achieve unanimity. The price to be paid would be that of ambiguity.

1. Ambiguity to Achieve Unanimity

§ 8

"Paul VI achieved, therefore, **this unanimity he so earnestly worked for. The consequence is that we are only halfway there. We could not go farther without causing ruptures,"** explains Fr. Yves Congar in a book interview. [10]

§ 9

The justification given by Cardinal Suenens at Toronto's International Theological Congress two years after the Council ended has a similar tenor. The Belgian Prelate stated:

"Another obstacle to the full flowering of the Council, astonishing as this may seem at first glance, **was the quest for this unanimity.** It is both the glory and the weakness of a Council to strive to win the assent of all its members to the proposed texts and decrees. ... In fact, the important votes were for the most part nearly unanimous.

"This unanimity, however, had its price. It can happen, in the course of debate with the interplay of numerous amendments ... **that certain texts lose their point, or at least their forcefulness.**

---

10. *Jean Puyo interroge le Père Congar – Une vie pour la verité* (Paris: Centurion, 1975), p. 149.

It will fall to future historians to disentangle here and there the central affirmation from the interpolations and embellishments. The quest for a 'common denominator' does not always do full justice to the underlying thought of the majority, and it is not easy to synthesize elements that originated in quite divergent currents of thought. **Hence the texts are sometimes far richer in what they imply than in what they openly affirm.**

"In the conciliar texts there are some formulas whose aim was to counterbalance other assertions or win wider assent; in some cases, like temporary stopping places on a long climb."[11]

§ 10   Fr. Rahner roughly concurs: "Naturally, here or there, **the unity of all** in liberty **was diligently sought and obtained in this Council through the tactic of leaving questions unsolved or by other means which,** at first sight, **may appear as an unfortunate compromise.** But even in these cases, true unity was attained in a climate of authentic freedom." [12]

§ 11   Equally elucidating is a concrete example described in great detail by Msgr. Philips, the main writer of *Lumen gentium*; its final lamentation is particularly expressive. Dealing with the vote on collegiality, Msgr. Philips says:

"One hundred and ninety-one Fathers voted *non placet* against the institution of the College of 12 Apostles; 322 Fathers opposed the existence of the College of Bishops; 325 refused to admit that a Bishop's consecration imparts the threefold sacred function in the Church. The number of opponents was a record for the 2,247 ballots cast. These voting rounds took place from September 21 to 30, 1964. One year earlier, on October 30, 1963, the number of opponents totaled 408. Therefore, this group appeared to shrink rather than grow; finally, it was almost entirely absorbed by the general current.

"In order to achieve this result the majority agreed to insert, in the exposition about the college, a certain number of subordinate propositions, emphasizing each time that the pontifical primacy remained intact. Now, it is certain that these additions made the text heavy to read. To gauge this effect, it suffices to put them between parentheses. **The multiplication of these safety measures pacified a certain number of Western Fathers;** on the other hand, especially the Eastern Fathers, who insisted that episcopal dignity be

---

11. Leo Józef Suenens, "Co-responsibility: Dominating Idea of the Council and its Pastoral Consequences," in V.A., *Theology of Renewal – Renewal of Religious Thought* (Montreal: Palm Pub., 1968), vol. II, p. 10.

12. Karl Rahner, *Vaticano II: Um começo de renovacão* (São Paulo: Herder, 1966), p. 12.

frankly recognized, were disappointed by so many restrictions marked by mistrust. How difficult it is to satisfy even one's own friends when in opposing fields!" [13]

2. Ambiguity to Prepare the Future [14]

§ 12   The fact that ambiguity was owed to this strategic need to carry a near-unanimity does not exclude – on the contrary, it even presupposes – that such ambiguity would be adroitly inoculated with the thinking of the progressivist current.

§ 13   Cardinal Suenens had insinuated that in the text cited above when he said: **"The texts are sometimes far richer in what they imply than in what they openly affirm."**

§ 14   Fr. Schillebeeckx gives an even clearer testimony as he states that **"a few intended to adopt formulas with double meaning so that the field would be open to their interpretation of 'papal collegiality.'"** [15]

§ 15   The same tactics can be noticed in the declaration of Fr. Giovanni Caprile, editor of the famous Jesuit magazine *La Civiltà Cattolica* and author of a highly regarded chronicle of Vatican II: **"The Council opened some doors. Other doors it left ajar because it saw that the times were still not ripe; however, it did not close them. It only left them ajar, saying: someone who comes after me will open them."** [16]

*

§ 16   Here we conclude this Chapter with the notion that ambiguity in the language of the Council obeyed strategic designs to facilitate handling the conservative reaction in the conciliar assembly. But it also served to pave the way for future and more explicit developments in the thought of the progressivist current.

* * *

---

13. G. Philips, *La Chiesa e il suo mistero nel Concilio Vaticano II,* p. 53.

14. In this Item we present only two texts to corroborate the statement in our subtitle, since Chapter V will deal with the same subject.

15. Edward Schillebeeckx, "Wij denken gepassioneerd en in cliche's," in *De Bazuin,* January 1965, in A. Acerbi, *Due ecclesiologie,* p. 472.

16. G. Caprile, Interview with the Author, Rome, February 3, 1983.

Chapter V

AFTER THE COUNCIL, AMBIGUITY STIMULATES PROGRESSIVISTS TO DRAW EVEN MORE RADICAL CONSEQUENCES FROM IT

§ 1   The leaders of conciliar and post-conciliar thought, consistent with their strategy, started emphasizing the fact that the Council, rather than saying everything that it had desired, had stopped halfway. Taking advantage of the texts' purposeful ambiguity (some of which had been proposed by the very authors who commented on them), those leaders encouraged interpretations that drew even more radical consequences.

§ 2   Cardinal Suenens, quoting Paul VI, comments: "For his part, Pope Paul VI wrote these far-reaching words that engage the future: **The Council's decrees, more than a point of arrival, are a point of departure toward new goals.** The Spirit and the renewing wind of the Council must continue to penetrate deeply into the life of the Church. **The germs of life sown by the Council in Church soil must reach their full maturity."** [1]

§ 3   Cardinal Döpfner, another moderator of the Council, speaks along the same lines: "There is something unusual in the Church that has emerged in the work of the Council: this openness, this readiness, this willingness to change, this departure from a rigidly delimited vital space to a vastness which it had long ignored. No, the **closure of the Council did not mark an end, but an inception, the beginning of a new way.** In truth, the words with which the Pope addressed the conciliar theologians in the audience he granted them on the penultimate day of the Council are valid for each member of the Church, whether Bishop, theologian or lay person, each in his own way: **'Continue your research and work; it is absolutely necessary!'"** [2]

§ 4   Also symptomatic is a statement by Fr. Schillebeeckx: **"We are saying things in a *diplomatic* way, but after the Council we will draw the implicit conclusions."** [3]

---

1. L. J. Suenens, *Discorso ufficiale d'apertura,* in V.A., *L'avvenire della Chiesa,* p. 46

2. Julius Döpfner, *La Chiesa vivente oggi* (Bari: Paoline, 1972), pp. 14-15.

3. *Apud* Romano Amerio, *"Sob a cúpola, o vazio,"* in *30 Dias* (São Paulo), January 1991, p. 25.

§ 5   Equally meaningful is a small discrepancy in opinion between Fr. Hans Küng and Fr. Yves Congar, narrated by the latter in a book containing some of his memoirs: **"Küng** certainly **recognized that the Council had done a very good job,** [4] but ... **one day I told him:** It's the story of the half-full and half-empty bottle. **You say it's half-empty; I say it's half-full; it's not that bad.'** [5] Indeed, I believe **the Council** has done a very good job. But it is true that **in numerous questions, it has stopped halfway.** It started a work that it did not finish, whether you're talking about collegiality, the role of lay people, the missions or even ecumenism." [6]

§ 6   In an interview to Vatican Radio about the expectations for the 1985 Synod of Bishops, Cardinal Suenens said: **"If we were looking at an elevator at the 10th floor of a 20-story building, we would say it's already on the 10th floor. But if we were looking at it from above, we would say that it was still at the 10th floor. This is more or less what happened with the Council."**[7]

§ 7   On December 12, 1965, four days after the closing of the Council, Karl Rahner gave a lecture in Munich on how that great ecclesiastical event should be seen. The lecture's title, *Vatican II: A*

---

4. In his book, *Veracidade - O futuro da Igreja* (p. 130), Hans Küng presents a list of the reforms undertaken by Vatican II and adds: "True, **the Council has not done everything it could have – from today's perspective. But it has done more than one would have dared expect of it back then."**

5. Here Fr. Congar is probably referring to the German adage: *"Der Pessimist: Die Flasche ist schon halb leer ... Der Optimist: O nein! Sie ist noch halb voll!"* [The pessimist: The bottle is already half-empty ... The optimist: Oh, no! It's still half-full!]

6. *Jean Puyo interroge le Père Congar,* p. 131.

7. Statement to Vatican Radio, transmission for Brazil, 11/7/1985.

The text of Suenen's statement reached our hands in typed form, sent by the TFP radio monitoring service. We asked Vatican Radio for a copy of the recording. Unfortunately, however, the magnetic tape had already been erased.

A reviewer of this Work wrote Cardinal Suenens asking him to confirm his statement. The Prelate kindly did so and indicated one of his works in which the same metaphor is used in analogous terms (L. J. Suenens, *Souvenirs et espérances,* p. 128).

The statement is also found in the Cardinal's comments to an Italian newspaper (L. J. Suenens, "Un nuovo battesimo per la Cristianita – I grandi testimoni del Vaticano II," interview granted to Silvano Stracca, in *Avvenire,* 10/23/1992, p. 15).

Beginning of Renewal, reflects well its thesis. In various parts this thesis comes to the surface in very clear words. For example:

"In fact, Vatican II established a beginning of *aggiornamento* [updating], an inception of renewal. It took steps of penance and conversion, always fruitful, by the way. But **this is only the beginning of a beginning.** It is very important, undoubtedly. **But it is nothing more than the start of a beginning. Everything, almost everything, is still only on paper. And written paper (Constitutions, Decrees) can be transformed into spirit and life,** service, faith and hope. **Not, however, automatically."** [8]

§ 8   Rahner adds some facts that corroborate his thesis: **"Much still has to be done in order that,** starting from this beginning of a beginning, **a true and real advance toward the future may materialize. We will even say that nearly everything remains to be done.** Indeed, the determinations of the Constitution on the Liturgy still need to be transformed into concrete liturgical forms so that they can be later inserted into the life of prayer of the Church as a true prayer to God in spirit and truth. Now it is necessary to start a generous, humble, persevering, optimistic and intelligent ecumenical dialogue. We still do not have deacons, for whose existence the Council opened new possibilities. The Council of Bishops [Synod] must now prove that it can, through new and living attitudes, make the principle of a personal and collegial government in the Church a reality. The promised reforms of the Roman Curia are still to be minutely codified so that it can be truly revitalized. We will still have to wait a long time for the *Code of Canon Law* is restructured so that it corresponds to the spirit and letter of Vatican II." [9]

§ 9   He continues: "The Directory related to ecumenical work still has to be concluded. The statutes of the Bishops' Conferences are still to be written. The Decree on the formation of future priests awaits its adaptation to different regional conditions to be made by the Bishops ... The work of codification of the Eastern *Canon Law,* already begun by Pius XII, still has to be adjusted to the Council's line." [10]

§ 10   Further on, Rahner says: "This is why Vatican II is no more than the beginning of a beginning. Undoubtedly, this is already a lot. However, **a severe judgment will weigh upon all of us,** shepherds and sheep, **if we limit ourselves to words without putting them**

---

8. K. Rahner, *Vaticano II: Urn começo de renovação,* p. 24.

9. *Ibid.,* pp. 26-27.

10. *Ibid.,* pp. 29-30.

into action, if we accommodate ourselves to the beginning of the road without trying to reach its end." [11]

§ 11   Suenens draws consequences of the Council's ecumenism in his speech to 223 theologians from around the world gathered in Brussels in September 1970 to celebrate the fifth anniversary of the magazine *Concilium*. The Primate of Belgium refers with ardent enthusiasm to a possible Vatican Council III or a Jerusalem Council II, as well as to the pan-religious unity he already foresees:

"You have before you, theologians and brothers in the Faith, a magnificent mission: **giving Vatican II its full continuation and preparing the next chapter in the History of the Church.** How will the future be? We do not know. But **we may expect that Vatican II was but a prologue, and that one day an Ecumenical Council bringing together representatives of all the world's Christians will be able to re-establish and proclaim the visible unity of all the Lord's disciples.** ... If the signs of the times do not deceive us, we may believe that the hour for Christians to return to unity is drawing near.

"The star that guided the Magi Kings to Bethlehem already shines in the sky of ecumenism. Pilgrims of unity have set out again; the road is always strewn with stones and the ways are uncertain; we are still crossing the desert. But, unlike the Magi Kings whose names come to us from the legends, today's pilgrims have well-known names ... they are called Paul VI, Athenagoras, Ramsey. ... I don't know where or when the decisive meeting will take place. **Will it be a Vatican III?** Perhaps.

"But since in a dream you can overcome all obstacles, **why couldn't the final meeting be in the same place that was the cradle of Christianity? Why couldn't the Council of reconciliation be a Second Council of Jerusalem?** This return of all of the Lord's disciples to the starting point, Jerusalem, seems to me to have been finely prefigured in these verses which I leave to you as a hope and an invitation:

'*We shall not cease from exploration,*
and the end of all our exploring
will be to arrive where we started,
and know the place for the first time.' (T. S. Elliot)" [12]

§ 12   Defending Vatican II from the attacks of some radicals who deem conciliar concessions to pneumatology to be too small, Bishop

---

11. *Ibid.,* p. 41.

12. L. J. Suenens, "Discorso ufficiale d'apertura," in V.A., *L'avvenire della Chiesa,* pp. 55-58.

Walter Kasper of Stuttgart-Rottenburg, says that the Council is only a starting point: "Y. Congar demonstrated that this censure is not true, but unilateral. H. Mühlen, G. Philips, C. Möhler, H. Careless and A. M. Chare, among others, have investigated the pneumatological statements of the Council. However, the malaise persists. On this, as on many other questions, one finds that **the texts of the Council are an impulse and a starting point rather than a conclusion and a complete answer."** [13]

§ 13   Concurring with statements that Vatican II is but a beginning is the testimony of Cardinal Ratzinger, ex-Prefect of the Congregation for the Doctrine of the Faith, and present day Pope: "Now, after the refusals of the last hundred years, the Council has taken the initiative to start the process of accepting this positive encounter to coordinate the Church and the modern world. ... **The fight of the conciliar Fathers over *Schema XIII* [*Gaudium et spes*] can be nothing but the beginning of a movement that continues."** [14]

§ 14   Many and dangerous are the consequences that these Prelates encourage us to draw from the "halfway" mark at which Vatican II halted. For example, let us look at a quotation from Nicola Colaianni, a Catholic professor who writes for the magazine *Concilium* and is a member of the editorial body of the magazine *Il Tetto* of Naples:

"Such criticism [made by Liberation Theology] is not outlandish ... It **represents a consistent development of many of the achievements ... in which ... the Council had stopped 'halfway.'** ... Indeed, **it is on the dogmatic level that the Council stopped 'halfway,' looking for compromised solutions not only ... in regard to contents but also to formulas, dogmatic *enunciations,*** precisely **because they could be interpreted with diverse and conflicting meanings."** [15]

§ 15   For his part, Msgr. Philips confirms: ***"Lumen gentium* did not say the last word about the priestly ministry,** but outlined an authentic and sincere explanation." [16]

---

13. Walter Kasper, "Espirito-Cristo-Igreja," in V.A., *A experiência do Espírito Santo* (Petrópolis: Vozes, 1979), p. 73.

14. Joseph Ratzinger, *Problemi e risultati del Concilio Vaticano II* (Brescia: Queriniana, 1967), pp. 10-11.

15. Nicola Colaianni, "Crítica ao Vaticano II na literatura atual," in *Concilium,* 1983/7, p. 127.

16. G. Philips, *La Chiesa e il suo mistero,* p. 325.

§ *16*   Let us see what are the immediate consequences of *Lumen gentium*'s failure to say the last word about ministry.

Fr. François Houtart, author of the introduction to *Gaudium et spes,* professor at the University of Louvain and Secretary General of the International Federation of Institutes for Social and Socio-Religious Research, states: **"One may say that the Vatican II is but a beginning in the institutional transformation of the Catholic Church. The future will undoubtedly see a much wider distribution of ministries, a much greater participation in the way the people in charge are designated,** more numerous communications shaped by a public opinion [inside the Church], a **less precise and less centrally organized system of norms, a very large variety of liturgical expressions and also of theological formulations."**[17]

§ *17*   Also bearing witness to the ambiguity of Vatican II, Cardinal Ratzinger agrees that the moral climate of dogmatic tolerance was established with the Council: "Under many aspects ... **almost more important than the solutions offered by the text [of *Gaudium et spes*] is the *'ethos'* behind it, which produced a new kind of ecclesiastical language:** the courage to approve **an open document that does not intend to be a concluding definition but rather a beginning that must continue.** This fundamental feeling contributed to make the Council rediscover its unity after its early difficulties, **notwithstanding many particular statements that remained insufficient."** [18]

§ *18*   Finally, there are also those who, for strategic reasons, admitting an evolutionist conception and having drawn nearly all the possible consequences from the ambiguity of the Council, as time went by began to consider it outdated and to prepare the minds of their followers for new changes. Several of the greatest theologians of the day are found among these. Here are only a few samples of their thinking, two by Fr. Congar, one by Fr. Rahner, and other by Fr. Huizing.

§ *19*   Fr. Congar: "One cannot seek a 're-launching' of Vatican II without recognizing that, from certain standpoints, we have moved beyond it, and that however rich and fecund it may be, **the Council cannot be treated only as a point of arrival,** a vast warehouse that it would suffice to exploit. So, giving ourselves time to digest Vatican

---

17. Francois Houtart, "Les religions comme réalités sociales," in V.A. *Bilan de la théologie du XXe. siècle,* vol. I, pp. 72-73.

18. J. Ratzinger, *Problemi e risultati del Concilio Vaticano II,* p. 125.

II (a Vatican III or Jerusalem II? Not so fast!!!), **we must realize that yet something else is needed.**" [19]

On a different occasion, Congar says: **"The Council,** being a moment in the life of the Church, **is absolutely not a definitive revelation.** One can see that in relation to many facts **the Council is already outdated.** There were things that it failed to perceive and others that it didn't. For example, the revolt of the youth, the fact that young people have broken with tradition. This the Council did not see!" [20]

§ 20   Karl Rahner, in a dialogue with his disciple Johann Baptist Metz who formulated a controversial political theology, [21] gives an idea of what may be the famous "starting point" or "halfway" point that progressivists talk about so much but whose final goal they fail to disclose. In that dialogue both theologians deem the achievements of Vatican II so timid as to be insufficient starting points to solve modern-day problems.

K. Rahner: **"The topics** explicitly **dealt with in Vatican Council II are not** properly **the central problems of the post-conciliar Church.** Except perhaps for the pastoral decree [sic] on the Church in today's world and the problems related to this subject, it seems to me that **all the** purely **conciliar problems** which have to do with the Church as such **are essentially secondary if compared to the urgent current problems in the Church.** With this **I am not criticizing the Church as if she had dealt only with unimportant**

---

19. *Y.* Congar, *Le Concile de Vatican II,* p. 107.

20. *Y.* Congar, Interview with the Author, Paris, February 19, 1983.

21. a. Ralph Wiltgen shows the leadership role the conciliar Fathers from the Rhine basin played in Vatican II. Among them, the German Episcopate played a decisive role, and its main theologian was none other than Karl Rahner, who authored a large number of the schemata accepted by the Council *(The Rhine Flows into the Tiber,* pp. 78-80).

During the second session of Vatican II the Archbishop of Freiburg in Breisgau introduced the Jesuit theologian to Paul VI, who praised both his work as a scholar and his theological work (Antoine Wenger, *Vatican II - Chronique de la deuxiéme session,* Paris: Centurion, 1964, p. 254; H. Fesquet, op. cit., p. 313). And at the end of Vatican II, Paul VI called Rahner to thank him for his contribution to the conciliar work (B. Mondin, *Os grandes teólogos do século vinte,* vol. I, p. 98).

b. As for Metz, many consider his political theology as the main source of inspiration for the so-called "Liberation Theology," notwithstanding the efforts of a certain media to bestow an aura of originality on several South American theologians.

things in Vatican II. **I am only** relating this simple **finding** about something entirely justified: **The Church must subject herself to a certain *aggiornamento*, she needs to prepare herself before tackling the problems ... that present themselves today.** Inasmuch as this work of preparation can depend on a Council, the Church carried it out in Vatican II. But **now the moment has come ... for the Church to face the really central problems** ... Do you agree?"

Metz: "I agree. I also believe that **the problems** explicitly **treated in the Council cannot serve as a starting point for us to determine the problems of the post-conciliar Church."** [22]

§ 21   Fr. Peter Huizing, SJ, professor of Law and History at the University of Nijmegen and consultant to the Commission for the Revision of the *Code of Canon Law*, goes so far as to speak about the "bankruptcy of Vatican II" and to ask for a Vatican III. He says: **"Vatican Council II did not translate its doctrine into the institutions of the Church. The declarations** on the collegiality of Bishops, the responsibility of the laity, the nature of Christian marriage, and so on **are useless if not anchored in institutions of the Church. This is the main reason for the bankruptcy of Vatican II. Vatican III should fill this gap."** [23]

§ 22   As a whole, these quotations provide evidence for something we touched on in the previous Chapter. The ambiguity in the Council's texts, so necessary, as we have seen, to achieve the unanimous support of the Conciliar Fathers, carried in its bosom a series of developments which, once Vatican II was over, would be stimulated and applied. Hence, important theologians, some of whom were great mentors of the Council, raised their voices in unison to say that the texts of Vatican II stopped "halfway" and were only "a starting point."

*

§ 23   Once again in this Chapter it becomes clear that ambiguity in the documents of the Council was "desired, intentional and conscious." [24] Further, this served as a strategy to stimulate the development of more radical positions in the post-conciliar period.

*   *   *

---

22. Karl Rahner in a dialogue with Johann Baptist Metz, in V.A., *Cinco problemas que desafiam a Igreja hoje,* pp. 149-150.

23. P. Huizing, "Vaticano III: Una costituzione sulla Chiesa," in V.A., *Verso la Chiesa del terzo millenio,* p. 167.

24. L. Sartori, "Il linguaggio del Vaticano II," p. 247; see Chap. III, § 5.

Chapter VI

AMBIGUITY: FRUIT OF THE CLASH BETWEEN TWO OPPOSING THOUGHTS

§ 1   Until now, our analysis and examples dealt only with the wording of the texts and the progressivist current's strategic interest in exploiting ambiguity.

We will now see how ambiguity in the Council's documents resulted from the clash of two opposing thoughts, two concepts of the Church confronting each other. [1] The texts of Vatican II are, as it were, a picture of the final phase of this battle in which one of the combatants – the progressivist current – was winning and the other – the group of conservatives – was being defeated. The texts recorded, at that moment, all the maneuvers of attack and defense by the contenders. In the next stage, that is, after the Council, the struggle may present the analyst with a quite different picture.

1. Two Concepts of the Church Confront Each Other

§ 2   The progressivist current, as we said, inherits the thought of J. A. Möhler, [2] to whom is attributed the foundation of the ecclesiology that triumphed at Vatican II. That ecclesiology aimed at replacing the centuries-old conception of the Church as *societas perfecta* that comes from her Tradition, made explicit by the Council of Trent and by St. Robert Bellarmine.

§ 3   Traditional ecclesiastical thinking is expressed by St. Robert Bellarmine in his work, *Disputationes de controversiis Christianae Fidei.*

"Our thesis," says the Saint, "is that there is only one Church, not two; and that the only one true Church is the community of men united by the profession of the true Christian Faith and the communion of the same Sacraments, under the government of legitimate Shepherds and, above all, of the sole Vicar of Christ on earth, the Roman Pontiff. From this definition one can easily see who belongs to the Church and who does not belong to her.

---

1. In notes to Chap. IV, we point out some intellectual foundations of the progressivist current.

2. Chap. IV, §§ 3, 4.

"Indeed, this definition is made up of three parts: profession of the true Faith, communion of the Sacraments and submission to the legitimate Shepherd, the Roman Pontiff. The first part excludes all infidels, those who were never in the Church such as the Jews, Turks and pagans, or those who once were in it and later fell away, like the heretics and apostates. The second part excludes the catechumens and excommunicated, since the former are not admitted to the Sacraments and the latter are excluded from them. The third part excludes the schismatics, who have the Faith and the Sacraments but do not submit to the legitimate Shepherd. ... All others are included, even if they are reprobates, delinquent and impious." [3]

The spirit of a Catholic faithful joyfully exults upon reading this sentence, so holy, consistent, limpid and secure. In contrast, it is filled with suspicion at the vagueness of Möhler's notion of Church, which we will see a little later.

St. Robert Bellarmine continues: "Between our declaration and the others there is this one difference: All the others require interior virtue to declare that someone is a member of the Church, and thereby make the true Church invisible. We, on the contrary, believe with certainty that in the Church are found all the virtues, Faith, Hope, Charity and the others; however, we do not believe that any interior virtue is required to be able to say that someone is somehow part of the true Church, of which the Scriptures speak, but only the external profession of Faith and the communion of the Sacraments, which can be perceived by the senses. Indeed, the Church is as visible and palpable a community of men as the community of the Roman people, the Kingdom of France or the Republic of Venice." [4]

Commenting on this passage, *La Civiltà Cattolica* – from which we have taken the quotation above – says: "At this point Bellarmine notes that in the Church there is soul and body. The soul is the gifts of the Holy Spirit, the theological virtues, etc.; the body is the external profession of Faith and the communion in the Sacraments. It so happens that some belong to the soul and to the body of the Church (the members who are alive to Faith and Charity), others belong to the soul but not to the body, like the catechumens and the excommunicated, if, as it can happen, they have Faith and Charity; still others belong to the body but not to the soul of the Church, such as those

---

3. St. Robert Bellarmine, *Disputationes de controversiis Christianae Fidei adversus huius temporis haereticus* (1586-1593) (Venice, 1721), 53, in *La Civiltà Cattolica,* Editorial: "Dalla 'società perfetta' alla Chiesa 'mistero,'" 1/19/1985, p. 107.

4. *Ibid.*

who have no interior virtue but nevertheless, out of hope or some temporal fear, profess the Faith and participate in the Sacraments under the government of the Shepherds; these are 'like the hairs or nails or the bad humors of the human body.' [5] " [6]

§ 4   *La Civiltà Cattolica* goes on to emphasize the contrast between the concepts of St. Robert Bellarmine and those of Möhler: "A change in perspective took place in the first decades of the 19th century when, under the influence of Romanticism ... there arose a desire to emphasize the vital, organic and mystical aspect of the Church. In this, the contribution by Johann Adam Möhler, author of two famous works, *Unity in the Church* and *Symbolik,* [7] played a decisive role."

"He conceives the Church as an organic unity of all faithful, produced by the presence in them of the Holy Spirit who makes use of her to communicate divine life. This organism is visible because the Holy Spirit tends to form his own body for himself. For this reason, the Holy Spirit is linked as much to the visible Church as to his own body.

"But where does the Hierarchy stand? Möhler answers: The Holy Spirit is the soul of the Church; just as the soul constitutes its organs, so also the Spirit builds the organs of his activity. These are the ecclesiastical ministries. However, in the constitution of the ecclesiastical Hierarchy there is also the action of the people insofar as it is a community of love animated by the Holy Spirit. This tends to reproduce in the Hierarchy the model of the Apostolic College, just as Jesus indicated, giving it a living image. This is the extent to which the hierarchical functions are a living expression of charity, given by the Holy Spirit to the totality of the faithful.

"This view of the Church ... leaves little room for the visible and hierarchical element in the Church," admits the well-known Jesuit magazine, adding: "This is why Möhler himself, in *Symbolik,* abandons the pneumaticism of his book *Unity in the Church* in order to better establish the Church upon Christ by showing that the Hierarchy continues Jesus' authority and that the visible side of the Church continues, in turn, the mediation of Christ's humanity. He adds, however,

---

5. St. Robert Bellarmine, *ibid.*

6. *La Civiltà Cattolica, ibid.*

7. Original titles: *Die Einheit in der Kirche oder das Prinzip des Katholizisntus dargestellt int Geiste der Kirchenvater der drei ersten Jahrhunderte* (Tübingen, 1825); *Symbolik, oder Distilling der dogmatist Gegensätze der Katholiken and Protestanten nach ihren Öffentlichen Bekenntnisschriften* (Mainz, 1832).

that in the Church the interior element is more important than the exterior one: 'We are not living members of the exterior Church unless we belong to the interior Church.'[8*] "[9]

§ 5   The notion of the Church as the body of the Holy Spirit, as Möhler conceives it in *Unity of the Church,* causes astonishment and suspicion. The egalitarian presentation of the people as the source of the Hierarchy comes close to the Romanticism of Rousseau and the myths of Illuminism and the French Revolution. The appearance of Christ in his second work, replacing the Holy Spirit in the first, judging from the context of the editorial in *La Civiltà Cattolica,* appears to be due more to a reshuffling in the nomenclature caused by adverse reactions than to a real change in concepts. This impression is strengthened by his final statement, which entirely confirms his first idea that only those who participate in the interior Church are members of the Church.

This is thoroughly opposed to the notion of a visible Church since, as St. Robert Bellarmine says, and we quote again, "Between our thesis and the others there is this one difference: all the others require interior virtue to declare that someone is a member of the Church, and thereby make the true Church invisible."

§ 6   Edmond Vermeil and A. Nicolas Fonck confirm the fact that the same conceptions found in *Unity* remained in *Symbolik:* "Vermeil believes that 'at depth, the master ideas remained the same.' It seems to me that he is totally right ... Möhler made of Christianity a conception inspired by the theories of Schleiermacher, which one sees he has not abandoned. One does not even conceive he could have abandonned them, since they were so deeply in accord with his mystical temperament; by this token, one may say that Möhler was an unconscious precursor of 'Catholic' Modernism."[10]

*

§ 7   These are, basically, the two conceptions of the Church that confronted each other in Vatican I and, a century later, in Vatican II. Vatican I was the glorification of the limpid and masterful conception made explicit by St. Robert Bellarmine. Vatican II, as we have pointed out, was the success of Möhler's conception.

*

8*. *Symbolik,* 2nd ed., § 48.

9. *La Civiltà Cattolica, ibid.,* pp. 108-109.

10. A. N. Fonck, *Moehler,* in DTC, vol. X, col. 2063.

§ 8   But how did Möhler's concept make it to our days?

La Civiltà Cattolica says that "J. A. Möhler died prematurely at age 38, [11] but his ideas had an enormous influence on later theology. By means of Fr. G. Perrone, a professor in the Roman College, they were passed on to his disciples, Passaglia, Schrader and Franzelin:

"It is thus understandable that Schrader and Franzelin, who were in charge of writing the *Constitutio de Ecclesia* to offer the Fathers of Vatican Council I a schema for discussion, entitled its first chapter *The Church Is the Mystical Body of Christ.* This is because, they say, if you want to define the Church you must start by examining her innermost nature ... so that people will not believe that the whole truth of the Church is reduced to her exterior and sensible aspect. Unfortunately, the Council was unable to debate this schema for lack of time ... only an excerpt of it was discussed – chapter XI, which dealt with papal primacy and infallibility. However, one may suppose that the schema raised problems among the Fathers, either because many of them were used to defining the Church by her exterior aspects, or because the expression 'mystical body' was suspect since it had been used and misinterpreted by the Synod of Pistoia."[12]

§ 9   Skipping over the period of Modernism, during which Möhler's ideas had a great influence, we arrive at the end of World War I (1918). The two currents continued to oppose each other during this time. Przywara writes, "The *'Corpus Christi mysticum'* has become the central idea in Catholic Germany in opposition to the *Ecclesia militans* and to the Church as a juridical formation, society, organization, institution." [13]

§ 10   In a lecture in the capital of Peru in July of 1986, Cardinal Joseph Ratzinger provides data that corroborate and further develop the words of Przywara. Ratzinger comments on Romano Guardini's statement that the Church "is a living reality" and not simply an organization. The following excerpt holds our attention:

"It is difficult to communicate the enthusiasm, the joy that there was then with this raising of awareness. During the time of liberal

---

11. There seems to have been a small error in the calculation of Möhler's age by the writer of *Civiltà Cattolica*. In fact, he died just before turning age 42 (May 6, 1796 to April 12, 1838) (*Ibid.*, cols. 2049-2050).

12. *La Civiltà Cattolica, ibid.,* p. 109.

13. Erich Przywara, "Corpus Christi mysticum. Eine Bilanz," in *Zeitschrift für Aszese and Mystik,* 15 (1940), p. 197, in A. Acerbi, *Due ecclesiologie,* p. 38.

thought, including up until the first World War, the Catholic Church was seen as a fossilized bureaucratic apparatus that tenaciously opposed the achievements of the modern era. Theology presented the question of the primacy as a vital issue to such a degree that it made the Church appear essentially as an institution articulated in a centralist way. It became a question tenaciously defended in the face of which, however, each one placed himself from the outside. Now, once again it has become clear that the Church is much more, that all of us make her vitally progress in the faith, just as she makes us progress.

"It became clear that the Church follows an organic growth through the centuries, which continues today. Likewise, in her the mystery of the Incarnation remains current: Christ still marches on through the times. If we ask ourselves what were the elements acquired at this starting point which later reappeared in Vatican II, we can answer: the first aspect was the Christological definition of the concept of Church.

"J. A. Möhler, the great regenerator of Catholic theology after the desolation of the Enlightenment, said: 'A certain erroneous theology could be caricatured in this phrase: 'In the beginning, Christ founded the Hierarchy and thus sufficiently provided for the Church until the end of time.' But in opposition to this is the fact that the Church is a mystical body, that is, that Christ Himself is always her new foundation and that He is never a past in her, but He is always and above all her present and future. ...

"She lives because of this: Christ is present in our hearts. Hence He forms His Church. Consequently, the first word of the Church is Christ and not herself; she remains whole to the degree that all of her attention is directed to Him.' Vatican II emphasized this conception so strongly as the apex of its considerations that the fundamental text on the Church begins precisely with the words: *Lumen gentium cum sit Christus*... .

"Secondly ... one must establish the aspect of interiority and the character of the communion of the Church. She grows from the inside out, and not vice-versa. The Church means first of all the most intimate communion with Christ; she is formed in the life of prayer, in sacramental life, in the fundamental attitudes of faith, hope and love ... The Church grows from the inside: this is what the expression 'Body of Christ' means."[14]

§ *11*   The notion of "mystical body" has taken on different names. Sometimes it returned to Möhler's radical pneumatology in *Unity of*

---

14. J. Ratzinger, "La eclesiologia del Vaticano," in *Iglesia-Mundo* (Madrid), October 1986, pp. 13-14.

the Church, receiving the title "Church of the Spirit;" other times it was called "ongoing Incarnation," "Church as mystery," "mystical person," "Church Sacrament," or "Sacrament of Salvation." Whatever the designation, the same latent conception was there, opposing the Church as *societas perfecta, inaequalis, hierarchica.*

§ 12   Under the guise of criticism, Fr. Congar makes an indirect defense of the "Church Sacrament" and the "Church as ongoing Incarnation," which reveals his opposition to the *societas perfecta* and his support of Möhler. The French Dominican writes:

"We can understand ... the insufficiency of presenting the Church as 'Sacrament,' a presentation which, in its own time and context, was itself a way of overcoming a wholly juridical and, in the final analysis, quite naturalistic conception of the Church. It is the presentation of the Church as the continuation of the Incarnation or ongoing Incarnation. It was dear to Möhler in *Symbolik* and, after him, to the Roman School. It is still found in numerous contemporary expositions. What makes it seductive is that it translates the structure of the Church as a visible and invisible reality at the same time, hence its analogy, from this standpoint, to the Christological mystery. But this still suffers from an excessively static view of the Church. Other criticisms can be made of the theme 'ongoing Incarnation,' as applied to the Church as Body of Christ " [15]

§ 13   In the next text, Congar emphasizes the difference between the two conceptions: "Until the ecclesiological renewal of the last 40 years, a renewal consecrated by the Council, the view of the Church commonly spread in manuals was dominated by the idea of a *societas inaequalis hierarchica,* instead of a community or people of God. The Mystical Body doctrine at times opened a breach in the clerical tower, but it was itself interpreted in the context of an unequal or hierarchical society ... People spontaneously had a clerical perspective of the Church." [16]

§ 14   The clash of currents dealt with in this Chapter also becomes clear in another statement by Fr. Congar in which he discloses the plans of Vatican II in this regard: "The idea of Church Sacrament ... was, on the part of the Council, a means to emerge from a predominantly juridical vision." [17]

---

15. Y. Congar, *Un people messianique* (Paris: Cerf, 1975), pp. 40-41.

16. Y. Congar, *Ministeri e communione ecclesiale* (Bologna, 1973), p. 34, in Piero A. Bonnet, "Le 'fidèle' récupéré comme protagoniste humain dans l'Eglise," in V.A., *Vatican II: Bilan et perspectives,* vol. I, p. 539.

17. Y. Congar, *Un people messianique,* p. 38.

§ 15   Thus, departing from Möhler, we arrive at Vatican II. The unity in the thinking indicates a current that wishes to destroy the notion of the Church as *societas perfecta, inaequalis, hierarchica.*

2. In the Murky Waters of Vatican II, a Meeting of Two Rivers

§ 16   With great lucidity, Fr. Raymond Schwager, SJ, in an interview with the Author, [18] let it be known that in order for Vatican II to be well understood, it must be considered as a meeting of the waters of Vatican I with those of a future Vatican III. It is no wonder that Vatican II is confusing: as time goes by, the more radical perspective of a future Vatican III will explain it.

The simple metaphor of the meeting of rivers easily explains the confusion and ambiguity that prevail in the texts of Vatican II, fruits of a clash between the two opposing currents.

The sequence of texts below is aimed at giving the Reader elements to make his own judgment of the Council's ambiguity as a result of the struggle between two opposing ecclesiological conceptions.

§ 17   The first text, by Cardinal Suenens, evokes the same metaphor. At the inaugural speech of the Congress of the magazine *Concilium* in 1970, after analyzing the "heated argument" about the collegiality of Bishops in regard to *Lumen gentium,* the Prelate says: "In a few words, a **job remains to be done: that of harmonizing two viewpoints and leading them to a perfect synthesis. There is in Ireland a place** well known to tourists **called *the meeting of the waters.* It is a valley in which two rivers impetuously throw themselves against each other to form, a little farther down, only one river with calm waters. I offer you this image as an invitation to bring to completion,** in a fraternal dialogue, **the marvelous symphony – unfortunately as incomplete as any human creation – of *Lumen gentium.*"** [19]

---

18. Fr. Karl Rahner set an appointment for an interview with the Author in Innsbruck. Unfortunately, on the eve of the interview, he was rushed to a Munich hospital where he remained interned with grave heart problems. Fr. Rahner's secretariat asked Fr. Raymond Schwager, SJ, a director of and professor at the Faculty of Theology of Innsbruck University, to replace him at the interview. Fr. Schwager kindly received the Author for two conversations, totaling four hours, on February 11, 1983.

19. L. J. Suenens, "Discorso ufficiale d'apertura," in V.A., *L'avvenire della Chiesa*, p. 48.

§ 18   Msgr. Luigi Sartori also describes the confrontation between the two currents present at the Council: "Considering the protagonists, **I believe that the factors of the Council's plurality of language can be grouped** in at least three ways: **First of all, the most radical difference that was lived and suffered was that of the shocking clash between a** predominantly **scholastic mentality ... and the mentality** that we can generally call **open ...**

"The first 'impasse' of the Council was, in fact, ascertaining and **verifying this coexistence (historic condensation?) between different generations.** *The Church's today should sew together yesterday with tomorrow.* True, **the first schemata** presented to the conciliar Fathers were withdrawn, because in fact they **were too openly linked with the outlook and language of the preceding Scholastic Theology** (accused of juridical formalism, manualism). Now this is something that did not happen, for example, in the Councils of Trent or Vatican I. Nevertheless, **one could not break totally with the past, even more so since the people with a Scholastic formation remained alive and functioning.** (How many were they? A few? Many? I am tempted to suppose that they were a majority. But that would need verification.)

"The texts should also know how to speak the old language, now more, now less, **so that they could be** understood and **approved by readers who had inherited the preceding formation. It is no wonder that the Church today faces the inconvenience of two different readings of the same texts:** concentrating one's attention on aspects of consonance and greater need can prevent or hinder a global and full discernment." [20]

§ 19   Fr. Cipriano Vagaggini, OSB, a conciliar *perito,* an important member of the International Theological Commission and a professor at Rome's Pontifical Atheneum of St. Anselm, in the preface to Antonio Acerbi's work, *Due Ecclesiologie,* says: **"This work demonstrates that the obligatory starting point for a later deepening** [of theoretical-practical problems] **in the present development of the life of the Church is the manner and the state in which such problems appear in the Council** itself. **Both manner and state are not always simple nor limpid.**

"Indeed, **the Council raised, broached upon, or implicitly outlined these problems, but only solved them partially and not always with maximum clarity and consistency; when it did more or less solve them, it was very far from drawing all their consequences either on the theoretical or practical levels.** As for the

---

20. L. Sartori, *Il linguaggio del Vaticano II,* p. 244.

rest, reading the work makes it obvious that **it could not have been otherwise given the ideas and currents that confronted each other in the Council** – and continue to do so in the post-Conciliar period – **as well as in the unfolding of the Council itself. The fact that arriving at a harmonization of the two viewpoints was often laborious is inevitably reflected in the texts themselves."** [21]

§ 20   Another author who confirms the double ecclesiology in the Council's texts is Fr. Gustave Martelet, SJ, a conciliar *perito* and professor at the well-known Faculty of Theology of Lyon-Fourvière, of the French Jesuits:

"Vatican II must reconcile a twofold requirement that leads some to say that it pays tribute to a double ecclesiology. The first would truly be 'communional,' as it has been called since then: in it appears the grandeur of Christians and their fundamental equality in the mystery of Christ; **the other ecclesiology would properly be 'juridical' and unduly reinstate a 'hierarchical' dependence of the faithful on a ministry that would govern them from the outside** and thereby compromise the free expression of their authentic grandeur! **Nobody will truly deny, and the Council less than anyone else, that it is difficult to achieve a synthesis of these two aspects, often opposed** at the discretion of their mutual distortions, **because of the very mystery that it must express."** [22]

§ 21   Fr. Angel Antón, SJ, says: **"The dynamics of the confrontation between the socio-juridical, abstract and apologetic ecclesiology** that prevailed since the Counter-Reformation, **and the new ecclesiology, historic and communional,** founded on Scripture and on the Fathers, which eventually imposed itself on the Council, **did not permit the desired synthesis to be achieved. It is necessary to recognize that the ecclesiology of Vatican II ... presents a certain** *juxtaposition* **of the two ecclesiological tendencies,** easily verified by comparing chapters I and II of LG with chapters III and IV." [23]

---

21. Cipriano Vagaggini, *Presentazione,* in A. Acerbi, *Due ecclesiologie,* p. 6.

22. Gustave Martelet, *Deux mille ans d'Eglise en question – Crise de la foi; crise du prêtre* (Paris: Cerf, 1984), p. 59.

23. A. Antón, "L'ecclesiologie postconciliaire," in V.A., *Vatican II: Bilan et perspectives,* vol. I, p. 419, pp. 426-427. For analogous observations on the role of sin in the world in the text of *Gaudium et spes,* see p. 436

§ 22   One of the most typical points of contention in the struggle between these two currents was the dispute on episcopal collegiality *versus* pontifical primacy. After giving ground in relation to most topics under discussion, the conservatives reacted a little more strongly when *Lumen gentium* dealt with episcopal collegiality. In the manner it was written, it paves the way for a more or less rapid erosion of papal primacy and the abolition of the monarchical principle inside the Church.

        So, the conservatives sought and obtained *a Preliminary Explanatory Note* through the intervention of "superior authority," which was to be attached to *Lumen gentium* saying in what sense chapter III on collegiality should be interpreted. The *Note* clearly defends papal primacy. The text, and especially the context, of chapter III defend the Bishops' collegiality to the detriment of papal primacy. How is it possible to read one part under the prism of the other when both wish the opposite as far as the primacy of the Pope is concerned? Nevertheless, the conservatives, who could have condemned the document as a whole or at least chapter III, contented themselves with the Pyrrhic victory of the *Preliminary Note.*

§ 23   This did not prevent Fr. Congar from considering the conservatives as allies, since conservative complaints obliged the progressivist theologians to take special care and be prudent with the final writing. Without such prudence this important point in the progressivist advance would have been left more exposed and vulnerable. [24]

§ 24   Cardinal Ratzinger, speaking out about this *Note* and its writing, makes ambiguity stand out as a fruit of the confrontation between

---

24. Indeed, addressing the conservatives, Congar says: "Brethren, let us work together! The very rigor of your demands can be beneficial to us. If the Council's Theological Commission was able to do a quite notable work as a whole, it owes this in part to a tenacious minority which obliged it to be more precise. See, for example, the explanatory *Note* preceding chapter III of *Lumen gentium"* (*La crisi nella Chiesa e Mons. Lefebvre,* Brescia: Queriniana, 1976, pp. 80-81).

On another occasion Fr. Congar explained what he meant by "working together" with conservatives: "The Council's preparation had been carried out under the domination – not only the influence, but domination – of the men from the Curia and the Holy Office. ... They held the reins of things; they knew their *métier.* The whole thing consisted, practically speaking, in leaving them in a minority, for they were nothing but a minority. ... I don't blame them. They have rendered us a great service by obliging us to make our thinking more precise and to lay the foundations of our reasonings" (*Jean Puyo interroge le Père Congar,* pp. 140-141).

the two currents and does not hide his sympathy for the progressivist thought:[25]

"The *Preliminary Explanatory Note,* as it is known, has helped to give a somewhat bitter flavor to the final journeys, filled with bold hopes, of the Council's third session. We would go too far if we wanted to analyze here in a precise fashion this very complicated text. Its result – to which we will limit ourselves – would be the recognition that this does not create a substantially new situation, but in principle continues the same dialectics."

---

25. a. The sympathy for Progressivism that the future Benedict XVI nurtured during the Council reveals itself in his poor reception of the *Preliminary Note.* As for the "bitter flavor" in the last meetings of the third session to which he refers, it appears to have been due to the fact that progressivists had expected to advance to the end of the road without encountering obstacles. In this regard, here is an interesting report on some "table talk" that took place during the Council:

"Fr. Ratzinger, personal theologian of Cardinal Frings, said one day over lunch with a group, that after obtaining a majority in the commissions, the progressivists thought they would have a free hand in the Council. Nevertheless, in the speeches and votes in the Assembly, he said, they began to note some resistance to their proposals, and the commissions had to take this into consideration when revising the schemata" (R. Wiltgen, *The Rhine Flows into the Tiber,* p. 150).

b. If someone were to cast into doubt Cardinal Joseph Ratzinger's affiliation with the progressivist current, he could find the Prelate's own acquiescence to this designation in the book-interview in which journalist Vittorio Messori calls him a "balanced progressivist" and points to him as one of the founders of the magazine *Concilium,* a meeting place for the so-called 'progressivist wing' of theology" (*Rapporto sulla Fede – Vittorio Messori a coloquio con Joseph Ratzinger,* Rome: Paoline, 1985, p. 14).

c. Ratzinger's statements to the same journalist, published by the magazine *Jesus,* are even clearer. Messori presents the Cardinal thus: "Perhaps what is most annoying is the fact that the supposed 'guardian of the faith' in reality has not only the stature of a great theologian ... but also of an open, modern theologian, open to the signs of the times. A *perito* of the German Episcopate at Vatican II, he is later found among the founders of *Concilium,* an international magazine that brings together the so-called 'progressivist wing' of Catholic theology.

"'Was it a sin of youth, Your Eminence, this engagement with *Concilium?*' I ask him, joshing. 'Absolutely not,' he answered. 'I did not change; they changed'" (J. Ratzinger, interview with Vittorio Messori, "Ecco perché la Fede è in crisi," in *Jesus,* November 1984, p. 69).

"The resulting ambiguity, as far as the actual competence of the episcopal college is concerned, is already inserted in the conciliar text itself. Undoubtedly, this dialectics was later weighted [sic] in favor of the pole for the primacy. But the text, under the impulse of this tendency by each statement, reintroduces on the side another statement and re-establishes the equilibrium, making it possible to interpret the whole both in the sense of the 'primacy' and in relation to the principle of collegiality. Therefore, one can easily speak of a certain intrinsic disharmony in the *Note*'s text, which reflects the disharmony among those who wrote it and attempted to reconcile conflicting tendencies. If the resulting text gives an impression of disharmony, this is a sign that a complete harmonization was not attained, nor was it possible."[26]

---

d. During a visit to Brazil in 1990, the Cardinal spoke to the press on the same subject:

Question: "What are the most marked differences between the Ratzinger of Council Vatican II and the Ratzinger of today? Who has changed more, you or the Church?"

Answer: "I do not see a real, profound difference between my work in Vatican Council II and my present work. On preparing this course for the Bishops, I reviewed a course of ecclesiology that I gave for the first time in 1956. Naturally, I found elements that need to be updated. But with respect to the fundamental vision, I found a complete identity, and what I proposed to the Bishops in Rio de Janeiro was the same fundamental vision that I put together then" (J. Ratzinger, interview to Walter Falceta, "Ratzinger reafirma identidade católica," in *O Estado de S. Paulo,* 7/29/ 1990).

e. Answering a journalist's question, the Cardinal confirms: "In my history as a theologian, I see no fracture, but a development" (J. Ratzinger, "Um passado que não lhes diz respeito," in *30 Dias,* January 1994, p. 72).

f. A renowned Protestant theologian bears testimony about the position of the then Cardinal-Prefect of the Congregation for the Doctrine of the Faith. He says:

Question: "How do you explain this dialogue with a personality who many Catholics see as reactionary and an enemy of ecumenical dialogue?"

Answer: "I do not understand. It is an erroneous opinion. I met Ratzinger 30 years ago, at Vatican Council II. He was the best of the so-called expert theologians, or *periti,* with a reputation for being a radical progressivist" (Oscar Cullmann, "O filho de Lutero é Ratzinger," interview with Lucio Brunelli and Alfred Labhart, in 30 *Dias,* March 1993, p. 13).

26. J. Ratzinger, *Problemi e risultati del Vaticano II,* pp. 64-65.

§ 25

The testimonies of these highly qualified theologians thus testify that the murky waters of Vatican II are the meeting point of two rivers: the progressivist and the conservative currents.

3. Synthesis: The Name Given to Ambiguity in order to Favor Progressivism

§ 26

Once it has become clear that at the Council there was a confrontation between progressivists and conservatives that is reflected in its final texts, it appears opportune to focus, albeit in passing, on a new maneuver apparently adopted to try to dampen conservative reaction after the Council. This was an attempt to present conciliar texts not as ambiguous, but rather as if they were written with the academic intent of seeking a transcendent, elevated and serene synthesis.

This tactic, it seems to us, is meant to divert attention from conciliar ambiguity and the clash of ideas to imply that the opposed interpretations are nothing but a temperamental confrontation between the hotheads on both sides. This clash of opposing views can then be viewed as mere "mischief-making" by the fervent partisans on either side. Therefore, the solution would be to leave the final word to the "moderates," who would supposedly have enough balance to find the *juste milieu,* the *via del mezzo,* the middle ground. This "middle of the road" position is presented as always being the ideal, sensible and impartial one. This is equivalent to saying that if one were presented with two glasses of water, one with poisoned, murky water and the other with pure, crystalline water, the right thing to do would be to drink out of a third glass with a mixture of the poisoned water and the pure water!

In fact, the defenders of this position want to legitimize progressivist victories in the Council and prevent a return to the *status quo ante.*

The argumentation of this position's proponents appears to us doctrinally inconsistent and easy to destroy. Nevertheless, it is a dangerous position because its adherents seek to catalyze in its favor the mentalities of the pseudo-moderates – those who dislike disputes and desire above all the petty comfort of their private lives.

The excerpts that follow have two things in view: *First,* they confirm what we have been dealing with in this Chapter, the existence of two opposing currents; *second,* they imply that the Council's ambiguity should not be understood as a victory of the progressivist wing (which it clearly was), but rather as a scholarly, elevated and balanced position.

§ 27   Which of the two currents the Council's ambiguity favored becomes obvious when we consider the statements by A. Acerbi in his work, *Due Ecclesiologie.* He confirms what we said in the beginning of this Chapter and defends the eclectic position:

"*Lumen gentium* often brings to the mind of an attentive reader the image of Moses who, after a long journey, gazes from the top of a hill at the land he will not enter. The Constitution is a frontier document, which hails from afar and looks upon new horizons, unable to explore them in depth.

"The starting point was the societal vision, whose guiding principle was that the Church's spiritual dimension has no bearing upon how she is understood by people; an adequate ecclesiology could and should emphasize only the societal dimension of the Church. ...

"The theology of the mystical body was a reaction against this vision. In fact, between the two [world] wars, the 'mystical body' indicated ... the most significant and essential reality for understanding the nature of the Church, which is not just a 'means' (an institution of salvation) in view of an end that is extrinsic to her (the salvation of souls). But she herself is the sanctification and communion of life with God in Christ. We know how this reaction, albeit just, brought with it the risk of subverting the affirmations of the societal tendency, without contradicting its logic of separation."[27]

§ 28   After upholding the idea that even long before the Council, a synthetic school had integrated the two currents and inspired Pius XII's Encyclical, *Mystici Corporis Christi,*[28] Acerbi continues:

---

27. A. Acerbi, *Due ecclesiologie,* p. 551.

28. a. With no desire to enter into a polemic about Acerbi's claim that a doctrinal synthesis between the two ecclesiologies would be possible, we would like to emphasize, in opposition to that, the statement by Msgr. G. Philips that the Encyclical *Mystici Corporis* represented an opening for the progressivist theological thought that prevailed at Vatican II: "Between the two [world] wars, many Catholics rediscovered, so to speak, the doctrine of the Church as mystical body. Pius XII's Encyclical, *Mystici Corporis,* published during the world conflict, places this theme under his aegis, against some conservative or fearful theologians. But there is more. This Encyclical concentrates attention on the spiritual element that reveals to the ecclesial community its full meaning: The professional theologians have contributed to this progress, stimulated by the progress in biblical studies, impelled by the liturgical movement and moved by the profound ecumenical aspirations that would show themselves a short time later" (G. Philips, *La Chiesa e il suo mistero,* p. 12).

b. Msgr. Philips's belief is corroborated by the forecited editorial in *La Civiltà Cattolica:* "The movement initiated by Möhler culminated with the Encyclical *Mystici Corporis* (June 29, 1943) of Pius XII and Vatican II."

"*Lumen gentium* welcomed the data of this theological reflection [of the supposed synthetic school], validating it with the authority of the Magisterium. But it attempted to do even more. By presenting the Church as the mystery of the divine action of salvation sacramentally manifested by means of the people of God, it upheld both the prevalence of the communion of life with God in Christ in the constitution of the Church, and the union of the social structure with the mystical nature; at the same time, it endeavored to show the tension that exists in the Church between *res* and *sacramentum.* Even though the two are united, in the Church's present condition as pilgrim they no longer harmonize perfectly. Furthermore, the communion of divine life is historically symbolized and accomplished not by means of a structure of authority, but rather by a communion of the mission and services, nonetheless directed by an authority which considers itself as a ministry among ministries." [29]

§ 29   The attempt to legitimize the Council's ambiguity by striving to present it as an elevated synthesis that superseded and integrated the two currents has already been implicitly refuted. As we have seen in the previous Chapter, a number of highly placed personalities involved in the Council testify, without a shadow of a doubt, that at the very root of the confusion in the Council's texts was a "meeting of waters," to use the expression of Cardinal Suenens, a clash of thoughts, a strategic measure dictated by concrete situations rather than a serene academic harmonization.

This notwithstanding, we will go on to present one more apologia for the supposed conciliar synthesis as a means of transcending the two mentioned currents. Afterward, in order to reinforce the certainty that this position is untenable, we will cite another unequivocal statement by Cardinal Suenens.

§ 30   The following text is by the then Archbishop Karol Wojtyla of Cracow, followed by a commentary of Rocco Buttiglione, a professor at Lateran University who studied Wojtyla's thinking and promoted it at international congresses. [30] Buttiglione is also the philosopher of the movement *Communione e Liberazione,* which is said to be partly inspired by Cardinal Ratzinger.

Summarizing the thinking of Archbishop Wojtyla, he says: "'Integration means ... an organic cohesion that acts simultaneously on both the thinking and acting of the Church as a community of believ-

---

29. A. Acerbi, *Due ecclesiologie*, p. 552.

30. In 1985 Buttiglione went to Brazil, where he gave a lecture at the International Congress promoted by the Archdiocese of Rio de Janeiro about the thinking of John Paul II.

ers. That is, it acts in such a way that on one hand we find and, so to speak, re-read the magisterium of the latest Council in the whole prior magisterium of the Church. On the other hand, we again find the whole preceding magisterium in the magisterium of the last Council, in whose context we somehow re-read it.'[31*] This principle of integrating novelty and tradition, through which the historical identity of the Church and her unity are constituted, is what leads directly beyond the controversy between integrists and neo-modernists on the way to understanding the Council's new synthesis." [32]

§ 31   Among the men who were privy to the most subtle aspects of the Council's intentions, it is difficult to find someone with stronger credentials to speak out than Cardinal Suenens. We recall here only three important facts regarding the Belgian Prelate's relevance: it was he who proposed the general plan adopted by Vatican II; [33] he exerted a great influence on the preparation of the Dogmatic Constitution *Lumen gentium*, [34] whose title, incidentally, came from one of his early speeches; [35] and he presented the proposal for the writing of *Gaudium et spes,* the boldest of all the documents of Vatican II. [36]

31*. Karol Wojtyla, *Alle fonti del rinnovamento,* p. 39.

32. Rocco Buttiglione, *Il pensiero di Karol Wojtyla* (Milan: Jaca Books, 1982), pp. 235-236.

33. The plan is transcribed *ipsis verbis* by the Cardinal in one of his works. L. J. Suenens, *Souvenirs et esperances,* pp. 72-79.

34. In his book, *La Chiesa e il suo mistero* (p. 25), Msgr. Gerard Philips, writer of the final version of *Lumen gentium,* says that Cardinal Suenens proposed an amendment changing 'the very skeleton of the [document's] schema.' That proposal was accepted without objection by the coordinating commission (see also L. J. Suenens, "Discorso ufficiale d'apertura," pp. 33, 84).

35. G. Philips, *Il Chiesa e il suo mistero nel Concilio Vaticano II,* p. 19.

36. Fr. Chenu thus describes the action undertaken by the Belgian Cardinal in favor of *Schema XIII:* "Everyone remembers the intervention of Cardinal Suenens at the end of the first session (December 4, 1962), immediately accepted by Cardinals Frings and Montini. Out of a confused agenda he extracted the decisive line of the Council: the Church has to define herself within herself, but also outside herself in a 'dialogue' with the world. This was the launching of the famous *Schema XIII,* a charismatic shock from which emanates the whole theology of renewal" (Marie-Dominique Chenu, "The History of Salvation and the Historicity of Man," in V.A., *Theology of Renewal,* vol. I, p. 155; L. J. Suenens, "Discorso ufficiale d'apertura," pp. 63, 84-85, 111; Antoine Wenger, *Chronique de la deuxième session,* p. 242).

In order to forestall any "temptation toward synthesis" that could come to the Reader's mind when he read the previous paragraph by Karol Wojtyla, we go on to add other statements by Cardinal Suenens.

What Suenens says about the current that won in the Council, and how it opposes the idea of a synthesis is noteworthy: **"The Second Vatican Council marked the end of an epoch, or even of several epochs, depending on one's historical perspective. It brought to a close the Constantinian era, the era of 'Christendom'** in the medieval sense, **the era of the Counter-Reformation and the era of Vatican I. With regard to that past, it marks a turning point in the History of the Church.**

"However, with regard to a more immediate past – namely, the first half of this century – **we see it** not as an end but **as a culmination, as the heir and beneficiary of those great currents of renewal which were and are at the very heart of the contemporary Church: scriptural, liturgical, patristic, theological and pastoral renewal. The Council caught and channeled the waters of these streams,** which had grown stronger and stronger under the influence of the Holy Spirit, **resolutely directing them towards the open sea,** which was its goal." [37]

In a more recent work, Suenens corroborates that opinion with respect to Vatican II: **"We were living at the end of an epoch which inherited a long past: from Constantine (4th century) to the Council of Trent (16th century), and from Trent to Vatican I** (19th century). Undoubtedly, [there was] a fundamental continuity, but also a **new perspective that would raise to a primary plane a vision of the Church enriched by a return to its sources. The theologians who had been a cause of concern for the Holy Office (Congar, Danielou, de Lubac, Rahner …) would,** as *periti,* **help to rescue that vision, a fact that constituted one more paradox."**[38]

§ 32   Given the clarity of the Belgian Prelate's words and what has been said so far in this Volume, how could someone reading texts such as those by Acerbi and Wojtyla-Buttiglione (among so many others that could be cited) [39] not have the impression that the preaching of that alleged synthesis in fact favors progressivist expansion in

---

37. L. J. Suenens, "Co-responsibility: Dominating Idea of the Council and its Pastoral Consequences," in V.A., *Theology of Renewal,* vol. II, p. 7.

38. L. J. Suenens, *Souvenirs et espérances,* pp. 63-64.

39. For example, Cardinal Alfonso Lopez Trujillo, A *los veinte años del Concilio* (Department of Publications of the Archdiocese of Medellin, 1985), pp. 18-19.

this post-conciliar period and staves off a possible awakening by the conservatives?

4. Pastoral Council? Dogmatic Council? *Chassé Croisé* of Interpretations. Who Profits from the Confusion?

§ 33   While we are dealing with the opposition between these two currents that generated the conciliar ambiguity, it is opportune to analyze one of the greatest ambiguities that to this day has not been entirely ascertained.

Was the Council a pastoral one? Or was it dogmatic? [40]

A. Theological Qualification of Vatican II

§ 34   There is confusion about the Council's theological qualification. Some say it was pastoral. As such, they understand in principle a Council primarily turned to the good of souls and the conversion of peoples. Dogmatic questions dealt with are supposedly mere repeti-

---

40. Some hermeneutic clarifications on this matter:

a. *Pastoral – a* word relating to the missionary effort of the Church to convert peoples by employing tactics and strategies which, without modifying the deposit of Faith, strives for the most efficient way of proselytizing.

b. *Doctrinal – first meaning:* a term concerning dogmatic and moral teaching of the ordinary and extraordinary ecclesiastical Magisterium which supposes some infallibility and which commands, in various degrees, the obedience of the faithful (Adolphus Tanquerey, *Synopsis Theologiae Dogmaticae,* Tournai: Desclée, 1937, vol. I, nn. 953-957, pp. 637-640); *second meaning:* a general term referring to the ensemble of non-theological theoretical principles that should orient the liturgical, canonical, exegetic, social, pastoral, etc. spheres.

c. The *pastoral* or *dogmatic* alternative, which usually arises when one seeks the theological qualification of the Council, could perhaps be better expressed by *pastoral* and *doctrinal* (first meaning); so that the Council would be generally related to Dogmatic Theology and Moral Theology. However, classifying a Council as *doctrinal* is less precise than it would appear at first sight, since there are several types of non-theological doctrine that do not directly require obedience from the faithful, for example, considerable parts of liturgical, canonical, exegetic, social and pastoral doctrine (second meaning).

Therefore, we believe it is better to use *pastoral* or *dogmatic and moral,* or simply *pastoral* or *dogmatic,* supposing the moral content of the dogmatic questions that orient the Council.

tions of the teachings of the Ordinary and Extraordinary Magisterium of the Church. In this case, it did not bring about doctrinal changes, but merely new doctrinal approaches in view of its pastoral goal. Others, on the contrary, deem it a dogmatic Council since, in fact, the subject matter dealt with has to do with topics directly related to the Faith.

Adding to the confusion, others say it was at times pastoral, at times dogmatic.

Faced with this picture, some conservatives allege that there is no need to obey Vatican Council II since the doctrine contained therein was intended to be nothing but pastoral.

However, there are progressivists, and a large number of them, who try with ever greater emphasis to present Vatican II as binding on all Catholics, assuming it as *ipso facto* dogmatic.[41]

Faced with such a variety of positions, it seems to us opportune to present some distinctions to try to diminish the confusion.

a. Two Qualifications – Dogmatic and Pastoral – Do Not Exclude Each Other

§ 35   An overview of the history of ecumenical councils suffices to show that they were not convened to deal with the subjects of interest to the Church in each epoch from only one standpoint.

The near totality of ecumenical councils dealt primarily with dogmatic and moral topics.[42] However, in doing so, the councils concomitantly issued disciplinary norms on ecclesiastical life, liturgy and exegetics,[43] expressed pastoral intentions,[44] and laid down socio-

---

41. See Section B, 4th and 6th phases.

42. Exceptions are, although not entirely, the First Council of Lyon (1245), which discussed mainly the deposition of Emperor Frederic II, and the Council of Vienne (1311-1312), which dealt primarily with the Order of the Temple and the Holy Land (V.A., *Conciliorum Oecumenicorum Decreta*, eds. G. Alberigo, P. Joannou, C. Leonardi and P. Prodi, Freiburg im Breisgau: Herder, 1962, pp. 286-287).

43. *Ibid., passim.*

44. For example, the Council of Basel-Ferrara-Florence-Rome (1431-1445), in sessions XIX and XXV in Basel, sought the union of the Greek Schismatic Church with the Catholic Church *(ibid.,* pp. 454-458, 486-488); also in session XIX the Council dealt with those who want to convert to the Catholic Faith *(ibid.,* p. 460); in session VIII, in Florence, a Bull was issued for the union of Armenians with the Holy Church *(ibid.,* p. 510); in session XI a Bull was issued for the union of the Copts *(ibid.,* p. 543); in session XIII, held in Rome, another Bull was issued for the

political orientations.[45] In reviewing the history of ecumenical councils, it is clear that the application of the ensemble of their teachings was never limited exclusively to one field. Their teachings are simultaneously dogmatic, moral, disciplinary, pastoral, socio-political, depending on the matter dealt with, for the good of the Church.

§ 36   Therefore, Vatican II could very well address both pastoral and dogmatic matters since they do not exclude each other.

In order to determine how the Council should be qualified, it is necessary first of all to see what matters it addressed.

b. According to the Subject Matter It Dealt with, Vatican II Is Simultaneously Dogmatic and Pastoral

§ 37   Two of the four Constitutions promulgated by the Council, *Lumen gentium* and *Dei Verbum,* are officially entitled Dogmatic Constitutions. This title is appropriate, since the first one addresses the doctrinal foundations of ecclesiology. Its topics are dogmatic from beginning to end. The second one deals primarily with Divine Revelation and secondarily provides guidelines for exegesis and makes an exhortation to read the Sacred Scriptures. Therefore, the topics covered by the two documents are principally dogmatic.

§ 38   In addition to pastoral matters, the Constitution *Gaudium et spes,* entitled a Pastoral Constitution, also covers innumerable points involving dogmatics and morals. For example: Part I, Chap. I: Man as the image of God; sin; dignity of moral conscience; the mystery of

---

union of the Syrians (*ibid.,* pp. 562-564) and in session XIV, a bull was issued for the union of the Chaldeans and the Moors from Cyprus (*ibid.,* pp. 565-567).

45. Thus, for instance:

• The Fourth Lateran Council (1215) addressed the question of whether duels could be fought by clergymen (*ibid., p.* 220), the limits of secular and ecclesiastical justice (*ibid.,* p. 229) and the subject of usury and the Jews (*ibid.,* p. 241); The First Council of Lyon (1245) dealt with usury in general (*ibid.,* pp. 269-271), financial assistance for the liberation of the Empire of Constantinople (*ibid.,* pp. 271-272) and the Crusades to the Holy Land (*ibid.,* pp. 273-277);

• The Second Council of Lyon (1274) dealt with extortion of the faithful by Church delegates (*ibid., p.* 303);

• The Fifth Lateran Council (1512-1517) stimulated the re-establishment of peace between Catholic and heretical princes (*ibid.,* pp. 582-584); issued a bull containing the Concordat between the Roman Pontiff and Francis I, King of France, on the abrogation of the Pragmatic Sanction (*ibid.,* pp. 614-621).

death; the attitude of the Church towards Atheism; Christ, the new Man. Chap. II: Communitarian nature of man's vocation in God's plan; respect and love for enemies; essential equality of all men: Social justice; need to transcend an individualistic morality; the Word made flesh and human solidarity.

Chap. III: Human activity infected by sin; human activity: its fulfillment in the paschal mystery. Chap. IV: What the Church receives from the modern world; Christ: Alpha and omega. Part II, Chap. I: Marriage and the family in today's world; holiness of marriage and the family; married love; the fruitfulness of marriage; married love and respect for human life; fostering marriage and the family: a duty for all. Chap. II, 2nd section: Faith and culture; multiple relations between culture and the good news of Christ.

These subheadings represent a little more than one-fourth of all the subheadings in the document.

Even though the other problems addressed by *Gaudium et spes* are not primarily dogmatic or moral, they involve delicate points which make up part of the Church's social doctrine but have serious dogmatic and moral implications. For example: Part II, Chap. III: Co-responsibility in enterprise and in the economic system as a whole; labor disputes; earthly goods destined for all men; ownership, private property, large estates. Chap. IV: Nature and purpose of the political community; the political community and the Church. Chap. V: Nature of peace; *First section:* Avoidance of war; curbing the savagery of war; total warfare; the arms race; total outlawing of war: International action to prevent war; *second section*: Establishment of an international community; the community of nations and international organizations; effective presence of the Church in the international community.

§ 39   The Constitution *Sacrosanctum Concilium,* which addresses the reform of the Liturgy, focuses on important dogmatic or closely dogmatic-related topics. For example: Chap. I: The work of Salvation, willed by God, is fulfilled in Christ; the work of Christ continues in the Church and is crowned in the Liturgy; the presence of Christ in the Liturgy; earthly liturgy and celestial liturgy; Liturgy does not exhaust all the Church's action; the sacrifice of the Eucharist is source of life in the Church. Chap. II: The most sacred mystery of the Eucharist; reform of the rite of the Mass, of the readings, the homily and common prayer; concelebration. Chap. III: The other Sacraments and the sacramentals; reform of the rites of all Sacraments.

§ 40   The Decree on Ecumenism, *Unitatis redintegratio,* tackles primarily dogmatic topics, to wit: Chap. I: The unity and oneness of the Church; relation of the heretics with the Catholic Church;

ecumenism. Chap. II: The practice of ecumenism; Church renewal; Conversion of the heart; the way of expressing and expounding the doctrine of Faith; cooperation with heretics.

§ 41   The Decree *Orientalium Ecclesiarum* refers to an important dogmatic subject as it discusses the relations of the Catholic Church with schismatics (nn. 26-28).

§ 42   The Decree *Ad gentes,* about the missionary activities of the Church, presents in Chap. I the missions of the Three Divine Persons as the foundation of the mission of the Church, a fundamentally dogmatic theme.

§ 43   The five decrees that follow: *Christus Dominus,* on the mission of Bishops; *Presbyterorum Ordinis,* on the ministry and life of priests; *Perfectae caritatis,* on the updating of religious; *Optatam totius,* on priestly formation; and *Apostolicam actuositatem,* on the lay apostolate, are moral, ecclesiastical, disciplinary, pastoral, educational and social norms founded upon the dogmatic points covered in the previous Constitutions and Decrees.

§ 44   The Decree *Inter mirifica,* on the means of social communication, is quite original as a conciliar document. It is, in fact, an exaltation of modern technology. The press, radio, television, cinema and other media are presented as tools for the pastoral action of the Church. There is nothing directly dogmatic in it.

§ 45   The Declaration on Christian Education, *Gravissimum educationis,* presents important moral and social questions, though not directly dogmatic.

§ 46   But the Declaration on Religious Liberty, *Dignitatis humanae,* is wholly based on a new concept of Faith and Morals, to wit: I: On the right of the person and communities to social and civil liberty in religious matters; the object and foundation of religious freedom; religious freedom and the relation of man with God; freedom of the religious communities; fostering religious freedom. II: religious freedom in the light of Revelation; the doctrine of religious freedom is rooted in Revelation; freedom of the act of faith; the conduct of Christ and the Apostles; the Church follows in the footsteps of Christ and the Apostles; freedom in the Church; the obligation of the Church.

§ 47   Finally, the Declaration on the Relation of the Church to Non-Christian Religions, *Nostra aetate*, is the dogmatic approach to relations with any of the false religions, especially the Muslim and Jewish.

§ 48   Thus having enumerated the subjects covered by Vatican II, in particular and as a whole, we can conclude that it discussed dogmatic topics at length and in depth. In addition, let it be stressed, it also addressed moral, ecclesiastical, liturgical, disciplinary, pastoral, educational and social topics.

Therefore, judging from the subject matter it dealt with, Vatican II covered topics of which the most important were dogmatic. Thus, it is stretching matters to conclude that it was an exclusively pastoral council.

As expounded here, the question of the theological qualification of Vatican II appears, up until now, quite clear.

c. Reasons of Convenience to Qualify Vatican II as Pastoral

§ 49 Before continuing to analyze the remaining elements that will enable us to qualify the Council, let us look at two reasons why the pastoral aspect of the Council was emphasized. We present these reasons as working hypotheses to help understand the pronouncements of John XXIII and Paul VI presented in Section d.

§ 50 The *first* concerns the convenience of using the material put together in the preparatory phase of the Council – the pre-Council. The *second* refers to taking advantage of the documents of Vatican II in the post-conciliar age.

On November 22, 1962, John XXIII rejected the schema *De fontibus Revelationis* (on the sources of Revelation) and with it nearly all other schemata of the pre-conciliar Theological Commission.[46] Now, the material prepared in the phase preceding Vatican II was essentially dogmatic,[47] seeking to present the errors opposed to

---

46. Chap. IV, Note 2.

47. Bishop Boaventura Kloppenburg, who participated in the preparatory works of the Council as a consultant to the Theological Commission, mentions some of the topics studied: "All questions of a purely doctrinal nature suggested by the Bishops (in the 15 volumes of the pre-preparatory documents) to be dealt with in the Council, were sent to our Commission.

"Once this basic material was gathered, it was first divided into five groups of different subjects, thus giving rise to the formation of five sub-commissions: 1. On the Church (ecclesiological questions left over from Vatican I and new ones that arose later, which, by the way, are not few; 2. On the sources of Revelation (some extremely delicate questions of exegesis and tradition); 3. On the complete custody of the deposit of Faith (with doctrines nowadays cast into doubt or denied by some); 4. On the moral order; 5. On the social order. Each of these sub-commissions was assigned between 7 and 12 members (there being no strict difference between 'member' and 'consultant'), one of whom was its president.

Catholic doctrine in today's world and condemn them according to the teachings of Vatican I.

It seems that even earlier, in the Council's *Opening Speech* on October 11, 1962, John XXIII was already preparing to reject the pre-conciliar schemata, which he did, as we will see in Section d. On that occasion, for the first time, he tried to avoid calling the Council dogmatic and presented it as "predominantly pastoral."[48]

It seems to us that for strategic reasons it was more convenient for John XXIII to impose the rejection of the pre-conciliar schemata in the name of pastoral necessity rather than on the claim of dogmatic principles. If, from the outset, he were to have presented the dogmatic ensemble that Vatican II actually approved, he would have run the risk of setting off a serious polemic and blocking the Assembly's work from moving in the direction he wanted it to go.

In our judgment, this was the first reason of convenience to emphasize the pastoral aspect of the Council.

§ 51 The *second* reason, also of a strategic nature, has to do with taking future advantage of the documents approved by the Council.

The dogmatic teaching of any ecumenical council requires the obedience of all Catholics. Now then, as a whole and in a large number of its points, the dogmatic teaching of Vatican II is opposed to the traditional doctrine of the Ecclesiastical Magisterium, as we intend to make clear in this Collection, especially beginning in Volume VI. If, soon after Vatican II, emphasis had been placed on the dogmatic aspect and obedience would have been demanded, this would probably have given rise to a reaction and people would have compared the Council's doctrine with the previous dogmatic doctrine. Such a reaction could have thwarted the advantages expected to be drawn from the approved documents.

Thus, we believe that the emphasis given to the pastoral aspect in the post-conciliar period and the absence of any demand for instant obedience greatly served the designs of those who conceived

---

"I was part of the third sub-commission (complete custody of the Faith), which was charged with preparing schemata on: 1. Human reason and the truths of the Faith; 2. The existence of God; 3. Creation and evolution; 4. Revelation and Faith; 5. Progress in doctrine ('evolution of the dogmas'); 6. Natural and supernatural order; 7. Spiritism, reincarnation and the four last things; 8. Monogenism; 9. Original sin; 10. Destiny of children who die without Baptism; 11. Vicarious Redemption" (*Concilio Vaticano II,* vol. I, pp. 157-158).

48. Text in § 52.

Vatican II and steered its application, by avoiding a reaction and assuring the ripening of its fruits.[49]

d. The Emphasis Given by John XXIII and Paul VI to the Pastoral Aspect of the Council Does Not Exclude Its Dogmatic Qualification

§ 52

In the *Opening Speech* (October 11, 1962), John XXIII thus indicated the Council's pastoral orientation:

"The *punctum saliens* [salient point] of this Council is not ... discussing one or the other article of the fundamental doctrine of the Church, repeating and proclaiming the teaching of the ancient and modern Fathers and theologians, which, we suppose, is quite present on and familiar to our minds.

"There would be no need of a Council for that. But from the renewed, serene and tranquil adhesion to the whole teaching of the Church in its integrity and exactness, as it shines in the conciliar acts from Trent to Vatican I, **the Christian,** Catholic and apostolic **spirit** in the whole world **expects progress in the doctrinal understanding, and formation of consciences in a more perfect correspondence with and fidelity to the authentic doctrine; but also that this be studied and expounded through the forms of questioning and literary formulation of modern thought. One is the substance of the ancient doctrine, the *depositum fidei* [deposit of Faith], and another is the formulation encasing it; and this is what we must** – with patience, if necessary – **take very much into account, measuring everything in the forms and proportions of a predominantly pastoral magisterium."**[50]

§ 53

Let us analyze this fundamental excerpt.

---

49. These reasons, which we present here only to facilitate the understanding of the possible intentions of John XXIII and Paul VI, which we will analyze now, are dealt with in more detail in Section B

50. In B. Kloppenburg, *Concílio Vaticano II*, vol. II, p. 310. Some observations on this translation of John XXIII's speech:

• The text by Kloppenburg that we transcribe is a faithful translation, verified by us, of the speech published in Italian by *L'Osservatore Romano* of 10/12/1962, p. 3. The speech was also distributed on October 10 to journalists stationed at the Holy See by the Vatican Press Service, linked to the Secretariat of State, to be part of the next day's news coverage and make possible a simultaneous translation of the Pope's speech (A. Wenger, *Chronique de la première session,* p. 47).

• This is why the same version is found in whole or in part in various *of* the main chronicles *of* the Council (G. Caprile, *Il Concilio Vaticano II,*

In the first paragraph John XXIII states that doctrinal discussion based on the traditional teaching of the Church will not be the keynote of the Council. This seems to be a first indirect attack against the conservatives. With it he appears to be preparing for the rejection of the pre-conciliar schemata, which he will do a little later. His language, however, is skillful: It does not definitely exclude traditional doctrine from the discussion but says it will not be the salient point. A door is thus left open either for a concession or a retreat of a conservative nature if John XXIII's program is not accepted by everyone.

He goes on to say that the "Christian spirit ... expects progress in the doctrinal penetration and formation of consciences in a more perfect correspondence with and fidelity to the authentic doctrine." A goal of the Council would be to fulfill that expectation. Now then, presenting "progress in the doctrinal penetration and formation of consciences" as a goal does not exclude dogmatic and moral topics but rather presupposes them as one of the Council's objectives.

John XXIII then provides the prism from which doctrine will be considered. It is that "this be studied and expounded through the forms of questioning and literary formulation of modern thought" Here we are faced with the first imprecise generalization: What are these forms of questioning of modern thought? Could they be, perchance, Kant's criticisms of reason? Nietzsche's of God? Darwin's of creation? Marx's of property? Freud's of morals? All these are outstanding authors of modern thought. John XXIII does not indicate clearly what modern thought is, and, as a consequence, one cannot know for

vol. II, pp. 2-7; René Laurentin, *Bilan de la première session,* pp. 12-15; Henri Fesquet, *Le journal du Concile,* pp. 27-28; A. Wenger, *Chronique de la première session,* p. 42).

• However, this unofficial version of Vatican II's opening speech is a relatively free translation of the official Latin text (John XXIII, *Discorsi, messaggi, colloqui del Santo Padre Giovanni XXIII,* Tipografia Poliglotta Vaticana, 1963, vol. IV, pp. 578-590; *L'Osservatore Romano,* 10/12/1962, pp. 1-2). There are, therefore, certain differences between the two texts.

• Such differences have caused polemics (Jean Madiran, "Autour du Concile," in *Itinéraires,* Paris, December 1962, pp. 10-26; February 1963, pp. 100-106, in A. Wenger, *Chronique de la première session,* pp. 46-50).

• But such polemics appear to have been resolved by the sheer weight of an argument of authority, since on December 23, 1962, responding in Italian to the Christmas wishes of Cardinal Tisserant, John XXIII used the same words in the unofficial Italian version when he described the meaning of the Council (*L'Osservatore Romano,* 12/24-25/1962, in *ibid,* p. 48*).*

We therefore believe the translation we have used is sufficiently authoritative.

sure what are the forms of questioning and literary formulation with which he proposes to "study and expound" Catholic doctrine. The fundamental criterion is ambiguous.

§ 54   Nevertheless, John XXIII goes on to explain: "One is the substance of the ancient doctrine ... and another is the formulation encasing it." Comparing this statement to the one preceding it, that Catholic doctrine must be expounded through the literary formulation of modern thought, this sounds like a justification. It would, therefore, be possible to modify the very formulation of dogmatic truth according to the canons of modern thought.

Was this what John XXIII affirmed? When we retun to the text we verify that what he says is only that there is a difference between the substance of the Faith and its formulation. That, of itself, is entirely true. Therefore, there is in the context a tendency that does not exist in the statement as such, taken separately. Once again it seems to us that we are faced with the use of ambiguity. One does not know for sure to what degree Catholic doctrine should be reformulated.

§ 55   First, he establishes the Council's goals: 1. Progress in doctrinal understanding; 2. Progress in the formation of consciences; 3. The study of doctrine through the forms of investigation of modern thought; 4. Expounding doctrine according to the literary formulation of modern thought. The first, third and fourth are dogmatic goals, and the second is a moral one.

Then, John XXIII explains how such goals should be attained: "And this is what we must take very much into account, measuring everything in the forms and proportions of a predominantly pastoral magisterium."

This phrase has a curious twist that calls one's attention. Taken in combination with the other excerpts of John XXIII's speech cited above, it can be understood either as an encouragement to progressivists or, on the contrary, as a warning of a conservative tone to them.

Some will interpret it as meaning: "To proceed earnestly with the study, exposition and reformulating of aspects of the Faith according to the criteria of modern thought, since such goals may be considered as included in the ambit of the pastoral magisterium." Others will take it as a word of caution: "Be very careful not to understand, reformulate and expound the Faith according to modern thought except in accordance with the criteria and limits of the pastoral magisterium." In our view, the possibility of giving rise to opposed interpretations configures the essential ambiguity of the phrase. [51]

---

51. Although we present only two interpretations, there would be others

If we analyze its ambiguous expressions, we will find:

• **Take very much into account** – can be understood as "take very earnestly" or "take great caution."

• **everything** – can refer either to modern thought or the reformation of the *depositum fidei*.

• **measuring** – if the direct object is modern thought, it can be understood as "considering:" considering modern thought *included in* the forms, etc.; or it can be taken as "judging:" judging modern thought *according to* the forms, etc. If the direct object is the reform of the *depositum fidei,* "measuring" can be understood as "adapting:" adapting the reformation of the *depositum fidei only* in the forms, etc. In addition to the verb's ambiguity, the omission in the sentence of any of the expressions emphasized in this paragraph makes the action being recommended even more ambiguous.

• **in the forms and proportions** – this expression can be understood as "in the ambit" or as synonymous with "according to the criteria and limits." Now since this expression is the point of reference for the action to be carried out, and since it is ambiguous, the whole action being recommended is left without direction, independent of the other ambiguities.

• **predominantly pastoral magisterium** – the adverb, "predominantly," can be taken as synonymous with: "nearly exclusively," thereby reflecting a great emphasis; "mainly," thus showing a smaller emphasis; or "preferentially," an even lesser emphasis. None of the meanings, however, excludes the dogmatic aspect of the ecclesiastical Magisterium as the ambit in which the Council will take place.

We have thus analyzed the ambiguities contained in the text in which John XXIII announced the goals of Vatican II. They are so numerous as to permit several other interpretations, with new combinations of meanings. However, we believe that the two mentioned above – one progressivist and the other conservative – are the landmarks between which are to be found the most likely interpretations.

§ 56   The analysis of ambiguities notwithstanding, we have seen that calling the Council "predominantly pastoral" does not preclude the fact that it may deal with dogmatic topics.

*

which we left out in order not to complicate the understanding of the subject.

§ 57

In an audience given to the participants of the Week of Pastoral Updating on September 6, 1963, Paul VI stresses the role of "pastoral" in the Council as well: **"We must** also **welcome another expression** that qualifies the activity of which you are promoters and disciples: **the word 'pastoral.' Nowadays this glorious word constitutes a whole program. As everyone knows, the Ecumenical Council has made it its own, polarizing in it its goals of reform and renewal."** [52]

The text adds nothing essential to the speech of John XXIII, but confirms it. The statement that the word pastoral "polarizes the Council's goals of reform and renewal" does not seem to exclude its dogmatic aspect.

§ 58

A little later, in the *Opening Speech* of the Council's second session, referring to John XXIII, Paul VI says: "You have called your brethren, the successors of the Apostles, not only for them to continue the doctrinal study interrupted (at Vatican I) and the legislative work that had been suspended, but also that they may feel united to the Pope in the same body and receive support and guidance from him so that the 'sacred deposit of Christian doctrine be better preserved and presented in a more efficacious manner.' [53*]

"Nevertheless, even while **pointing out** in this way **the most elevated objective of the Council, you added to it another goal, more urgent and at present of a more beneficial nature, the pastoral goal ... We shall not forget the norms that you yourself** [John XXIII], the first Father of the Council ... **drew up for it and we are pleased to repeat: 'one will have recourse to a manner of presenting things that better corresponds to a teaching, above all, of a pastoral character.'** [54*]" [55]

Stating that "one will have recourse to a manner of presenting things that better corresponds to a teaching, above all, of a pastoral character" adds nothing essential to what was said by John XXIII.

§ 59

The same can be noted in the Brief *In Spiritu Sancto,* with which Paul VI closed Vatican II. In it he says: **"Vatican Council II** ... must undoubtedly be considered one of the great events in the Church.

---

52. Paul VI, "Audience to the Members of the l3th Week of Pastoral Updating," September 6, 1963, in B. Kloppenburg, *Concílio Vaticano II,* vol. III, p. 501.

53*. *AAS,* 1962, p. 790.

54*. *Ibid., pp.* 791-792.

55. In B. Kloppenburg, *Concílio Vaticano II,* vol. III, pp. 510-511.

Indeed, it was the largest as far as the number of Fathers who came to the Seat of Peter is concerned, ... the richest one in topics, ... finally, it was the most opportune, because having in mind the needs of the present time, **it confronted above all the pastoral necessities.**" [56]

The statement that the Council "confronted above all the pastoral necessities" seems to confirm that the dogmatic aspect was not excluded.

e. The Dogmatic Tone Is Accentuated in the Promulgation of the Documents

§ 60

In the solemn manner that Paul VI promulgates each conciliar document, the keynote is of a dogmatic teaching. Indeed, it even appears to fulfill the conditions characterizing the Extraordinary Magisterium of the Pope. [57]

The Pope calls upon the representation of Christ and the assistance of the Holy Spirit with such great solemnity that one wonders whether he is making use of papal infallibility. In fact, he declares: "The whole ensemble and each of the points that have been enunciated in this Dogmatic Constitution appeared sound to the Fathers of the Sacrosanct Council. And **we, by the apostolic power entrusted to us by Christ,** together with the venerable Fathers, **in the Holy**

---

56. *Ibid.,* vol. V, p. 516.

57. Studying the conditions for an *ex cathedra* pontifical pronouncement to take place, A. V. Xavier da Silveira summarizes the thought of Diekamp, Billot, Choupin, Hervé, Journet, Nau, Salaverri and Cartechini, and points out four conditions: "1. That the Pope speak in his capacity as universal Doctor and Shepherd; 2. That he use the fullness of his apostolic authority; 3. That he manifest a will to define; 4. That he deal with a matter of Faith or Morals" ("Qual a autoridade doutrinária dos documentos pontifícios e conciliares?" in *Catolicismo,* October 1967).

He then notes: "The crucial point of the question is in the third condition: that he manifest a will to define. How is that intention manifested? Is it by employing the words 'we define'? Is it by excommunicating whoever says the opposite? Is it by the juridical nature of the document? None of these signs is apodictic (Sisto Cartechini, "Dall'opinione al domma," Rome: *La Civiltà Cattolica,* 1953, pp. 29, 31, 36, 54). The fundamental thing is that it must be clear, in any way whatsoever, that the Pope wants to define a dogma.

"For this reason, **in solemn definitions, the Holy Pontiffs use a number of verbs to make their intention unmistakable: We *'promulgate, decree, define, declare, proclaim,'* etc.** In other cases, while such verbs may be absent, the circumstances surrounding the document will

Spirit, approve it, decree it, and enact it. And we order that what has thus been decided in the Council **be promulgated** for the greater glory of God." [58]

Imperative characteristics that usually follow official dogmatic and moral declarations by the Extraordinary Magisterium of the Church are also used in the Brief *In Spiritu Sancto,* which closed the Council: **"With our apostolic authority ... we order and command ... that all that was established by the Synod be religiously observed by all faithful ... These things we have sanctioned and established, decreeing that the present letters be permanent** and continue firm, valid and efficacious, **that they be fulfilled and attain full and complete effects, and that they be fully validated by those on whom it will or may behoove in the future. Thus it must be judged and defined. And all that is done contrary to this by any individual or authority,** consciously or out of ignorance, **must be considered, from this moment onward, null and void"** [59]

One can see, therefore, that the tone is imperative and solemn, typical of the most important dogmatic documents and appropriate to oblige acceptance by all Catholics. [60]

---

show that there was a will to define. This is what happens when the Pope imposes on the whole Church the acceptance of a formula of faith." (A. V. Xavier da Silveira, "Qual a autoridade doutrinária dos documentos pontifícios e conciliares?").

58. These words are the formula of promulgation of *Lumen gentium.* A similar formula – only one or the other word having been replaced, in addition to the title (Dogmatic Constitution with Pastoral Constitution, Constitution, Decree or Declaration) – was used for promulgating the other documents (V.A., *Documentos do Vaticano II – Constituições, decretos e declarações,* eds. B. Kloppenburg and F. Vier; Portuguese edition reviewed by the undersecretaries of the National Conference of Brazilian Bishops, Petrópolis: Vozes, 1966, pp. 133, 252, 299, 327, 342, 394, 429, 475, 496, 517, 557, 573, 592, 611, 621).

59. Brief *In Spiritu Sancto,* December 7, 1965, in B. Kloppenburg, *Concílio Vaticano II,* vol. V, p. 516.

60. A precise analysis of the scope of the application of such formulas and the manifestation of such intentions from the standpoint of Canon Law and the tradition of the Pontifical Magisterium goes beyond the bounds of the present Collection. On reading the above-cited promulgations and the Brief, we limit ourselves to stating the opinion of Catholics based primarily on the *sensus fidelium.*

f. The Pastoral Characteristic Is Stressed in the Preliminary Notes

§ 61   When the schema *De Ecclesia,* which would come to be the Dogmatic Constitution *Lumen gentium,* was discussed, there was a serious polemic about episcopal collegiality. Many conservatives saw in it an attempt to undermine the monarchic and absolute power of the Sovereign Pontiff. So the *Preliminary Explanatory Note,* which safeguards traditional doctrine on the matter, was written. [61]

The *Announcement* [62] that precedes the *Preliminary Explanatory Note* to *Lumen gentium* says: "Taking into account conciliar practice and the pastoral purpose of the present council, the sacred synod has defined as binding on the Church only those matters of faith and morals which it has expressly put forward as such."

----

61. On the disagreements that arose about this matter, see Section B, 3rd phase, §§ 100-102.

62. Here is the full text of the *Announcement* made by the Secretary General of the Council in the 123rd General Assembly on November 16, 1964:

"A query has been made as to what is the *theological qualification* of the doctrine expounded in the schema *De Ecclesia,* on which a vote is to be taken.

"The doctrinal commission has thus replied to this query in appraising the *modi* proposed for the third chapter of the schema *De Ecclesia:*

" 'As is evident, a conciliar text should always be interpreted in harmony with the general rules known to everyone.'

"In this regard, the doctrinal commission calls attention to its *Declaration* of 6 March, 1964, whose text we transcribe below:

" 'Taking into account conciliar practice and the pastoral purpose of Council Vatican II, this Sacred Synod intends to issue, in matters of faith and morals, only the definitions it openly declares as such.

" 'Everything else that the Council proposes as doctrine of the Supreme Magisterium of the Church is to be acknowledged and accepted by each and every member of the faithful according to the mind of the Council which is clear from the subject matter and its formulation, following the norms of theological interpretation.'

" 'By superior authority, a previous explanatory note on the *modi* presented in regard to chapter III of the schema *De Ecclesia* has been communicated to the Fathers. The doctrine expounded in this chapter III should be explained and understood according to the spirit and meaning of this note" (Pericle Felici, "Notificações," November 16, 1964, in V.A., *Atas do Concílio Ecumênico Vaticano II,* in V.A., *Documentos do Vaticano II,* pp. 108-109).

One could say, therefore, that this pronouncement exempts Vatican II as a whole from any dogmatic responsibility and *ipso facto* does not oblige any of the faithful to accept it.

§ 62   Nevertheless, the second and seventh paragraphs of the *Announcement* appear to indicate that such an exemption from responsibility refers exclusively to chapter III of *Lumen Gentium,* which deals with the subject of collegiality. Except for that, what is said in the third paragraph seems to prevail, to wit:

"As is self-evident, the conciliar text is to be interpreted in accordance with the general rules which are known to all."

Therefore, there is an imprecision about the limits for applying the criteria mentioned: Is it the Council as a whole or only chapter III of *Lumen gentium?* This imprecision will necessarily generate ambiguity in the interpretation of the *Announcement* and, consequently, in the theological qualification of Vatican II.

Taken in their broader sense, the intentions stated in the fifth paragraph of the *Announcement* seem to clash with the words of promulgation Paul VI used to enact the contents of *Lumen gentium* and the other conciliar documents. For as we have seen above, he used the normal formulas of the Extraordinary Magisterium of the Pope.

In order to avoid such a clash, the intentions under scrutiny should be understood as restricted to chapter III of *Lumen gentium.*

We point out that this *Announcement,* interpreted in its broadest meaning, is the only document that could be claimed to argue that the Council was not simultaneously dogmatic and pastoral.

§ 63   In the initial *Note* referring to the title of *Gaudium et spes,* even though it affirms the prevalence of the pastoral aspect in this Constitution, the usual interpretation of councils that are both dogmatic and pastoral already appears. It says: "Although it consists of two parts, the Pastoral Constitution 'The Church in the World Today' constitutes an organic unity. The Constitution is called 'pastoral' because, while resting on doctrinal principles, it seeks to set forth the relation of the Church to the world and to the men of today. In Part I, therefore, the pastoral emphasis is not overlooked, nor is the doctrinal emphasis overlooked in Part II."[63]

The initial *Note* of *Gaudium et spes* is such as to confirm our interpretation of the Council – that it is both dogmatic and pastoral – and therefore appears to restrict the explanations of the *Announce-*

---

63. *Constituição pastoral Gaudium et spes sobre a Igreja no mundo de hoje,*note regarding the title in V.A., *Documentos do Vaticano II,* p. 137.

ment to the *Preliminary Explanatory Note* to *Lumen gentium* only to chapter III of that Dogmatic Constitution.

§ 64   On ending the analysis about the theological qualification of the Council, we may conclude this Section A by saying that it was at the same time dogmatic and pastoral. Fundamental ambiguities remain, however, on how the Council's proposed goals should be achieved, namely the adaptation of dogmatics to modern thought, and how cogent the Council's dogmatic characteristics are. To be consistent with Catholic doctrine and the tradition of the councils, such characteristics should demand acceptance by all Catholics, and should any point diverge from Catholic dogma, it should be judged by traditional doctrine.

In our view, this analysis reduces as much as possible, but does not eliminate, the Council's ambiguity from the standpoint of its theological qualification.

B. A Practical Consideration: Ambiguity in Theological Qualification Serves as a Tool of Progressivist Victory

§ 65   A complete ambiguity generally hovers over the theological qualification of the Council, independent of the above analysis. When conservatives say it is dogmatic so they can judge it according to traditional Catholic doctrine, progressivists contend it is pastoral; when the former agree it is pastoral and consequently refuse to obey it, the latter, in flagrant contradiction to what they had maintained, say that the Council is dogmatic and requires obedience. Thus, what happens in practice is that the progressivists methodically use ambiguity regarding Vatican II's theological qualification in order to obtain advantages for their current.

§ 66   Now we will attempt to clarify this method by presenting to the Reader, as an hypothesis, a concatenation of phases showing the oscillation in the meanings the progressivists use to qualify the Council. This concatenation is based on observation and founded on facts and texts by various authors.

§ 67   Someone could object that it is not licit to attribute to the progressivist current such an underhanded maneuver based on the alternate employment of the dogmatic or pastoral nature of the Council, since, contrary to Church practice, that would entail judging intentions.

To this we would answer:

- Several progressivist authors of great renown have stated – as we have already documented [64] – that ambiguity in the conciliar texts was due to a strategic maneuver to attain unanimity and to prepare the future.
- The modernists – whose successors are the progressivists[65] – are known to have frequently resorted to such tricks in order to deceive the unwary. [66]
- The employment of ambiguity to define the Council gives the progressivists elements to carry out a maneuver similar to those they avowedly have used in the past and to the ones employed by their modernist ancestors.
- Therefore, it seems to us entirely licit to suppose that they carried out this maneuver. To deny such a supposition, we believe, would be unforgivable naiveté.

Nevertheless, on raising an hypothesis about this maneuver, we do not intend to go beyond the bounds of conjecture. We lack the data and information necessary to affirm this with certainty; such information is perhaps accessible only to those more closely involved with the strategic and doctrinal plans of Progressivism.

*

§ 68   As one analyzes the use of ambiguity in the theological qualification of the Council, one can distinguish in the confrontation between progressivists and conservatives the following intertwining of chronological strategic phases:

§ 69   **1st phase**   • **The conservatives arrive at the Council not organized among themselves but confident that the dogmatic schemata prepared in the pre-Council will be approved.**
- **The progressivists arrive very well organized and ready to make their best efforts, but uncertain of victory.**

---

64. Chaps. IV, V, VI.2.3.

65. Chap. VI.1.

66. *Pascendi Dominici gregis*, n. 4.

§ 70   **2ⁿᵈ phase**

- Right at the opening of Vatican II, by declaring that the Council was to be predominantly pastoral and relegating dogmatic questions based on the traditional teaching to a secondary plane, John XXIII disorients the conservatives.

- With the withdrawal of the schema *De fontibus Revelationis* by the express desire of John XXIII, nearly all the remaining schemata of the pre-Council are dropped from the agenda.

- The conservatives show discouragement and resignation.

§ 71   **3ʳᵈ phase**

- Alleging pastoral actions, the progressivists introduce into the schemata ideas of adaptation to the world and different religions.

- The conservatives protest against some of them.

- Paul VI, directly or indirectly, uses his authority to silence the conservatives and give the victory to progressivists.

- Faced with contradictions with traditional doctrine, the conservatives accept them only by force of the pontifical authority and under the allegation that they are pastoral actions.

- This tactic is used until the end of the Council.

§ 72   **4ᵗʰ phase**

- Once Vatican II is over and victory clearly won by the progressivists, they gradually begin to say that the Council was not only pastoral, but also dogmatic.

- Their tendency is to accentuate the doctrinal aspect of the victories obtained.

§ 73   **5ᵗʰ phase**

- The conservatives, on the contrary, once Vatican II is over, begin to stress its pastoral aspect.

- Their apology seeks to demonstrate that since the Council was pastoral, it does not require obedience like dogmatic ones.

§ 74   **6ᵗʰ phase**   • **In the post-conciliar period, when the possibility of a conservative reaction arises, the Vatican leadership uses its power and prestige to try to destroy the reaction by alleging that the Council was dogmatic.**

§ 75   **7ᵗʰ phase**   • **When, in the post-conciliar era, the progressivists have problems with their grassroots who complain about Vatican II's ambiguity, the leadership call to mind the dogmatic victories in the Council and stress the need for making them more explicit in the future.**

*

We now present documents to corroborate these phases of a hypothetical progressivist maneuver.

1ˢᵗ phase   • **The conservatives arrive at the Council not organized among themselves but confident that the dogmatic schemata prepared in the pre-Council will be approved.**
              • **The progressivists arrive very well organized and ready to make their best efforts, but uncertain of victory.**

§ 76   With respect to the disorganization and consequent unpreparedness of some episcopates, especially from more conservative countries, these words by Archbishop Guglielmo Montolese of Taranto, appear expressive of the **1ˢᵗ phase: "In general we Italian Bishops were not very prepared, unlike those of France, Germany and the other countries of Central Europe.** Along with four other Italian Bishops, I was part of a work group that included several French Prelates. We would meet at Rome's French College to compare each other's positions. Suddenly, I realized the difference in preparedness."[67]

§ 77   His opinion is somewhat confirmed by Archbishop Aurelio Sorrentino of Reggio Calabria, who says: **"I must honestly recognize that I, like many others, I believe, arrived at the Council**

---

67. Guglielmo Montolese, "La Chiesa, compagna di viaggio dell'uomo – I grandi testimoni del Vaticano 11/7," interview with Silvano Stracca, in *Avvenire,* 11/27/1992.

absolutely unprepared both with respect to the themes to be discussed as well as the method to be followed."[68]

§ 78   Cardinal Suenens tells how early in the Council he was assigned by John XXIII to "clear up" the schemata which had been written *grosso modo* by conservatives. He confirms the progressivist articulation in this **1ˢᵗ phase** as follows:

> **"During an audience in March 1962, I complained to Pope John XXIII about** what I felt was **the abusive number of schemata prepared for the coming conciliar discussion.** There were 70, I believe, of very unequal value and in any case of an excessive weight, preventing *a priori* a fruitful and valid work in the Council. **John XXIII asked me to clear the way and make him a plan** based on these schemata. **After studying these documents, I sent John XXIII a preliminary note aimed at uncluttering the Council** and placing it into a true pastoral perspective. ... **The preliminary note was intended to remove excessively juridical conceptions away from the Council. It fully suited the views of John XXIII, who gave it his personal approval."** [69]

Suenens, after transcribing his note, continues to explain how he prepared the plan that would be adopted by the Council, and the political contacts he organized, partly under the orientation of John XXIII himself:

> **"The road having been thus cleared, I worked to prepare a plan. At the end of April 1962 the plan was ready.** In it I inserted, as much as possible, the themes that were dear to me, with the constant concern of promoting the pastoral adaptations I deemed of first importance. **The confidential document remained strictly personal until the moment I found it useful to communicate it to some Cardinal friends, among whom was Cardinal Montini. In** my files I find a letter from Cardinal Liénart, dated June 14, 1962: **'Your plan is fully satisfactory to me** and I do not want to wait until evening to tell you this in a mere phone call. **I fully approve** the apostolic spirit with which you conceived [the plan], the disposition of its parts as you outlined them, and the broadness of the perspectives that you opened.' **Other Cardinals reacted,** orally, **in the same sense. For his part,** on May 19, 1962, **Cardinal Cicognani,** the Secretary of State, **by order of John XXIII, sent photocopies of**

---

68. Aurelio Sorrentino, "La Chiesa, compagna di viaggio dell'uomo," *ibid.*

69. L. J. Suenens, *Souvenirs et espérances,* pp. 65-66.

this plan to a certain number of Cardinals, so that they might be informed of it.

"John XXIII wanted to gain the adhesion of some influential Cardinals to this plan so that, at the opportune moment, he would be able to present it under their collective sponsorship. Toward this end, he asked me to go to some whom he himself indicated. " [70]

After naming Cardinals with whom he met and who supported him – Montini, Döpfner, Liénart, Siri – the Belgian Prelate alludes to the Pontiff's tacit endorsement of his plan:

"John XXIII, for his part, adopted it in its major parts as his own. One can read this between the lines in his memorable radio message of September 12, 1962, announcing and presenting the Council to be inaugurated a few weeks later. ... The Holy Father's speech explicitly adopted the proposed distinction between the Church *ad intra* and the Church *ad extra,* which was the mainstay of the plan." [71]

These testimonies show without a doubt how the progressivist current, in its most high-ranking members, arrived at the Council entirely organized.

§ 79   Fr. Bernard Häring, CSSR, describes the role he played before the beginning of the Council to sound out reactions and arrange for the rejection of the conservative schemata:

"Cardinals Suenens and Döpfner charged me, after the closure of the preparatory works, to survey the largest possible number of Bishops and Cardinals about the positions they would take at the Council regarding the 72 previous schemata. Shortly before the opening of the Council, I explained to some of our friendly Cardinals that, based on all these contacts, it was certain that only the schema on liturgical reform would have some probability of being accepted and discussed. For certain, more than one-third of the votes would be against the other 71 schemata. My friends and I took advantage of every possibility to explain our assessment of these schemata to the largest possible number of Bishops and to linguistic groups." [72]

---

70. *Ibid.,* p. 69.

71. *Ibid.,* p. 70.

72. Bernard Haring, "Minha participação no Concílio Vaticano II," in *Revista Eclesiástica Brasileira,* June 1994, p. 382.

§ 80   Confirming the **1st phase,** the group presided over by Cardinal Gerlier of Lyon displays a typical example of the progressivists' close-knit organization. The well-informed Fr. Chenu writes:

"About 50 Bishops and 30 *periti* ...had gathered at the Belgian College on October 26, 1962. ... **This commission,** which held private sessions in its workings, **was in constant contact with Council officials.** In the first place, it was **efficaciously presided over by Cardinal Gerlier,** Archbishop of Lyon; furthermore, **it never failed to keep Cardinal Lercaro, who informed the Pope, abreast of events. The intervention by various of its members in the Assembly opened up its debates to the [conciliar] experiences, analyses, doctrines and projects. Various documents of great scope came out of this group, which,** incidentally, **had imposed extreme discretion on itself as a duty."**[73]

§ 81   Fr. Schillebeeckx, a *perito* of the Dutch Episcopate and the author of many of Cardinal Alfrink's interventions, gives a meaningful testimony on the well-organized progressivist scheme, which continued until the end of the Council:

"Undoubtedly Alfrink played a great role in the Council. He was not alone. He would always meet with other Cardinals: Liénart, Döpfner, König. They formed a small college and discussed above all the strategy to be adopted. The idea of collegiality was taken ahead by Alfrink. It was he who proposed to establish the synod [of Bishops], which he then described as the crown's counsel." [74]

§ 82   As to the uncertainties of victory on the part of the progressivists, Hans Küng himself testifies: **"The Council** did not do everything... But **it did more than one would have dared expect of it back then."** [75]

2nd phase • **Right at the opening of Vatican II, by declaring that the Council was to be predominantly pastoral and relegating dogmatic questions based on the traditional teaching to a secondary plane, John XXIII disorients the conservatives.**

---

73. M. D. Chenu, "A Igreja dos pobres no Vaticano II," in *Concilium,* 1977, No. 4, p. 64.

74. Edward Schillebeeckx, "Dio é un dono non una garanzia," interview with Francesco Strazzari, in *Il Regno* 6/15/1990, p. 332.

75. H. Kung, *Veracidade,* p. 130.

- **With the withdrawal of the schema *De fontibus Revelationis* by the express desire of John XXIII, nearly all the remaining schemata of the pre-Council are dropped from the agenda.**
- **The conservatives show discouragement and resignation.**

§ 83   We have thus analyzed the Council's *Opening Speech,* in which John XXIII states the predominantly pastoral goal of Vatican II and relegates traditional dogmatic teaching to a secondary plane.[76]

In an interview with the Author, Fr. Chenu confirms the **2nd phase** as he describes the surprise and disconcertment the Council's *Opening Speech* caused among conservatives:

"Adaptation to the needs of the times is indeed a principle of the Council, according to **John XXIII, who made an *Opening Speech* saying that the Church must look at the world in order to adapt herself to it. It is the opposite of what had been prepared.** You know that there was a preparatory commission that had written the schemata. And on the opening day the Pope said the opposite. I was there in Rome. **Traditional theologians were disconcerted.**"[77]

The following excerpt by Fr. Chenu depicts the impasse in which the speech of John XXIII left the conservatives:

"On the one hand, there was John XXIII's opening speech defining the reasons for convening [the Council] and, on the other, an interview by Cardinal Siri, Archbishop of Genoa, published in the Italian weekly *Oggi.* '**A Council,**' said the latter, '**is being held to reinvigorate the truth that finds itself threatened; therefore, it is above all dogmatic.**' ... **In opposition** to the doctrinally-oriented people of the Siri type, **John XXIII spoke of a 'pastoral' action.**"[78]

§ 84   In addition, to confirm this **2nd phase** is John XXIII's typical interference in closing the debate on the sources of Revelation, which was the object of great quarrels between conservatives and progressivists. After successive discussions, the vote was held on November 21, 1962. Out of 2,211 voters, 1,368 opposed keeping the schema for discussion; 822, on the contrary, desired it procede as planned. The progressivists had failed to muster the two-thirds majority needed for the schema to be definitively rejected.

---

76. Cf. §§ 52-56.

77. M. D. Chenu, Interview with the Author, Paris, February 20, 1983.

78. *Jacques Duquesne interroge le Père Chenu* (Paris: Centurion, 1975), p. 175.

So, in this very strict sense, the conservatives were holding the upper hand. But the following day, the Secretary General, Cardinal Pericle Felice, on behalf of the Secretary of State Cardinal Amleto Cicognani, transmitted to the Assembly a pontifical communiqué withdrawing the matter from debate and entrusting it to a special commission charged with rewriting it.[79]

Thus, the victory that the conservatives – even though a minority – were about to celebrate was turned into a defeat.

3rd phase   • **Alleging pastoral actions, the progressivists introduce into the schemata ideas of adaptation to the world and different religions.**

• **The conservatives protest against some of them.**

• **Paul VI, directly or indirectly, uses his authority to silence the conservatives and give the victory to progressivists.**

• **Faced with contradictions with traditional doctrine, the conservatives accept them only by force of the pontifical authority and under the allegation that they are pastoral actions.**

• **This tactic is used until the end of the Council.**

§ 85   Corroborating what we said about the **3rd phase,** perhaps the most typical boycott carried out against the conservative wing was the one of a petition asking for the condemnation of Communism and Socialism. Here is a summary of what happened.[80]

On December 3, 1963, as the second session was coming to an end, Bishop Castro Mayer, Bishop of Campos, Brazil, delivered to the Secretary of State Cardinal Amleto Cicognani a petition signed by 213 Fathers of the Council from 54 countries asking the following of Paul VI: That he might deign to "order the study and preparation of a schema of a conciliar constitution in which: 1. Catholic social doctrine would be expounded with great clarity and the errors of Marx-

---

79. B. Kloppenburg, *Concilio Vaticano II,* vol. II, p. 190; R. Laurentin, *Bilan de la première session,* pp. 44-45; H. Fesquet, *Le journal du Concile,* pp. 114-119.

80. See the report by Henrique Chaves, "Desfazendo manobras astuciosas de Moscou, duzentos Padres conciliares pedem nova condenação do Comunismo e do Socialismo," in *Catolicismo,* January 1964.

ism, Socialism and Communism from the philosophical, sociological and economic standpoints would be condemned; 2. The errors and mentality that prepare the minds of Catholics to accept Socialism and Communism and give them a propensity to the latter would be eradicated." [81]

§ 86   The text of this petition – in support of which two Brazilian Bishops worked – takes a stand against the great process of the de-Christianization of the West – the Revolution – expounded in the essay, *Revolution and Counter-Revolution* by Plinio Corrêa de Oliveira. It also presents a close logical connection with his study, *The Freedom of the Church in the Communist State,* in which the Catholic thinker demonstrates the unfeasibility of setting up *a modus vivendi* between the Church and the communist regimes.

This timely essay by Prof. Corrêa de Oliveira was sent to all the conciliar Fathers [82] and, along with the petition, undoubtedly played an important role [83] in creating the favorable climate that later enabled important Prelates to feel at ease as they questioned, in the plenary assembly, the reasons for the ominous refusal of tackling the question of Communism.

§ 87   By his silence, Paul VI rejected the request of the 213 conciliar fathers. [84] A few months later, shortly before the start of the third session, in the Encyclical *Ecclesiam suam,* he spoke of a "dialogue of salvation" in which he did not rule out the hypothesis of including the Communists. [85]

---

81. The full text of the petition was published by the monthly journal on religion and culture, *Catolicismo,* January 1964.

82. A. Wenger, *Chronique de la deuxième session,* p. 240.

83. The petition by the 213 conciliar Fathers and the distribution of *The Freedom of the Church in the Communist State* had ample repercussion in the Italian press. The following newspapers published reports on the topic: *Il Tempo, Il Messagero, Il Secolo* and the *Daily American* of the American community of Rome, *Corriere della Sera,* the magazine *Il Borghese* of Milan, the daily *Roma* and *Il Mattutino* of Naples, *Il Resto del Carlino* of Bologna, *La Nazione* of Florence, *Arena* of Verona, *Il Giornale* of Vicenza, *Alto Adige* of Bolzano, *Il Giornale del Popolo* of Bergamo, *La Provinzia* of Cremona, *Messaggero-Veneto* of Udine, *Gazetta* of Mantua, *Gazetta* of Reggio Emilia, *Gazetta Emiliana* of Modena, *Gazetta Padana* of Ferrara, *Gazetta di Parma, Tribuna del Mezzogiorno* of Messina and *Il Giornale di Sicilia* of Palermo.

84. R. Wiltgen, *The Rhine Flows into the Tiber,* p. 273.

85. Encyclical *Ecclesiam suam,* August 6, 1964, in *Insegnamenti di Paolo VI,* 1963-1970, Encicliche, pp. 45-48.

§ 88   As the third session began on October 20, 1964, *Schema XIII* on "the presence of the Church in the modern world" came up for discussion. At that meeting and subsequent ones, the conciliar Fathers debated at length about the part of the schema dealing with Atheism, but carefully avoided the word Communism. Several Prelates, both orally and in writing, lamented such an omission. [86]

---

86. a. Bishop Luigi Carli of Segni, in a collaboration entitled "Il Comunismo e il Concilio Vaticano II" for the book by G. Scantamburlo, *Perché il Concilio no ha condannato il Comunismo* (Rome: L'Appennino Ed., 1967), presents a collection of the main interventions by conciliar Fathers criticizing *Schema XIII's* failure to mention Communism. Here are some of the most significant criticisms:

b. Archbishop William Conway of Armagh, Ireland: "The schema ... does not speak of the persecution of the Church in certain countries. One may object that this silence is intentional, so as not to hinder the dialogue with Atheism, but truth and sincerity are essential conditions of any dialogue" (in L. Carli, "Il Comunismo e il Concilio Vaticano II," pp. 201-202).

c. Ukrainian Archbishop Maximo Hermaniuk of Winnipeg, Canada: "It is necessary ... to show clearly what is the vocation of man that atheist Marxism wants to reduce to a mere force of production. ... It would be deplorable to forget the testimony of the martyrs and confessors of the faith" *(ibid., p. 202)*.

d. Bishop Joseph Stimpfle of Augsburg, Germany: "The schema should speak openly about the militant Atheism spread in so many countries which has caused so much harm to the Church and contemporary humanity. How can one maintain a tranquil conscience if one fails to speak about and even mention the Marxist phenomenon, the real and gravest danger to humanity today, a humanity of which the Council claims to want to take pastoral care?" *(ibid.)*.

e. Bishop Raffaele Barbieri of Cassano all'Ionio, Italy: "The principal goal of this Council is pastoral ... but it would be a scandal for many faithful if the Council would give the impression that it is afraid to condemn the greatest crime of our time, scientific and practical Atheism, which is worse than the atomic bomb itself because of its consequences in the moral and spiritual planes" *(ibid., pp. 202-203)*.

f. Cardinal Yu Pin, Archbishop of Nankin (China), speaking in the name of 70 conciliar Fathers: "The schema puts a great emphasis on the signs of the times, but appears to ignore that Communism and Marxist materialism are the greatest and saddest characteristic signs of our times. A declaration about this point is necessary in order to defend the truth, since Communism, materialism and militant Atheism represent the apex of all heresies. We must also remember that wherever Communism exists, there is no lack of bloody or at least destructive persecution. Likewise, the doctrine of peaceful coexistence, the policy of the

§ 89   On April 7, 1965, during the recess between the third and fourth sessions and while *Schema XIII* (which gave rise to the Pastoral Constitution *Gaudium et spes)* was being revised, Paul VI created the Secretariat for Unbelievers, with the aim of fomenting dialogue with atheists.

§ 90   The second version of *Schema XIII,* sent to be examined by the conciliar Fathers on May 27, 1965, also omitted any explicit reference to Communism. Thus, in the fourth session, when the schema was debated in the Assembly, there were criticisms of the document and requests that Communism be condemned. [87]

§ 91   On September 29, 1965, faced with such a flagrant and repeated omission, 25 Bishops from various countries took up an initiative by *Coetus Internationalis Patrum* [88] and sent the conciliar Fathers a circular letter expounding a series of reasons why it was indispensable that "after paragraph 19 of the schema on Atheism, *The Church in the Modern World,* a new and adequate paragraph dealing expressly with the problem of Communism should be added."[89]

---

extended hand, and the concept of the so-called Catholic Communism are sources of dangerous confusions. In order to fulfill the expectations of peoples, especially those who suffer and groan under the communist yoke; in order to give the schema a greater balance and correspondence to the present situation in the world, it would be necessary to complete it with a chapter dedicated exclusively to Marxist ideology and its political expression, Communism, accompanied by an explicit condemnation" (*ibid.,* pp. 203-204).

g. Also speaking at the conciliar assembly along these same lines were Archbishop S. Garcia de Sierra of Burgos (Spain); Archbishop G. Bolatti of Rosario (Argentina); Archbishop J. Pogacnikof Liubliana (Yugoslavia); Bishop J. Wright of Pittsburgh, Penn. (USA) *(ibid.,* pp. 204-206). Bishop Luigi Carli himself should also be included in his list.

87. A. Wenger, *Chronique de la quatrième session,* pp. 156-158, 159-161, 164-166; R. Laurentin, *Bilan de la quatrième session,* pp. 117, 166-167; H. Fesquet, *Le journal du Concile,* pp. 1012-1013.

88. This International Group of Fathers was set up at the beginning of the Council on the initiative of some conservative Bishops, among them Luigi Carli, Marcel Lefebvre, Geraldo P. Sigaud and Antonio C. Mayer. Its goal was to disseminate and defend viewpoints of traditional Catholic doctrine. In addition to coordinating the activities of its members in the conciliar Assembly, it promoted contacts with influential personalities of the Hierarchy, sponsored public lectures, issued press releases, etc. For more information on the *Coetus* see R. Wiltgen, *The Rhine Flows into the Tiber,* pp. 148-150, 231, 235-236, 240, 247-249, 274.

89. Giovanni Caprile, *Il Concilio Vaticano II,* vol. V, p. 119.

This exposition, [90] initially supported by 334, and later 435 conciliar Fathers, [91] was accompanied by a proposed addition to *Schema XIII.* [92]

In this circular letter the *Coetus* warned, "Tomorrow the Council will be blamed – and quite justly so – for its silence in regard to Communism, a silence that will be taken as a sign of cowardice and connivance." [93]

On October 9, within the required deadline, the text of the amendment to *Schema XIII* and its formal preamble, with the 334 signatures gathered by the *Coetus* supporting the proposal, were delivered to the General Secretariat of the Council by Archbishops Geraldo Sigaud and Marcel Lefebvre.

§ 92

Nevertheless, the third version of the *Schema,* distributed on November 13, again failed to make any reference to Communism. There is more. In the official report presented by Cardinal Garrone, the commission in charge of reviewing the text did not mention the amendment proposed by the 435 conciliar Fathers; it only said that "two Fathers asked that Atheism be called by its proper name. But the commission was not of this opinion." [94] This was a flagrant violation of the *Procedural Rules,* which mandated that all proposed amendments be made known to the plenary Assembly, even if introduced by only one Father. [95]

Invoking papal authority to justify that refusal, Cardinal Garrone explained: "It seemed to the commission that this manner of proceeding agrees very well both with the pastoral ordination of the Council and the **express will of Popes John and Paul.**" [96] Soon thereafter,

---

90. *Ibid.,* pp. 119-121.

91. R. Wiltgen, *The Rhine Flows into the Tiber,* p. 277.

92. Full text in L. Carli, "Il Comunismo e il Concilio Vaticano II," in G. Scantamburlo, *Perché il Concilio no ha condannato il Comunismo,* pp. 217-219. It was also published by the magazine *30 Dias, "A* petição 'desaparecida,'" August-September 1989, pp. 54-55.

93. R. Wiltgen, *The Rhine Flows into the Tiber,* p. 274.

94. *Schema constitutionis pastoralis de Ecclesia in mundo huius temporis. Textus recognitus et relationis,* Pars I (*sub-secreto*), Typ. Polygl. Vat. 1965, p. 24, in L. Carli, "Il Comunismo e it Concilio Vaticano II," p. 228.

95. *Ibid.*

96. In a footnote, Giovani Caprile reports that Cardinal Garrone had been received in an audience by Paul VI in the first weeks of November 1965. In order to lay out clearly the position of Paul VI, opposed to that of the conservative Fathers, he cites Fr. Tucci, a member of the

Fr. Caprile, of *La Civiltà Cattolica,* commented: "This part of the report contained ... an indirect but clear answer to those who proposed an explicit mention of Communism; this measure, as has been insinuated, was also ruled out by the prudent and qualified advisors of a specialized secretariat. The path chosen by the commission was in line with the pastoral guidelines given to the Council by John XXIII and also corresponded to the wishes of Paul VI." [97]

§ 93   Conservative conciliar Fathers were left perplexed. On that same day, Bishop Luigi Carli filed an appeal with the Council's presidency. Voting on the *Schema* would take place on Monday the 15th. So the *Coetus* members still had the option of reintroducing the amendment as *a modus*. However, Luigi Carli comments: "The battle was already lost. In fact, at least 700 votes would be needed to have the commission re-examine the *Schema;* unfortunately, it was not humanly possible to collect them in an Assembly that had ignored not only the text but even the amendment about Communism." [98] So the collection had to be made that very Monday at the entrance of St. Peter's Basilica. Even then, 220 conciliar Fathers introduced the *modi* to the text of the third version.

§ 94   The whole case was widely reported by the Divine Word News Service. [99] The Italian press commented on it widely, making a considerable impact on Catholic public opinion. [100]

Commission in charge of reviewing *Schema XIII:* "We have good reasons to believe that Cardinal Garrone dealt with this matter with the Holy Father ... This seems to be confirmed by the spoken statements added at this point of the exposition" (Roberto Tucci, "Introduzione storico-dottrinale alla costituzione pastorale *Gaudium et spes,*" in *La Costituzione pastorale sulla Chiesa nel mondo contemporaneo,* Turin, 1966, p. 116, note 111, in G. Caprile, *Il Concilio Vaticano II,* vol. V, p. 403).

97. *Ibid.*

98. L. Carli, "Il Comunismo e il Concilio Vaticano II," p. *230.*

99. *Divine Word News Service,* a news agency set up in Rome by the Society of the Divine Word, was headed during the Council's sessions by Fr. Ralph M. Wiltgen, SVD. This Catholic agency, whose dispatches were sent to 3,000 subscribers in 97 countries (including all international news agencies), rendered a great assistance to the *Coetus Internationalis Patrum,* reporting on its actions and disseminating its documents, which a certain media generally relegated to a secondary plane or simply boycotted. When Vatican II ended, Fr. Wiltgen published his important book, *The Rhine Flows into the Tiber,* revealing the intimate cohesion among the Prelates of the "European alliance," whose progressivist orientation prevailed in the Council.

100. Fr. Wiltgen's agency contributed to that end by carrying in its bulletin unpublished news on the efforts of the *Coetus* and the sabotage

§ 95   Fr. Roberto Tucci, SJ, a *perito* on the revision commission and later coordinator of John Paul II's trips, [101] said in a press conference that the amendment had not come to the knowledge of his commission's members perhaps because it had been barred by a "red light." In view of the general disconcertion created by the case, Cardinal Tisserant decided to set up an inquiry to clarify irregularities.

It was found that the "red light" had been the work of Msgr. Achille Glorieux, Secretary of the commission for revising the Schema on the Church in the World, secretary of the Commission for the Apostolate of the Laity and also a holder of other Vatican posts. Although the amendment had been delivered to the general secretariat on time, the secretary of the revision commission had "shelved it," preventing it from reaching the hands of other commission members. [102] There is no news of any sanction ever having been given the French churchman for this arbitrary action so beneficial to pro-Communist designs.

§ 96   Fr. Häring also played a salient role in the "veto" of the Bishops' request: "In a recently published book-interview, German theologian Bernard Häring, who was secretary-coordinator of the committee in charge of writing *Gaudium et spes,* recounts: 'When about 200 Bishops asked for a solemn condemnation of Communism, Msgr. Glorieux, secretary of the Commission for the Apostolate of the Laity and of the mixed commission, and I were accused in particular as scapegoats. I have no reason to deny that I did everything possible to avoid this condemnation, which clearly resounded as a political condemnation. I knew that John XXIII had promised the Moscow authorities that the Council would not condemn Communism in order to make possible the participation of observers from the Russian Orthodox Church." [103]

---

to which the conservatives were subject. Such news made front-page headlines in the Italian newspapers *Il Giornale d'Italia, Il Messaggero, Il Tempo, Il Popolo, Il Secolo, L'Avennire d'Italia,* and was published on inside pages of *Il Giorno, La Stampa, Paese Sera, Corriere della Sera,* and the Communist Party daily, *L'Unità* (R. Wiltgen, *The Rhine Flows into the Tiber,* pp. 275-276).

101. Lucio Brunelli, 1994 – "Ao som de Bill e da família," in *30 Dias,* December 1993, p. 10.

102. R. Wiltgen, *op. cit.,* p. 276; Tommaso Ricci, "A 'distração' do Concílio," in *30 Dias,* August/September 1989, pp. 53-54.

103. Bernard Häring, *apud* T. Ricci, "O mistério do pacto Roma-Moscou," *30 Dias,* October 1989, p. 55.

§ 97   On December 2, the definitive text was distributed to the Fathers. Its section on Atheism said not even a word about Communism. According to the official report, "It is not advisable to mention Communism since this word contains political and economic concepts that are not dealt with here. Furthermore, strictly speaking, Marxism constitutes a philosophical system that would require a long exposition. For this reason, it is better that the word not be used."[104]

§ 98   The epilogue is that the petition for a special schema condemning Communism and Socialism was turned down and the proposed amendment to the Constitution *Gaudium et spes* did not even come up for consideration. Nor were the votes modifying those documents taken into account. As a "consolation prize" for defeated conservatives, a note was inserted in the fourth and definitive version of the Schema making a brief mention of documents by previous Pontiffs that referred to Communism. Here again the forbidden word Communism was not mentioned, [105] and the conservative wing was thus defeated by an action that could not but have been known and approved by Paul VI.

§ 99   A telltale sign of the effort to shackle the action by conservative Bishops that we are studying in the **3rd phase** is a letter that the Vatican Secretary of State, Cardinal Cicognani – presumably under instructions from Paul VI – sent to Bishop Luigi Carli, coordinator of *Coetus Internationalis Patrum*. In it the Cardinal expressed surprise that the Bishops of *Coetus* share similar viewpoints in theological and pastoral matters and claimed that they provoke the "accentuation of tendencies and divisions among the conciliar Fathers." He finished by advising that the *Coetus* be closed down.

Here is the full text of Cardinal Cicognani's letter:

"Most Reverend Excellency: As the IV session of the Ecumenical Council Vatican II approached, the letter which Your Excellency, along with other conciliar Fathers, sent to the Holy Pontiff to present some requests in order to make the work of this session more agile and fruitful has recently come into my hands. It was my duty to refer its contents to His Holiness, who paid careful attention to the proposals suggested.

---

104. *Schema constitutionis pastoralis de Ecclesia in mundo huius temporis,* p. 76, in L. Carli, "Il comunismo e it Concilio Vaticano II," p. 234.

105. Pastoral Constitution *Gaudium et Spes,* P.I, chap. I, n. 21 (Relation of the Church with Atheism), note 16, in V.A., *Documentos do Vaticano II,* p. 157.

"However, I must tell Your Excellency that a certain surprise was caused by the fact that the request was presented in the name of a *Coetus Internationalis Patrum, idem in re theological ac pastorali sententium,* that is, of a particular group in the bosom of the Council. This initiative could authorize the official appearance of other 'alliances' to the detriment of the Conciliar Assembly, something which, in fact, as Your Excellency understands, hampers the Fathers' liberty of judgment and choice that must be guaranteed above all private interest, and accentuates tendencies and divisions among the Fathers themselves, whereas every measure should be taken to attenuate them in favor of serenity and concord, for the success of the Council and the honor of the Church. This initiative cannot, therefore, be approved, and it is advisable for the said *Coetus* not to function as an organ representing the positions of the Fathers affiliated with it.

"As for the proposed suggestions, offered with a desire for a fecund progress of the works in the coming session, they will be examined with all diligence in view of the high goal at which they must aim.

"Upon expressing my heartfelt thanks for Your solicitude and attention, I am pleased to take advantage of this circumstance to manifest my distinctly courteous sentiments.

"To Your Most Reverend Excellency,

Most devoted *in Domino,*

Amleto Cardinal Cicognani." [106]

*

§ 100   Another pontifical interference directly aimed against the conservatives took place in regard to the discussion about collegiality in chapter III of *Lumen gentium.* Such interference also shows the difficulties encountered by the conservatives in accepting conciliar doctrine, pointed out in the **3ʳᵈ phase.**

John XXIII was succeeded by Cardinal Montini, who had been one of the most ardent progressivist leaders in the defense of collegiality to the detriment of pontifical primacy. As Pope, he went so far as to send several suggestions on collegiality to the theological commission. [107]

§ 101   Paul VI's direct interference to disarm conservatives did not stop at this. On the day following the opening of the third session, Archbishop Dino Staffa, then secretary of the Congregation for Semi-

---

106. From *Corrispondenza Romana,* Agenzia di Informazioni per la Stampa, 3/28/1990.

107. R. Wiltgen, *The Rhine Flows into the Tiber,* p. 230.

naries and Universities, asked to speak to the Assembly before the vote on the subject was taken. His request was based on the *Procedural Rules* [108] and was further supported by the signatures of 70 conciliar Fathers who thought as he did. His request was turned down by the Council's presidency, and the subcommittee in charge of reviewing the text on collegiality ignored his objections.

Archbishop Staffa wrote the Pope a long letter dated November 7, 1964, expressing his problem of conscience with accepting collegiality, which was opposed to the traditional teaching of the Church. He said that he felt obliged to vote against it. He added that the action of the Moderators (whom the Pontiff had personally chosen as his representatives and vested with full authority) forbidding him to speak had been illegal.

Paul VI asked for an investigation to examine the violations of procedure and forwarded Archbishop Staffa's observations of a theological nature to the theological commission. Archbishop Staffa was not given the opportunity to speak. [109]

§ *102*   Also corroborating the **3ʳᵈ phase,** 35 Cardinals and five Superior Generals of large religious Orders wrote the Pope saying that the text on collegiality was ambiguous and that, after the Council, it would certainly be interpreted according to the tenets of the extreme progressivist current.

Paul VI wrote Cardinal Arcadio Larraona who headed the list – his name Fr. Wiltgen does not mention in his chronicle – criticizing the arguments that had been presented. This Cardinal went to speak with Paul VI in the name of the group to explain their suspicions. Paul VI did nothing. [110]

The Cardinal also suggested that a debate involving theologians be held in the presence of the Pope. Paul VI did not accept this suggestion.

It was at that point that a progressivist representative boasted, in writing, about the ambiguity of the texts on collegiality and indicated how his partisans would interpret it after the Council. This document came to the knowledge of the wary group of Cardinals and Religious Superiors. Thus, faced with a clear progressivist admission of how they would take advantage of this ambiguity, the Cardinal, who represented these 34 Prelates and the five Superior Generals, went again for an interview with Paul VI.

---

108. See a. 57, sec. 6, *Procedural Rules.*

109. R. Wiltgen, *The Rhine Flows into the Tiber*, pp. 230-231.

110. *Ibid.,* pp. 231-232. As for the Cardinal's name, Andrea Tornielli, "O Timoneiro do Concílio," in *30 Dias,* July 1992, p. 38.

It was only then that, as a consequence of an imprudence by a progressivist hothead, Paul VI ordered the famous *Preliminary Explanatory Note* to be written. Even so, he did not want it incorporated into the text of the document. [111]

§ 103 We conclude our comments on this **3rd phase** with the words of Henri Fesquet on the confrontation between progressivists and conservatives and the tenacious papal action opposed to the latter. He gives his opinion as he starts his report on the fourth session:

"Conciliar mechanics – as is normal after functioning for four years – has come a long way. The [progressivist] majority has become aware of its youthful energy, formerly unimagined. It learned to avoid clashes with the minority. It discovered less onerous methods to gain ground. For its part, the minority became aware of its true limitations. Facing harsh realities, it learned how to draw consequences from its failures. It has less pretension of being the custodian of orthodoxy after having perceived that the two last Popes, though remaining above the fray, not only failed automatically to support it, but also untiringly incited it to carry out its *aggiornamento*." [112]

*

§ 104 Perhaps it would not be superfluous to point out the final defeat of conservatives, who, led by Cardinal Ottaviani, head of the Holy Office at the time, made their *ralliement* with Progressivism by signing the documents they had opposed.

Indeed, as rumors circulated about the imminent reform of the Holy Office, Cardinal Ottaviani gave an interview in which he said:

"I am the soldier who watches over the gold reserve. Do you think I would fulfill my duty by arguing, abandoning my post, turning a blind eye? My son, seventy-five years are seventy-five years! I lived them defending certain principles and certain laws. If you tell the old soldier that the laws are going to change, it is obvious that ... he will do all he can so they will not change. But, if they nonetheless change, God will certainly give him the strength to place himself in the defense of a new treasure in which he believes. Once the new laws become the treasure of the Church, an enrichment of the gold reserve, only one principle counts: to serve the Church. And this service means to be faithful to her laws. [113]

---

111. R. Wiltgen, *The Rhine Flows into the Tiber.,* pp. 231-232.; see in this Chapter, §§ 61-62.

112. H. Fesquet, *Le journal du Concile,* pp. 860-861.

113. Alfredo Ottaviani, interview with *Corriere della Sera,* 10/28/1965, in H. Fesquet, *Le journal du Concile,* p. 1019.

§ 105   In addition to Cardinal Ottaviani, another lamentable example of *ralliement* with Progressivism was made by Cardinal Pietro Parente, another exponent of the Holy Office and a model of "conservatism." Referring to his action in the Council, he says: "Inspired by God, John XXIII carried out Vatican Council II, which suffers from the crisis [of the *nouvelle théologie*] but is able to contain it. I actively participated in this magnificent 'ecumenical assembly' and remember two of my interventions: on collegiality and on Mary's mediation. I strongly fought in favor of the former. ... Some people were surprised at my stand because of my position as an aide to the Holy Office. But collegiality was approved unanimously: only five no's out of 2,156 Fathers! The rumor spread that I was the cause." [114]

§ 106   Regarding the general defection of the conservative conciliar Fathers, the journalist of *Le Monde* comments: "Attached to a past that has just died, despising the present world whose grandeur and advantages the last two Popes have strived to make them see, the opposition Fathers (from 50 to 300?) finally adhered, not without grandeur of soul [sic!], to the schemata that prickle their sensibilities and transform their mental habits." [115]

§ 107   It is no wonder that the post-conciliar conservative opposition was profoundly affected by such actions hardly compatible with Catholic heroism.

4ᵗʰ phase   • **Once Vatican II is over and victory clearly won by the progressivists, they gradually begin to say that the Council was not only pastoral, but also dogmatic.**

• **Their tendency is to accentuate the doctrinal aspect of the victories obtained.**

§ 108   These words by Paul VI a few months after the end of Vatican II are characteristic of this **4ᵗʰ phase**:

"There are those who ask what authority, what theological qualification the Council intended to give to its teachings, knowing that it avoided issuing solemn dogmatic definitions engaging the infallibility of the ecclesiastical Magisterium. The answer is known by who-

---

114. Pietro Parente, "Cristo, Maria, la Chiesa: I punti nevralgici della mia ricerca teologica," interview with Gino Concetti, in *L'Osservatore Romano,* 12/19/1985.

115. H. Fesquet, *Le journal du Concile,* p. 1033.

ever remembers the conciliar declaration of March 6, 1964, repeated on November 16, 1964: given the Council's pastoral character, it avoided pronouncing, in an extraordinary manner, dogmas endowed with the note of infallibility. However, **it gave its teachings the authority of the Supreme Ordinary Magisterium, which [being] the Ordinary Magisterium and thereby manifestly authentic, must be docilely and sincerely accepted by all the faithful according to the Council's intention with respect to the nature and ends of each of the documents."** [116]

§ 109   In 1966, Fr. Umberto Betti, OFM, professor of Fundamental Theology at Rome's Antonianum, wrote about Vatican II, confirming what has been said about this **4ᵗʰ phase:**

"Even if its infallibility and, consequently, **its irreformability were not explicitly declared, one must not thereby think it does not exist.** Indeed, **just as an infallible definition always expresses the conviction of the universal Church, so also the conviction of the universal Church indicates the doctrine that is its infallible object."** [117]

§ 110   These statements by Fr. Karl Rahner, two years after the end of the Council (1967), confirm the **4ᵗʰ phase:**

"What form must the Church give today to this legitimate influence in face of a secular world? ... How must the Church herself be presented in her concrete structure and in the mentality of her members if she, in fact, wants to exercise an influence such as this on secular society? To begin to answer the first question, it would be advisable first of all to reflect a little on a distinctive trait of certain encyclicals of John XXIII (*Mater et Magistra, Pacem in terris*), of Paul VI's encyclical *Populorum progressio,* and especially of the Pastoral Constitution *Gaudium et spes* of Vatican II. What is characteristic of these documents?

"They contain, to be sure, **a good number of fundamental, theoretical and ever valid 'doctrinal' truths (with good reason, it must be said, and necessarily),** but the salient point of these texts, **what in them is stimulating and 'shocking' for the pure theoretician,** rests in their intention, which can be described first of all (in the terminology of Vatican II) as 'pastoral.' Nevertheless, **one would underestimate and misconstrue this 'pastoral' element**

---

116. Paul VI, General Audience of January 12, 1966, in *Insegnamenti di Paolo VI,* vol. IV, p. 700.

117. Umberto Betti, "Qualification théologique de la Constitution," in V.A., *L'Eglise de Vatican II,* vol. II, p. 217.

in its essence for understanding it as a series of purely practical consequences, whose certain and compelling deduction from general principles the merest glance at the present-day situation of the world would suffice to bring about. **The intent of these documents is clearly present in 'imperatives,' in emphases,** in an historical program that calls the world to take this decision." [118]

§ 111   Even though this item is not intended to analyze the doctrine underlying the notion of 'pastoral,' [119] it would be well to point out in passing that behind the Council's pastoral approach, often presented merely as an overflowing of its mercy for the world, is a doctrinal background.

§ 112   The following remarks by Fr. Chenu also confirm the characteristics of the **4ᵗʰ phase,** as they raise the question of the Council's doctrinal character:

"**The *demarche* by the Council has been very significant. This Council, while retaining the two words [pastoral and dogmatic], prepared ... a double constitution, one said to be 'dogmatic,' and the other 'pastoral,'** but both of them true 'constitutions' **without, however, effecting a formal dogmatization. A preliminary explanatory note to the Constitution *Gaudium et spes* would later clarify the ambiguity that still remained in people's minds** and express in an excellent fashion the organizational unity that commanded the proceedings. **But in the beginning and during the writing of *Gaudium et spes,* with all its vicissitudes, a certain indetermination would still persist even in regard to the objective of the Council.**" [120]

§ 113   Also supporting the **4ᵗʰ phase** is a statement by Bishop Clemente Riva, then Auxiliary Bishop of Rome and co-author of a book commenting of the document on religious liberty, along with Cardinal Jean-Jerome Hamer, later Prefect of the Congregation for Religious:

"First of all, **we cannot fail to recognize the *doctrinal* importance the Declaration [*Dignitatis humanae*] takes on in the progress of Catholic doctrine.** The problem of freedom of conscience and religious liberty, coupled with the duty of the apostolate and evangelization, offers a very broad perspective for the thinking and action of Christians. ... **Applying this theological consideration,**

---

118. Karl Rahner, "Theological Reflections on the Problem of Secularization," in V.A., *Theology of Renewal,* vol. I, pp. 179-180.

119. Chap. VII.

120. *Jacques Duquesne interroge le Père Chenu,* pp. 175-176.

not only to the idealistic-objective values of truth, but also to real-personal values, cannot fail to confer a much broader panorama and a possibility of a further deepening for a theological doctrine itself. ... This conciliar document ... also represents a stimulus and a basis for deepening a doctrine which opens itself to immense theological, juridical, sociological and practical developments."[121]

§ 114   This excerpt by Msgr. Philips also corroborates the **4th phase** of the hypothesis raised above at the beginning of Section B:

"Certainly one can loyally recognize that the Council did not proclaim any new thesis as *de fide definita*. But **to state that the Fathers limited themselves to giving practical guidelines and taking merely disciplinary measures is to want to deny the brightness of the sun.** ...

"Fr. Semmelroth touches the crux of the matter when he writes that **the Council, even though it did not promulgate definitions of faith strictly speaking, did resolve various more or less disputed questions. Although these 'decisions' are valid, the magisterium that published them did not want to say the last word since the Fathers were quite conscious of the progressive nature of the knowledge of truth that the people of God acquire along their pilgrimage. This explains the dynamic character the Council deliberately imparted to its sentences.** It is not advisable to burn the stages [by moving too fast]; but, on the other hand, it is not worthwhile to convene an ecumenical Council only to tread once again an already beaten path."[122]

§ 115   The remarks of Fernand Dumont, professor of Sociological Theology at Laval University, Canada, on the new conception of Pastoral Theology and its opposition to Dogmatic Theology, also apply to progressivist desires for Vatican II and confirm this **4th phase:**

"In a Church that wishes to be both missionary and engaged in her own reform, **it was inevitable that in recent decades there should have been great activity in pastoral theology. It is considered less and less as a heteroclite ensemble of practices and prescriptions on the fringe of the main body of doctrine and has become, progressively, a comprehensive vision of the Church in its project of continual construction. One can** even

---

121. Jèrôme Hamer and Clemente Riva, *La libertà religiosa nel Vaticano II* (Turin: Elie Di Ci, 1967), pp. 260, 262.

122. G. Philips, *La Chiesa e it suo Mistero, p.* 603.

think, as we suggested elsewhere, [123*] that ... pastoral theology will soon question the most profound foundations of systematic theology. ...

"If pastoral theology and theological anthropology continue to develop along the lines indicated thus far, it is unlikely that they will limit themselves to adding new tracts to the *corpus* of theology. They will suggest new, comprehensive perspectives for all of theology, an opening – so far badly defined – for the concrete historical situations of man." [124]

§ 116   Fr. Raymond Schwager, SJ, in a dialogue with the Author of these lines, expressed his opinion about the dogmatic character of Vatican II in this way:

"It is a way of interpreting the Council to say: 'All this is solely pastoral.' In the end, the document on the Church, *Lumen gentium,* is not a pastoral document but a very dogmatic document. There are people who wish to diminish the scope of this document by saying that it is only pastoral, but this is already a strategy. It is a strategy to reduce the document's scope." [125]

§ 117   The year 1988 saw the publication of an important collection about the Council, *Vatican II: Bilan et perspectives, vingt-cinq ans après (1962-1987).* It was issued under the auspices of Rome's Gregorian University, Biblical Institute and Eastern Institute and under the direction of Fr. René Latourelle, SJ. In the *Introduction* to the three-volume work, Fr. Latourelle makes an apologia of Vatican II. His exposition, which compares Vatican II to other milestone councils outstanding for their dogmatic importance, is useful to show the growing doctrinal role being attributed to Vatican II. Thus, confirming the **4th phase,** Latourelle says:

"Vatican II is undoubtedly the vastest operation of reform ever undertaken in the Church, not only on account of the number of conciliar Fathers ... but above all because of the breadth of the topics covered: Revelation, the Church (its nature, constitution, members, pastoral and missionary activity), the Liturgy, the Sacraments, the other Christian communities and the other religions,

---

123*. Fernand Dumont, *Pour la conversion de la pensée chrétienne,* 1964, pp. 205-207.

124. F. Dumont, "The Sociology of Religion and the Renewal of Theology," in V.A., *Theology of Renewal,* vol. II, pp. 271-272.

125. Raymond Schwager, interview granted to the Author, Innsbruck, February 11, 1983.

the laity, religious life, the reform of ecclesiastical studies, **religious liberty, relations between faith and culture,** the means of social communication.

"Vatican II represents an event of a unique originality. For the most part, the previous Councils were provoked by heresies or particular, that is, regional, deviations. Even the Council of Trent evolved within clearly limited doctrinal borders: the relation between the Scripture and Traditions, original sin, justification, the Sacraments. **In Vatican II, you have an operation that affects the universal Church at all levels and under all aspects.** ...

"In 1987 twenty-five years will have gone by since the beginning of the Council (1962). The Church has gone ... from a past which still has not disappeared to a future that is only beginning. **The Council of Trent gave its name to a 400-year period. Now, Vatican II marks a much more profound change. ... Vatican II is a planetary and simultaneous event,** but one must not forget that it is also a great sign in History." [126]

About the doctrinal content of the texts, Latourelle notes: **"The texts are presented** not as dogmatic definitions, but **as broad doctrinal expositions** with a pastoral visualization." [127]

§ 118 And Msgr. Philippe Delhaye, confirming the **4th phase,** emphatically declares: Our research "is sufficient to show that, **on a certain number of doctrinal points, Vatican II wanted to bear witness to the faith of the Church with authority. Such authority is, more explicitly than in the past, based on fidelity to Revelation, continuity of the Magisterium,** but also on the consciousness of being able to express itself on points that complement the knowledge of the mystery of Christ and of the Church. **To speak only about points of doctrine that have never been established, let us cite, for example, the sacramentality of the Episcopate, and the collegial character of the authority of Bishops** gathered around the Pope. **These texts of Vatican II certainly oblige as much as the constitutions of Vatican I,** which at times they imitate." [128]

§ 119 Perhaps one of the most categorical confirmations that the Vatican strives to present the Council as dogmatic comes from Cardinal

---

126. René Latourelle, *Introduction,* in V.A., *Vatican II – Bilan et perspectives,* vol. I, pp. 7-8.

127. *Ibid.,* p. 17.

128. Philippe Delhaye, "Vatican II: Autorité des textes conciliaires," in DTC, *Tables,* vol. III, col. 4335.

Willebrands, then President of the Secretariat for the Union of Christians, in a speech to the Jews about the authority of the Declaration *Nostra aetate*. In the excerpt below, the Cardinal appears to defend the infallibility of this conciliar document by saying it was supported by the assistance of the Holy Ghost. His words are important inasmuch as they reflect an intention to present Vatican II under a light different from the initial, preponderantly "pastoral," one. As such, they indirectly confirm the **4th phase**. Willebrands says:

"If the Jews over the last years have come to better appreciate the novelty and **the** practically **unique character of the text of** *Nostra aetate,* **we Catholics have realized** better **how it is** really **in accordance** with a deeper layer of our tradition and even **with the Word of God in the two Testaments. It could not have been otherwise, since this would be approved by an Ecumenical Council. The conciliar documents,** I am sure that you all know this, in traditional Catholic teaching **are considered as having** ultimately **issued from the Holy Spirit, who assists, illuminates and,** if necessary, **corrects the human process of reflection and decision-making. Therefore, if God is behind the text of** *Nostra aetate* **and also behind** *Lumen gentium* (n. 16) ... **then the new relations with Judaism are not a matter of practical [pastoral] decision,** however noble and great the alleged reasons may be. **It is for us, as Catholics, a question of fidelity to our own vocation, one part of our response to God."** [129]

5th phase   • **The conservatives, on the contrary, once Vatican II is over, begin to stress its pastoral aspect.**

            • **Their apology seeks to demonstrate that since the Council was pastoral, it does not require obedience like dogmatic ones.**

§ 120   Fr. Congar corroborates the **5th phase** as he castigates the "unacceptable attitude" of those who, by regarding the Council merely as "pastoral," deem themselves not obliged to follow its teaching: [130]

"Vatican II was doctrinal. The fact that it did not 'define' new dogmas takes nothing from its doctrinal value, according to

---

129. Jan Willebrands, "Allocution au Comité International de liaison du dialogue judéo-chrétien," in *La Documentation Catholique* (Paris), *Bilan du dialogue judéo-chrétien,* 1/19/1986, p. 122.

130. Congar's document also confirms the **4th phase** we have just analyzed.

the qualifications classic theology gives in various degrees to the documents that it promulgated. Some are 'dogmatic,' expressing common doctrine. They would be comparable to the great doctrinal encyclicals. ... Such is the case of *Lumen gentium,* of the doctrinal parts of *Dei Verbum,* of the Constitution on the Liturgy and *Gaudium et spes,* but also of various 'decrees' and the Declaration *Dignitatis humanae personae.*

"Other texts or parts of these same documents are of a purely 'pastoral' nature, that is, they provide practical guidelines in accordance with the supernatural prudence of the shepherds gathered in the Council. ... In these parts of a 'pastoral' character of the conciliar teaching, based more or less directly on Revelation, there is a content that goes beyond the development of the deposit of Faith as such, which does not come from a pure deduction of the articles in that deposit. It is what the Body of Shepherds, gathered in prayer and reflection, dares to say about historical situations which traditional Faith must clarify beyond its classically acquired propositions. ...

"**It is,** we believe, precisely **this aspect of openness, of induction, of guidelines given according to the circumstances, that certain minds refuse. Since then, these men have said: This Council was nothing but 'pastoral,' and did not intend to be anything but that. Therefore, it does not oblige, it remains debatable and free [to be obeyed or not]. This is an unacceptable attitude: What we have just said shows it well.**" [131]

§ *121*   Archbishop Marcel Lefebvre shows a sense of irony as he defends the pastoral character of the Council in opposition to the "dogmatism" of "liberal" theologians who want to impose acceptance of Vatican II:

"I believe you have noticed in Maritain, Yves Congar and their like, the perversity of historic-doctrinal relativism. We are dealing with people who have no notion of the truth, no idea of what an immutable truth may be. It is strange to learn that **these same relativist liberals, who were the real authors of Vatican II, now end up** by **dogmatizing this Council which,** nevertheless, **they used to call pastoral, and by seeking to impose conciliar novelties upon us as definitive and untouchable doctrines.**" [132]

131. *Y.* Congar, *Le Concile de Vatican II,* pp. 64f.

132. M. Lefebvre, *Its l'ont découronné – Du libéralisme à l'apostasie – La tragédie conciliare* (Escurolles: Fideliter, 1987), p. 136.

§ 122   The first successor to Archbishop Lefebvre, Fr. Schmidberger, emphasizes the pastoral aspect of the Council: "**Vatican Council II is not a super dogma, but, by the manifest will of two conciliar Popes, John XXIII and Paul VI, is a simple pastoral Council** that expressly renounced condemnations and new definitions. This is a completely new fact in the History of the Church. **For this reason, it is not the Council that guarantees infallibility,** but the conformity of each of its texts with the doctrine of the Church." [133]

§ 123   Lay author Anne Roche Muggeridge also corroborates the 5th phase as she alludes to the conservative position while referring to the progressivist maneuver we describe here:

"Only two of the documents of Vatican II, the Dogmatic Constitutions on the Church *Lumen gentium* and on Divine Revelation *Dei Verbum,* were termed 'dogmatic.' The others were described as 'pastoral,' a distinction upon which both radicals and conservatives seized, the radicals 'in order to obtain the passage of certain formulations with a modern tendency,' as Edward Schillebeeckx, a leading radical theologian at the Council, admits; **the conservatives to discredit these new departures as 'merely pastoral,' not having the force of doctrine.** 'This gap between doctrinal and pastoral, which was used as a pawn, will continue to have a bearing on the interpretation of the Council and is, in my opinion, one of the most important shadows cast on the Council debates ...' [134*] Schillebeeckx is right. The double voice of the Council has been a major cause of post-Conciliar confusion in the Church." [135]

§ 124   Bishop Rudolf Graber, a typical leader of the "conciliar right," says that the keynote of conciliar documents is pastoral, even though he admits to an "opalescent ambivalence" in the goal of the topics covered:

"It is still early to formulate a definitive judgment of the Council. But the terrible thing is that events as grand as this one touch several levels and develop on different planes. The texts certainly are entirely orthodox [sic], and some passages are formulated in a classic fashion. It will be our task, for a long time, to struggle with the Council's words in order to prevent it from being distorted, especially by the famous

---

133. Franz Schmidberger, "Mas eu respondo a König," interview to Stefano Pacci, in *30 Dias,* November 1992, p. 60.

134*. E. Schillebeeckx, *The Real Achievement of Vatican II* (New York: Herder & Herder,1967), pp. 84-85.

135. A. R. Muggeridge, *The Desolate City – Revolution in the Catholic Church* (San Francisco: Harper & Row, 1990), p. 56.

'spirit' of the Council. However, **since the Council aimed above all at a pastoral orientation and, therefore, stopped short of promulgating dogmatically definitive sentences and from dissociating itself from errors and false doctrines by issuing clear anathemas, many questions have taken on an opalescent ambivalence, which has given a certain credence to those who speak about the spirit of the Council.** Furthermore, as we have seen, a series of concepts arose, such as collegiality, ecumenism, religious liberty, which may undoubtedly have been well-founded but have also had a boomerang effect." [136]

6th phase   • **In the post-conciliar period, when the possibility of a conservative reaction arises, the Vatican leadership uses its power and prestige to try to destroy the reaction by alleging that the Council was dogmatic.**

§ 125   Substantiating the **6th phase** is the categorical statement by Paul VI in a letter to Archbishop Lefebvre on June 29, 1975 that Vatican Council II "is no less authoritative, and under certain aspects is even more important than that of Nicea." [137]

§ 126   John Paul II speaks out in the same vein: **"We nourish the profound conviction that the Spirit of truth that speaks to the Church** (Apoc 2:7, 11, 17 *et allii)* **spoke in a particularly solemn and authoritative way through Vatican Council II,** preparing the Church to enter the third millennium after Christ." [138]

§ 127   Cardinal Ratzinger, speaking about conservative criticisms of the doctrine of collegiality, also establishes that **"Vatican II is sustained by the same authority as Vatican I and Trent. ...** From the standpoint of content, we recall that Vatican II places itself in strict continuity with the two preceding Councils and literally repeats them on decisive points." [139]

---

136. R. Graber, *Athanasius and die Kirche unserer Zeit,* pp. 70-71.

137. Paul VI, Letter to Msgr. Lefebvre, June 29, 1975, in Anton Holzer, *Vatikanum II - Reformkonzil oder Konstituante einer neuen Kirche* (Basel: Sala, 1977), p. 58.

138. John Paul II, letter to Cardinal Joseph Ratzinger about the possibility of accord with Msgr. Lefebvre, published under the title, "Lettera di Giovanni Paolo II al Cardinale Joseph Ratzinger," in *L'Osservatore Romano,* 4/9/1988, pp. 1, 5.

139. J. Ratzinger, *Rapporto sulla Fede,* p. 26.

§ 128

An indirect but cogent argument confirming the **6th phase** is provided by the two documents that lay down the conditions for granting the right to celebrate Mass according to the 1962 Missal.

Indeed, it is an indirect argument, for the two official documents do not refer to the doctrinal force of the Council, but to the doctrinal force of the liturgical reform of 1970. However, it is notorious that such reform started mainly with the Constitution *Sacrosanctum Concilium* of Vatican II. While dealing with various aspects of liturgy in the Church, the Constitution's most important point is found in chapter II, when it establishes general norms for reforming the Ordinary of the Mass. [140]

The modification of the *Ordo Missae*, which was the nucleus of Paul VI's liturgical reform, was nothing but a development and application of the norms of *Sacrosanctum Concilium*. Therefore, what is said about the "doctrinal force" of the liturgical reform obviously applies to the conciliar Constitution that was its "seed." [141]

---

140. SC 47-58. About the reform of the *Ordo Missae,* see Chap. IX.1.A.

141. a. Commenting on the approval of the Constitution *Sacrosanctum Concilium* during the second conciliar session, Fr. René Laurentin says: "The liturgical Constitution is part of a dynamic balance. Indeed, **it is not a dead letter, but a seed of reform**" *(Bilan de la deuxième session,* p. 244). Further on, he continues: **"The Constitution does not propose** new rubrics, but a doctrine, a spirit, and **a program of reforms spread out over a long term.** *First stage*: Missal, Ritual of the Sacraments and sacramentals, Divine Office (Breviary), Liturgical Year will all be reviewed in Rome by post-conciliar commissions. *Second stage*: Once implemented, these reforms will be applied in different parts of the Catholic world by Bishops' Conferences, which will add the necessary adaptations according to countries, climates, languages, mentalities, etc. ... The reforms should start 'as early as possible.' But they will not reach their term for some years" *(ibid.,* pp. 245-246; 247-260).

b. This statement also confirms our opinion: "The extraordinary Synod in homage to Vatican II, **the Synod of 1985 ... also speaks of liturgical renewal as 'the most apparent fruit of the whole conciliar work'"** *(Relatio finalis,* II.B.b; *Enchiridion Vaticanum* 9/1798, in Giuseppe Dossetti, "Vaticano II: Quale recezione," in *Il Regno,* 12/1/1991, p. 696).

c. The Holy See published (March 29, 1994) the *IV Instruction for a Correct Application of the Conciliar Constitution on the Sacred Liturgy,* whose title shows that to this day the *Sacrosanctum Concilium* continues to be the central document of the whole post-conciliar reform (G. Mocellin, "IV Istruzione Liturgica – 30 anni dopo pensando all'Africa," in *Il Regno,* 4/15/1994, p. 204).

§ 129   The first document that permits the celebration of the Mass according to the *Roman Missal* of 1962 is a letter sent by the Congregation for Divine Worship to the presidents of the Bishops' Conferences dated October 3, 1984 and signed respectively by Cardinal Paul Augustin Mayer, Pro-Prefect, and Archbishop, later Cardinal, Virgilio Noè, Secretary.

As for the question of those who remain "attached to the so-called Tridentine rite," the document rules: "The Supreme Pontiff, wishing to be generous toward these groups, grants diocesan Bishops the faculty of using the Indult, whereby the priests and faithful who are explicitly mentioned in a petition to be presented to their Bishop may celebrate the Mass using the *Roman Missal* according to the typical edition of 1962, on condition that the following norms be observed: a) **That it be known publicly and without ambiguity that the said priest and faithful have nothing to do with those who cast doubt on the legitimate doctrinal force, and correction of, the *Roman Missal* promulgated in 1970 by the Roman Pontiff Paul VI.**" [142]

The document is quite clear. Only those who accept the doctrinal principles contained in the liturgical reform of Paul VI, that is, the principles of the Constitution *Sacrosanctum Concilium* and their applications, are to benefit from the "indult."

Later, finding that this "indult" was still too restrictive by virtue of the disciplinary conditions set out in sections b-e of the document, which we have not transcribed, a commission of Cardinals proposed a more generous application of the "indult," on the sole condition that the doctrinal validity of the new liturgy be accepted. Cardinal Mayer narrates the fact:

"The Bishops often took into account only the first indult of October 3, 1984, which established very restrictive conditions for the celebration of Mass according to the old rite. **A commission of Cardinals** assembled in December 1986 **examined this indult and found that its conditions were very restrictive. It** then **proposed that they be relaxed, keeping the recognition of the juridical and doctrinal validity of the new liturgy as the only necessary condition for someone wishing to benefit from the indult.** The *motu proprio* of July 2, 1988 [*Ecclesia Dei*] adopted these suggestions, asking the Bishops to be generous in the application of the indult." [143]

---

142. Congregation for Divine Worship, "Epistula – De usu Missalis Romani iuxta editionem typicam anni MCMLXII," of October 3, 1984, in *Acta Apostolicae Sedis,* Ed. Typis Polyglottis Vaticanis, vol. LXXVI, 12/1/1984, pp. 1088-1089.

143. Paul Augustin Mayer, "Cardeal anti-cisma," interview to Stefano M. Paci, in *30 Dias,* June 1991, p. 60.

§ 130   The second official document on the matter is the Apostolic Letter *Ecclesia Dei,* to which Cardinal Mayer referred above. In it, as a matter of fact, John Paul II recommends this: "The will of those who feel linked to Latin liturgical tradition should be respected everywhere by means of an ample and generous application of the directives issued by the Holy See some time ago for the use of the *Roman Missal* according to the typical edition of 1962." [144]

The requirement remains, therefore, of accepting the "doctrinal force" of the liturgical reform, that is, of the Constitution *Sacrosanctum Concilium* and of Vatican II.

7ᵗʰ phase **• When, in the post-conciliar era, the progressivists have problems with their grassroots who complain about Vatican II's ambiguity, the leadership call to mind the dogmatic victories in the Council and stress the need for making them more explicit in the future.**

§ 131   Another text by the forecited author, Nicola Colaianni, corroborates what we define as the **7ᵗʰ phase:**

"As the demand for new institutions intensified and gained urgency ... the Council seemed ... 'generic and vague' (Basset), 'with omissions and ambiguous points' (Waif), to such an extent that **at the most recent international congresses, questions were raised on whether Vatican II was still of current interest.** And even though **the timeliness of a new council, a Vatican III** [145*] **was not envisaged, it became evident that on account of the ambiguity of the conciliar texts,** when considered separately, **'the ecclesiology of Vatican II can still be a project of current interest for the Church so long as it is appraised,** in its main lines, according to a global reading ... **and offers perspectives of development.'** [146*]" [147]

§ 132   In order to close this topic on the pastoral and dogmatic natures of the Council, let us consider this excerpt by Cardinal Suenens that substantiates the **7ᵗʰ phase:**

---

144. John Paul II, Apostolic Letter *Ecclesia Dei,* July 2, 1988, in *Insegnamenti di Giovanni Paolo II,* vol. XI/3, p. 12.

145*. Congress of Notre Dame, 1977.

146*. Congress of Bologna, 1980.

147. N. Colaiani, "Crítica ao Vaticano II na literatura atual," in *Concilium,* 1983/7, p. 126.

"The invitation now is to locate Vatican II in the context of the future. For the Church is a Church that is on her way, a pilgrim Church; she never has the right to come to a full stop, and her pauses are only in preparation for new stages on her journey. In some respects, **the Church is always 'transient.'** John XXIII used to like to say, 'They call me a transition Pope.' He added: 'It's true, but the continuity of the Church is made up of transition after transition.' **Whether we wish it or not, we are now on the way towards some Vatican III,** whose outlines are still vague and indiscernible. **This Vatican III must,** in its turn, **draw out what Vatican II contained only in germ; it must unfold what is now only potential, and make explicit its riches for the future. ... We must live the experience of Vatican II in that perspective, which will lead us from the present stage to the next one,** from the 'already' to the 'not yet.'"** [148]

Cardinal Suenens' references to the "pilgrim Church," to a certain evolutionary view of the Church and to the theory of the "already but not yet" should be kept in mind for the next Chapter.

*

§ 133   As we end this presentation of the proofs that substantiate the chronological-strategic concatenation of phases in the various usages of qualifying the Council theologically, it is quite difficult not to conclude that as a whole it favors the progressivist current. In view of this fact, it is possible to conjecture that the process was premeditated and executed following a certain methodology and, therefore, that it was a strategic maneuver.

*

§ 134   Was Vatican Council II pastoral? Was it dogmatic? We have seen that *de facto* it was simultaneously dogmatic and pastoral. However, for the progressivists it is convenient to have clouds of ambiguity hovering over the theological qualification of the Council. That enables them to confound possible reactions and to avoid comparisons between their doctrine and the constant and universal teaching of the ecclesiastical Magisterium.

*   *   *

---

148. L. J. Suenens, "Co-responsibility: Dominating Idea of the Council and its Pastoral Consequences," in V.A., *Theology of Renewal,* vol. II, p. 9.

Chapter VII

IS THERE A DOCTRINE
UNDERLYING THE AMBIGUITY?

§ 1

One becomes perplexed in the face of so many statements by renowned authors about the ambiguity of the Council and so many facts proving that it was indeed utilized to favor Progressivism.

Would there be, in addition to the strategic reasons already presented, a more profound explanation for such a lack of precision in conciliar language?

Would there be a new doctrine that justified the introduction of this ambiguity so alien to the habits of the ecclesiastical Magisterium?

This Chapter is not intended to present a definitive answer to such questions. We attempt to do that in another place in this Collection.[1] Nevertheless, as one considers the following texts by famous authors, a certain consistency already begins to show in this confused picture. *Needed to create*

Order out of chaos

1. A Hesitating Theology Is Supposedly Normal

To change the church

Novus ordo

§ 2

The text below by Fr. Karl Rahner gives rise to the idea that an insecure theology, subject to errors and pluralistic in its expressions, would be a normal thing:

"**Present-day theology** (based on exegesis, philosophy, contemporary spiritual life) **is faced with such a large number of problems,** has such a variety of instruments and conceptual enunciations at its disposal, **and is conscious of the ambiguity of all statements to such a point that it is no longer as easy as it used to be to oppose a real** or supposed **error with a new, positive statement immune from all confusion** and that gives all honest scholars the impression that it not only says something exact but also satisfies their own viewpoint. **This situation must be considered dispassionately** and then clarified, for only thus can one search for a more just and efficacious behavior for the Church and her Magisterium."[2]

---

1. Vol. VI, *Inveniet Fidem?,* Chaps. II, III.5, IV.2, 3; *Vol. VII, Destructio Dei,* Chaps. II.2, 3.B, III.3, IV.2.C; Vol. VII, *Fumus Satanae, passim*; Vol. IX, *Creatio,* Chaps. I, II, III, V; Vol. X, *Peccatum – Redemptio,* Chaps. V, VII, IX.

2. Karl Rahner, *Magistero e teologia dopo il Concilio* (Brescia: Queriniana, 1967), p. 32.

§ 3   Not satisfied with putting forward such surprising principles, Rahner goes so far as to conclude, no less disconcertingly, that one can legitimately disagree with the centuries-old teaching of the Church:

"The situation is one of a pluralism of methods, of a scientific theological terminology, of the vastness of the theological question in face of which a theologian on his own **can no longer be a specialist in an adequate way.** Because of this, **the theses of theologians are no longer a simple and clear** *yes* or *no* **to a doctrine presented in the traditional manner, formulated in an established way, but are often laid down in singular disagreement with traditional doctrine."** [3]

§ 4   Rahner goes on to frontally combat the clarity of the theological teaching before the Council, which he brands as "planned monolithism." He then pretends that he is opposed to excesses in theological pluralism. Nevertheless, he fails to define the limits that supposedly set apart his position – which he considers to be that of Vatican II – from the excesses he seems to oppose. In his clear combat against clarity and in his confused distinction regarding confusion, the notion prevails that theology should be always ambiguous and hesitating. Here is the text:

"Today, above all, **it is not the case of** simply saying the old truth, defending it in an authoritarian manner and **saying** *no* **to deviations.** It is necessary to defend this truth in such a way that it will have an effect and be accepted as true in good will and based on reality itself. To do that, it is not sufficient to appeal to the formal juridical authority of the Pope and the Bishops – regardless of whether this is done correctly from the formal doctrinal standpoint. Whether we like it or not, **we find ourselves in need of finding an intermediate path between a 'planned monolithism,' which made everything clear and** where everything of importance could be easily and, above all, swiftly decided with clarity, even decided upon by some form of papal declaration (encyclical, papal speech, statement by the Holy Office, etc.), and a **disconcerting confusion in which theologians and laity believe they may think and say anything they please in matters of faith.**   *"Says who?"*

"**The first route ... is no longer possible. It is clear that Vatican II preferred another method: it** was prudent and reserved in its dogmatic enunciations, **gave a more ample space to 'dialogue' within the Church, let the diverse theological tendencies be expressed more freely, etc.** It was seen that formulating a clear

---

3. *Ibid.,* pp. 32-33.

and binding doctrine [dogma] is not as easy as one would still have thought 20 years ago. ... **The second way is a road adulterated by a peculiar Catholic conception of faith and the Church: in the Church there must be a confession of faith; in the Church there simply is no room for equally legitimate but most different, disparate and even contradictory 'interpretations.'"** [4]

§ 5   Just prior to the next text, the German theologian emphatically praises Kant, German Idealism, Phenomenology, Existentialism, and the modernist Maurice Blondel. He then returns to his apologia for ambiguity:

Wrong - Thomism was clear, ordered!

"This internal ambiguity, however, is not only a mark of modern philosophy, but also of every human work and, therefore, of philosophy in all epochs; [5] **it must neither prevent us** from seeing what is Christian in the historic situation of modern times nor, consequently, **from understanding this situation in its essence as an element which a current theology, inasmuch as it is Christian philosophy, can no longer do without."** [6]

§ 6   Such principles are vehemently defended by Msgr. Luigi Sartori who, in his eagerness to praise ambiguity, boldly brands the distinction between good and evil, and truth and error, as "Manichaeism." This amounts to a violent, albeit indirect, criticism of the whole Catholic teaching that preceded Vatican II. Here is how he puts it:

it is ambiguous because evil people reconstruct historical events! - Sartori

"The ambiguity of History does not refer only to the world. I have already repeated innumerable times, and am more and more convinced, that Manichaeism is the most dangerous, the most latent, the most persistent heresy and temptation for the faithful: that of dividing the world into two distinct parts, here and there, good and evil people, we being among the good and having the truth. On the contrary, ambiguity in History also includes us, the Church." [7]

we must know good & evil! Sicut!

Rahner attacks Catholic Tradition, Scholastic Theology!

---

4. *Ibid.,* pp. 24-26.

5. It should be noted, in passing, that Rahner is laying down here a general principle. Ambiguity is a characteristic of philosophy in all epochs. Now then, since Catholic philosophy – and to a paramount degree Scholastic philosophy – is known to have been always characterized by crystalline clarity, by defending ambiguity Rahner implicitly combats the philosophy of the Church and, as a consequence, theology as a whole.

6. K. Rahner, "Théologie et anthropologie," in V.A., *Théologie d'aujourd'hui et de demain* (Paris: Cerf, 1967), p. 112.

7. Luigi Sartori, "Spirito Santo e storia," in V.A., *Lo Spirito Santo pegno e primizia del Regno – Atti della XIX Sessione di formazione ecumenica*

The way out indicated by this theologian to resolve the
§ 7 ambiguity of History, which supposedly also touches the Church, is to allow the latter to be judged by the sciences of the world. A rather curious criterion to be uttered by the president of the Italian Theological Association. Sartori goes on:

"Then, convinced of universal ambiguity, we will discern but also let ourselves be discerned and make ourselves discerned. I want to be practical. **One of the faithful – a theologian, a priest, a teacher – must, for example, submit his behavior and act of faith ... to the analysis of a psychologist, a pedagogue, a sociologist, an historian. As we preach, as we make theology, as we express the Faith, how many things must be discerned, diagnosed, even through the sciences! ... This principle obliges the Church and Christians to submit themselves to the judgment of others,** rather than only laying down their own."[8]

§ 8 Supposing an ever-vacillating theology, this same criterion establishing an equivalence between modern science and matters of Faith, is also taken up by Msgr. Carlo Molari, a theologian highly regarded for his many years as a teacher in Roman universities and as a member of the Sacred Congregation for the Doctrine of the Faith. Commenting on the "sensibility to the signs of the times" in a passage of *Gaudium et spes,* he pronounces it to be law. He then refers to the "profound meaning" of the conciliar term "pastoral." Molari says:

"The Council clearly expressed this law. It recognized that **in order for the Church 'to understand revealed truth more deeply' [and therefore, Molari comments, to apprehend the 'profound meaning' of its formulas] 'she has a special need for the help of those who, believers or non-believers, living in the world, are specialized in the various institutions and disciplines** and understand her profound mentality' (GS 44). **The reason for the dialogue which the Council invited believers to carry out with atheists,** Christians with followers of other religions, and Catholics with all Christians, **is not a tactical measure,** a missionary rule: **It is a requirement of faith."**[9]

According to Molari, Catholic doctrine is, then, habitually uncertain and hesitant. In order to remedy such defects and attain truth in its "profound meaning," the Church must resort to dialoguing

---

organizzata dal Segretariato Attivita Ecumeniche, Trento (Turin: Elie Di Ci, 1982), p. 79.

8. *Ibid., pp.* 79-80.

9. Carlo Molari, "La problematica del linguaggio teologico," in V.A., *Il linguaggio teologico oggi,* p. 89.

with those who are in error. [10] That is quite a singular notion of Faith to be preached by one of the best-known theologians in Italy!

*

§ 9

We call to mind that in this Item we will not analyze in depth what this notion of Faith is. Before delving into a more detailed analysis, we will highlight other important characteristics mentioned by these authors.

What we want to make clear is that there are numerous doctrinal explanations for the systematic use of ambiguity. They form the basis of a philosophy and theology that is uncertain and hesitant out of principle.

2. Subjacent to Ambiguity, the Doctrine of Universal Evolution

§ 10

A first impression comes to the mind of an analyst who wants to determine the doctrinal background underlying the systematic ambiguity of the Council: he notices that the Catholic Church, hitherto immutable in its doctrine and fixed in its structures, is presented as a 'Church in transition.'

Theologian Fr. Hans Küng writes: **"Just as John XXIII became a transition Pope ... and Council Vatican II was a transition council, so also is the Catholic Church today a transition Church**: it is in transition from a past still not completely elapsed to a future that is just beginning to appear." [11]

§ 11

Given his often radical stands, it would not be surprising if it were only Hans Küng who made such a statement. Nevertheless, authors as important as Fr. Chenu, inspirer of the conciliar Fathers' *Message to the World* in the beginning of the Council, [12] also admit, like Küng, the same principle of transition applied to the Church and her doctrine. They even go further as they define this transitional phase and link it to evolutionist principles.

---

10. Molari's thesis also has curious and equally grave consequences in the individual sphere: Since all aspects of reality are equivalent whether expressed by science or by the Faith, it would behoove man to pick those aspects he deems most adequate to construct the edifice of his own internal thinking. This is tantamount to saying that truth becomes a subjective reality.

11. H. Küng, *Veracidade*, p. 112.

12. *Jean Puyo interroge le Père Congar*, p. 128; R. Laurentin, *Bilan de la première session*, pp. 123-124; H. Fesquet, *Le journal de Concile*, p. 49.

From several standpoints, Fr. Chenu celebrates the introduction of the idea and the word *evolution* into conciliar texts.

First, from the standpoint of the formulation of the Faith: "Relative used to be a dangerous word ... up until the Council. **'Official' theology deemed the formulas expressing the faith to be immutable realities and would not even allow the word evolution, which the Council introduces, into its vocabulary."** [13]

Continuing from the point of view of dogmatic formulation, Fr. Chenu says: "That she [the Church] may be at the same time one and varied; that she may be one and multiform. For **humanity itself is in a multiform evolution. ... The dogmatic forms, which used to be considered absolute, are relative; relative to time, places, circumstances, evolution.** The same realities have different formulas." [14]

§ 12   *Second,* from the standpoint of the aim toward which the Church should tend: **"The very word evolution, obstinately placed under suspicion until then, was introduced three or four times, in spite of the negative reactions, into the text at critical points of *Gaudium et spes* as a reinforcement to the word 'history'**... I am pleased to quote Paul VI, then still Cardinal Montini, who makes an excellent comment: **'The order toward which Christianity tends is not a static one; it is an order in permanent evolution toward a better form; it is an equilibrium in movement.'"** [15]

§ 13   *Third,* regarding the essence of evolution, which is supposedly the "Spirit of God:" "Already chapter II [of *Gaudium et spes*], on describing the promotion of the common good in the human community, affirmed the presence of the Spirit in the 'evolution' of the world: 'The Spirit of God, who, with wondrous providence, directs the course of time and renews the face of the earth, assists at this development' (GS 26)." [16]

§ 14   Fr. Chenu then begins to develop the inner core of the conciliar doctrine by defending that it evolves according to the "signs of the times" that are revealed in History:

---

13. *Jacques Duquesne interroge le Père Chenu*, p. 47.

14. Marie-Dominique Chenu, Interview with the Author, Paris, February 20, 1983.

15. *Jacques Duquesne interroge le Père Chenu,* pp. 185-186.

16. M. D. Chenu, "Les signs des temps – Reflexions théologiques," in V.A., *L'Eglise dons le monde de ce temps – Constitution pastorale "Gaudium et spes,"* eds. Y. Congar and M. Peuchmaurd (Paris: Cerf, 1967), vol. II, p. 212.

"If one should qualify the Council by a main trait, I would propose to call it 'prophetic' in the full force and technical meaning of the word both in theological language and in the sociological vocabulary. A prophet is one who knows how to discern in current events that which places them in the continuity and ruptures of a History on the move. The prophet does not analyze structures and notions in their static condition, but in their dynamism. Thus, according to the famous formula, the future is already present. ...

"The *aggiornamento* of which John XXIII spoke is not an updating after which one again returns to the road with definitive formulas; it is a continuous application of one's intelligence to understand the 'signs of the times,' which emerge from the new values of the Gospel in a world in progress ... Evidently, the constitution *Gaudium et spes* is where this prophetism is more palpable. ... And if inspires many other declarations or decrees. This is why, gauging well the word and [applying it] in this sense, **one can say that Vatican II is obsolete.**

"To the extent that its basic element is prophetic, it requires its own outdating. If it is projected – in the proper sense – **toward the future,** the texts take on a new density inasmuch as the future is present. Needless to say, **it is difficult to define fidelity to the first inspiration, but it [fidelity] is the profound law. So, if I limit myself to only one commentary, only one discourse, I will actually be unfaithful.** This is why **it is normal for those responsible at all levels in their day-to-day decisions not always to be in agreement, as though there were a set of norms to be applied or a dogmatic formula to be taught.** One must undoubtedly lament deviations and ramblings, but they do not compromise the most important character of the Council's innovations."[17]

If one were to admit Fr. Chenu's explanation and draw only the major consequences from it, one sees that it would legitimize the abandonment of the dogmatic formulas of the past. Attachment to them would be "infidelity." The lack of unity in Church teaching would be considered normal, and a corollary would be to deny to the authority – especially that of the Pope – the competence to teach the same thing always and everywhere.

Historicity applied to the dogmas of Faith and to authority in the Church makes them relative to such an extent that one could ask whether such concept of historicity differs from Luther's principle of free interpretation. Since free interpretation relativizes the teaching of Catholic exegetic tradition and historicity extends relativism to the field

---

17. *Jacques Duquesne interroge le Père Chenu,* pp. 191-192.

of exegesis in dogmatics and ecclesiastical authority, one would say that historicity differs from free interpretation only in that it surpasses the latter in its developments, even though both adopt the same principles.

In his explanation of the new, historic and evolutionary view of the universe, Fr. Chenu provides elements of an anthropology according to which man should be considered as essentially linked to the evolutionary process. These doctrines, he claims, are the foundations of Vatican II. Fr. Chenu says:

"It is not by chance that the Christian is becoming more attentive to the peculiar character of the economy of salvation at a moment when man is becoming vitally aware of the historicity of his own nature. This is a normal convergence if it is true that faith, incarnate in the human subject, adjusts itself to man's structures and evolutions. We observe this, moreover, in the Council. **To the extent that the Council elaborated its Christological vision of a universe in movement, it experienced the need,** a need albeit inadequately satisfied, **for an anthropology.**

"Now, **in this 'Christian' anthropology, as it is being set forth more or less explicitly in theological statements, three attributes, three co-essential attributes of man are emerging:** *First,* that man is by nature social; *second,* **that he is so linked to the universe that the very matter of the cosmos is engaged in his destiny; and** *third,* **that man exists in History. Let us understand this** threefold **value ... written into man's nature and in some way, too, issuing from it, as distinct from abstract analysis or anything resembling either a timeless idea or an immutable definition.**

"**Thus it is that even in its vocabulary, the Council speaks rather of the human** *condition* **than of human** *nature* **as such, in contrast with Vatican I.** Without setting aside an essentialist philosophy, **one can readily have recourse to existential analyses.**"[18]

One sees that Fr. Chenu only broaches on some central ideas of the so-called Christian anthropology, its evolutionary character, its warm reception by the Council and its relations with Existentialism. But such ideas appear sufficient to confirm the impression that an evolutionary doctrine is subjacent to, and latent in, conciliar ambiguity.

---

18. M. D. Chenu, "The History of Salvation and the Historicity of Man in the Renewal of Theology," in V.A., *Theology of Renewal,* vol. I, pp. 163-164.

Evolutionary Doctrine

§ 16   This Item limits itself to verifying the emergence of evolution-ary doctrine as one of the principal characteristics of Vatican II. An analysis of this doctrine will be made further on. [19]

§ 17   Fr. Yves Congar, who worked on 10 of the 16 schemata of Vatican II, [20] also rejoices over the introduction of the concepts of evolution and historicity in the Council, historicity that he links with the idea of eschatology.

"One of the great novelties of Vatican II, as far as documents of the 'magisterium' are concerned, was the introduction of the eschatological point of view [21] **and, therefore, also of historicity.** That was lacking, and this grave lack had to do with the predominance of the juridical aspect. **Vatican II sees the Spirit of God present in the evolution of the human community, directing the course of time** and renewing the face of the earth (GS 26)."[22]

§ 18   Consistent with his admiration for the harbingers of the *nouvelle théologie,* [23] Cardinal Wojtyla in his book, *Alle fonti del Rinnovamento,* comments on the Constitution *Gaudium et spes.* He endorses the same principles defended by Congar and Chenu, taking evolution as a doctrinal substratum of conciliar ecclesiology:

---

19. Vol. III, *Animus Injuriandi II,* Chap. VI; Vol. VI, *Inveniet Fidem?,* Chap. IV. 2; Vol. VII, *Destructio Dei,* Chap. II; Vol. IX, *Creatio,* Chaps. II, III; Vol. X, *Peccatum – Redemptio,* Chap. V.

20. Alain Woodrow, "A Rome: Trente théologiens du monde entier pour accomplir le Concile," in *Informations Catholiques Internationales,* 5/15/1969, p. 9.

In a book-interview, Congar himself confirms: "I was quite involved with the preparation of most of the great conciliar texts: *Lumen gentium,* above all chapter II; *Gaudium et spes; Dei Verbum,* the texts on Revelation; ecumenism; religious liberty; the Declaration on relations with non-Christians; the missions. I also worked very much with the commission of the clergy that elaborated the text *Presbyterorum ordinis"* (*Jean Puyo interroge le Père Congar,* p. 149).

21. About the progressivist notion of eschatology, see Vol. III, *Animus Injuriandi II,* Chap. V.2.

22. Y. Congar, *Le Concile de Vatican II,* p. 170.

23. According to Fr. Mieczyslaw Malinski, a friend of Cardinal Wojtyla, in a study circle held at the Polish College during the Council: the latter stated: "Prominent theologians like Henri de Lubac, J. Danielou, Y. Congar, Hans Küng, R. Lombardi, K. Rahner and others, played an extraordinary role in these preparatory works [of the Council]" (*Mon ami Karol Wojtyla,* Paris: Centurion, 1980, p. 189).

"**The Church,** with the consciousness of the history of salvation that is her own, **goes out to meet that multiform evolution and the consciousness of today's man, which is linked to it.** ... **The paschal mystery of Jesus Christ is as open to eschatology** (in fact, it awakens 'the desire for the future world') **as it is to the evolution of the world, which the Council understands above all as a commitment to make the life of humanity and of men 'more humane.' Vatican II stressed the ethical meaning of evolution** ...

"**According to the doctrine of Vatican II, the Church participates in the evolution of the world** not only because the ideal of an ever more humane world is in accordance with the Gospel, but also because the history of salvation, in which the ultimate reality is prepared, necessarily passes by the realization of this world.

"Furthermore, this reality, almost embryonically and in a mysterious way, is already present in the world through the Church. So, **it is worthwhile,** above all, **to pay attention to the way in which the Church, according to the doctrine of the Council, participates in evolution and in progress toward an ever more humane world and, therefore, the way that she, in her conscience, continuously surpasses this evolution by orienting herself to the ultimate reality that will also be the 'plenitude of the kingdom of God.'**

"**In many passages,** but perhaps **primarily** in chapters III and IV of the Constitution *Gaudium et spes* (first part), **Vatican II speaks to us about the active participation of the 'kingdom' in the evolution of the world.** ...

"**The Church, as is evident, participates in the evolution of the world also by means of her own evolution. Vatican II expresses a mature consciousness of this truth and makes it one of the fundamental principles of the program of renewal. Here the historic consciousness of the Church is manifested in a particularly clear way. One may say that the whole conciliar conception of *'aggiornamento' (renovatio acomodata)* expresses, above all, this consciousness. By emphasizing the**

Rocco Buttiglione is no less explicit in this regard: "By stating that the work of Creation is included in that of Redemption and stressing the close connection between them, Wojtyla takes a stand in favor of the *nouvelle théologie* against positions that distinguish a pure order of nature, in which man fulfills himself as a purely natural being, from an order of grace ... This was the position of 'Roman theology' and was labeled as 'rightist.' ... From this standpoint, Wojtyla is certainly an innovator and aligns himself with the *progressivist* wing of the Council" *(Il pensiero di Karol Wojtyla, pp. 226-227).*

Social Kingship of J.C.

participation of the Church in the evolution of the 'world,' even by means of her own evolution; and, moreover, by proclaiming its necessity, Vatican II takes a stand in regard to the past and, simultaneously, **to the future**.

"This is a particular expression of the historic consciousness of the Church, for the usual category of history is only the past; the history of salvation, on the contrary, continuously reports to a dimension at the same time eschatological, essential and dynamic, and has, in itself, a unique reason to face the future. It is only in the totality of these dimensions that the Church preserves a full consciousness of her own identity; in it she also finds the basis of the whole program of renewal and *aggiornamento*. Only with this fundamental condition can the Church participate in the evolution of the world through her own 'evolution.' One may say that this is the most profound substratum of the 'historic consciousness' of the Church."[24]

*

§ 19   Several characteristics appear in the texts cited in this Item 2 that point to the evolutionist conception as the foundation of conciliar doctrine.

In brief, this concept of evolution is supposed to influence the teaching of Vatican II by:

- Justifying the relativization of dogmatic formulations.
- Making the Church tend toward an order continuously in movement.
- Reflecting the actual "Spirit of God"
- Making the Church and Catholic doctrine adapt continuously to the "signs of the times."
- Providing the basis for the Christological vision of a universe in movement and the "Christian" anthropology explained by Vatican II.
- Being present in the very essence of human nature.
- Being the foundation of conciliar eschatology.
- Being the prism for understanding the new ecclesiology born out of the Council.

---

24. Karol Wojtyla, *Alle fonti del rinnovamento – Studio sull'attuazione del Concilio Vaticano Secondo* (Vatican City: Libreria Editrice Vaticana, 1981), pp. 151-157.

It is hard not to see, therefore, that the doctrinal substratum of conciliar ambiguity appears to be a new vision of the universe, of man, of the Church and of God Himself. We will opportunely analyze them in this Collection. Here we will limit ourselves to noting that there is a subjacent doctrine supporting ambiguity in the conciliar documents, and that this doctrine is evolution.

3. *Ecclesia Semper Reformanda*

§ 20   The adoption of ambiguity as a norm of language starting from the principle that theology must be hesitating, uncertain and groping [25] and the notion of an evolving dogmatic teaching modifies the very conception of the Church. If such premises were to be admitted, the Church would come to be uncertain in her teaching: Now she would be right, now wrong. In order to know where truth is, she would have to consult a pluralistic array of theologians with contrasting opinions and to count on the help of other religions and the world; she would become insecure in choosing the means to fulfill her mission; she could have made mistakes and even sinned in her past, so she would have to repent and do penance; she would need to have a continuous reform in her customs and institutions.

Since the premises are absurd, so are the conclusions and consequences.

The Council is consistent in that it takes to the final consequences the premises of evolutionary ambiguity and hesitation; it concludes that the Church must always subject herself to a continuing reform. In so doing, it echoes the Lutheran-flavored principle of a "reformed Church" updated by Fr. Antonio Rosmini with the well-known expression, *Ecclesia semper reformanda* (Church always to be reformed).

§ 21   The introduction of the concept *Ecclesia semper reformanda* can be found in *Lumen gentium:* "The Church, however, clasping sinners to her bosom, at once holy and always in need of purification, follows constantly the path of penance and renewal." (LG 8)

§ 22   The same notion is present in the Decree *Unitatis redintegratio:* "Every renewal of the Church essentially consists in an increase of fidelity to her own calling. ... Christ summons the Church, as she goes her pilgrim way, to that continual reformation of which she

---

25. "Vatican II groped. No one directed it in a somewhat systematic way," says Fr. Congar *(Le Concile de Vatican II,* p. 18).

always has need, insofar as she is an institution of men here on earth. Consequently, if in various times and circumstances, there have been deficiencies in moral conduct or in Church discipline or even in the way that Church teaching has been formulated ... these should be set right at the opportune moment and in the proper way." (UR 6)

§ 23   Since no one whosoever is excluded from this process of "Church renewal," how can it avoid being influenced by the most censurable excesses? How can a Döllinger or even a Lenin or a Marx be rejected? What are the limits to this constant reform in the Church? How could one deny that she could be shaken constantly and almost routinely at her very foundations?

§ 24   How can one deny the validity of the premises and the consistency of the reasoning of Fr. Hans Küng as he makes explicit the immediate consequences of the two conciliar texts cited above?

Indeed, the theologian from Tübingen writes: **"External forms and structures of the Church make difficult and,** in certain circumstances, **even impossible the realization of good intentions."** [26]

He continues: **"Authentic reform is attentive to the creation of new structures** needed at the present time. Therefore, it is not only a simple restoration, but rather, and once again, a renewal. **We have already seen that this cannot be attained by an interior reform of hearts that would overlook a reform of the structures, institutions and regulations. ... What becomes continuously necessary is a reform that creates situations and structures,** one that does not dissolve the essence of the Church but that replaces it and makes it appear in all its credibility. ...

"That which men institute and constitute in this divine institution and constitution **participates in human imperfection and sinfulness and, therefore, needs continuous reform.** But since, as we have noted, its essence and historic realization cannot be adequately separated, **there are no domains that cannot be reformed. There is no stone or place of the ecclesiastical building not in need of constant reform. ...**

"Of the conciliar texts already cited, let us repeat only these two decisive phrases. 'Christ summons the Church, as she goes her pilgrim way, to that continual reformation *(ad hanc perennem reformationem)* of which she always has need, insofar as she is an institution of men here on earth' (UR 6). 'The Church, at

---

26. Hans Küng, *A Igreja* (Lisbon: Moraes, 1970), vol. II, p. 118.

once holy and **always in need of purification** *(semper purificanda),* **follows constantly the path of penance and renewal** *(poenitentiam et reformationem)*' (LG 8)." [27]

§ 25   Fr. Mario von Galli, SJ, of the magazine *Orientierung,* of Zurich, who followed the works of the Council as a *perito,* says this about applying the conciliar principles of reform to the liturgy:

"Thanks to the Council, we have learned that the Church is a congregation in perpetual movement, in incessant transformation; and if the liturgy is the living nucleus of the Church, it also changes to the rhythm of that evolution. **It was a gross error for us to have so doggedly attached ourselves to the same forms for four centuries. We have to become accustomed to the idea that the liturgy is something that must be in constant evolution.**" [28]

§ 26   Fr. Ansgar Ahlbrecht, OSB, likens the cited excerpt from *Unitatis redintegratio* on *Ecclesia semper reformanda* to another passage about the exercise of the Pope's authority, concluding in favor of a dialogue with the Protestants, who preach such a "reform" in the Church and combat papal authority:

"In its Decree on Ecumenism, **Vatican Council II says that the Church needs a continual reform.** ... In the Constitution on the Church, **the Church is presented less as an official society headed by the Pope than as the holy people of God, in which all authority has only a function of service. This** sacred **people** of God **appears,** in turn, **as a people filled with faults and imperfections, on pilgrimage through History, and also [it is filled with faults] regarding the division of the Church. This guilt is confessed with frankness,** thus creating a first premise for conversation with the separated brethren." [29]

§ 27   There is but a step from admitting guilt in the Church to admitting a "sinning Church." Such a step is taken with ease by the well-known Jesuit authors Maurizio Flick and Zoltán Alszeghy, professors at Gregorian University, whose works are widely publicized and frequently used as textbooks by Catholic institutions at the university level. About the genesis of the concept of a "sinning Church," the authors state:

---

27. *Ibid.,* pp. 124-125.

28. Mario von Galli, "La nueva liturgia," in V.A., *La reforma que llega de Roma* (Barcelona: Plaza & Janes, 1970), p. 53.

29. Ansgar Ahlbrecht, "Dialogo con los protestantes," in V.A., *La reforma que llega de Roma,* pp. 124-125.

"The Church is weak not only from the sociological stand-point **but also from the moral aspect** inasmuch as she fails to conform with that ideal of holiness that she must promote with her preaching and sacraments. ... **The Fathers of the Church and ecclesiastical writers before the Protestant reformation had no difficulty finding, in the biblical images of Rahab, Babylon, and the harlot of the** *Apocalypse,* **the type of Church that saves albeit being herself a sinner.** [30]

"**Only when the scorching criticism of the reformers concluded that the perverted Roman Church could not be the true Church of Christ was the sanctity of the Church unilaterally emphasized** and empirically demonstrated on the basis of an apologetic argumentation. Even in the 19th century, Rosmini was censured for speaking of the five wounds of the Church; **it was necessary to wait until Vatican Council II for it to be again recognized that the pilgrim Church is called by Christ to a continual reformation** 'of which she always has need insofar as she is an institution of men here on earth. Consequently, if in various times and circumstances there have been deficiencies in moral conduct or in Church discipline, or even in the way that Church teaching has been formulated ... these should be set right at the opportune moment and in the proper way' (UR 6). **As Rahner's analyses show,** [31*] **the Council, though not applying the adjective 'sinful' to the Church, in effect admits her sinful aspect."** [32]

§ 28   One may conclude that the underlying thought that oriented the Council, besides containing an evolutionist substratum in its texts and indicating a "Copernican" transformation of the vision of the universe and man, adopts a specific concept of Church: a Church in continual reform which, in turn, presupposes or generates – depending upon how you look at it – a "sinful Church."

*

---

30. On the progressivist emphasis given to the "sinful" aspect which they claim exists in the essence of the Church; on the appropriateness of the use of the metaphor of harlot to express that aspect; as well as on the studies of Patristics regarding the matter, see Vol. II, *Animus Injuriandi I,* Chap. IV; Appendix II, *passim.*

31*. K. Rahner, *La Chiesa peccatrice nei decreti del Concilio Vaticano II* (Rome, 1968), pp. 443-478.

32. Maurizio Flick and Zoltán Alszeghy, *Il mistero della croce – Saggio di teologia sistematica* (Brescia: Queriniana, 1978), pp. 411-412.

§ 29

Even though the analysis typical of this Volume I essentially consists in demonstrating the existence of ambiguity in the Council and it could, therefore, stop here, it is also opportune to ask what consequences this new concept of Church will entail.

Is not this conciliar view of the Church disorienting for a Catholic? How can one admit that she, the light of the world, may present her truth as wavering and ambiguous? How can one imagine that she, one in her Faith, infallible in her extraordinary Magisterium as well as in certain conditions in her ordinary Magisterium, [33] by the special assistance of the Holy Spirit, now shows herself to be hesitating in her dogma, unsteady in her morals, fragmented by contrasting opinions? How can she assume a confused "theological pluralism" to replace the unity and clarity of her teaching of old?

With such premises, how can she not abandon this secure assistance from the Holy Spirit to look for direction in the broken compass of other religions or the often fleeting certainties of modern sciences? How can a cry of affliction be restrained when one sees her, most holy in her institution, structures, laws and customs, being treated as a vile sinner, given second place to heresy – as was Our Lord to Barabbas – pronounced guilty and almost forced to ask pardon for crimes she has never committed? How can one not remember the Way of the Cross and the Calvary as one sees her, the innocent one, being led as a malefactor to the gallows where she is expected to reject her perennial mission of Queen and Mistress?

§ 30

What an atrocious affliction! All the more so since it is confirmed by the "clinical" analysis of great Shepherds who can think of no "medicine" for her other than perpetual adaptation.

Let us look, for example, at the testimony of Cardinal Döpfner, moderator of the sessions of Vatican II, then Archbishop of Munich. In a homily addressed to German Catholic politicians a few years after the Council, Döpfner says:

"An unusual picture has now taken shape. The Church, which until today has answered everything with so much assurance, is now asking questions. She who was used to sovereignly defending herself, is recognizing errors of the past. She, who conveyed an impression of solidity and cohesion (How proud we were of it!) now appears to be dissolving in contrasting opinions. This disorients and disturbs many Catholic Christians. Including you, who are out there in faraway mis-

---

33. On the ordinary and extraordinary Magisterium, see A. V. Xavier da Silveira, "Qual a autoridade doutrinária dos documentos pontifícios e conciliares?," in *Catolicismo,* October 1967.

sionary posts in the world ... who saw the Church as a solid support with her dependable guidelines, her cohesion, her courage with a force and clarity that were not modern. At times it will seem to you as though you have lost your support, and that is understandable: **The image of the post-conciliar Church is multi-faceted and polyvalent.**" [34]

What is the solution that Cardinal Döpfner offers his perplexed audience? He continues:

"Now, [each one] must place himself in the correct position, attain the right perspective. It is of fundamental importance to firmly believe that the Council was a unique, pentecostal event, that it carried out an authentic testimony of Christ. It is necessary to see the correlations with the whole, the relation between cause and effect starting from the fixed center, which is now seen with a new clarity. We must visualize from this center the apparently convulsive oscillations in the magnetic needle of Church life. We must commit ourselves deeply to the general lines of the Council and the balanced coordination of each of its declarations; there is need for a clarifying dialogue. Above all, we should not isolate ourselves and set ourselves apart like Thomas during Easter week ... Through cooperation, we understand better what the Church is properly aiming at, even though many forms are still imperfect and marked by experience and transition." [35]

This excerpt by the German Cardinal does not seem to provide any answer to the anguishing problems he raises: The only measures suggested are not to isolate oneself and to dialogue. So, he leaves up in the air the tragic picture described above and does not say how to avoid or stop it. One is left without knowing whether or not it is a goal of the post-conciliar Church to present herself as a Church without assurance, defense or cohesion, a Church diluted by contrasting opinions and thus causing disorientation among the faithful.

The description by Cardinal Döpfner and his "answer" are cited here as characteristic and symptomatic of the attitude of many Prelates faced with the same problem.

*

§ 31   So, in this Item, we have seen one more important consequence of ambiguity and the hesitant and evolutionist doctrine: It is a new conception of Church, *Ecclesia semper reformanda.*

*

---

34. Julius Döpfner, *La Chiesa vivente oggi,* p. 379.

35. *Ibid.,* pp. 379-380.

As a conclusion to this Chapter, we are led to state that in the conciliar ambiguity, described in the many texts mentioned here, a new doctrine of an evolutionist nature, which supposes a new conception of the Church and also of the Faith,[36] finds it easy to cloak itself.

*   *   *

---

36. The new progressivist conception of the Faith is dealt with in Vol. VI, *Inveniet Fidem?* and the new vision of the Church in Vol. XI, *Ecclesia.*

Chapter VIII

ANOTHER SOURCE OF AMBIGUITY –
TENDENTIOUS OMISSIONS

§ 1   Having thus looked at several aspects of the polyvalent conciliar language, it is timely to note that there is also another type of ambiguity: tendentious omissions. It was through omissions that Vatican II introduced ambiguity into several official texts on topics that both the Magisterium and Church tradition had already unequivocally defined. Not a few authors believe that such omissions, as we shall see in this Chapter, were made intentionally to open the way for certain ideas cherished by the progressivist current.

It is obviously more delicate to analyze an omission in a text than an ambiguous word that actually appears in it. In this Volume we do not intend to hold as indisputable the interpretations of Vatican II omissions emitted by the authors cited below. Nevertheless, they are well worth noting on account of their consistency with everything we have seen so far on the purpose and doctrine underlying conciliar ambiguities.

It seems indispensable for a Reader intent on forming an overall view of the question of ambiguity to know several of such omissions and the comments to which they gave rise. This is why, by way of a sampling, this Chapter focuses on them.

We will cite some of these omissions accompanied by comments of progressivist authors.

1. Virginity of Mary Most Holy

§ 2   Negation of Our Lady's virginity is a frequent fixture in progressivist circles. Some deny it directly, others indirectly by vaguely speaking about some spiritual virginity while downplaying bodily virginity. It is characteristic of this tendency no longer to attribute virginal conception exclusively to Our Lady.[1]

§ 3   Msgr. Gerard Philips, the primary writer of the final text of *Lumen gentium*, explains the sinuous circumlocutions he employed when dealing with the virginity of Mary during childbirth:

---

1. Highly expressive of this general tendency among progressivists is the thesis of Rahner, one of the most relevant thinkers of the Council, which denies Our Lady's *virginitas in partu* [virginity during childbirth]. This thesis is analyzed in Vol. II *Animus Injuriandi I,* Chap. VII.4.

"The conciliar text [LG 57] did not avoid the expression of the Gospel, but pointed out another fact of undeniable importance: 'The Son did not diminish her virginal integrity, but rather consecrated it.' This circumlocution is very simple, and the formula chosen is liturgical and traditional." [2]

Msgr. Philips thus justifies this circumlocution: "It is known that many questions, especially of late, have been raised about *virginitas in partu*." [3]

Philips later explains that some Bishops reacted to this and wanted the text to affirm without subterfuge the characteristic of Mary: *Virgo ante partum, in partu, et post partum* – Virgin before childbirth, in childbirth, and after childbirth. But their reaction was not taken into account. "The Council considered that the terminology employed could suffice for that end, without entering into biological details" [sic].[4]

The official conciliar writer goes on: "One thing is certain: **the virginity in question ... is not taught as a personal privilege of Mary.**" [5]

Basing his argument vaguely on the Church Fathers, Msgr. Philips continues his text, not cited here, trying to overestimate the spiritual aspect of virginity to the detriment of the bodily aspect, considered merely as a "symbol." [6]

2. Original Sin

§ 4

The following text by Canon Jacques Mouroux, a theologian held in considerable renown for works written before the Council, refers to an intentional omission which, he points out, weakens the doctrine on Original Sin.

"One cannot describe the human condition without including the tragic reality of sin. One of the first texts[7] contained an item about original sin. Text I no longer carried any development on it. Many [conciliar] Fathers rightly considered the text to be 'exaggeratedly optimistic,' and so this tragic dimension of human condition was rein-

---

2. G. Philips, *La Chiesa e it suo Mistero*, p. 544.

3. *Ibid.*

4. *Ibid.*

5. *Ibid.*

6. *Ibid.*

7. The final text of *Gaudium et spes* approved by the conciliar Fathers on December 7, 1965, was preceded by several drafts, of which Mouroux mentions three in an abbreviated manner as Tx. I, Tx. II and Tx. III.

troduced. [8*] Incidentally, the Council wanted neither to add original sin to the title of chap. I, 'On the Corruption of Nature,' [9*] nor to expressly mention original sin and certain doctrinal precisions [10*] since that was not necessary for its objective. [11*] Always pursuing its pastoral objective, it therefore limited itself, as far as this point was concerned, to the doctrinal minimum indispensable for the equilibrium of Christian truth and the clarification of man's painful condition." [12]

§ 5   Commenting on the three most important statements in *Gaudium et spes* on man's decayed condition, Mouroux points out the text's discretion in topic 18 (the mystery of death), as it mentions the sin of Adam: "Note, by the way, the text's discretion: it explicitly mentions original sin (GS 18b) without, however, making any precise comments. It says that the depth of evil harkens back to Romans 1:21-25, [13] which aims not at original sin, but rather at the behavior of sinful humanity as such." [14]

§ 6   If the comment by Mouroux about *Gaudium et spes* is well-founded, as we are inclined to believe, the way would be open for the negation of the sin of Adam and Eve and for the defense of the notion – opposed to dogma – that at its source original sin was not the sin of a couple but that of "all humanity."

8*. Rel. by Msgr. Garrone, Tx. II, p. 6.

9*. Tx. III, p. 154.

10*. Resuming Rom 1:21-25 and 5:12-21.

11*. Tx. III, 1, p. 157; 4 and 6, p. 158.

12. Jacques Mouroux, "Situation et signification du chapitre I (de la *Gaudium et spes):* Sur la dignité de la personne humaine," in V.A., *L'Eglise dans le monde de ce temps,* vol. I, p. 237.

13. Perhaps due to some reviewing oversight, Jacques Mouroux transcribes the conciliar text referring to Rom. 1:21-25, whereas *Gaudium et spes* quotes Rom. 5:21 and 6:23.

In fact, here is the reference to original sin: "The Christian faith teaches that bodily death, from which man would have been immune had he not sinned (Wis 1:13; 2:23-24; Rom 5:21; 6:23; Jas 1:15) will be overcome when that wholeness which he lost through his own fault will be given once again to him by his almighty and merciful Savio." (GS 18b).

Another confusion is caused by Mouroux's statement in the first quotation that the "Council did not want ... to mention original sin expressly," whereas in another quote on the same page of his book he says that the text "explicitly mentions original sin." It is hard not to see the contradiction between the two statements.

14. J. Mouroux, "Situation et signification du chapitre I," p. 237.

The premise of this theory is that Adam could be a generic, cosmic reality: humanity. The designation *man* supposedly means not so much an individual, but the human genre. By the same token, *Christ* would also be a generic and cosmic reality. *Adam,* then, would be mankind in its initial stage; and the resurrected Christ, mankind in its final stage, representing the beginning of divinized humanity. [15]

The author says that the Council did not define whether Adam was an individual or a group. Hence doors are opened for a progressivist conception of a sin of humanity rather than the sin of a first couple. Indeed, Mouroux affirms: "The mystery of Christ and that of man finally make up only one mystery. And this is why the Council ... directly relates the mystery of the first man to that of the Word Incarnate. By saying 'Adam, the first man,' the Council repeats a biblical expression, [16*] but it does not intend to resolve here whether Adam was an individual or a group. [17*]" [18]

3. The Existence of Hell

§ 7

Hans Küng assembles documents of the perennial teaching of the Church on this topic and contrasts them with statements of Vatican II. He shows that the Council's omission about the eternal punishment of those who find themselves outside the Church, especially atheists, brings into question the very existence of Hell, which, therefore, is supposedly "an unresolved matter." Küng writes:

"In 1442 the Council of Florence ... pronounced a whole series of human groups worthy of condemnation ... 'The Holy Roman Church ... firmly believes, confesses and proclaims that no one outside of the Catholic Church, be he a pagan or a Jew, a non-believer or separated from its unity, takes part in eternal life, but on the contrary, falls into the eternal fire prepared by the Devil and his angels unless he unites himself to her (the Catholic Church) before his death.' That which Benedict XII defined in the Constitution *Benedictus Deus* (1336) also holds true for Catholics: 'We define: Just as God universally ordered, the souls of those who die having committed a mortal sin go

---

15. This strange doctrine is broached in Vol. VIII, *Fumus Satanae,* Chaps. II, IV, V.4.B; Vol. *X, Peccatum-Redemptio,* Chaps. V, VI, VII, VIII.2.E, IX.2.

16*. 1 Cor 15:45-47.

17*. Tx. III, n. 3, p. 186.

18. J. Mouroux, "Situation et signification du chapitre I," p. 249.

immediately to Hell, where they are tormented by eternal punishments.'...

"Instead, **Vatican Council II** (even **without revoking or** expressly **correcting the definition of Florence** ...) **declares that even atheists in good faith can reach eternal salvation.** With this, evidently, **the question of Hell is not resolved,** since it was not dealt with directly in Vatican Council II." [19]

Now then, if everyone can be saved, both those who are in the Catholic Church and those outside of her, it does not make any sense, from this progressivist perspective, for Hell to exist. This is tantamount to denying its existence. Hence one can better understand Küng's general affirmation that the "question of Hell is not resolved."

§ 8
For his part, Fr. René Laurentin, author of a well-known chronicle of the Council, on assembling a "list of silences" of Vatican II, comments:

"**Another category of silences: those concerning disregarded sectors in which some maintain their beliefs in an archaic and somehow shameful form, while others abandon them. [This is the case regarding] Angels, about whom the Council said nothing, the cult of Saints, or Hell. The problem of Hell was only materially raised and superficially resolved by adding a quote from Scripture to the** *Constitution on the Church* **(LG 48); nevertheless, the terrible mystery of the refusal of love**

---

19. Hans Küng, *Vida Eterna?* (Madrid: Cristiandad, 1983), pp. 218-219.

Küng is right in saying that Vatican II did not directly deal with Hell. The only two references made by *Lumen gentium* do not mention it by name and broach the topic only in passing:

"But since we know neither the day nor the hour, we should follow the advice of the Lord and watch constantly so that, when the single course of our earthly life is completed (Heb 9:27), we may merit to enter with Him into the marriage feast and be numbered among the blessed (Matt 25:31-46), and not, like the wicked and slothful servants (Matt 25:26), be ordered to depart into the eternal fire (Matt 25:41), into the outer darkness where 'men will weep and gnash their teeth' (Matt 22:13 and 25:30)" (LG 48c).

The other conciliar text that deals with condemnation to Hell clears the way for the salvation of non-Christians by vaguely declaring: "But very often, deceived by the Evil One, men have become vain in their reasonings, have exchanged the truth of God for a lie and served the world rather than the Creator (Rom 1:21, *25).* Or else, living and dying in this world without God, they are exposed to ultimate despair" (LG 16).

and its eternal consequences should not have been put under the table." [20]

§ 9   Incidentally, the deliberate omission of the word Hell in the chapter of *Lumen gentium* on the eschatological origin of the Church disconcerted innumerable conciliar Fathers, some of whom expressed their perplexities in the plenary Assembly. In spite of that, the final text of the document did not include it. According to a summary by Kloppenburg, several Prelates intervened during the 80th general congregation held on September 15, 1964. They expressed themselves in this way:

Cardinal Rufini, Archbishop of Palermo: "There are repetitions in the text [he gives three examples]. And **there are omissions: Why does it not speak about Hell?** Why is Purgatory, whose existence is a dogma of Faith, hardly mentioned? *Schema capitis VII iterum retractetur.*" [21]

§ 10   Latin Patriarch of Jerusalem Alberto Gori: "It is certainly opportune to stress the eschatological nature of the human vocation. But **n. 48** [of *Lumen gentium*] **should also remind us of Hell,** of which Revelation and all of Tradition speak to us. **Such an omission on the part of a Council would be inadmissible.**"

The orator then goes on to expound the three reasons why the text must also mention Hell: because it is an indisputable reality of Christian revelation; because the knowledge of this truth is of great importance for every human person; and because such a mention is especially needed at the present time:

"For the quest for a better material life and hedonism destroy man's esteem for friendship with God and the sense of sin; as a consequence, the consideration of Hell is cast aside as inopportune and even condemned as opposed to the present-day mentality. The preachers no longer want to talk about it. So the conviction can prevail, among the faithful, that Hell is something obsolete, whose reality can be legitimately cast into doubt. **Therefore, the Council must expressly mention the doctrine on Hell.**" [22]

§ 11   Archbishop Enrico Nicodemo of Bari: "Also **missing** [in this chapter VII] **is a word about Hell,** which is the penalty for sin. And sin is a treason against the vocation for holiness." [23]

---

20. R. Laurentin, *Bilan de la quatrième session,* pp. 356-358.

21. Ernesto Ruffini, Comments on the Existence of Hell, in B. Kloppenburg, *Concilio Vaticano II,* vol. IV, p. 15.

22. Alberto Gori, Comments on the Existence of Hell, p. 16.

23. Enrico Nicodemo, Comments on the Existence of Hell, p. 17.

§ 12   Archbishop Secundo Garcia de Sierra y Méndez of Burgos: "What is said about Purgatory may be ecumenical, but it is little. Vague allusions are not sufficient. There are pastoral reasons for one to speak clearly. Also the fear of God must be announced to today's naturalistic man. But **Hell is not even mentioned throughout the chapter.**"[24]

§ 13   The following day, during the 81st general congregation, Bishop Biagio d'Agostino of Vallo di Lucania, Italy, also criticized chapter VII's omission in regard to the question of Hell:

"The naturalist and materialist mentality of our times requires that we stress the truths of the *Novissimis* more. Unfortunately, current preaching deals little with them. And the present text is weak. It makes only a timid allusion to Purgatory. Everyone knows the doctrine of the separated brethren on this subject. For this reason we must clearly enunciate our doctrine. And **in the whole text not a word is found about Hell. Today, as we see ourselves oppressed by public and private delinquency, it is wholesome to call to mind not only the mercy, but also the justice of the eternal Judge.**"[25]

§ 14   Therefore, it is very difficult to argue that the failure to mention Hell in *Lumen gentium* and the other conciliar documents was not deliberate.

4. Distinction between the Church Militant and the Church Triumphant

§ 15   *Lumen gentium* mentions only once the distinction between the celestial Church and the terrestrial Church. Delving into this matter would have been opposed to the progressivist desire to unify the two realities. A statement by Msgr. Philips sheds light on why the distinction was enunciated only once and on the depth of the Council's thinking about the matter:

"The terms, 'celestial Church,' 'Church on earth,' could lead us astray toward a certain dualism, as if there were two Churches, one below and another up above. Our commentary deliberately avoids this language. Needless to say, there is only one Church, but the situation of its members varies. The following article (LG 50) insists on

---

24. Secundo Garcia de Sierra y Mendez, Comments on the Existence of Hell in the Conciliar Assembly, p. 19.

25. Biagio d'Agostino, Comments on the Existence of Hell in the Conciliar Assembly, p. 21.

this unity, even though the terminology 'terrestrial Church,' 'celestial Church' is stained by a certain division and localization." [26]

Eliminating the distinction between the Church Triumphant and the Church Militant, which, according to Philips would have been ideal, leads to confusion and ambiguity, and casts a shadow on the fight, which is indissociable from the earthly mission of Holy Church.

5. The Roman Character of the Church

§ 16   Philips and Congar, two conciliar *periti* who worked assiduously on Council documents, especially on the text of the Constitution on the Church, refer to the conscious omission of the Roman character of the Church in topic 8a.

Msgr. Philips, who wrote the final text of *Lumen gentium,* states: "We profess in the Creed one, holy, Catholic and apostolic Church ... Where shall we find this Church? Concretely it is incarnated in the society governed by the Successor of Peter and the Bishops in communion with him. The text does not say: The Church is the Catholic community; and it even omits the adjective, 'Roman,' which is found in the Tridentine profession of Faith, because it aims to stress that which is of fundamental importance, particularly the succession beginning with Peter and the Apostles." [27]

§ 17   Fr. Congar also attests to the omission of the 'Roman' character of the Church in *Lumen gentium*: "But it remains to be known whether *Lumen gentium* strictly, that is, exclusively, identifies this Church Body of Christ with the Roman Catholic Church, as did the Encyclical *Mystici Corporis.* One can doubt this since one finds that not only the attribute 'Roman' is missing, something of little importance since there is mention of the Church 'governed by the successor of Peter and the Bishops in communion with him,' but also avoids saying that only Catholics are members of the mystical body." [28]

§ 18   According to Fr. Schillebeeckx, also a conciliar *perito, Lumen gentium*'s omission of the Roman character of the Church also extends to the Holy Pontiff, as the document, in the above-mentioned topic 8a, emphasizes the title "successor of Peter":

---

26. G. Philips, *La Chiesa e it suo Mistero,* pp. 484-485.

27. *Ibid.,* pp. 110-111.

28. Y. Congar, *Le Concile de Vatican II,* p. 160.

"It is typical that the *Dogmatic Constitution on the Church* completely lacks the statement that the Bishop of Rome governs the Church ... in his capacity as Pope. Preference is given to the formal reason for his primacy, the 'successor of Peter,' so that the qualification 'Roman' in the formulas 'Roman Pontiff' and 'Roman Church' only have material significance." [29]

As Congar pointed out, the omission of the Roman character of Holy Church is done to facilitate ecumenism. It favors ambiguity in determining who is a member of the "Church of Christ."

6. Survival of the Western Patriarchates

§ 19

The existence of Patriarchs in the Church, according to a venerable tradition, is an honorific prerogative of the Seats that have been personally governed by St. Peter. There are thus the Patriarchates of Rome, Jerusalem, Antioch and Alexandria. [30] Patriarchates also exist by special privileges granted to communities with their own history, like those of Constantinople, Venice, Lisbon, the Western Indies (Toledo) and the Eastern Indies (Goa), in addition to the Armenian, Chaldean, Copt, Melkite, and Maronite Patriarchates. [31]

In the Decree *Orientalium ecclesiarum,* even though the Eastern Patriarchs are mentioned, [32] not the least reference is made to the Patriarchs of the West. According to Philips, this was done in order to strengthen the position of the Bishops' Conferences. Yet it seems to point to a tendency toward extinguishing this elevated honorific prerogative.

---

29. E. Schillebeeckx, "Igreja ou igrejas?" in V.A., *Cinco problemas que desafiam a Igreja hoje,* p. 32.

30. Alexandria was considered to be indirectly governed by St. Peter since his disciple St. Mark had been there once. Eusebius of Cesarea, *Historia eclesiastica* (Buenos Aires: Ed. Nova, 1950), lib. II, chaps. 16, 24, pp. 75, 93-94; St. Jerome, *De viris illustribus,* XXXVI, in Jules Lebreton, *L'Ecole Chrétienne d'Alexandrie avant Origène,* in V.A., *Histoire de l'Eglise,* vol. II, p. 226; Jacques Zeiller, *La propagation du Christianisme,* in V.A., *Histoire de l'Eglise,* vol. I, p. 283; J. Baptista Pighi, *Institutions Historiae Ecclesiasticae* (Verome: Bibliopolae Editoris Pontificii, 1922), vol. I, p. 30.

31. In addition to the honorific prerogatives we are stressing, some of these Patriarchates also have a greater or lesser power of jurisdiction. For greater details, see Raymond Vancourt, *"Patriarcats,"* in DTC, vol. XI, cols. 2253-2297.

32. OE 7-11.

§ 20

      Gérard Philips comments on this matter: "To create a new Patriarchate, for example, for a continent other than Eurasia, would not appear to us to be a very opportune idea. Such an institution would be artificial and obsolete ... **The honorific Patriarchates have lost their meaning in the West.** On the contrary, the Bishops' Conferences ... have a great future ... Collegial solidarity will find here a vast and important field of application. **An attentive reader will not have failed to notice the silence of the conciliar text about the Patriarch of the West, who is none other than the Roman Pontiff.**[33] [Those who work with] the ecumenical question strive to define this inevitable problem and to find a peaceful solution for it."[34]

7. The Council's Position Regarding Freudian Psychoanalysis

§ 21

      It is well to make one more observation in this Chapter on tendentious omissions, not about doctrinal points or ecclesiastical institutions that the Council left in the shadows, but about a new doctrine that apparently it wants to impose. The text of *Gaudium et spes* is remiss about modern science and, especially, Freudian psychoanalysis,

---

33. As one recalls, among the factors that caused the Schism of the East was the demand that the Papacy and the Patriarchate of Constantinople be placed on equal footing.

Beginning with the illegal succession of Photius to the See of Constantinople (858-859), this demand grew stronger (Emile Amann, "L'époque carolingienne," in V.A., *Histoire de l'Eglise,* vol. VI, pp. 471, 494). After his death Photius became the symbol of an imagined equality between Constantinople and Rome (*ibid.,* p. 501), which later fermented and helped to cause the Eastern Schism.

Ever since, one of the strongest resentments that the Eastern Schismatics have nourished against the Pope is his superiority, of divine right, over every Seat in Christendom, which cannot even be compared to the schismatic seat of Constantinople, self-named orthodox (St. Robert Bellarmine, *De Romano Pontifice,* lib. I, chap. 23; lib. II, chap. 12, in *Opera omnia,* vol. I, pp. 354-345, 383; Louis Billot, *De Ecclesia Christi,* Rome: Aedes Universitatis Gregoriannae, 1921, q. XIV, tes. 23, p. 593; H. Hurter, *Theologiae dogmaticae compendium,* Paris/ Innsbruck: Lib. Academica Wagneriana, 1883, vol. I, pp. 379-380).

Therefore, the silence about the Patriarchate in the West apparently is also aimed at avoiding an affirmation of the primacy of the Pope over the Patriarchate of Constantinople, considered as the *primus inter pares* [first among equals] of the Greek Schismatic Church.

34. G. Philips, *La Chiesa e it suo Mistero,* p. 277.

which it should have criticized. In so doing, it appears to open the gates to the doctrine of the Austrian analyst.

It is Jacques Mouroux who notes the omission and defends this opinion: "By pointing primarily to the conquest of the material world, the Council, needless to say, leaves the door open to 'human sciences,' which are increasingly important for the knowledge and equilibrium of present-day man and, therefore, for pastoral care(GS 54, 62b). [35] If the Council explicitly refused to consider psychoanalysis, it was undoubtedly because the question – as it was posed – did not appear to be mature and was fraught with dangerous ambiguities. But even this silence leaves the door open for prudent research afterward." [36]

§ 22

Mouroux appears to be right when he interprets the opening to culture and sciences as being, in the final analysis, an opening to Freud. Indeed, these words by Fr. Congar resound with the same meaning. He says that ancient culture "no longer touches today's man, who seeks a different culture whose Fathers will be neither Athanasius nor Augustine but Marx, Freud and modem technology. The Catholic Church herself is abandoning her old culture, which has been hers ever since Constantine up to Vatican II." [37]

*

§ 23

It is not our intent to conclude that such omissions indisputably mean exactly what each author has commented on the various matters. We only affirm that these omissions are such as to give rise to these and other comments, thereby leading us to conjecture that the Council also used ambiguous omissions as a resort to favor Progressivism.

*   *   *

---

35. Here is the part of *Gaudium et spes* to which Mouroux refers as opening the door to psychoanalysis: "In pastoral care, sufficient use should be made not only of theological principles but also of the findings of secular sciences, especially psychology and sociology." (GS 62b)

36. J. Mouroux, *La Chiesa e it suo Mistero*, p. 241.

37. Y. Congar, "Salvación y liberación," in V.A., *Conversaciones de Toledo – Teología de la liberación* (Burgos: Aldecoa, 1973), p. 202.

Chapter IX

A DOCTRINAL CONSEQUENCE: AMBIGUITY IMPLIES CONCESSIONS TO THE OTHER RELIGIONS AND TO THE MODERN WORLD [1]

§ 1   Having seen how the ambiguity in the texts and doctrine of Vatican II favors a new concept of the world, of man and of the Church, we will now analyze how such a procedure also implies a virtual denial of the traditional missionary and militant characters of the Church.[2] Nothing could appear more consistent. Once the Church has been denied her condition of

---

1. Volume V of this Collection will study in more detail the concessions of the conciliar Church to the other religions and the modern world. This Volume looks at the doctrinal underpinnings of the ecclesiastical Magisterium that condemn both types of concession and the apparent or real opposition of Vatican II to traditional Church doctrine in this matter (Vol. V, *Animus Delendi II*, Part I, Premises 1, 2; Part II, Premises 1, 2). We will not cite the pontifical condemnations here.

2. It is necessary to distinguish two concepts of missionary Church and the missions. Until Vatican II, the goal of the missions was to convert heretics, schismatics, Jews and pagans from the errors they professed in order to bring them into the bosom of the Church. After Vatican II, the "missions" came to signify a movement of the Church toward the heretics, schismatics, Jews and pagans without asking any conversion of them. What prevails is the orientation made explicit by Msgr. Louis Pelatre, apostolic Vicar of Constantinople: "Proselytism is banned" ("Islam: la paura ingiustificata," interview with Francesco Strazzari, in *Il Regno,* 3/15/1993, p. 147). According to this conception, it is the Church that must adapt to others.

This Volume I refers to the perennial missionary character of the Church, which it deems as the exclusive fountain of all truth, that is, the one that preceded the Council and is based on the mandate of the Savior: "Go ye into the whole world, and preach the Gospel to every creature. He that believeth and is baptized, shall be saved; but he that believeth not shall be condemned" (Mark 16:15-16).

On the clash between the traditional character of the missions with the neo-missiology *aggiornata,* see the work by Plinio Corrêa de Oliveira, *Tribalismo indígena: ideal comuno-missionário para o Brasil no século XXI* (São Paulo: Vera Cruz, 1977).

indefectible Mistress of the truth through the concept *Ecclesia semper reformanda,* and her santicty through the concept of "sinning Church," it becomes implicitly untenable that she continue to be militant "against the perfidy of heretics" and missionary to become Queen of peoples and builder of cultures and civilizations.

What will follow are excerpts from the works of highly regarded commentators of the Council who clearly affirm the need, based on the premises of the Council, to abolish the defense and propagation of the Faith both with respect to the other religions and to the modern world.

1. Concessions to the Other Religions [3]

§ 2

In this Item 1, which is intended to deal with the concessions to the other religions arising from ambiguity in the conciliar texts, the subject matter is divided into two parts. *First,* we wish to focus our attention, although not exhaustively, on one of the most important and debated religious topics: the liturgical reform and the consequent reform of the Ordinary of the Mass. *Second,* we bring to the Reader's consideration a certain number of testimonies by theologians with sufficient credentials to deal with the doctrinal concessions that came from a desire to move ecumenism forward.

---

3. Even though the texts of this Item deal primarily with the concessions that the Church supposedly should make to the other religions, they also contain some applications of conciliar doctrinal premises regarding the modern world and vice versa: Some excerpts on the modern world (Item 2) also deal with concessions to the other religions. This is quite understandable, since the principles that guide both types of concession are the same. The titles presented here only aim to make it easier for the Reader to follow the matter by means of a general order that is not intended to be a definitive classification.

Two distinct methods will be used to expound the documents corroborating Items 1 and 2. In Item 1, the subject matter is appropriate for uniform development. This is not the case with Item 2, in which the matter will be divided into segments preceded by a letter, a, b, c, etc. The reason for this is that it is easy to organize a direct doctrinal exposition about concessions to the other religions. In contrast, with regard to concessions made to the world, due to their multiple consequences and the ambiguity of the word "world," the exposition is indirect and multifaceted.

A. Ambiguities in the Conciliar and Post-conciliar Language Regarding the Liturgical Reform of the Holy Sacrifice of the Mass

§ 3

Pope Pius XII made a first attempt at liturgical reform. [4] That reform was probably a fruit of the preparatory commission that the Pontiff had established in view of a coming Council. [5]

---

4. "This rotation of the tendencies [in the liturgy] was not made brusquely. It was prepared, stimulated for a long time, because the return to the sources in the liturgical sphere, which had been sought for more than 20 years, had already had its effect. ... Pius XII admitted and at times applied, during Holy Week, for example, the principle of an adaptation of the liturgy." These are the words of the highly regarded *perito* and conciliar chronicler Fr. René Laurentin *(L'Enjeu et le bilan du Concile,* vol. II, p. 80).

The same author states: "The conciliar schema [regarding the liturgy] inserted itself during the long period of liturgical reform initiated by Pius XII. It was concerned foremost with promoting or, better, with restoring a lively participation of the faithful in the liturgy. It followed three inter-related orientations to achieve this end: adaptation to our time, differentiation according to the needs of the people and, finally, restoration of the powers of the Bishops in the collegial college" *(ibid.,* p. 23).

• Fr. Pedro Romano Rocha, SJ, professor of the Pontifical Gregorian University, offers more data: "Already in 1956, the rubrics of the new *Ordo* of Holy Week mentioned the people and their intervention [in the ceremonies]" ("La principale manifestation de l'Eglise," in V. A., *Vatican II - Bilan et perspectives,* vol. II, p. 21, note 11).

• Cardinal Silvio Oddi comments: "Let us not forget it was he [Pius XII] who initiated the liturgical reform. It was he who reduced to three hours the period of obligatory fast before communion" *(Il tenero mastino di Dio,* Rome: Progetti Museali Editore, 1995, pp. 48-49).

• In the Apostolic Constitution *Missale Romanum,* of March 4, 1969, Paul VI said: "Given that the liturgical movement began to grow and spread among the Christian people ... it became clear that the formulas of the Roman Missal should be restored and enriched. Our predecessor Pius XII undertook such a reform" (in *Ordo Missae,* Rome: Typis Polyglottis Vaticanis, 1969, pp. 7-8).

5. This can be inferred from the words of Fr. R. Laurentin: "The liturgical commission brought together specialists from around the world, including those from the Curia, men well-trained in research and the study of sources, and prepared for this dialogue that was developing between Rome and the rest of the Church. This dialogue existed between the Congregation of the Rites and the promoters of the liturgical movement,

§ 4

What is certain is that only two of the several schemata preparing for the Council remained essentially unchanged: the schema on liturgical reform and the one dealing with the communications media.[6] The others were abrogated by John XXIII when he rejected the schema *De fontibus Revelationis.* Cardinal Suenens remodeled the schemata and gave them a new focus following his own plan of "covering the topics most dear to him."[7]

Sacrosanctum Concilium, the constitution on liturgy, was the first document to be discussed and approved by the Council (11/14/1962), promulgated by Vatican II (11/21/1963), and officially ratified and promulgated by Paul VI (12/4/1963). The Constitution substantially adopted the schema prepared by the aforementioned commission. Soon after that proceeding, the liturgical reform went into force.

a. Excerpts from *Sacrosanctum Concilium* that Open the Way for Changes in the Liturgy of the Mass

§ 5

Let us analyze some excerpts of this important conciliar document. We do not consider these excerpts to be unequivocally erroneous. Although one or the other might be so, it is not our goal to analyze them in detail. Our aim is solely to present the Reader with a number of passages of the said Constitution so that he is able to see that, due to their ambiguous language, many excerpts directly or indirectly open the way for the desacralization of the principal act of worship of the Catholic Church and facilitate rapprochement with the false religions. Often times, this rapprochement is made to the detriment of the orthodoxy of some of the most fundamental dogmas of the Creed.

---

which was born in Germany, Belgium, France and other places during the last 30 years. This commission set the fundamental basis for a true reform – not without much friction and many obstacles and new starts, which makes one think of Penelope and her loom. Thus, John XXIII made use of a text capable of opening in a positive and fecund way the discussion of Vatican II: It was a single text, but a text of worth" *(L'Enjeu et le bilan du Concile,* vol. VI, p. 12).

Regarding the intention of Pius XII in preparing a new ecumenical Council, see Vol. IV of this Collection, *Animus Delendi I,* Chap. I.1.A.

6. R. Laurentin, *L'Enjeu et le bilan du Concile,* p. 16.

7. Commenting on the plan that he himself presented in the first session of December 4, 1962, Card. Jósef Suenens, in a book recording his conciliar activities, says: "I inserted there [in the plan] as many as possible of the themes that were dear to me" (*Souvenirs et esperances,* p. 69).

Let us, therefore, transcribe excerpts from *Sacrosanctum Concilium,* each one preceded by a short subtitle in italics indicating its tendency toward ambiguity.

§ 6
• *Adaptation to the world and to the false religions*: "The sacred Council has set out to impart an ever-increasing vigor to the Christian life of the faithful; to adapt more closely to the needs of our age those institutions which are subject to change; to foster whatever can promote union among all who believe in Christ. ... Accordingly it sees particularly cogent reasons for undertaking the reform and promotion of the liturgy." (SC 1a).

§ 7
• *Confusion between the various types of presence of Our Lord in the Church*: "Christ is always present in his Church, especially in her liturgical celebrations. He is present in the Sacrifice of the Mass not only in the person of his minister ... but especially in the Eucharistic species. By his power he is present in the Sacraments ... He is present in his word since it is he himself who speaks when the Holy Scriptures are read in the Church. Lastly, he is present when the Church prays and sings, for he has promised 'where two or three are gathered together in my name there am I in the midst of them' (Matt 18:20)" (SC 7a).

§ 8
• *The priesthood of the faithful is placed on the same level as that of the priest*: "Mother Church earnestly desires that all the faithful should be led to that full, conscious, and active participation in liturgical celebrations which is demanded by the very nature of the liturgy, and to which the Christian people, 'a chosen race, a royal priesthood, a holy nation, a redeemed people' (1 Ptr 2:9, 4-5) have a right and obligation by reason of their baptism. In the restoration and promotion of the sacred liturgy the full and active participation by all the people is the aim to be considered before all else" (SC 14a, b).

§ 9
• *Desacralizing ceremonies and rendering the celebration of the Mass democratic*: "In this restoration both texts and rites should be drawn up so as to express more clearly the holy things which they signify. The Christian people, as far as is possible, should be able to understand them with ease and take part in them fully, actively, and as a community" (SC 21b). "With the passage of time, however, there have crept into the rites of the sacraments and sacramentals certain features which have rendered their nature and purpose far from clear to the people of today. Hence some changes are necessary to adapt them to present-day needs. For that reason the sacred Council decrees as follows concerning their revision" (SC 62).

§ 10
• *Exaltation of Scripture to please Protestants*: "In order to achieve the restoration, progress, and adaptation of the sacred

liturgy it is essential to promote that sweet and living love for Sacred Scripture to which the venerable tradition of Eastern and Western rites gives testimony" (SC 24). "In sacred celebrations a more ample, more varied, and more suitable reading from Sacred Scripture should be restored." (SC 35.1).

§ 11

• *Rendering the liturgy less sacred and more democratic, and imitating Protestant and pentecostal customs*: "To promote active participation, the people should be encouraged to take part by means of acclamations, responses, psalms, antiphons, hymns, as well as by actions, gestures and bodily attitudes" (SC 30).

§ 12

• *Indirect mention of the Protestant doctrine on the two tables*: "The Church, therefore, earnestly desires that Christ's faithful ... through a good understanding of the rites and prayers ... should take part in the sacred action, conscious of what they are doing, with devotion and full collaboration. They should be instructed by God's word, and be nourished at the table of the Lord's Body. They should give thanks to God" (SC 48). "The treasures of the Bible are to be opened up more lavishly so that a richer fare may be provided for the faithful at the table of God's word" (SC 51).

§ 13

• *Rushing liturgical reform and Bishops' collegiality*: "The liturgical books are to be revised as soon as possible. Experts are to be employed on this task, and Bishops from various parts of the world are to be consulted" (SC 25).

§ 14

• *Attributing a messianic character to the reform*: "Zeal for the promotion and restoration of the sacred liturgy is rightly held to be a sign of the providential disposition of God in our time, and as a movement of the Holy Spirit in his Church" (SC 43).

§ 15

• *Exaltation of the Bishop's power to the detriment of papal power*: "The Bishop is to be considered as the High Priest of his flock from whom the life in Christ of his faithful is in some way derived and upon whom it in some way depends" (SC 41a).

§ 16

• *Promoting equality among the faithful and a disdain for higher classes*: "In the liturgy ... no special exception is to be made for any private person or classes of persons whether in the ceremonies or by external display" (SC 32).

§ 17

• *The priest as president of the community:* "In the liturgy God speaks to his people, and Christ is still proclaiming his Gospel. And the people reply to God both by song and prayer. Moreover the prayers addressed to God by the priest who, in the person of Christ, presides over the assembly, are said in the name of the entire holy people and of all present" (SC 33a, b).

§ 18 • *Encouraging use of the vernacular*: "But since the use of the vernacular, whether in the Mass, the administration of the Sacraments, or in other parts of the liturgy, may frequently be of great advantage to the people, a wider use may be made of it. ... These norms being observed, it is for the competent territorial ecclesiastical authority ... to decide whether, and to what extent, the vernacular language is to be used" (SC 36-2,3).

§ 19 • *Ending the primacy of the Latin Rite and establishing inculturation*: "Even in the liturgy the Church does not wish to impose a rigid uniformity in matters which do not involve the faith or the good of the whole community. Rather does she respect and foster the qualities and talents of the various races and nations. Anything in these people's ways of life which is not indissolubly bound up with superstition and error she studies with sympathy and, if possible, preserves intact. She sometimes even admits such things into the liturgy itself" (SC 37). "In some places and circumstances ... an even more radical adaptation of the liturgy is needed ... The competent territorial ecclesiastical authority ... must ... consider which elements of traditions and cultures of individual peoples might appropriately be admitted into divine worship" (SC 40-1). "The Church, indeed, approves of all forms of true art ... and admits them into divine worship" (SC 112c). "The art of our own times from every race and country shall also be given free scope in the Church" (SC 123).

§ 20 • *Opening the gates to liturgical abuse*: "The canons and ecclesiastical statutes which govern the provision of external things which pertain to sacred worship should be revised as soon as possible, together with the liturgical books. ... These laws refer especially to the worthy and well-planned construction of sacred buildings, the shape and construction of altars, the nobility, placing and security of the eucharistic tabernacle, the suitability and dignity of the baptistery, the proper ordering of sacred images, and the scheme of decoration and embellishment. Laws that seem less suited to the reformed liturgy should be amended or abolished. Those which are helpful are to be retained, or introduced if lacking. In this matter, especially as regards the material and form of sacred furnishing and vestments ... powers are given to territorial episcopal conferences to adapt such things to the needs and customs of their different regions" (SC 128a, b)

b. The Modifications of the 1969 Missal and the Remodeling of 1970

§ 21

In order to carry out the "opening up" of *Sacrosanctum Concilium*, Paul VI established a new commission to reform the liturgy of the Mass: the Pontifical Commission for the Application of the Constitution on the Sacred Liturgy.[8] The commission was headed by Fr. Annibale Bugnini,[9] and included Protestant observers.[10] The fruit of these studies was the Apostolic Constitution *Missale Romanum* of Paul VI, published on April 3, 1969.

§ 22

This Apostolic Constitution promulgated two documents regarding the reform of the Mass: the *Institutio Generalis Missalis Romani* and the new *Ordo Missae.* These documents officially came into force on November 30, 1969, vested with papal authority.[11]

The *Institutio* includes 341 articles in which the new rites are minutely explained. At the same time, it establishes theoretical and practical principles for the Eucharistic celebration.[12]

---

8. *Consilium Pontificium ad Exsequendam Constitutionem de Sacra Liturgia.*

9. Fr. Bugnini played a very relevant role in bringing about liturgical changes in the Church. Already as far back as 1956, he was co-author of the Holy See's unofficial commentaries regarding the reform of Pius XII (A. Bugnini and C. Braga, *Ordo Hedomadae Sanctae instauratus,* Rome, 1956, in P. Romano Rocha, *ibid.*).

Fr. Bugnini, later raised to the Episcopate, also played a key role in the preparatory phase of the schema on the liturgy. Unlike nearly all the other secretaries of preparatory commissions, his defense of the changes and the strong reactions they caused prevented him from automatically becoming the secretary of the Council's liturgical commission (R. Laurentin, *L'Enjeu et le bilan du Concile,* vol. II, pp. 23, 25; vol. VI, p. 242). However, as a manifestation of his content with Bugnini's work, Paul VI designated him secretary of the post-conciliar liturgical commission. Accordingly, the most important task of preparing the reform of the Mass was also entrusted primarily to him.

10. On April 10, 1970, Paul VI received the commission that prepared the new *Ordo Missae.* As a picture of the audience was about to be taken, the Pontiff chose to appear at the side of the observers from "non-Catholic ecclesial communities." In the foreground, next to Paul VI, appears Max Thurian, of the community of Taizé (A. V. Xavier da Silveira, *La nouvelle messe de Paul VI,* cover).

11. *Ibid.,* p. 12.

12. *Ibid.*

The 1969 *Ordo* includes the new text of the Mass and the new rubrics for its celebration.

Paul VI declared that the promulgation of those documents had not been improvised but was rather the result of long and profound studies. [13] However, in May 1970, when the Latin edition of the new *Roman Missal* was published, the *Institutio* and the *Ordo* of 1969 appeared in it with numerous modifications. This is certainly surprising. In fact, the alterations of 1970 were introduced in an attempt to somehow reduce the grounds for the numerous criticisms provoked by the ambiguities of the text and its tendency to make a rapprochement with Protestantism.

In the exposition below, we will examine whether those modifications actually attenuated the gravity of the ambiguities found in the *Institutio* and in the *Ordo Missae*. [14]

c. An Example of Tendentious Ambiguity: The Priestly Role of the People

§ 23   We have chosen one example, among many worthy of note, of instances in which the rite of the Mass was modified [15] in essential points: the role of the people in the new concept of the Mass. Although there are other points of even greater relevance, we chose this one because it can be easily understood.

---

13. Paul VI, *Missale Romanum,* Typis Polyglottis Vaticanis, 1970, pp. 8-9.

14. Note that the *Institutio* of 1969 and the *Ordo Missae* of 1969 used by the author on whom we based ourselves (sections b–f) were not part of the multiple vernacular versions published, but the actual Latin text of the Apostolic Constitution in its official edition entitled *Ordo Missae* (in A. V. Xavier da Silveira, *La nouvelle messe de Paul VI*, p. 11, note 1). The texts of 1970 quoted by the author are from the *Missale Romanum,* in its official Latin edition *(ibid.,* p. 13, note 9).

15. About the history of the rite of the Holy Mass designated in current parlance as the "Mass of St. Pius V," of its formulas and its dogmatic value that harken back at least to the time of St. Gregory the Great, we recommend the timely study by Prof. Remi Amelunxen and Fr. Paul Trinchard, "Historical Prelude: A Brief History of the Holy Mass from the Canonized Liturgy to the *Novus Ordus* English Liturgy," in P. Trinchard, *New Mass in Light of the Old,* Monrovia, CA: Marian Publications, 1995.

In the *Institutio* of 1969

§ 24

According to the teaching of the Council of Trent, the priesthood "was instituted by that same Lord Our Savior, who gave to the Apostles and their successors in the priesthood the power of consecrating, offering and administering His Body and Blood, and also of forgiving and retaining sins."[16]

For this reason the Church teaches that the power of consecrating belongs exclusively to the priest and can in no way be attributed to the people. The reference to the "priesthood of the faithful" that appears in Sacred Scriptures and in certain Church teachings should be understood *lato sensu* (in a broad sense). It does not indicate the power of consecrating and of forgiving sins, but only the consecration of the Catholic that proceeds from Baptism, that is, the desire of dedicating oneself to the cause of the Church and to the divine work in union with Christ.

To confuse the priesthood of the faithful people with that of the priest is to accept the thesis of Protestants, who, since the 16th century, have held that the celebration of the "Lord's supper" is realized jointly by the priest and the people in equal conditions. The pastor only presides over the assembly in the liturgical celebration as a delegate of those assisting.

§ 25

With regard to this subject, **the *Institutio* is ambiguous.** As **Xavier da Silveira points out, it** "maintains some expressions found in traditional doctrine, but **introduces** along with them **notions and principles that insinuate or contain the Protestant theses.** Thus, one reads in n. 10 that the priest 'presides over the assembly representing Christ (*personam Christi gerens*),' and in n. 60 that 'the priest ... presides over the gathered assembly acting in the place of Christ (*in personam Christi praeest*).' Number 48 says that the priest 'represents Christ (*Christum Dominum repraesentans*).'

"As one sees, these expressions have an altogether traditional *tonus,* being even the technical terms to designate the manner by which the celebrant acts in the place of Our Lord. Such expressions, however, appear in **the *Institutio*** in a context that causes a certain perplexity. On the one hand, **it does not say *exactly* what is meant by 'acting in the place of Christ' or 'representing Him.'** On the other hand, **the *Institutio* contains numerous passages that insinuate that the celebrant is a mere president of the assembly, and that**

16. DS 1764.

his *principal function* in the Mass consists in *representing* the faithful gathered there."[17]

§ 26   These imprecisions, according to this same author, **open the door for an interpretation of the "representation" of Christ in a broader sense that dilutes the specific notion of the hierarchical and visible priesthood,** in function of which the priest lends his lips and voice to Our Lord at the moment of the Consecration.

• **In n. 7** of the first edition of the document, **the priest is qualified only as president of the "assembly of the people of God."**

• **In n. 10, after the affirmation that the priest presides over the assembly, the document states that the Eucharistic prayer constitutes a "presidential prayer."** The same article defines the presidential prayers as those that **"are directed to God in the name of all the holy people and of all here present."**

"Undoubtedly," Xavier da Silveira observes, "there are parts of the Eucharistic prayer that are directed to God in the name of the people. But **its principal part, the Consecration, is said exclusively by the priest in the name of Our Lord. It is impossible for a Catholic to admit any ambiguity on this point.** Therefore, n. 10 of the *Institutio* is one of the most censurable of the whole document."[18]

• In n. 12, we find this affirmation: "The *nature* of the 'presidential' parts demands that they be pronounced in a loud and clear voice, and be listened to attentively by all. Therefore, when the priest is pronouncing them, let there be no other prayers or hymns, and let the organ and any other musical instruments be silent."

"Likewise," comments the forecited author, **"that the words of the Consecration should be pronounced under those conditions insinuates once more that, at that moment, the priest acts specifically as a delegate of the people. Furthermore, this item of the *Institutio* contains a flagrant and grave contradiction to the rubric of the traditional *Ordo,* according to which the Canon is not said in a 'loud and distinct' voice.**

This fact is particularly worthy of attention in view of the following anathema issued by the Council of Trent: 'If anyone says that the rite of the Roman Church whereby a part of the Canon and the words of the Consecration are pronounced

---

17. A. V. Xavier da Silveira, *La nouvelle messe de Paul VI,* p. 31.

18. *Ibid.,* p. 32.

in a low voice must be condemned ... let him be anathema.' [19] **By stating that the** *nature* **of the 'presidential' parts** (and therefore the Eucharistic prayer and the words of the Consecration) *demand that they be pronounced in a loud and clear voice, the* Institutio **establishes a principle valid for all times and therefore implicitly affirms that the Council of Trent erred on this point."** [20]

• Number 271 formulates a new criticism of the traditional Mass, also based upon the false notion of the "presidential" function of the celebrant: "'The seat of the celebrant ought to signify his function as president of the assembly and director of prayer. For this reason, its most suitable position is facing the people, in the center rear of the sanctuary.' According to the Roman *Ordo,* the priest is normally facing the altar for he is above all the one who sacrifices, who presents himself before the Eternal Father in the name of the Word Incarnate. This modification is based upon a notion of 'presidency' of the 'assembly' that conflicts with traditional doctrine."

§ 27   In a note, Xavier da Silveira says: "We observe that, according to traditional Church practice, this is not an exclusive practice. In numerous rites, for example, the Mass is celebrated *versus populum* (facing the people). **What causes perplexity is the fact that the new** *Ordo* **proscribes the Mass not celebrated** *versus populum* **as a less adequate means since it fails to appropriately express the priest's 'presidential function.'"**

In the Prologue of the 1970 *Institutio*

§ 28   The 1970 edition of the *Institutio* was preceded by a prologue that manifests the concern of presenting principles of Catholic doctrine that were not presented or were presented insufficiently in the *Institutio.* However, a careful study of this prologue shows that the changes introduced did not substantially change the document of 1969.

Articles in the prologue that are presented with completely insufficient formulations and require important reservations include the following:

• Article 4, which affirms: "The nature of the ministerial priesthood, proper to the priest – who in the place of Christ (*in persona Christi*) offers the Sacrifice and presides over the assembly of the

---

19. DS 1759.

20. A. V. Xavier da Silveira, *La nouvelle messe de Paul VI,* pp. 32-33. Number 12 of the *Institutio* was not modified in 1970.

holy people – makes itself manifest in the very form of the rite, by means of a greater eminence of the position and function of the priest in relation to the people. The principles of this function are expounded and explained more clearly in the thanksgiving of the Mass of the blessing of the Holy Chrism on Holy Thursday, the day on which the institution of the priesthood is commemorated. For this text emphasizes the conferring of the priestly power that is realized by the imposition of hands. Enumerating each of its functions, it describes this same power that is a continuation of the power of Christ, the High Priest of the New Testament."

§ 29   This article contains some indisputable truths: that the priest acts in the place of Christ and that the power with which he is invested proceeds from Our Lord. However, **one** also **notes a dangerous approximation between the 'offering of the Sacrifice' and the 'presiding over the assembly of the holy people.'**

For the latter function, notes Xavier da Silveira, is "secondary, accidental and a simple consequence of the first. Even in the absence of an 'assembly of the holy people,' the celebrant fully exercises his priestly function at the Mass. **The importance** thus **given to the 'presidential' role of the priest in the Mass favors the impression among the faithful that the Sacrifice is celebrated by both them and by the priest.** ...

"Therefore, given the context of the *Institution,* given the criticisms that have rightly been made of it on this point, and given the erroneous interpretations that have arisen, **it would be suitable and even indispensable for the *Institutio,* in its corrected version, to have eliminated once and for all this very dangerous error, which completely destroys the doctrine on the Catholic priesthood. It would be necessary to affirm not only the *ministerial* character of the priesthood but also its *hierarchical* nature, which places it essentially above any other representation of Christ that might exist in, or proceed from, the people."** [21]

• Article 5 of the Prologue is even more serious than the former, because it confirms and amplifies the tendencies manifested there. It reads: "But, alongside considerations of this nature on the ministerial priesthood, another reality of great importance is also placed in its true light, that is, the royal (*regale*) priesthood of the faithful, whose spiritual sacrifice is insinuated by the ministry of the priest in union with the sacrifice of Christ, the sole Mediator. Indeed, *the cel-*

---

21. *Ibid.,* pp. 101-102.

ebration of the Eucharist is the action of the whole Church; [22] and in this action, each one should do only and entirely that which behooves him in view of the position he holds in the people of God. For this reason, we have also paid greater attention to certain aspects of the celebration that have attracted less interest over the centuries. Indeed, this people of God, redeemed by the Blood of Christ, reunited by the Lord, nourished with His word; *a people called to carry to God the prayers of the whole human family*; a people that give thanks in Christ for the mystery of salvation, *offering his sacrifice*; a people, finally, that grows in unity through communion in the Body and Blood of Christ. This people, while holy in its origin, nevertheless continuously grows in its sanctity through the same conscious, active, and fruitful participation in the Eucharistic mystery."

§ 30

Commenting upon this article, Xavier da Silveira observes:

"When we consider carefully the terms of article 5, we see that they clearly reaffirm the notion of the priesthood of the people, which we previously pointed out as unacceptable. Indeed, what are these 'aspects of the celebration that have attracted less interest over the centuries'? One of them is the fact that the holy people are 'called to carry to God the prayers of the whole human family.' Another is the fact that this people, '*offering* his sacrifice, gives thanks in Christ for the mystery of salvation.' **As can be seen, we come back to the same kinds of imprecision and ambiguity that existed in the previous text of the *Institutio*. ...**

"Incidentally, this passage establishes a strange distinction between the 'people of God' and the 'human family.' For it says that the

---

22. In a note, the author says: "The 'celebration of the Eucharist' in its proper sense is exclusively an action *of* Christ and of the priest who represents Him at Mass. In the Encyclical *Mediator Dei,* Pius XII condemned the statement that 'the eucharistic sacrifice' is an authentic concelebration of the priest as well as of the people present (AAS, 1947, p. 553). The faithful can and should unite with the celebrant to offer the victim that is immolated, and in this sense the Mass really is an action of the whole Church. But the offering made by the faithful is essentially distinct from that of Our Lord. One may not say, in any case, that, on account of this offering, the common faithful become authentic 'celebrants' of the Mass. There is no doubt that, analogically, the term 'celebration' can have broader meanings. But **it is not legitimate to distort those meanings so as to insinuate that the faithful have a function of 'celebration' properly speaking. For this reason, in the context of item 5 of the Prologue, the expression 'the concelebration of the Eucharist is an action of. the whole Church,' is ambiguous.**"

former, by the priestly action that it exercises in the Mass, carries to God the prayers 'of the whole human family.' **Taken in its natural sense, this expression indicates that the 'people of God' exercise, properly speaking, a priestly function of mediation between the whole human race ... and God.**

"Even more: since the phrase that follows immediately attributes to this same 'people of God' the faculty of 'offering the Sacrifice to Christ,' it appears that throughout the Mass the prayers of *all men* taken indiscriminately, that is, including non-Catholics, non-Christians, polytheists, atheists, etc., are presented to God and made agreeable to Him. **Such a conception of the Mass is all the stranger in that it agrees with a certain heterodox ecumenism that is spreading in large sectors of the Catholic public.**

"In view of all these dangerous ambiguities, the fears that we expressed above in regard to article 4 are aggravated in article 5 of the Prologue. Indeed, in article 5, **not only the silence about the *hierarchical character* of the priestly ministry of the celebrant, but also the absence of a clear conception of the *representation of Christ by the priest,* favor and prepare for an erroneous notion of the priesthood of the faithful.**" [23]

In the *Institutio of* 1970

Number 7 of the *Institutio,* which raised a polemic, was rewritten in the 1970 edition. It says: "In the Mass or Supper of the Lord, the people of God are united under the presidency of the priest, who acts in the place of Christ (*personam Christi gerente*) to celebrate the memorial of the Lord or the Eucharistic sacrifice. Accordingly, for this local gathering of the Holy Church, the promise of Christ, 'Wherever two or three are gathered together in My name, I am there, in the midst of them' (Matt 18:20), holds in an eminent way. Indeed, in the celebration of the Mass, in which the sacrifice of the Cross is perpetuated, Christ is really present in the very assembly gathered in His name, in the person of the minister, in His words, and moreover, substantially, and permanently under the Eucharistic species."

§ 31   Even with this new rendering, n. 7 can still be the object of the same criticisms made about the former version. With regard to this, Xavier da Silveira makes this analysis: "In this new text, n. 7 is still susceptible to corrections almost as serious as before. ... **The grav-**

---

23. *Ibid.,* pp. 102-105

est fault consists in affirming that it is the *people* who celebrate the memorial of the Lord or Eucharistic sacrifice. Note, indeed, that the word *celebrandum* has as subject *populus Dei.* After all we have said about the gravity of this concept, we think it would be superfluous to spend more time on this point. Let us simply note that **this same concept can be found in various places in the new text of the *Institutio.* This alone would suffice to show how the document strays from the teachings of the Church.**

"Even in the new text of n. 7, one observes that the strange imprecisions about the diverse manners of 'presence' of Our Lord in the Mass continue. In fact, it is said that His presence under the Eucharistic species is 'substantial and permanent.' The expression is absolutely exact. But the [Latin] word *enim* [because] establishes an unclear and very dangerous connection between that substantial presence and the principle enunciated above: 'Where two or three are gathered together in My name, there I am in the midst of them.' What relation would there be between these two 'presences'? Would the 'communitarian' nature of the 'assembly gathered in the name of Christ' contribute to His becoming present under the Eucharistic species? Or would it cause this second presence to be more fully attained? Or does the assembled 'people of God' exercise some active function to make effective the substantial presence of Our Lord in the Eucharist?

"The text allows dangerous ambiguities to remain about this point, particularly since it was said above that the 'people of God' *celebrate* **the sacrifice.** Nor are the necessary distinctions established between the diverse modes of the non-substantial presence of Christ: that is, in the gathered assembly, in the person of the minister, and in the word of Scripture. **The fact that the assembly is mentioned before the minister is telltale since it could indicate that the presence of Our Lord in the people is, if not superior, at least more fundamental to the Eucharistic celebration than His presence in the person of the minister."** [24]

The Affinity of "Communitarian" Liturgy with Protestantism

§ 32

To what could one liken this effort of the post-conciliar period to introduce through ambiguous formulas the notion of a priestly ministry of the faithful?

An answer comes, *a contrario sensu* [from the opposite side], from Luther Reed, a Lutheran pastor in the United States. Expounding on the "communitarian" nature of the worship established by Luther,

---

24. *Ibid.,* pp. 117-119.

he says: "The medieval Church destroyed the earlier unity and the sense of corporate worship by emphasizing the priestly class and by removing the laity from all active participation. The Reformation corrected this and duly restored the priesthood of believers and the congregational character of worship. Masses without communicants were forbidden and actual communion by the people was promoted. The use of the vernacular, together with the development of hymnody and of popular preaching, were significant factors. The worldwide liturgical movement in the Roman Church today is a belated effort to develop intelligent active lay participation in the Mass so that the people may think of themselves as 'co-celebrants' with the priest." [25]

d. Two Extremely Important Points

§ 34   Our concern with synthesis throughout this section does not prevent us from pointing generically to two principal points of the Mass that were modified by the *Novus Ordo,* that is to say, the Offertory and the Consecration. In these points we also note a tendency to accommodate the rite of the Mass to the doctrinal and liturgical desires of the Protestants.

Omissions and Tendentious Deletions in the Offertory

§ 35   How is the Offertory in the Mass of St. Pius V understood?

The true sacrificial oblation that is made in the Mass is not in the Offertory, but in the offering that Jesus Christ, at the moment of Consecration, makes of Himself to the Most Holy Trinity. The true Victim in the Sacrifice of the Mass is not the bread and wine nor the faithful there present, but Jesus Christ Himself.

The oblation that Our Lord makes of Himself is not visible to us since He does not present Himself in a manner perceptible to our senses. Thus, it is proper that there be perceptible elements that express the nature of the Sacrifice that will take place as well as the diverse offerings that will be made. This is the object of the Roman Offertory. As a consequence, during the course of the Offertory, it is stated what is the sacrificial oblation properly speaking, as well as the offering of ourselves to God. The propitiatory end of the Mass is likewise affirmed.

---

25. Luther Reed, *The Lutheran Liturgy* (Philadelphia: Fortress Press, 1959), p. 334, *in ibid.,* p. 143.

§ 36
The fundamental characteristics of the Offertory can, therefore, be reduced to three elements:

⊙ The oblation of Our Lord truly takes place at the moment of the Consecration, but to make the sacrificial nature evident from the very beginning, the *Roman Missal* contains an ensemble of prayers that tell us who is the true Victim to be immolated and, by way of anticipation, offers this Victim to the Most Holy Trinity.

⊙ The oblation of ourselves to God by means of Jesus Christ is symbolized by the offering of the bread and wine. Secondarily, it is symbolized by the offering of other material goods. We should note that the symbolism only becomes effective if the bread and wine, at the moment when they are placed upon the altar, are not just presented to God, but are truly offered in a sacrificial spirit. In other words, the gifts are consecrated to God.

• The Roman Offertory, through many of its prayers, clearly shows the propitiatory character of the Sacrifice. [26]

§ 37
Xavier da Silveira notes this about the changes: "**These three elements have disappeared in the new Offertory, replaced by a simple 'preparation of the offerings' or 'preparation of the gifts,' which corresponds to** *a conception of the Offertory that is fundamentally different from that of St. Pius V.* **In addition to this, various expressions of the other principles that distinguished Catholic doctrine from Protestantism were suppressed or attenuated.** The allusion to the fall of our first parents was eliminated. The invocation to Our Lady, the Angels and the Saints disappeared. The principle that the sacrifice should be accepted by God for it to be agreeable to Him became less clear. The manifestations of humility and compunction for one's own sins were weakened, as well as the affirmation of the hierarchical priesthood of the celebrant. And there is no longer any explicit reference to the faithful departed."[27]

§ 38
Perhaps one of the most important confusions in the Offertory concerns the concept of Transubstantiation. Only an allusion to the Transubstantiation of the bread occurs, i.e.: "That this bread may become for us the bread of life." **Here also we note the presence of ambiguity, since the word of God is also the bread of life** according to the words of Jesus Christ: "Man does not live by bread alone, but by every word that comes out of the mouth of God" (Matt 4:4). The *Mysterium Fidei,* Transubstantiation, the bodily presence of Christ after the Consecration, is obviously not just spiritual bread.

---

26. *Ibid.,* pp. 64-66.

27. *Ibid.,* p. 66.

The words "bread of life" suggest misinterpretations such as transignification instead of Transubstantiation.

Although we do not want to prolong the presentation of this subject beyond the indispensable necessary for this Volume, let us at least mention that there are indisputable protestantizing consequences to the elimination of the fundamental prayers of the Offertory such as the *Suscipe Sancte Pater,* the *Offerimus Tibi Domini,* the *Deus Qui Humanae Substantiae* and the *Veni Sanctificator.*[28]

Essential Modifications in the Consecration

§ 39

There was a modification in the formula of the Canon of the Mass, or the Roman Canon, also now called the Eucharistic Prayer. The text of the new formula tends to accommodate the conception of the Eucharist as a simple *agape* realized by the community in commemoration of the Passion and Resurrection of Our Lord.[29]

In the *Novus Ordo,* three new formulas of Eucharistic prayers are introduced, thus giving the celebrant a choice from four formulas. **A true Canon of the Mass, that is, an exclusive rule according to which the sacrifice must be celebrated, ceases *ipso facto* to exist. The new Eucharistic prayers desacralize the traditional Roman Canon and sound strange to pious ears while they make, in a certain way, the central part of the Mass acceptable to Protestants.**[30] **The fact that the central part of the Mass has become less removed from Protestantism tends to create confusions that are inadmissible and extremely prejudicial to the Faith.**

The consecratory formula has been fused into the preparatory prayer of the Consecration, *Qui Pridie,* and the two together have become "the Narration of the Institution."[31] By this fusion, **it is implied that the Mass has been changed from a Sacrifice to merely a memorial supper.** Importantly, the form of the Consecration of the Holy Sacrifice of the Mass was definitively expressed at the dogmatic Council of Florence in 1442, reiterated at the dogmatic

---

28. *Ibid.,* pp. 66-76.

29. *Ibid.,* pp. 76-81.

30. *Ibid., pp.* 81-86.

31. Dietrich von Hildebrand and John McManemin, "Why the Tridentine Mass?," in *Una Voce Pamphlets on the Liturgy,* § 2 (St. Paul: Remnant Press, n.d.).

Council of Trent in 1545, and the *Missale Romanum* was codified by Pope St. Pius V in 1570 in the Bull *Quo primum tempore.*[32]

§ 40   **The removal of the words *"mysterium Fidei"* from the consecratory formula of the wine in the *Novus Ordo* contradicts these two dogmatic Councils and *Quo primum,* and could appear to be a deliberate attempt to eliminate the sacrificial nature of the Mass. This facilitates an acceptance of the *Novus Ordo* by Protestants and places grave doubts about Transubstantiation in the minds of Catholics.** Doubts of this magnitude can without question contribute powerfully to increase the extraordinary crisis of faith that is shaking large parts of the clergy.

The removal of the words *pro multis* from the ICEL (International Committee on English in the Liturgy) version of the Consecratory formula of the wine in the *Novus Ordo* contradicts Sacred Scripture (Matt 26: 26-28; Mark 14: 22-24). As explained in the *Catechism of the Council of Trent,* the words "for all" are not used because, with the miracle of Transubstantiation, the fruits of the Passion are alone spoken of, and to the elect only did His Passion bring the fruit of salvation.[33] With the changes in the consecratory formula of the wine, the heart of the Holy Sacrifice of the Mass has been profoundly modified by the *Novus Ordo.*

e. Other Topics, Not Studied Here, on the Reform of the Mass

The work by Xavier da Silveira analyzes other topics in addition to the priesthood of the faithful, the Offertory and the Consecration. His study is always punctilious and dispassionate, and its conclusions are always coherent, as the Reader can gauge from the examples cited. He covers the *Institutio* and the *Ordo* both of 1969 and of 1970.

§ 41   For the Reader's information, we mention below some of the most important topics analyzed by the author.

---

32. *Canons and Decrees of the Council of Trent,* trans. by H. J. Schroeder (St. Louis, MO: B. Herder, 1941); *Missale Romanum, Ex decreto sacrosancti concilii tridentini restutum;* St. Pius V, Bull *Quo primum tempore,* of 1570.

33. *Catechism of the Council of Trent,* trans. by John A. McHugh and Charles J. Callan (New York, 1923).

In the *Institutio* of 1969

• The absence of any mention of the dogma of Transubstantiation favors heresy.

• A definition of the Mass, presented in n. 7, opposes that of the Council of Trent.

• The omission of the notion of propitiatory sacrifice incurs the anathema of the Council of Trent.

• A tendency to place the "liturgy of the Word" and the "Eucharistic liturgy" on the same footing echoes heresies that deny the value of Tradition.

• The Mass is presented as a memorial of the Resurrection and the Ascension. [34]

In the *Ordo* of 1969

§ 42

• In the rite of Communion, the general tendency is to suppress the signs that distinguished the celebrant from the assembly and to introduce prayers and symbols conducive to creating confusion between the priesthood of the celebrant and that of the faithful. [35]

In the Prologue of the *Institutio* of 1970

§ 43

• The Prologue implies that doctrinal errors in relation to Eucharistic worship no longer exist. As a consequence, one may introduce the vernacular, Communion under both species for the common faithful, new texts of prayers in the Mass, formulations adapted to modern theological language, etc.

• It repeats the tendency of the *Institutio* of *1969* to consider the action of the faithful as an essential element of the Sacrifice of the Mass. [36]

In the *Institutio* of 1970

§ 44

• The *Institutio* no longer mentions the propitiatory nature of the Sacrifice of the Mass. Such precision appears only in n. 2 of the Prologue. Thus, the prior judgment about the *Institutio* prevails.

---

34. *Ibid.*, pp. 16-42.

35. *Ibid.*, pp. 86-90.

36. *Ibid.*, pp. 109-113.

• It insists excessively upon the fact that the Eucharist commemorates the Resurrection, and thus glosses over the sacrificial and propitiatory character of the Mass.

• The new text, which alludes to the priestly function of the priest, absolutely fails to clarify the ambiguities about the "celebration" of the people. [37]

In the *Ordo* of 1970

§ 45   The new modifications introduced in the *Ordo* of 1970 do not alter the criticisms made about the text of 1969.

f. The Ambiguities in the New Documents Contain Profound Affinities with Protestant Rites

§ 46   We will present below some points of Protestant doctrine and rites regarding the mass as a point of reference to analyze ambiguities in the liturgical reform.

• For Luther and Melanchthon, the mass is no longer a sacrifice; teaching replaces sacrifice, the lectern takes the place of the altar.

• All Christians are priests and therefore receive communion under both species.

• Jesus Christ is not constantly present in the Eucharist. Protestants deny Transubstantiation.

• Vernacular is introduced in worship and replaces Latin.

• Primary importance is given to the sermon, then prayer and confession of faith, and finally, the supper.

• Zwingli celebrated facing the assembly instead of the altar.

• Acolytes distributed the bread to the faithful in the pews. Each took a piece of bread in his hands and put it in his own mouth.[38]

• The same heresiarch insisted that wooden chalices be used for the wine in order to reject all display of pomp and ceremony.

• Luther and Melanchthon defended the principle of the universal priesthood, thus confusing the priesthood of the priest with that of the people.

---

37. *Ibid.*. pp. 120-122.

38. *Ibid., pp.* 130-160.

• Some parts of the Lutheran *confiteor* are said by the minister, others are said alternately by him and the people, and others said simultaneously by both the minister and the people. This also occurs in the new *Ordo Missae.*

• The pseudo-reformers confessed only to God and omitted all references to the intercession of the Virgin and the Saints. The "penitential rite" [*Confiteor*] of the new *Ordo* consists of three formulas from which the priest chooses the one he deems most appropriate. The second and third formulas contain no reference to Mary or to the Saints.

• The Catholic Offertory is a legitimate and laudable "anticipation" of the true offering of Our Lord to God the Father, which is made at the Consecration. The Lutherans reduced the offertory to a presentation of the offerings by the people and the preparation of the bread and the wine for communion. In the *Novus Ordo,* the Offertory also appears to have taken this direction.

• As for the Canon of the Consecration of the Mass, Zwingli replaced its formula with four prayers. Luther was against its recitation in low voice. [39] In the footsteps of the two heresiarchs, the new *Ordo* also has four formulas for the Canon, which is recited aloud.

g. Conclusions on the Protestantization of the Church Beginning with the Liturgical Reform

§ 47

It is very difficult for one not to conclude that the reform of the Mass, and by extension, the liturgical reform, disfigured venerable characteristics of Catholic doctrine and ritual so as to bring them closer to important Protestant tenets. This conclusion inevitably arises from the exposition we have just made. It is not, however, ours alone. Let us look at the position of the late Cardinal Suenens, who had undeniable credentials to represent the progressivist current, which is totally opposed to our way of thinking and judging.

In a long article published in *L'Osservatore Romano,* from which the most important excerpts are quoted in his memoirs, the Cardinal touches on the topic of the Pseudo-Reformation, relating it to Vatican Council II. He says that the revolt of Luther and his cohorts was an understandable consequence of the "evils" that supposedly afflicted Holy Church at the time. The Church allegedly erred by presenting herself as hierarchical and militant. This is what he appears to

---

39. *Ibid., pp.* 135-152.

indicate when he uses the expressions "abuses, juridical strictures, and Latin scholastics." In order to remedy these "errors," Vatican II would exercise a function of "complementarity" by drawing closer to the heretics in many of their characteristics. Let us see what the last of the four moderators of the Council left as record before presenting himself before God.

§ 48   The Reformation, he says, "reacted to a large extent against abuses, juridical strictures, and Latin scholastics. As I see it, even if there had not been a decree on ecumenism at Vatican II, this Council would have remained eminently ecumenical by virtue of its very complementarity. Think about the insistence of the Council on the notions of Church and people of God, on the collegiality of Bishops and local Churches; think about the relevance given to *epiklesis,* [40] to the liturgy in a living language, to concelebration, to Communion under both species, to the permanent diaconate, etc. Reinstating and re-emphasizing all this has had an effect on the present internal and ecumenical evolution in the Church. This whole contribution is laden with promise and hope." [41]

Does the ensemble of conciliar reforms analyzed here and praised by Cardinal Suenens mean that the Catholic Church has become entirely Protestant? This is not what he, or we, have said. But this does not lessen the gravity of the situation, since in relation to the Faith and to the Sacred Liturgy, this adage prevails: *Bonum est integra causa, malum ex quocumque defectu* [good is the purity of the entire cause, evil is any defect].

Thus, the attenuating circumstance, that is, the fact that the reforms of the rite of the Mass are not *entirely* Protestant, could only please someone who does not truly love the Catholic Church. It would be like the situation of someone who, seeing how the insults and blows inflicted upon Our Lord Jesus Christ physically disfigured Him, were to comment, "After all, He still is not totally disfigured. Some parts in

---

40. According to a current progressivist notion, Our Lord's presence in the Holy Mass would not take place at the moment of Consecration, in which Christ becomes really present in the Eucharistic species. Instead, it would take place during the invocation for the coming of the Holy Spirit, a part of the Mass called *epiklesis.* This is yet another confusion between the Real Presence and other divine presences that may occur during the Mass; it is also a virtual negation of the Real Presence. Furthermore, this invocation of the Holy Spirit has taken on pentecostal connotations with strong Protestant overtones.

41. L. J. Suenens, *Souvenirs et esperances,* p. 285.

Him are still whole." Could someone who thinks like this still deserve the honorable name of follower of Christ, of Catholic?

§ 49   Some people, nevertheless, have rejoiced at such reforms and even wish them to continue toward a full identification with Protestantism. At least, so it would appear from the words Cardinal Suenens attributes to Paul VI.

Narrating a visit to the Anglican cathedral in York, England, the Prelate told of a theretofore unknown episode in the ecumenical relations of Paul VI. He said: "In the sacristy they showed me the chalice into which was set the ring of Cardinal Mercier given to Lord Halifax on the eve of his death. Paul VI drew inspiration from that gesture to offer an episcopal ring to Anglican archbishop Ramsey with these words: 'This is not yet a wedding ring, but it is already an engagement ring.'" [42]

To what "engagement" could Paul VI have alluded if not the rapprochement of the Conciliar Church with Protestantism, of which Anglicanism is a denomination? If such an "engagement" implied carrying out the change in the Church that we are now analyzing, how far will the rapprochement have gone when the "wedding" takes place? We leave the answer for the Reader to ponder.

Once again we are clearly faced with the disastrous results produced by the ambiguities in the texts of the liturgical reform of the Constitution *Sacrosanctum Concilium* and the documents of 1969 and 1970 relating to the Mass in particular and to all acts of worship in general.

B. Multiple Concessions to the False Religions

§ 50   Two pages written by Msgr. Luigi Sartori are particularly enlightening in regard to concessions by the Church to the false religions. So we do not hesitate to transcribe them here: "The pastoral character of Vatican II is further determined by the profound intention of *dialogue.* Paul VI's orientation gave this subject a greater clarity and decisiveness. **To positively mix [in the conciliar text] ... perspectives as varied as possible** has precisely this goal: On the one hand, it **enriches the doctrinal position** (and therefore the living possession of the truth) **of the interlocutor called the Catholic Church,** and on the other hand it favors dialogue with the others. The Council favors and promotes the plurality of theologies inside the

---

42. *Ibid.,* p. 171.

Church. I would almost say it discovers their value, properly as a consequence of the external stimulus from interlocutors of the Church.

"She is asked by the Protestants to become more sensitive and open to biblical language and that of the origin of Christianity. She is stimulated by the Jews and Muslims to return more decisively to the very origins of the History of salvation. She is called by the non-Christian religions and by all of humanity to go beyond the letter of the Bible and fix her attention on history in general and on creation in order to be able to speak the language of every man on this earth who has spoken, speaks, or will speak about God, himself and the universe. ... And finally I would like to note what seems to me ... the *punctum saliens* of ecumenical dialogue in Vatican II: the updating of the missionary spirit for an opening and dialogue of the Church with the world. The insistence of Paul VI in this regard was decisive.

"Someone who reflects a little will not have difficulty discovering the increasing expansion of the ecumenical program for unity of the believers: the successive creation of the three secretariats [43] is a symbol of that. Finally, **the Council made the Church rediscover her universal mission in a perspective of openness (centrifugal and not centripetal,** one would say) and, therefore, of dialogue: **triumphant over the perils of colonialism** (which was spoken about in the Council, precisely in regard to the missions) **by means of a superior provision for 'mutual interchange'** in relations with men and the world, that is to say, as she gives and receives in a spirit of humility and charity, and of poverty and abundance all at the same time.

"This is the dialogue which, in a certain sense, conditions all the others: from the living dialogue with brethren inside the Church to that with separated brethren, to that with all those who believe in God. Then **the capacity to understand** (and not just that of making oneself understood) **becomes important for the language of the Church in relation to all of humanity. Here you have a total victory [of openness] over the esoteric "closedness" in theological language and in the announcement of the faith**. ... I believe that the Council's effort, especially in *Gaudium et spes,* to adopt categories of thought and expression from contemporary culture to announce the faith is, therefore, of utmost importance. [44]

---

43. Secretariat for the Promotion of the Unity of Christians (7/5/1960); Secretariat for Non-Christians (5/19/1964); Secretariat for Unbelievers (4/9/1965).

44. L. Sartori, "Il linguaggio del Vaticano II," in V.A., *Il linguaggio teologico oggi,* pp. 253-254.

It is difficult not to see Msgr. Sartori's comment as a confirmation of what was said above about the new position of the Church in regard to heretics and pagans.

§ 51 Furthermore, Cardinal Suenens reveals the surreptitious meaning of a passage of the decree *Unitatis redintegratio,* which is supposed to contain the key to ecumenism:

"In the *Decree on Ecumenism,* a small phrase was inserted, almost in passing, that must be examined in depth. Article 11 says: 'Furthermore, in ecumenical dialogue, Catholic theologians, standing fast by the teaching of the Church yet searching the divine mysteries together with separated brethren, should do so with love for the truth, charity and humility. When comparing doctrines with one another, they should remember that *in* Catholic *doctrine there exists an order or 'hierarchy' of truths,* since they vary in their relation to the foundation of the Christian faith. Thus the way will be opened whereby this kind of fraternal rivalry will incite all to a deeper realization and a clearer expression of the unfathomable riches of Christ!' ...

"A precious phrase is this one that speaks of an 'hierarchy of truths.' Yes, every truth is true, but not every truth is equally central and vital to the Christian mystery. Did the Lord perchance not say that He is 'the way, the truth and the life'? **A convergence of all Christians around the truths closer to the Lord and to the mystery of salvation,** when possible, **has a considerable importance in ecumenism.**

"What is central and vital in the Lord's Revelation? What is at the center of the indispensable communion of faith, preliminary to any ecumenical understanding? This question is capital: in its bosom lies all ecumenical hope. **Here also Vatican II did not say the last word, but the one it gave us is a germ of life, a mustard seed that could become the great tree of which the Scripture speaks, where all the birds of the sky could gather."** [45]

Although he does not give explicit answers to the question he raises, Cardinal Suenens makes it clear that the foundation of ecumenism – the mustard seed, according to him – is the notion of a "hierarchy of truths" admitted by the conciliar Church.

The notion of "hierarchy of truths" to which Cardinal Suenens refers is common in post-conciliar jargon. In order to explain it better, the progressivists imagine a metaphor in which the Catholic Church is higher up the mountain that leads to Christ, the other "Christian"

---

45. L. J. Suenens, "Discorso ufficiale d'apertura," in V.A., *L'avvenire della Chiesa,* pp. 50-51.

religions are somewhere below, those that believe in God even further below, and finally, at the base of the mountain, the atheists, who believe in nothing but vague principles. Principles are more general and encompassing to the degree that one comes down the mountain. They become more specific and selective as one climbs. In this way, it would be possible to promote ecumenism with everyone starting from the general principles. After this one should ascend only without risking any harm to those general principles. This is the concept of "hierarchy of truths" which the Council talks about and Cardinal Suenens has just expanded upon.

That this relativistic conception participates in religious indifferentism is an indisputable fact.

We would like to emphasize, in accordance with the goal of this Item, that such a concept collides head-on with the Church's militancy and her missionary character.

The principle underlying the notion of a "hierarchy of truths" is that the Catholic Church should not have a total and exclusive possession of the Truth and the Faith. And consequently, she should not be the only representative of Jesus Christ.

§ 52   Fr. Edward Schillebeeckx, the famous theologian from Nijmegen and influential conciliar *perito,* is quite straightforward as he explains the crux of the question:

"By admitting that the other Christian communities are also the Church, the Council passes judgment on the incapacity of its own Church to achieve the plenitude and unity desired by Christ. It is difficult to say that the Catholic Church is still one, Catholic and apostolic when one says that the others are equally one, Catholic and apostolic, albeit to a lesser degree. Although maintaining the conviction that the Church of Christ in its apostolic plenitude is essential for salvation, **at Vatican Council II the Roman Catholic Church officially abandoned its monopoly over the Christian religion. In the conciliar documents, belonging to the Church no longer has one single meaning but an analogous meaning.**

"The whole problem now consists in knowing whether one should continue to see the analogy of the Church in such a way that the Roman Catholic Church is the *princeps analogatum,* whereas the other churches would be only *analogata,* called churches only inasmuch as they approach the Roman Catholic Church. **It seems to me that it would be better to say that all the churches, and therefore also the Roman Catholic one, are *analogata* to that which in the Bible is called 'the Church of Christ.'** All of them are local churches of Christ. **The criterion of comparison is not the Roman Catholic Church as such,** but the apostolic plenitude, the plenitude of the messianic promise. **This is the perspective of Vatican Council II in the *Dogmatic Constitution on Divine Revelation.*** " [46]

In Schillebeeckx' words about the final goal of ecumenism, the end of the Church's militant and missionary character is presented as a premise:

"**The final objective [of ecumenism] must be that all churches recognize themselves and their own faiths in the other churches and not that all the other churches return to the Catholic Church. Unity implies first that the Catholic Church,** the Roman Catholic Church, see herself **reflected in that which we call the Protestant Church, and that the Protestant churches plainly recognize themselves in the local Catholic churches** without excluding all the local differences that may exist."

Here Schillebeeckx interrupts these startling statements – though consistent from the ecumenical standpoint – to observe, in a note: "As I explained elsewhere, based on the recognition proclaimed by the Council of the ecclesial elements in non-Catholic Christian churches, **we may even say that these churches, precisely because of their character of [Protestant] reformation, historically have an essential function to fulfill in relation to the indefectibility of the Church** in the form of a constantly renewed purification."

The author returns to his text: "Finding oneself in others is already unity. **From the moment that we understand that the differences of faith are not differences of *faith*, but only theological differences, it will become clear that the differentiation and plurality of forms can be preserved. The multiformity of the other churches actually constitutes an enrichment for all parties**. ... Unity in the Church does not mean uniformity; there is no difficulty with admitting diverse modalities of Christian piety, to experiment with living the same fundamental reality in different thematic [doctrinal] expressions. ... This is also possible.

"Thus, **to the degree that study and ecumenical experience show that current divergences are not fundamental dogmatic differences** but primarily theological differences, **we will be able to say that the various churches together constitute only one *sacramentum mundi* and that,** in their turn, **the local churches are signs of this great sacrament in the one Church** as the

46. E. Schillebeeckx, *"Igreja ou igrejas?"* in V.A., *Cinco problemas que desafiam a Igreja hoje,* pp. 26-27.

'sacrament or sign of communion with God and of unity among all men' (LG 1)." [47]

§ 53
Fr. Hans Küng, also a *perito* at Vatican II, reinforces the statements of Schillebeeckx, basing himself on conciliar documents. He explains that the official writers wanted to leave the text ambiguous so as to foster ecumenism. He also attests to the contradictions between the attitudes of Vatican II and the perennial teaching of the Church:

"Even though some obscure points still remain, **Vatican Council II reviewed the attitude of the Catholic Church toward the other Christian churches** in regard to very important points.

"1. **The Catholic Church used to only use the terms heretics and schismatics** (whom at depth she considered to be in bad faith); **today, she addresses the remaining Christians generally as separated brethren.**

"2. **Whereas she used to recognize only isolated Christians outside the Church, today she recognizes the existence of communities of Christians** *('christianae communiones,'* UR 1) **outside the Church.**

"3. **She considers these communities not only as sociological quantities but as 'churches' or 'ecclesial communities'** (*'Ecclesiae vel communitates ecclesiasticae,'* LG 15; UR 3).

"4. She also recognizes the association of these churches among themselves in the ecumenical movement born outside the Catholic Church and, in so doing, cites the basic formula of the Ecumenical Council of Churches: 'Everywhere large numbers have felt the impulse of this grace, and among our separated brethren a movement, fostered by the grace of the Holy Spirit, for the restoration of unity among all Christians grows daily. Taking part in this movement, which is called ecumenical, are those who invoke the Triune God and confess Jesus as Lord and Savior. They do this not merely as individuals, but also as members of the corporate groups in which they have heard the Gospel and which each regards as his Church and indeed, God's (UR 1).

"5. In this way, notwithstanding the presence of other slightly variant formulas, **the Catholic Church no longer identifies herself purely and simply with the Church of Christ.** At least in relation to one point, an explicit revision has been achieved: Instead of the identifying formula first proposed by the commission: 'The sole Church that we confess in the Creed as One, Holy, Catholic and Apostolic ... *is (est)* the Catholic Church, governed by the successor of Peter and by the Bishops in communion with him,' this formula was admitted: ...

---

47. *Ibid.,* pp. 33-34.

'subsists in the Catholic Church' *(subsistit in)* (LG 8). **In order to justify the rejection, the first time ever, of the identifying formula** (something of transcendental importance and which can give rise to grave consequences), **the commission added this explanation: 'So that this expression be in greater accord with the statement that elements of the Church also exist in other parts.'** [48] The commission means to refer here to the 'churches or other ecclesial communities' mentioned in LG 15. **The new formula was consciously kept as vague as possible in order not to prevent a broader theological implication,** which was absolutely necessary in so difficult a question." [49]

§ 54   To corroborate these explanations by renowned theologians, we would like to quote Fr. Bernard Sesboüé, a member of the International Theological Commission. By denying that the Catholic Church is the sole Church of Christ, he confirms what we have said so far about the end of the Church Militant and of her missionary character. Furthermore, he attests to the influence of the Tübingen School at Vatican II, as we noted above. [50]

Here are Sesboüé's words: "Fortunately, in the beginning of the 19th century, the romantic school of Tübingen brought a whole new stimulus to Catholic ecclesiology, whose weak propositions were becoming, it should be confessed, not very evangelical. ... **The work of Vatican II appears** then **to be the conclusion of that whole germination and the definitive turnaround of the official perspectives.** ... **The Church is not yet the Kingdom,** but rather the place where the latter progresses. **The Council also explicitly recognizes that outside the Catholic Church, there are other ecclesial communities that belong to the mystery of the Church regardless of their deficiencies. The borders of the Church of Christ are far from coinciding with the boundaries of the Roman Catholic Church.**" [51]

§ 55   Also of interest is the testimony of Fr. Giuseppe Alberigo, a well-known professor of Church History at the University of Bologna, Secretary of the Institute for Religious Sciences of that city, journalist, director of the magazine *Cristianesimo nella Storia,* the 1960 Borgia Prize winner, and a member of the editorial staff of the magazine *Concilium.* He stresses an end to the doctrine that considers

---

48. *Schema Constitutionis De Ecclesia* (Rome, 1964), pp. 15-25.

49. H. Küng, *A Igreja,* vol. II, pp. 39-40.

50. Chap. VI.1.

51. Bernard Sesboüé, O *Evangelho na Igreja – A tradição viva da fé* (São Paulo: Paulinas, 1977), pp. 81-82.

the Catholic Church as the sole Church of Christ and, consequently, the end of the era of militancy and propagation of the Faith.

Alberigo states: "After the first seven ecumenical councils, the successive general councils signaled a confirmation from the global Christian standpoint of a gradual reduction of Christianity to one of its constituent traditions, the primeval western tradition from Trent onward, which is the Western-Roman tradition. With Vatican I, this tendency radicalized to the point that some were led to think that Catholicism had passed beyond its very possibility to hold councils.

"In regard to this itinerary, **Vatican II expresses an embryonic reversal of this tendency.** Indeed, although it is still a general council of the Catholic Church, posing the problem of announcing the Christian [message] to today's man and updating the question of unity (also with the decree, *Unitatis redintegratio,* and the presence of observers), **it explicitly raises questions that transcend the area and forces of each of the traditional confessions and challenge all of contemporary Christianity."** [52]

Alberigo goes on to criticize the "timidity" of Vatican II and to label the part of *Lumen gentium* that still considers the constitution of the Church to be hierarchic as "ecclesiocentric deformations": **"The** concrete **development of the works of Vatican II was only timidly consistent with such orientation,** above all to the degree that the Council concentrated on the ecclesiological question **with ecclesiocentric deformations,** [53] **as was perhaps inevitable, given its exclusive Catholic composition."** [54]

*

§ 56   Based on the authors cited above, we conclude this Section B on concessions to the other religions by saying that the ambiguity of conciliar texts was intentional. To admit that the other religions are churches or that the Holy Spirit acts in them and that there is salvation in them is implicitly to deny the exclusivity of the true Faith and the authenticity of the Catholic Church; this is confirmed by the difference established between the Catholic Church and the "Church of Christ." As a direct consequence, such principles negate the militant character of the Church. She should no longer fear the attacks by schismatics, heretics and pagans, but instead approach them incautiously in an

---

52. Giuseppe Alberigo, "Per un Concilio ecumenico cristiano nella prospettiva dell'unità della Chiesa," in V.A., *Verso la Chiesa del terzo millennio,* p. 63.

53. Chap. III of *Lumen gentium.*

54. G. Alberigo, "Per un Concilio ecumenico cristiano," p. *63.*

attitude of dialogue. Finally, they deny the missionary character of the Church in the propagation of the Faith, [55] for if she is not considered the exclusive guardian of the Faith of Christ, trying to convert others would be nothing but an egocentric attitude, qualified as "spiritual colonialism." [56]

2. Concessions to the Modern World

§ 57   It would be well to make a few preliminary distinctions about the much-trumpeted adaptation of the Church to the modern world, *aggiornamento.*

A. Ambiguity in Conciliar Language regarding the Concept of World

§ 58   The concept of *world* in Church moral teaching is not open to equivocation: The faithful are recommended to stay away from worldly things. The same cannot be said for its socio-political teaching in which the word *world* can be interpreted in different ways:

§ 59   *First,* world can be considered the ensemble of men established as a society. In this sense, the Catholic Church is established in the world, since the ensemble of faithful is in the world. Also, the State is founded in the world, of which all of its citizens make a part. Thus, in this sense, world is the place where both the Church and the State exert their influence. Therefore, the word *world* here has an ambivalent meaning.

§ 60   *Second,* world can be taken as synonymous with the temporal order, that is, the political constitution of the State. In this case, relations between the Church and the world are the same as relations between the Church and the State, and the teachings that the Magisterium has laid down through the centuries would be applied to them.

§ 61   *Third,* world, and especially the modern world, can be understood as "modern civilization." This would be that ensemble made up by the modern State born out of the French Revolution, derived from the Enlightenment, developed by modern philosophy and modern science and based on Positivism and modern technology. Also,

---

55. On the dialogue of the Church with the world, see Vol. V, *Animus Delendi II,* Part I, Chap. II.

56. The expression is by Cardinal Lercaro, addressing the Brazilian Bishops gathered in Rome during the first conciliar phase (in B. Kloppenburg, A *eclesiologia do Vaticano II,* p. 154).

the modern world would include the egalitarian and liberal customs that were adapted, at a first stage, to the habits of a bourgeois consumerism, later to a proletarian Communism, and today are moving swiftly toward an indigenous tribalism of a self-managing type.

§ 62   When we ask ourselves which of the various meanings of the word was adopted by the Council, we see that ambiguity prevailed also here. Even though the keynote is adaptation of the Church to modern civilization (third meaning), the word is sometimes used to designate relations between Church and State (second meaning), or mankind as a whole (first meaning). [57]

---

57. a. In the texts of Vatican II we find the word *world* used in all three meanings:

1ˢᵗ meaning: "Proceeding from the love of the eternal Father, **the Church** was founded by Christ in time and gathered into one by the Holy Spirit. It has a saving and eschatological purpose which can be fully attained only in the next life. But it **is now present here on earth and is composed of men;** they, the **members of the earthly city,** are **called to form the family of the children of God** even in this present history of mankind and to increase it continually until the Lord comes ... **Thus the Church,** at once 'a visible organization and a spiritual community,' **travels the same journey as all mankind and shares the same earthly lot with the world; it is** to be a **leaven and,** as it were, the **soul of human society** in its renewal by Christ and transformation into the family of God" (GS 40b; PO 22b).

b. *2nd meaning:* **"All we have said up to now about the dignity of the human person, the community of mankind, and the deep significance of human activity provides a basis for discussing the relationship between the Church and the world and the dialogue between them"** (GS 40a).

c. *3rd meaning:* **"The Church, moreover, acknowledges the good to be found in the social dynamism of today, particularly progress towards unity, healthy socialization, and civil and economic cooperation. The encouragement of unity is in harmony with the deepest nature of the Church's mission,** for it 'is in the nature of a sacrament – a sign and instrument – that is of communion with God and of unity among all men.' It shows to the world that social and exterior union comes from a union of hearts and minds" (GS 42c, 23a, 34c, 54, 62b, f, g).

d. In the considerations below by Fr. Angel Antón, his letter b is close to our 1st meaning; his letter c is not far from the 2nd meaning; his letter a has something in common with the following Item in this Work (Section B). His introductory remarks also confirm this Section A:

"It is necessary to indicate as the key point in *Gaudium et spes* its concept of 'world' adopted in the preamble and abundantly described in other passages of the Constitution. Though it is evident that the Council tried to stress the positive aspects of the world as a work of the Creator, **Gaudium et spes left us a hardly elaborated concept of world from the theological standpoint. Ratzinger wrote that this concept is still in its pre-theological stage** (J. Ratzinger, *Der Weltdienst der Kirche: Zehn Jahre nach Vaticanum II*, eds. A. Bauch, A. Glasser and M. Seybold, Regensburg, 1976, p. 37). **Hence it is necessary for post-conciliar theology to make it more precise**.

"It is no less true that *Gaudium et spes* pointed out some positive aspects of the polyvalent notion of world: a. Although in the language of the Bible, whence it passed onto Christian literature, this concept has a pejorative *nuance* that comes from sin and the powers of the Evil One for working in the world, its positive aspects echoed by *Gaudium et spes* far outnumber [that nuance] as being the ensemble of God's creation renewed in Christ. b. *Gaudium et spes* also understands by 'world' the men who inhabit the earth, some of whom are good while others are bad in the moral and spiritual sense mentioned above, some being Christians, believers or atheists. This does not mean that one must simply dissociate oneself from the latter. Without being of this world, the Church lives in the world and for the world. c. Finally, *Gaudium et spes* includes in the concept of world the earthly realities and the *temporal* tasks that man was called to carry out during his existence on earth. The realities of this world, created by God, have a certain autonomy that man must respect. By establishing the principle of distinction between the Church and human society, *Gaudium et spes* affirmed this relative autonomy of the temporal. But such a distinction does not mean that the two realities exclude all permutation and reciprocal influence. Incidentally, *Gaudium et spes* does not support the thesis that a Christian's profession of faith and his existence in the world unfold in two separate and impermeable domains" (A. Anton, "L'ecclésiologie postconciliaire," in V.A., *Vatican II: Bilan et perspectives*, vol. I, p. 437).

e. A particular excerpt of *Gaudium et spes* about the *world* calls for our attention: "The Second Vatican Council ... longs to set forth the way it understands the presence and function of the Church in the world of today. Therefore, the world that the Council has in mind is the whole human family seen in the context of everything that envelopes it: It is the world as the theater of human history, bearing the marks of its travail, its triumphs and failures, the world, which in the Christian vision has been created and is sustained by the love of its Maker, which has been freed from the slavery of sin by Christ, who was crucified and rose again in order to break the stranglehold of the Evil One, so that it might be fashioned anew according to God's design and brought to its fulfillment" (GS 2).

Commenting on this excerpt and more generally on the position of *Gaudium et spes* toward the world, Cardinal Ratzinger calls it a "counter-*Syllabus*," confirming the presence of both the second and third meaning presented above. He states: **"If one is looking for a global diagnosis of the text, one could say that it (in connection with the texts on religious liberty and the world's religions) is a revision of the *Syllabus* of Pius IX, a kind of counter-*Syllabus*.** As is known, Harnack interpreted the *Syllabus* of Pius IX simply as a challenge to its century. What is true is that it drew a line of separation before the determining forces of the 19th century: the scientific and political conceptions of Liberalism. In the modernist controversy, this double boundary line was once again reinforced and fortified.

"Undoubtedly, many things have changed since then. The new ecclesiastical policy of Pius IX established a certain openness toward the liberal conception of State. In a silent but persevering combat, exegesis and Church History increasingly adopted the postulates of liberal science; on the other hand, facing the great political upheavals of the 20th century, Liberalism was obliged to accept notable corrections. This happened because, first in central Europe, conditioned by the situation, the unilateral dependence on the positions taken by the Church through the initiatives of Pius IX and Pius X against the new period of History opened by the French Revolution was to a large extent corrected *per via facti*; but a fundamental new determination of relations with the world as it had been since 1789 was still lacking.

"In reality, in the countries with strong Catholic majorities, the mentality that preceded the Revolution still reigned; today almost no one denies that the Spanish and Italian concordats tried to conserve too many things from a conception of the world that for a long time had not correspond to reality. Likewise, almost no one can deny that this dependence on an obsolete conception of relations between Church and State was matched by similar anachronisms in the domain of education and the attitude taken toward the modern historic-critical method. Only a detailed inquiry into the various ways in which the different parts of the Church welcomed the modern world could undo the complicated entanglement of causes that contributed to give shape to the pastoral constitution *[Gaudium et spes],* and only in this way could the drama of the history of its influence be clarified. Let us content ourselves here with stating that **the text plays the role of a counter-*Syllabus* to the degree that it represents an official attempt to officially reconcile the Church with the world as it had become after 1789.** On the one hand, this visualization alone clarifies the ghetto complex which we mentioned before. On the other hand, it permits us to understand the meaning of this new relationship of the Church with the world. **'World' is understood here, in depth, as the spirit of modern times with which the group consciousness of the Church felt itself as a separate subject,** and, after the hot and cold wars were over, it sought dialogue and cooperation with this spirit" (J. Ratzinger, *Les principes de la théologie catholique – Esquisse et materiaux,* Paris: Tequi, 1985, pp. 426-427. See also J. Ratzinger, *Principles of Catholic Theology: Building Stones for a Fundamental Theology,* San Francisco: Ignatius Press, 1987, pp. 381-382.).

An evaluation of the adaptation of the Church to the world, such as the one the Council defended, should therefore take into account the polyvalent meanings with which the word was used.

B. Adaptation of the Church to the World: General Considerations

§ 63   Among the great novelties of Vatican II is its opening to the modern world.

Up until that novelty was introduced, the Church had always considered the world as a territory in which good and evil disputed. Since man was conceived in the sin of our first parents, an inherited stain that affected human nature in its very origin, it would not be conceivable for society itself to escape the consequences of sin. The coming of Our Lord and Savior Jesus Christ redeemed mankind from original sin. Nevertheless, it did not do so automatically, but in an inchoate manner. That is to say, even though Redemption was entirely accomplished by the Death and Resurrection of the Son of God, in order for the fruits of that Redemption to reach their plenitude, they require – after Baptism – the fidelity of every man to Faith and Morals inside the Divine Institution that Our Lord founded.

Only thus can those fruits expand throughout the world. Hence the divine mandate: "Go ye into the whole world, and preach the Gospel to every creature; he that believeth and is baptized shall be saved; but **he that believeth not shall be condemned**" (Mark 16:15-16). St. Matthew also puts forward the same mission entrusted to the Apostles and the Church: "All power is given to me in heaven and in earth. Going therefore, teach ye all nations: baptizing them in the name of the Father, and of the Son, and of the Holy Ghost, **teaching them to observe all things whatsoever I have commanded you**" (Matt 28:18-20). This divine mandate is also repeated in the Gospel of St. Luke: "**And thus it behooved Christ to suffer, and to rise again from the dead,** the third day; **and that penance and the remission of sins should be preached in his name, unto all nations,** beginning at Jerusalem" (Luke 24:46-47).

The premise of the divine mandate is, evidently, that the world is placed under the aegis of original sin: *Mundus totus positus est in maligno* [The whole world is seated in wickedness] (1 John 5:19).

Therefore, the world is good only to the degree that it consciously and explicitly accepts the fruits of the Redemption of Our Divine Savior and subjects itself to the divine mandate given to the Apostles and, consequently, to the Church.

§ 64

The acceptance of a doctrine by an ensemble of men – society or world – must be reflected in clear positions expressed in laws, customs and institutions. A group of men and, *a fortiori,* a society or the world, does not have a soul of its own to be saved or condemned. For this reason, its acceptance of the true Faith must favor men, considered individually, who are susceptible to salvation or condemnation. It would make no sense to speak of an acceptance by the world of the graces of Our Lord through the Church that would not be reflected, sooner or later, in laws, customs and institutions. [58]

§ 65

As one seeks out the laws, customs and institutions generated by the modern world, one sees that they are to a large extent the opposite of what was laid down as characteristic of a Catholic society. Born out of the deist philosophy of the Enlightenment and the Encyclopedists, synthesized in the trilogy Liberty – Equality – Fraternity and expressed in the *Declaration of the Rights of Man and of the Citizen,* it does nothing but generate laws, customs and institutions that it proudly presents as secular and, therefore, separated from the Church and the saving fruits of Redemption. Moreover, this world has always struggled for the destruction of Christian Civilization shaped by the evangelical principles.

The final utopia desired by the modern world and its agents is to establish a universal brotherhood independent of God, if not opposed to Him. Attempts at achieving this utopia were first sketched by the League of Nations, founded in 1919 with headquarters in Geneva and, after World War II, by the United Nations, headquartered in New York.

§ 66

Hence the fact that the Church has always exercised the greatest vigilance in regard to the modern world. [59]

---

58. True Catholic culture and civilization flourish precisely from this correspondence to grace. Prof. Plinio Corrêa de Oliveira expounds upon this topic in his work, *Revolution and Counter-Revolution* (Part I, chap. VII.2.B): "A soul in the state of grace possesses all virtues to a greater or lesser degree. Illuminated by faith, it has the elements to form the only true vision of the universe. The fundamental element of Catholic culture is the vision of the universe elaborated according to the doctrine of the Church. ... Catholic civilization is the structuring of all human relations, of all human institutions and of the State itself according to the doctrine of the Church."

59. On the errors of the modern world and the condemnations it has received from the ecclesiastical Magisterium, see the list of documents in Chap. I, Note 14. Also, about the Church's traditional teaching on modern errors, see Vol. *V, Animus Delendi II,* Part I, Chap.I, Premise 1.

C. The Church Should No Longer Orient and Influence the Temporal Order, but Adapt Herself to It

§ 67 Great theologians whose thought has marked the post-conciliar period take a stand on Church-world relations by giving their doctrine on adaptation.

Fr. Hans Urs von Balthasar, the first theologian to be awarded the "Paul VI International Prize," was highly praised by John Paul II when he received the prize at Vatican Palace's Clementine Hall. The Pontiff quoted phrases of von Balthasar and called them "grave, prophetic statements." [60]

In his work *De l'Intégration,* von Balthasar says: "It is certain that **the Church as a whole, in all of its members, but above all in its responsible Hierarchy, must adapt its structures ... to the historic situation;** ... but **then it appears clearly that the factor of development is found first on the side of earthly History, and only in second place and by way of consequence, on the side of the Church."** [61]

He continues: **"It is not so much the Church that develops in herself this face** [the visible face of God] **so as to adapt humanity to it; it is humanity, in its own development, that requires the Church to adapt herself to each human situation."** [62]

§ 68 Fr. Chenu develops the progressivist doctrine on Church-world relations:

"Ecclesia ad extra: **With this formula one hears the announcement of the Gospel and, therefore, the 'presence' of the Church *in* the** world – see the title of the new *Schema XIII* [The Church in the Modern World]. **It is not, for this reason, an extension of a previously constituted Church, nor an** *'excursus'* **about ecclesiastical society to affirm its rights over humanity. Here the very nature of the Church is what is at stake.** All the problems that she raises about herself, her structure, her government (*ad intra*) are imposed by her reason for existence: to propagate the Word

---

60. "Giovanni Paolo II alla consegna del Premio Internazionale Paulo VI – Hans Urs von Balthasar ha messo la sua conoscenza al servizio del vero que promana da Cristo," in *L'Osservatore Romano,* 6/24/1984; Vol. II, *Animus Injuriandi II,* Chap. I.1.

61. Hans Urs von Balthasar, *De l'intégration – Aspects d 'une théólogie de l'Histoire* (Brouges: Desclée de Brouwer, 1970), p. 136.

62. *Ibid.,* p. 137.

of God to men (*ad extra*) as the Mystical Body of Christ, after the Incarnation. **The Word of God and the Church** doubtlessly come from above ... nevertheless, they **are not superposed on the world, but incarnate themselves in it every day, according to the course of History that is formed gradually by successive generations.**[63]

§ 69   Fr. Chenu points out the first part of *Gaudium et spes* as an example of the Church's adaptation to the world:

"[At the Council] it was an inductive method that manifested itself everywhere, but very particularly in this famous *Schema XIII*. It is also the first time in the history of councils that a text of this kind was preceded by a secular introductory analysis rather than by a preliminary exposé of the Church position. **The authors of the text began by detaching themselves** in a certain way **from the problem of the Church to study the world in itself.** ... **The Church, officially becoming conscious of herself, obliges herself to be conscious of how the world is changing. That is to say, a Church that used to rest on an established order decides that from now on she must be known in the movement of the world.**"

"**In these** five or six **introductory pages** to Part I **of** *Gaudium et spes,* **there are very strong statements.** For example: 'We are entitled ... to speak of a real social and cultural transformation'; '**Ours is a new age of history**'; '**We are faced with a crisis of growth that shakes the world.**' I re-read all these texts complacently** as an historian as well as a theologian, not because they make an unsettling observation on novelties, but **because they go to the technical and economic roots, something the Church had never done until then** ... In other words, **she has assumed in her behavior these realities which she neither mastered nor had to direct,** but which were her own inasmuch as they are the place in which she should utter the Word of God."[64]

§ 70   The same new concept of Church *vis-à-vis* the world, stemming from *Gaudium et spes, is* confirmed by Fr. Congar:

"**It is not enough to see the Church and the world as two powers outside each other or placed face-to-face** (juxtaposed to each other) [sic]: '**The world' is no longer simply the power of the State, it is humanity working;** it is ready for the Church and clamoring for her if the Church is understood as the one who reveals to the world its own ultimate meaning.

---

63. M. D. Chenu, "La Chiesa e il mondo," in V.A., *I grandi temi del Concilio* (Rome: Paoline, 1965), p. 834.

64. *Jacques Duquesne interroge le Père Chenu,* p. 183.

"Thus, seen in its existential and concrete condition, the world is no longer a competitor opposed to the Church, but rather it is part of the substance of the Church, open to and ontologically or covertly oriented to her. *Gaudium et spes* often reveals the world affected by the hidden presence of Christ or his Holy Spirit." [65]

§ 71   This is ratified by Fr. Leo von Geusau, founder of the Dutch Documentation Center (DOC) and later of the well-known IDOC: [66]

"In the context of the Church as perfect society and its current variation expressed by the ecumenical movement, its place and implications in the world were not yet seen as a problem. Only in the last few years have a growing number of thinkers attempted to formulate the question in clear and explicit terms. It is extremely interesting and suggestive to briefly follow the process whereby **the world –**

---

65. Y. Congar, "Le rôle de l'Eglise dans le monde de ce temps," in V.A., *L'Eglise dans le monde de ce temps, vol.* II, pp. 315-316.

66. The IDOC promoted a series of lectures by personalities such as Frs. Chenu, Kung and Schillebeeckx outside of the Council's sessions. When Fr. Schillebeeckx spoke about *Schema XIII,* he was introduced by none other than Cardinal Alfrink, who congratulated IDOC on the work of its information service (H. Fesquet, *Le Journal du Concile,* p. 425). IDOC is a huge international network, a progressivist media superpower.

Both organizations were initially denounced by the magazines *Approaches* of Scotland and *Ecclesia* of Spain as semi-clandestine organizations plotting to subvert the Church by transforming her into an atheistic, desacralized, demythified, egalitarian New Church placed at the service of Communism. Based on those denunciations, Prof. Plinio Corrêa de Oliveira wrote several articles in *Folha de S. Paulo,* namely: "A propaganda progressista: um dinossauro discreto" (3/26/1969); "Artigo-bomba explode em Madrid" (5/7/1969); "Da infiltração à subversão" (5/14/1969); and "Os 'grupos proféticos' à serviço da Igreja-Nova e do Comunismo" (5/21/1969). He also wrote the article, "A Igreja Católica infiltrada por adversários velados," the introduction to a special edition entitled "Grupos ocultos tramam a subversào na Igreja" This special edition of 170,000 copies was spread widely throughout Brazil by the TFP. It was also reproduced by the magazines of the TFPs in Argentina, Chile, Colombia, Peru and the United States.

Involved with IDOC are theologians such as Frs. Bernard Lonergan, John Courtney Murray, Gregory Baum and Johann Baptist Metz; publishing houses like Herder & Herder, MacMillan & Sheed & Ward; newspapers and magazines such as the *National Catholic Reporter* (USA), *Informations Catholiques Internationales,* later called *Actualités Religieuses clans le monde* (France) and *Znak* (Poland).

which was considered a reality 'outside' the Church – was transformed into something which is essential to the very nature of the Church.** Perhaps the most macroscopic example was offered to us by the history of Vatican Council II and, above all, by the itinerary followed by the *Schema on the Church and the world*." [67]

§ 72   Msgr. Pierre Eyt of Bordeaux, a member of the International Theological Commission, dean of the famous *Institut Catholique* of Paris, later Archbishop of Bordeaux was made a Cardinal in 1994. His comments on *Gaudium et spes* reveal a categorical and straightforward spirit:

"In History, even recent History, there was a great temptation to conceive the Church and the world in a relationship of opposition and reciprocal exteriority, encamped and poised in a pathetic confrontation. *Gaudium et spes* **was intended to do away with this image and make us become more vividly aware of the convergence between the two vitally united movements.** ... Indeed, **on the one hand the world (the whole world) is inhabited by a powerful dynamism that orients it toward the Church. On the other hand, the Church is,** in the hands of God, **the living instrument of the passage of the world and of every man to the Kingdom. Nothing that interests the world can be foreign to the Church."** [68]

§ 73   Finally, Hans Küng, taking up the same doctrine, presents as an ideal the Church as a servant of the world:

"A Church which, in these times, forgets that she exists only for the generous service of men, her enemies and the world, loses her dignity, her power to convince, and her reason for existing, because she truly gives up following Christ. However, **a Church that remains aware that it will not be herself, but rather the Kingdom of God, that will come** in power and majesty' **finds in her smallness her true grandeur."** [69]

*

67. Leo Alting von Geusau, "La Chiesa 'scandalo' del mondo," in V.A., *La fine della Chiesa come società perfetta* (Verona: Mondadori, 1968), p. 157

68. Pierre Eyt, "Igreja e mutações sócio-culturais," in V.A., *Igreja do futuro* (Petrópolis: Vozes, 1973), pp. 17-18.

69. H. Küng, A *Igreja,* vol. I, p. 144.

D. On Adapting the Church to the World, the Limits between the Spiritual and Temporal Spheres Begin to Dissolve

§ 74   Among the most important consequences of conciliar doctrine on the adaptation of the Church to the world is the virtual disappearance of the limits between the spiritual and temporal spheres. Hence the two become mixed.

This paragraph by Leo von Geusau expresses well the consequence of this conciliar doctrine:

"After Christ the limits between the 'chosen people' and the rest of humanity became increasingly vague, and it became impossible to draw a line separating the two fields. The differences between the people of God and the rest of humanity ('the world') will never correspond to precise limits, be they geographical or moral, racial or confessional, historic or cultural. **Nor can one speak any longer of a distinction between the Church and the world in terms of the redeemed and the non-redeemed, the kingdom and the darkness."** [70]

A little later, Geusau adds: **"If,** therefore, **the Church exists because of the world, there must be a function related to this actual world.** A majority of Protestant and Catholic theologians already agree on this, and **chapter II of the Dogmatic Constitution on the Church** [*Lumen gentium*] **made this view its own. It no longer speaks of the 'missionary duty' of the Church as though it were something beyond and above her 'normal' life, but of the 'missionary nature of the Church,' which implies a relationship with the world that is part and parcel of the Church herself. When the Church is mentioned as the 'sacrament' of the kingdom of God, it is understood that the Church no longer faces the world in an attitude of conquest. The Church no longer identifies with the kingdom of God,** so that the very kingdom may be extended to the degree that the number of people who belong to the Church increases." [71]

In brief, von Geusau, whose words are cited here as an example of the general thinking of the progressivist current, draws from conciliar doctrine a consequence of such great import as to revolutionize the very concept of the spiritual sphere and the temporal sphere. One would dissolve within the other. What will result from that? A theocratic State, a secularized Church, or an absolute confusion?

---

70. L. A. von Geusau, "La Chiesa 'scandalo' del mondo," p. 178.

71. *Ibid.,* pp. 181-182.

E. Behind the Concept of Adaptation Looms the Notion of Divine Revelation in the World and in History...

§ 75

If we try to analyze in depth the underlying doctrinal perspective of the various authors cited in this Item, we will see that the change in the nature and mission of the Church is based on a new conception of Revelation. The latter would no longer be the ensemble of principles contained in the teachings and examples that Christ bequeathed to men during His life, the legacy of which the Church is the custodian and interpreter. Revelation would be the manifestation of a "cosmic Christ" immanent inside every man, in the ensemble of men – humanity – and in the evolution of the world through the ages, that is, History. So the world and History would have immanences of revelation that the Church does not know, and they would be, properly speaking, the vehicles of revelation. Hence the need for the Church to open up and constantly adapt herself to this world, to History in general, and to the cosmos, all of them mysteriously "Christified." [72]

Let us look at some conciliar theologians who present History as a vehicle for divine revelation.

§ 76

In his work *Level the Ramparts,* published before the Council and which later exerted considerable influence, von Balthasar preaches the self-destruction of the Church. [73] In it he comes up with a new doctrine according to which the distinction between God and the world is coming to an end. Consequently, the world would have become a vehicle for revelation. Here is what "perhaps the most learned man of our time," in the words of Cardinal de Lubac, [74] wrote:

"At first, the spaces of creation with its generic revelation of God and the space of Redemption and the Church as a special guide of truth and grace ... were separate. At least in the realm of ideas, it was possible to carefully cross the threshold. **Here also walls have crumbled; and although the order of Creation**

---

72. On the "cosmic Christ" see Vol. VI, *Inveniet Fidei?,* Chap. V.6.B, D.a; Vol. VII, *Destructio Dei,* Chaps. II.2, III.3; Vol. VIII, *Fumus Satanae,* Chaps. I.3.C, II, V.3; Vol. IX, *Creatio,* Chaps. IV.3.B, V; Vol. X, *Peccatum-Redemptio,* Chaps. V.1, VII.I, VII1.2, IX.2.

73. An overview of the destructive intentions of *Level the Ramparts* is given in Vol. IV, *Animus Delendi I,* Chap. II, Note 25.

74. Hans Urs von Balthasar is "perhaps the most learned man of his time," says Fr. Henri de Lubac in a chapter dedicated to an apologia for his oldest disciple, in the work *Paradoxe et mystère de l'Eglise* (Paris: Aubier-Montaigne, 1967), p. 184.

and the order of Redemption, world and Church, must always remain distinct, [75] we hear as new the words of Christ who, alpha and omega of everything created, **recapitulates in Himself everything in heaven and earth;** and who was thus destined, already before the Creation of the world, to report to the Father the world that was made through Him, with Him and in Him. He is not the world; but even though He is younger than that world into which He descended and from which He took his nature and being, He is at the same time older. In a mysterious sense, the world was made to his image ...

"This high wall between God and the world was kept standing for an exceedingly long time. For this reason, anyone who wished to turn to God had to abandon the world for a time or forever. Now also this last wall is falling ... Crumbling walls can bury many things which, formerly protected by them, appeared to be alive. But in the space that is thus made, there is a more ample participation." [76]

§ 77   De Lubac is author of the book *Catholicisme,* which became "the object of the worst suspicions" when it was published in 1938. He later wrote *Surnaturel* attacking "certain complications of modern Scholastics." [77] That did not prevent him from being sent a letter of encouragement by Pius XII, [78] invited to participate in the Council's Preparatory Commission, named a conciliar *perito* by John XXIII, praised by Paul VI and elevated to Cardinal by John Paul II. His opinion is regarded as one of the most authentic interpretations of the Council; even his old work is now seen as having been a forerunning sign of the Council. This is why we quote from it. In his book, the Jesuit says:

---

75. Von Balthasar admits, *pro forma,* that the world and the Church "must remain always distinct." In this he shows less radicality than von Geusau, cited above. Nevertheless, the explanation of a world that supposedly became divinized in the end leads to the same consequence.

76. Hans Urs von Balthasar, *Abbattere i bastioni* (Turin: Borla, 1966), pp. 115-116.

77. H. de Lubac, *Entretien autour de Vatican II* (Paris: Cerf, 1985), pp. 10-11.

78. In an interview with Marco Politi, the then newly designated Cardinal de Lubac comments on his "rehabilitation" by Pius XII: "Mind you that I've received from Pius XII an excellent letter; it had no shadow of a censure, it was very encouraging." "Irrequieto ma ubbidiente – La Chiesa e i suoi protagonisti, Henri de Lubac," in *Il Messaggero,* 2/2/1983, p. 3.

"God acts in History, God reveals himself through History. More, God inserts himself in History, thus giving it a 'religious consecration' that obliges one to take it seriously. **Historical realities therefore have a depth, they must be understood from the spiritual standpoint:** *historika pneumatikos;* **and in turn, spiritual realities appear in the making and must be understood spiritually:** *pneumatika historikos* ... **If our salvation is essentially social, all of History becomes the obligatory interpreter between God and each one of us."** [79]

§ 78   The following excerpts by Fr. Chenu make very clear the progressivist notion that divine revelation takes place uninterruptedly in History and in the world:

* "Evangelical truth will be, therefore, of a type different from metaphysical truth. ... The very word 'truth' in biblical language, which the exegetes have masterly analyzed, is impregnated with an original density: truth and fidelity, justice, certainty, peace, uprightness. 'Do the truth' says St. John (John 3:21; 1 John 1:6); an unintelligible expression for a certain intellectualism. It **[the truth]** therefore does not derive from propositions placed outside of time, which we manipulate according to the structures of logic in a kind of sacred metaphysics under the custody of an authority. Rather, it **proceeds from a History guided by God in events of salvation in which He reveals Himself. Revelation is the act by which God revealed Himself in the course of History and continues to reveal Himself, by an extension that unfolds through the centuries until the total realization fulfilled by Christ in the plenitude of time.**

"God speaks today in the Christian community starting from this 'Christological concentration' that the Spirit ... distributes and reveals in a multiplicity of signs announcing the things of the future, that is, the new order of things born out of the death and Resurrection of Christ.

"Time enters into the fabric of revelation. Thus, the theology that comes from it is tightly stretched between two poles: the eternal truth of its object and the contingent situation in time. It must fulfill two fundamental conditions: Provide a [new] expression to the truth of the Christian message and adapt that same expression to all situations. The 'situation' includes the totality of the creative consciousness that man has of himself at a given moment, the synthesis of scientific, artistic, economic, political, social

---

79. H. de Lubac, *Catholicisme – Les aspects sociaux du dogme* (Paris: Cerf, 1947), pp. 133-134.

or moral forms in which the conscience of a generation finds the fulfillment of its hopes in its own expression.

"From this standpoint, in the new civilization, 'secularization' as an awareness of the promotion of man and his autonomy gives the theologian an auspicious occasion for its understanding. In the final analysis, language itself ... must be a product of the community in a state of effervescence and expression of the Spirit. **By its nature, in the realm of faith theology is,** therefore, **in a state of inquiry."**[80]

* "The evangelical aspirations to universal brotherhood become theologically clear when 'neighbor' is defined in terms of a worldwide socialization. **The solidarity of the world and the diversity of its civilizations form, in the laborious creation of a 'human community,' an admirable picture and ... a challenge for the Catholicity of the Church,** which has been too long confined, her theology included, to the West. **The theologian finds here something like a second inspiration of the transcendence of the Word of God. These are so many 'signs of the times' of God spelled out in secular realities.**

"Does not this kind of historicity ruin the speculative construction of theology, or will it not at least reduce theology to a rather artificial superstructure? The blunders of a type of pseudo-evangelical Positivism might make us fear so. But let us leave them to their failure. Let us rather observe that any articulation of a 'speculative' science on History, that is, in the present case, any constructing of a science-theology on the History of salvation, will not proceed without problems or without risk." [81]

F. ... that Demands a New Theology

§ 79   Fr. Chenu applies these principles to a new conception of theology:

"Such, then, is the economy of revelation in the Old and the New Covenants: It is not a History in which a revelation occurred, but a History revealing itself. This introduces a serious problem for theology. It will oblige theology not to occupy itself with ontological relations and with definitions of essences, but

---

80. M. D. Chenu, "Omelia tenuta nel Corso della celebrazione Eucaristica," in V.A., *L'avvenire della Chiesa,* pp. 62-63.

81. M. D. Chenu, "The History of Salvation," in V.A., *Theology of Renewal,* vol. I, p. 163.

to be primarily a reflection on a becoming, on a plan of salvation. It is within a History that theology encounters the problem of ontological relations.

"The theologian, then, in the use he makes of the documents, will have to respect both their authority and their origin, and this he cannot do except by integrating them into an historical pattern of thought, rather than using them merely as a point of departure."[82]

How then, should this new theology in the making be? Should theology no longer be deduced from the eternal principles contained in Revelation and in its sources, the Scriptures and Tradition? Would it become a continuous adaptation to History and the world and, therefore, an empirical science?

§ 80   The answer is clearly given by the well-known Canadian theologian, Fr. Bernard Lonergan,[83] a professor at Rome's Pontifical Urbanian University:

"Before [the Council] ... theology was a deductive, and had become largely an empirical science. It was a deductive science in the sense that its theses were conclusions to be proven from the premises provided by Scripture and Tradition. It has become an empirical science in the sense that Scripture and Tradition now supply not premises, but data. The data has to be viewed in its historical perspective. It has to be interpreted in the light of contemporary techniques and procedures.

'Whereas before the step from premise to conclusion was brief, simple, and certain, today the steps from data to interpretation are long, arduous and, at best, probable. An empirical science does not demonstrate. It accumulates information, develops understanding, increasingly masters its materials, but it does not preclude the uncovering of further relevant data, the emergence of new insights, the attainment of a more comprehensive view."[84]

In another passage, Lonergan says: "So a contemporary Catholic theology has to be not only Catholic but also ecumenical. Its concerns must extend not only to Christians but also non-Christians and atheists. It has to learn to draw not only on

82. *Ibid.*, p. 159.

83. Battista Mondin places him among the ten greatest theologians of this century. *Os grandes teólogos do século vinte*, vol. I, pp. 269-282.

84. Bernard Lonergan, "Theology in its New Context," in V.A., *Theology of Renewal,* vol. I, pp. 37-38.

the modern philosophies, but also on the relatively new sciences of religion, psychology, sociology, and the new techniques of the communication arts." [85]

§ 81   In a part of his previously cited homily, Fr. Chenu returns to his conception of the new theology, this time buttressing his arguments with quotes from *Gaudium et spes*:

"Theology ... is oriented by its goal, that is, the daily interpretation of the Gospel. Therefore **every theological enunciation must be verified in the event that reveals and harvests the reality (GS 3f, 10f, 22, 40, 42f etc.) and in the event that efficaciously transforms reality. Vice-versa, the 'signs of the times' have a hermeneutic and maieutic [86] function to discover new aspects of the faith hitherto unrevealed or hardly revealed at all (GS 40, 44, 62) ...**

"Theology, then, be it in the Scripture, in the 'world' or in its philosophical self-interpretation enters into a critical confrontation that prevents it from closing itself inside its problems and systems and moving only within the consecrated circle of its problems." [87]

§ 82   Journalist Fr. Bartolomeo Sorge, SJ, analyzes the failure of the modern world and the rise of the post-modern world. Sorge claims that Vatican II had an intuition of the end of the modern world and seeks to show how conciliar guidelines suit well the new world supposedly being born. In the transition he describes, he sees above all one danger: an attempt to return to the "medieval cultural experience." As he expounds his thesis, it becomes clear that in its adaptations to the modern world, the Conciliar Church abandoned the theological and sociological standards of the past to which, in his view, it could no longer return. A new theology, therefore, becomes imperative. In fact, Sorge says:

"No less dangerous than absence [that is, the attitude of those who defend the modern world without taking into account its crisis and replacement by the post-modern one] would be a presence conceived according to the paradigm of the 'medieval cultural experience.' The temptation is real. Indeed, some ask themselves

---

85. *Ibid.,* p. 41.

86. Maieutics: Socrates' dialectic and pedagogic method of asking a great number of questions in order to form from particular and concrete cases, by way of induction, a general concept about the object in question.

87. M. D. Chenu, "Omelia tenuta nel corso della celebrazione eucaristica," in V.A., *L'avvenire della Chiesa,* pp. 70-71.

whether restoring to man the sense of transcendence and primacy of the person over structures can mean anything other than repeating the 'medieval cultural experience.' But that is not how things present themselves. The world reality is profoundly distinct.

"There are acquisitions of the modern world that are already irreversible, such as the pluralism of cultures and views of life or the awareness of the autonomy and the laic nature of temporal realities. They make unthinkable and impossible the homogeneity typical of 'medieval Christendom.' ... At the same **time, the Church's awareness of her nature and mission also has grown profoundly, to the point of making unthinkable the medieval conception of Church-world relations.**

"As for the rest, the history of the 'modern world' and its crisis should contribute to remove any doubt. **The presence of a Church, which for an exceedingly long time remained anchored to the paradigm of the 'medieval cultural experience,' only pro-duced an even graver rupture with the modern world. The con-demnation of the 'pretended freedom of conscience' which Gre-gory XVI defined as a 'delirium'** (*deliramentum*), **the** *Syllabus* **of Pius IX, the anti-Modernism of the days of Pius X,** notwith-standing its historic justification, **did not help the 'modern world' to open itself to the whole truth, but ended by leaving it in its con-tradiction and crisis. For this reason, the Council,** at the dawn of the post-modern world and taking into account the changes that oc-curred, **has characterized the Church's new attitude as one of dialogue and mediation."** [88]

Further on, Sorge offers an outline for a new social theology: "Why should it mean a 'compromise' – as is feared – to **achieve together a society based on respect for freedom of conscience, on the principle that all men are equal and have the same hu-man and civil rights, on the right of peoples to self-determina-tion,** on liberty of culture and scientific research, **on the principle of tolerance and pluralism – even religious, and on respect for every man, even when he errs?"** [89]

It is no wonder that Fr. Sorge, on advocating a new theologi-cal conception of the Church in consonance with the modern and post-modern worlds, combats memorable documents that represent the struggle of the Church against the French Revolution, Liberalism

---

88. Bartolomeo Sorge, "I cristiani nel mondo postmoderno – Presenza, assenza, mediazione?," in *La Civiltà Cattolica*, 5/7/1983, p. 249.

89. *Ibid.,* p. 251.

and Modernism. Indeed, how could conciliar theology feel at ease alongside the teaching of the Magisterium that judges and condemns it? Sorge, therefore, vehemently "anathematizes" those documents to which, incidentally, he renders an evolutionist homage.

§ 83   In this particular instance, Cardinal Ratzinger takes an analogous position. He labels as "provisional dispositions" the anti-Liberal and anti-Modernist documents of the pontifical Magisterium. In an official pronouncement on the launching of the *Instruction on the Theologian's Ecclesial Vocation,* the then Prefect of the Congregation for the Doctrine of the Faith issues this extremely grave opinion:

"The text also presents the various forms of bonds that rise from the different degrees of magisterial teaching. It affirms – perhaps for the first time with this clarity – that **there are decisions of the Magisterium that cannot be a last word on the matter** as such, **but are,** in an essential determination of the problem, **above all an expression of pastoral prudence, a kind of provisional disposition. Its nucleus remains valid, but the particulars,** which the circumstances of the times have influenced, **may need further corrections.**

"In this regard, one may think of the declarations of Popes in the last century about religious liberty, as well as the anti-Modernist decisions at the beginning of this century, above all, the decisions of the Biblical Commission of the time. As a cry of alarm in the face of hasty and superficial adaptations, they remain fully justified. A personage such as Johann Baptist Metz said, for example, that **the Church's anti-Modernist decisions render the great service of preserving her from falling into the liberal-bourgeois world. But in the details of the determinations they contain, they became obsolete** after having fulfilled their pastoral mission in their own time." [90]

§ 84   The most important consequence of the adaptation of the Church to the world is its effect on theology. Theology used to be founded on Revelation and on the infallible teaching of the Magisterium, which scrutinized the Scriptures and Tradition, the sources of Revelation. Now, God is supposedly immanent in creation, and revelation is to be found inside man, in the world and in History ... a real "Copernican revolution" [91] at the very foundation of the Faith.

---

90. Joseph Ratzinger, "Instruction on the Theologian's Ecclesial Vocation," published with the title "Rinnovato dialogo fra Magistero e Teologia," in *L'Osservatore Romano,* 6/27/1990, p. 6.

91. a. The expression is by Emmanuel Lanne, OSB, commenting on the conciliar concept of the local Church. "L'Eglise locale et l'Eglise

G. Such Doctrine Also Implies the Virtual Destruction of Christendom ...

§ 85

     As the Reader can see, the conciliar concept of adapting the Church to the world is fraught with consequences. One of them deserves special attention as far as Church-State relations are concerned. Within the framework of the conciliar principles of adaptation and the virtual promiscuity of the spiritual and temporal spheres, the notion of Christendom appears to lose its meaning and be doomed to disappear. Indeed, Christendom has always been understood as a projection of the Catholic Church onto the temporal sphere. Christendom is established to the degree that the principles of Catholic doctrine shape the customs, laws and institutions in autonomous and sovereign States, which, as such, become gradually more Catholic, constituting the temporal Kingdom of Our Lord Jesus Christ in the concert of nations.

     So, in order for Christendom to exist, the Church must take upon herself the mission of expanding the principles of her doctrine so that the two spheres are distinct from each other and the temporal sphere allows itself to be docilely shaped by the wholesome action of the Church.

     Now then, these elements, as we have seen above, are apparently denied by the conciliar doctrine on adaptation. It is no won-

---

universelle," in *Irenikon* (Chevetogne, Belgium, 1970) 43, p. 490, in Y. Congar, *Le Concile de Vatican II,* pp. 170-171.

b. Although the metaphor was originally employed with regard to relations between the universal Church and local churches, it later took on by way of analogy broader meanings such as those mentioned. It is, for example, what Cardinal Suenens notes about the precedence that *Lumen gentium* gives to the 'people of God' in relation to the Hierarchy: "The first question: 'Church of God, what are you?' was answered with the constitution *Lumen gentium,* which is the principal text of Vatican II, the key. **It sought to give a vision of the Church that was no longer traditional, but which contained the essential, the quintessence of the essential – to such a point that it ended by deciding that the second chapter should be dedicated to the people of God.** 'Church of God, what are you?' **First of all it is the Church of the baptized. The Pope is no more baptized than you or I. And this is fundamental: to place the emphasis above all on that which makes us common. I believe that this is what has been called 'Copernican revolution.'** The idea is not mine, but I greatly appreciate it" ("Un nuovo battesimo per la Cristianita," interview to S. Stracca, in *Avvenire,* 10/23/ 1992).

der, then, that the negation of the ideal of Christendom is attributed to this doctrine.

§ 86   Speaking after the Council, Cardinal Jean Daniélou, a conciliar *perito* and a consultant to the Secretariat for Unbelievers, announces the end of Christendom:

"One of the aspects of the present crisis is that we are witnessing the end of a particular form of the incarnation of Christianity in Western culture. We refer to so-called Christendom, which started with Constantine and was the reality of the Western world until the 19th century, founded on the fact that Christianity became, so to speak, the inspiration of all Western literary, philosophical and artistic culture. It was the expression of Christianity in civilization itself. **This form today is not only going through a crisis, but its very value is ever more profoundly being cast into doubt. ... Perhaps we are entering a world in which Christianity will no longer have the same representation in culture and civilization. We will have to give up the idea of a Christian civilization and even of a Christian humanism."** [92]

§ 87   For his part, Cardinal Suenens says: **"Sociological Christianity is falling like a scaffold around a building. I have never attributed the same importance to scaffold and building. We must return to our roots."** [93]

§ 88   Cardinal Congar says basically the same, attributing this change to the conciliar documents. He refers to Christendom generally as "relations between the spiritual and the temporal inherited from the Middle Ages:"

"In full consonance with the dogmatic constitution *Lumen gentium*, *Gaudium et spes* profoundly changes the manner, inherited from the Middle Ages, of viewing the relationships between the spiritual and the temporal, something that weighed on classic teaching until the Preparatory Theological Commission introduced chapter IX of *De Ecclesia*. **We will see that this change amounts less to a contradiction [with the past] than to an evolution [from it]: It is the problem that has changed. It has switched from the juridical and political planes to that of anthropology and personal faith. ... One may say that, with documents such as *Gaudium et spes* or the *Declaration on Religious Liberty*, Vatican II has definitively turned the page of the**

---

92. Jean Daniélou, "Relações entre Igreja e civilização," in V.A., *Cinco problemas que desafiam a Igreja hoje,* p. 139.

93. L. J. Suenens, *ibid.*

Middle Ages. Indeed, the perspectives of *Gaudium et spes* are quite different." [94]

§ 89   In another work, Congar takes up an analogous thesis, emphasizing that any "nostalgia for a Christianization" must come to an end:

"Some mentalities are still taken up by the nostalgia for a new baptism of Clovis ... **With the *Declaration on Religious Liberty* and the pastoral constitution *Gaudium et spes* on the Church in the modern world** – a meaningful title! – **the Church of Vatican II has clearly placed herself in today's pluralist world and,** without denying what greatness there was, **she cut the ropes that kept her moored to the banks of the Middle Ages."** [95]

§ 90   A similar opinion is upheld by a theologian from Louvain, Antoine Vergote, professor of psychology and philosophy at that city's university and member of various scientific associations. He expounded his theses to 223 theologians from around the world gathered for the fifth congress of the magazine *Concilium.* From his talk, we chose these words:

"It is often said: Christendom died. And we are all agreed to bury it in the cultural past. No political or international institution will base its principles on Faith in God and in Jesus Christ any longer. ... The death of sociological and political Christendom has liberated man and the world." [96]

§ 91   Also Chenu, commenting on *Gaudium et spes,* appears to announce an opposition between Vatican II's doctrine and the concept of Christendom:

"'The Church is in the world.' In today's world, the Council specifies. ... **[The Church] is 'missionary' to such a point that she is only herself** when she comes out of herself, if one may say this. **And this is so not because of a tiresome concession, but by nature.** There are no two churches, just as there are no two beliefs: The same faith is at the same time communion with Christ and witness in the world. **In contrast with a certain image of Christendom, what we have here, we believe, is not a growth due to a fervor**

---

94. *Y.* Congar, "Le rôle de l'Eglise dans le monde de ce temps," in V.A., *L'Eglise dans le monde de ce temps,* vol. II, pp. 311-312.

95. *Y.* Congar, *La crisi nella Chiesa e Mons. Lefebvre,* p. 52.

96. Antoine Vergote, "La presenza della Chiesa nella società di domani - Riflessioni bibliche," in V.A., *L'avvenire della Chiesa,* pp. 163, 165.

that springs up during a second phase, when one is heavily laden with goods, as if this were a supplementary need, almost an appendix. It is only one thing." [97]

§ 92   As we can see, it is habitual for theologians who interpret the documents of Vatican II to show the existing opposition between conciliar doctrine and the concept of Christendom. To give a few more examples, we now quote excerpts from two who hold apparently opposed positions. On the one hand, we have Fr. Gustavo Gutierrez, OP, the controversial Peruvian intellectual considered the "father" of Liberation Theology. On the other is Fr. Gustave Martelet, SJ, a disciple of Cardinal de Lubac, conciliar *perito* and professor at the Jesuit Faculties of Lyon-Fourviere, certainly a "moderate" in comparison to the first.

The *ardito* Gutierrez writes:

"It is classic to say that Vatican II has put an end to the mentality of Christendom. It is time for dialogue and service to the world ... John XXIII stressed in the Council the task of opening up to the world, finding an appropriate theological language, bearing witness to a Church of the poor." [98]

For his part, the "moderate" Martelet says:

§ 93   **"Compared to a time in which the Church could appear as encompassing all of society, Christendom no longer has conditions to represent the status of the Church in our present societies.** Even more, **in the eyes of the Church herself, Christendom is not an essential ideal for her.** The Church did not wait for Vatican II to realize this and say it ... Vatican II should not turn back to condemn or praise a system of relations which, having played its role, should still not be discredited. Nevertheless, **the manner in which the Council defines the mission of the Church in the world visibly excludes every possible return to formulas which the development of human and Christian consciousness has made obsolete."** [99]

These excerpts are quite expressive and dispense with the need for any comment.

---

97. M. D. Chenu, "'Vox populi, vox Dei'. L'opinione pubblica nell'ambito del popolo di Dio," in V.A., *La fine delta Chiesa come società perfetta,* pp. 222-223.

98. Gustavo Gutierrez, "Os pobres na Igreja," in *Concilium,* 1977/4, p. 89.

99. Gustave Martelet, *Deux mille ans d'Eglise en question,* p. 38.

H. ... and the Preaching of Socialism

§ 94
Assuming that the promiscuity between the spiritual and temporal spheres had been established, several conciliar thinkers began to present "theologies" of socio-political realities. For this purpose, they interpret Socialism at times as a temporal expression of religious principles, and at other times as a "sign of the times" provided by the modern world to which the Church must pay heed.

Let us see, as examples, an excerpt by Schillebeeckx in the first sense and one by Chenu in the second.

§ 95
Schillebeeckx states: **"The discovery of the human being in his full secularity** ... also **characterizes the present attitude of the Church in a fundamental fashion. Today's Church,** without giving up her faith in grace and in the kingdom of God ... **must believe in man more than ever.** When man becomes conscious of himself, we find ourselves faced with a reality that discloses its more intimate secret only through the revelation of the kingdom of God. **Spiritual goods ... must be fraternally distributed among men as a sign of the return of Christ. This earthly Christian Socialism, if we can so express ourselves ... this Christian messianism,** which as a collective force must reinforce hope in this world also in the realm of an earthly life established in justice and love, **is a sign that points to Christ not only as head of the Church but also as sovereign of the world.** ...

"The humanization of the world, and in it, the humanization of man, essentially belong to the wealth of messianic goods that Christ conquered for us with the sacrifice of his life and which Christians, co-heirs of Christ, must therefore fraternally share among themselves. Appreciating human value in the cultural, social and economic fields, and providing all men with the same living conditions, helping under-developed countries, etc. are not profane, secular tasks to be fulfilled only with a Christian spirit. They are, above all, a profound realization of the Christian consciousness of its own vocation." [100]

Alluding to Marxists, Schillebeeckx continues:

"Also, **we Christians have left this messianism too much to non-Christians, causing the most profound inspiration of messianism to be reduced to a purely earthly messianic dynamism."** [101]

---

100. E. Schillebeeckx, "I laici nel popolo di Dio," in V.A., *La fine della Chiesa come società perfetta,* pp. 207-208.

101. *Ibid.,* p. 208.

Finally, the theologian from Nijmegen concludes: **"Only if Christian lay people again bring to the world this earthly aspect of religious messianism will the Church appear to the world as a reality that speaks to hearts."** [102]

§ 96   While Schillebeeckx presents the Church as an agent transforming Socialism into religious messianism, Chenu, in the next text, pretends that the world gives the Church socialization as a "sign of the times" according to which she should reinterpret herself.

Chenu comments on excerpts of *Gaudium et spes*: "It is not the faithful alone who in their personal lives give light and benefit through their presence in the world ... but the Church herself as community of the word. '**The Church** has a visible social structure which is a sign of its unity in Christ: As such, she **can be enriched and is being enriched by the evolution of social life,** not as if something were missing in the constitution which Christ gave the Church, but **in order to understand this constitution more deeply, express it better and adapt it more successfully to our times.'**

"Such a statement by the Council (GS 44), fundamental in itself, establishes the nature, causes and criteria for a presence in the world: in this relation, **the world, 'through the evolution of social life,' and through the massive phenomenon of socialization today helps the Church in the act of evangelization."** [103]

§ 97   According to these authors, [104] the preaching of Socialism and the assimilation of socialization appear as matter-of-fact consequences of the new conciliar doctrine of adapting the Church to the modern world.

*

§ 98   Based on the aforementioned authors, we conclude this Item 2 on the concessions of the conciliar Church to the modern world by saying that:

- The texts of the conciliar documents are ambiguous about the concept of world;

- In the adaptation of the Church to the world, the Council appears implicitly to deny the divine mandate of Our Lord to

---

102. *Ibid.*

103. M. D. Chenu, Vox populi, vox Dei.' L'opinione pubblica nell'ambito del popolo di Dio," p. 223.

104. The Reader will find analogous testimonies by other conciliar theologians in Vol. V, *Animus Delendi II,* Part I, Chap. IV.3.

the Church and to accept, also implicitly, the errors of the modern world;

- From every indication, the superiority of the Church regarding the temporal sphere is denied; as well as her mission to orient and influence it;

- Consistent with the conciliar concept of adaptation, the limits between the spiritual and temporal spheres are diluted;

- The notion of a divine immanence in the cosmos, supposedly manifested by divine revelation in the world and in History, appears to loom behind the doctrine of adaptation;

- Such a doctrine revolutionizes theology, which was deductive based on Revelation, and now becomes inductive based on human and historic realities;

- Important teachings of the Church's previously anti-Liberal and anti-Modernist doctrine are "anathematized" in the name of theological adaptation;

- Another consequence of the doctrine of adaptation is the virtual destruction of Christendom and the banishment of its ideal among men. A messianic-religious Socialism is advocated for society and a secular socialization for the Church as a result of the reversibility between the two spheres.

As we see it, these are, in synthesis, the grave doctrinal concessions stemming from conciliar ambiguity in regard to adaptation to the modern world.

*

§ 99

If we add to these the conclusions reached in Item 1, we find that it is difficult to conceive a broader doctrinal panorama than the one which unfolds as we consider the concessions Vatican II made to the false religions and the modern world.

As a rule, such concessions are a direct fruit of the ambiguity in conciliar documents.

*   *   *

Chapter X

OTHER CONSEQUENCES: CONCILIAR
AMBIGUITY PROVOKES A CRISIS OF DISCIPLINE,
GENERATING A CRISIS OF FAITH AND MORALS

§ 1

As we have seen above, [1] ambiguity in conciliar texts harbored old tendencies and doctrines which, defeated at Vatican I and condemned by St. Pius X, had still not died. As a matter of fact, in spite of some counter-measures taken in the period from Benedict XV to Pius XII, they became stronger. At Vatican II, they won. [2]

With its attitude of "lowering the drawbridge" of the Church citadel to her enemies, [3] "opening doors and windows for the new currents," [4] "leveling the ramparts" of the Holy City, [5] Vatican II inevitably gave those currents a great impetus and an unmistakable hope of imposing their designs on the whole Church.

§ 2

Furthermore, the ambiguity in the conciliar texts caused a certain reservation in conservative Catholic opinion. However hard some Prelates, representative of conservatism, strove to present the Council as a continuation of the ancient doctrines, [6] as time went by and the

---

1. Chap. III.

2. Chaps. IV, VI.1.

3. Y. Congar, *Eglise Catholique et France moderne* (Paris: Hachette, 1978), p. 47.

4. *Ibid.,* p. 55.

5. *Ibid.,* p. 47; see also H. U. von Balthasar, *Abbatere i bastioni.*

6. The words of Bishop Rudolf Graber of Regensburg present a typical illustration of this: "The attribution of an anti-conciliar position to the so-called 'conservatives' can be deemed an imputation that borders on bad faith. There is nothing so false as that. On the contrary, we claim an attitude of the greatest fidelity to the Council, of which we have made ourselves the defenders. What happens is that we interpret its texts just as they were written. By uniting ourselves to Pope Paul VI, we vigorously oppose the so-called 'post-conciliar mentality,' which completely ignores the 'identification of the Council, in its precepts and teachings, with the doctrine and tradition bequeathed to the Church, even if it is an extraordinary evolution' (in *Adhortatio Apostolica Petrum et Paulum,* February 22, 1967). This is the sense in which the considerations we are about to make must be interpreted. Therefore, by no means are they directed against the Council, but are meant instead as a cry of alert in the face of certain symptoms of crisis that are multiplying in an alarming fashion" (R. Graber, *Por que a Igreja está em crise,* Rio de Janeiro: Grifo, 1971, pp. 19-20).

Council was applied, a large part of the faithful realized that this was not the case. They saw that the Church was facing a reform which, considering the broad scope of the themes it covered, the importance of the changes in direction that it entailed and its profound consequences on contemporary Catholic theological thinking, constitutes a development of unparalleled importance in ecclesiastical History.[7] The reservations of the faithful increased in greater or lesser degree as the fruits of the Council developed and the enthusiasm of the progressivist *arditi* increased.

Since Vatican II was ambiguous, both positions – of the ardent progressivists and of the cautious mass of Catholic faithful – were more or less inevitable. Such states of mind are the logical fruits of the process of the development of conciliar ambiguity. It was to be expected that the progressivist advance would become accentuated and that the reaction of the faithful against it would crystallize more and more.

Thus, what was predictable began to happen. The crisis in the Church became patent.

*

---

7. On this matter, Prof. Plinio Corrêa de Oliveira comments: "It is painful to say this. But, in this sense, the evidence singles out the *Second Vatican Council* as one of the greatest calamities, if not the greatest, in the history of the Church. From the Council, the *'smoke of Satan' (Sermon* of Paul VI on June 29, 1972) penetrated the Church in unbelievable proportions. And this smoke is spreading day by day, with the terrible force of gases in expansion. To the scandal of countless souls, the Mystical Body of Christ entered, as it were, a sinister process of self-destruction.

"History narrates the innumerable dramas the Church has suffered in the 20 centuries of her existence: oppositions that germinated outside her and tried to destroy her from outside; malignancies that formed within her, were cut off by her, and thereafter ferociously tried to destroy her from outside. When, however, has history witnessed an attempted demolition of the Church like the present one? No longer undertaken by an adversary, it was termed a *'self-destruction'* in a most lofty pronouncement having worldwide repercussion *(Allocution* of Paul VI to the Lombard Seminary on December 7, 1968). From this resulted an immense debacle for the Church and what still remains of Christian civilization. The *'Ostpolitik'* of the Vatican, for example, and the massive infiltration of Communism into Catholic circles are effects of all these calamities" *(Revolution and Counter-Revolution,* York, PA: The American Society for the Defense of Tradition, Family and Property, 1993, P. III, chap. II.4.A, pp. 145, 148-149).

§ 3   If an analyst of public opinion were to follow in depth the acceptance of Vatican II, he could state, in round numbers and therefore in a somewhat simplified fashion, that in the post-conciliar period from 1965 to 1975 the progressivist current expanded very swiftly in the Church. From 1975 to 1985 there was a quiet but gradual increase in the reservations of the ensemble of faithful;[8] from 1985 on the Vatican leadership sought to present a "moderate" view of Vatican II so as to make it accepted by those with objections and reservations.

---

8. Describing how this phenomenon of passive resistance in Catholic public opinion took place, analyzing the natural mechanism of such resistance and the role of authentic or counterfeit leadership, as well as the power and importance of these reactions, muted for the most part but often inexorable, goes beyond the scope of this Work. History will perhaps one day explain what we are just mentioning here.

As a confirmation of what the text is saying, we quote here the anguish-filled words of Fr. Gilles Pelland, SJ, describing the emptiness into which the new conciliar preaching fell in the early 70's: "An unfortunate experiment ended up, in many cases, leading to the same gap [the 'nonchalant disinterestedness' of modern man for Church preaching in the post-conciliar era]. After striving to 'adapt themselves' and 'become closer to the man-in-the-street' in his concerns and language, [churchmen] began to have doubts: 'Are we not simply repeating what everyone says, covering with religious names the most common merchandise, evoking 'mystery,' 'revelation,' 'tradition' to disseminate those already widespread and often worn-out truths about liberty, dialogue or progress? In short, are we not just echoing others (though with a little more archaic language) without having anything to say? From this standpoint, we would not be speaking in a vacuum, but of a vacuum. The vacuum would not only be in front of us, but in us' (M. de Certeau, "La parole du croyant dans le language de l'homme," in *Esprit,* 55, 1967, pp. 463-464).

"The malaise or diffused inquietute of the faithful often won over even Pastors to the degree they were closer to those whom their mission assigned them to guide. ... Priests formed in a very hierarchical view of the Magisterium were repeatedly told that they had to change their mentality and make the service of the word a priority; but, at the same time, the Christian assembly was melting like snow in the sun! As soon as they [the priests] had been recycled, they faced the difficult experience of the 'place of solitude,' finding themselves facing a dispersed people who expected nothing from them nor found anything 'significant' in their words. ... Such a context encouraged no one to boast and cry victory! After May 1968 and during the early 70's, what was seen was, above all, a reverse triumphalism: that of bitter criticism, a 'savoring sadness.' If the Church before the Council could fall into triumphalism, afterward she showed herself to be restless, when not indecisive" (Gilles Peiland, "à propos de triomphalisme," in V.A., *Vatican II: Bilan et perspectives,* vol. I, pp. 126-127).

The advance of the process set in motion by the Council was thus jeopardized in the decade of 1975-1985.

§ 4   Even during the sessions of Vatican II, the progressivist wing had encountered difficulties in attaining victories due to the conservative reactions of a certain number of Prelates. Much skill was required from the leadership, as we have seen,[9] to neutralize the reaction and incorporate it into the progressivist stream.

In the post-conciliar period, analogous attempts were made, although with ever greater skill, to cancel out the reaction of a large part of Catholic public opinion and foist the new theories on it.

Just as unanimity among the Prelates was sought during the Council to prevent them from offering any future reaction, a great effort has been made after the Council to avoid, as much as possible, any serious disagreements with conservative leaders of Catholic opinion, which could polarize the diffused discontent. When it is not possible to avoid such disagreements, they are circumscribed as much as possible. This strategy is quite understandable from the progressivist standpoint. For if the progressivists, who hold key posts in the Church, were to react to a polarization by condemning this or that leader of the discontented faithful and thus break the unanimity, they would break the cohesion in the Church and in the mentality of the faithful. In the short and the long run, that could only harm them.

In the short run, should the unanimity be lost – and thus a certain mentality of consensus that goes with it, which is an efficient anesthetic for deep-seated malaise and anguish – it would bring down a series of psychological barriers inherited from the past. Such barriers, which are maintained by respect for and fidelity to highly-placed authorities in the Church, prevents the faithful from asking themselves whether or not evil has also reached the highest Church echelons. Furthermore, a climate of polemics and possible doctrinal condemnations would bring into question the "opening" toward enemies, the *aggiornamento* with a neopagan world and "dialogue" with everybody. How can one believe in "mercy" for enemies and at the same time fulminate with condemnations of one's own children in the Church? Above all, how can ecumenism be carried out with the outlaws of yesterday while maintaining and even multiplying anathemas against the new "outlaws"?

In the long run, the loss of unanimity in the Church would also harm progressivists. Condemnations by "moderate" or *ardite* ecclesiastical authorities against conservatives who somehow catalyzed a

---

9. Chap. IV.

diffuse mentality of discontent would cause the latter to withdraw into silence only to resume the fight at the first prudent opportunity, just as the Liberals and Modernists did *contrario sensu* after the pontificates of Pius IX and St. Pius X. And through that time of condemnantion and silence, one could well imagine that such conservatives would constitute a pole of attraction for the discontented "silent majority."

It would be impossible to prevent conservatives, convinced of their just right despite having been condemned, from feeling that the eighth Beatitude was speaking of them: "Blessed are they that suffer persecution for justice' sake: for theirs is the kingdom of heaven" (Matt. 5:10) and from remembering the Condemned One on the Cross and asking themselves: Did He not draw all things to Himself? *"Et ego si exaltatus fuero a terra, omnia traham ad me ipsum"* (John 12:32).[10]

For these reasons – there are others we shall not expound for the sake of brevity – one sees that one of the underpinnings of the post-conciliar progressivist strategy is the need for unanimity in directing Catholic public opinion.

§ 5   In order to achieve such unanimity, as was done in the Council, concessions must be made to conservative public opinion. Here, the authorities permit or promulgate a catechism with certain traditional aspects; there, they tolerate the use of Latin; elsewhere, they admit a paltry return to the Mass said *versus Deum*; further, they admonish some theology more open to Marxism or some excess of the "homosexual ministry." However, the concession that has caused the most pain among the progressivist "moderates" who execute the maneuvers and that has elicited the greatest impatience among the *arditi* is the long delay in moving forward the conciliar process.[11]

---

10. "And I, if I be lifted up from the earth, will draw all things to myself."

11. In the text we emphasized the role of ecclesiastical authorities and a certain number of concessions made to appease conservative Catholic opinion in the quest for a unanimous acceptance of the Council's application. Such factors act as anesthetics, bringing on a certain lethargy and preventing reactions. However, a relevant factor that should be emphasized, albeit in passing, is the establishment of a criteriological chaos among those elements capable of leading some anti-conciliar reaction.

Indeed, both the "conciliar revolution" and its consequences are so vast and require so much study that practically no one has ever put together, in a clear and systematic fashion, the reasons for disagreeing with the Council so as to seriously hinder the avalanche of reforms that was unleashed upon the Church. This difficulty, which was already great

Slowness is the tribute that the discontented "silent majority" demands from progressivist "moderates" as a precondition for a *modus vivendi*. Slowness is also the main cause for the erosion in the enthusiasm of the *arditi* and their disciplinary protests. Failing to fully understand the advantages of the "moderates" strategy, the *arditi* accuse them of having a "bourgeois spirit," "tepidity" in their progressivist fervor, "softness" in their orientation, and so on.

Now then, what is the so-called post-conciliar crisis?

§ 6   In order to carry Catholic public opinion with them, the "moderates" are obliged to slow down the application of conciliar reforms. This slow pace exasperates the progressivists and leads them to revolt against the "moderate" authorities. Some *arditi* come up with bolder doctrinal explications of far-reaching consequences. These daring manifestations of revolt and far-flung doctrines confirm the fears of the conservative masses, which thus become even more wary and morose. This obliges the "moderates" to make new concessions to the "silent majority"

If this cycle of mutual erosion is not interrupted, it will give rise to a series of reactions that may destroy the conciliar process. This is the outline of the post-conciliar crisis.

*

§ 7   But, regarding the awakening of the "silent majority," the Reader may ask how can it be explained that the reaction of the faithful only began to manifest itself in 1975? What could have prevented it from showing itself until then? What factor was added which allowed it to happen?

---

among those who had reservations about the Council, increased among those who accepted in good faith the directives of ecclesiastical authorities. In this part of Catholic public opinion - certainly a great majority - disorientation and perplexity took hold as a result of the Council's contradictions with traditional Church teaching.

Thus was born a criteriological chaos among the common faithful and in the conservative milieu.

The media played no small a role in the installation of such chaos. In general, it reported on conciliar changes in such a way as to favor the indolence and discourage reactions.

Chaos is, therefore, an important factor in the acceptance of the "conciliar revolution."

While anesthesia instils torpor in Catholic opinion, chaos obscures its vision. A fecund reaction could rise only to the degree that both of these elements were eliminated.

Even though the phenomenon essentially lies in a crystallization against excesses, the question is pertinent: An analysis of the situation seems to reveal that there was indeed a factor obliging Catholic opinion to accept the Council and its fruits, and that this factor ceased to have an effect.

It is useful to recall that also in the conciliar assembly there appears to have been some impediment that slowed the action of conservatives, rejected their presentation of the pre-conciliar schemata, [12] treated them in a pejorative fashion, [13] discouraged them by

---

12. B. Kloppenburg, A eclesiologia do Vaticano II, p. 13.

13. a. In the Council's Opening Speech John XXIII reprimanded the "prophets of doom" who saw only "prevarications and ruins." His censure is impregnated with that "naive optimism" - which Schillebeeckx pointed out in the Council (see letter c below). Which would later be dampened by the crisis sweeping the Church and temporal society. John XXIII said: "In the daily exercise of our pastoral ministry, insinuations come to our ears made by souls doubtless ardent with zeal but not endowed with a great sense of discernment and moderation. In the modern times they see nothing but prevarications and ruins; they repeat tirelessly that our time, in comparison with past ones, has become worse; and they behave as though they have learned nothing from History, which also is the mistress of truth. ... But it seems to us that we must disagree with these prophets of doom, who are always announcing ominous developments as though the end of the world were imminent" (in B. Kloppenburg, Concilio Vaticano II, vol. II, p. 308).

b. According to H. Fesquet, with these words John XXIII denounced the "integrist" tendency that the conciliar majority would have to combat (Le journal du Concile, p. 27).

c. Two decades after the utterance of these words about conservatives, Fr. Schillebeeckx, a perito and aide to the Dutch episcopate during the Council, showed how the optimism of John XXIII was devoid of any foundation: "It is an irony of History that Vatican Council II accepted the 'modern era' at a moment in which 'modernity' itself came under the focus of universal criticism. ... The uneasiness and aloofness of youth toward the Council must be sought not in Church factors, but in the general change of climate in Western society. The contrast with the beginning of the '60s, when the Council took place, could not be greater. We then had a world emerging from the chaos of the Second World War, which radiated with joy at economic development and the perspective of international peace. We find something of this 'naive optimism' even in the Pastoral Constitution Gaudium et spes: the role that the Church should play in this great process toward universal well-being! From the '70s onward, the winds of austerity began to blow" (E. Schillebeeckx, Gott ist jeden Tag neu – Ein Gespräch, Mainz: Mathias Grunewald, 1984, pp. 171-172, in Orientierung, 1/31/1985, p. 13).

failing to support their initiatives, [14] fought them publicly, [15] criticized them privately; [16] and so on. To the contrary, the same factor served to accelerate and encourage the progressivist current. This factor was the use that John XXIII and Paul VI made of their pontifical authority.

§ 8

Analogously, after the Council, the respect of the faithful for papal authority and the Hierarchy's authority *in genere* prevented the "silent majority" from showing suspicion of the Council.

Nevertheless, as the first 10 years of the Council's application unfolded with ever more disconcerting changes in Church practices, the authorities gradually lost their influence. A widespread malaise took hold among the faithful that came from a heart-rending problem of conscience: on the one hand, a filial desire to obey the Sovereign Pontiff and his hierarchical representatives; on the other hand, the self-evidence of the facts, which made resistance an imperative.

In our view, the symbolic landmark and principal factor, which represented the apex of this conflict took place in Brazil, and by extension, in South America.

---

14. Chap. VI.4.B. 3rd phase.

15. Msgr. Philips comments on the attitude of Paul VI toward the debate on collegiality: "No one had any doubt about it. The argument that would dominate the last discussions about the schema on the Church would be the doctrine on the college of Bishops. That was the pivotal point to which a conciliar minority obstinately clung in an attempt to defend the pontifical primacy, which they believed to be threatened, and to preserve it intact at all costs. In his inaugural speech of September 14, 1964, Pope Paul VI had to call attention to this central point, doubtless in order to reduce the resistance of those last hesitating few" (*Chiesa e it suo mistero nel Concilio Vaticano II*, p. 49).

16. Nothing is more expressive in this matter than Cardinal Cicognani's letter to Bishop Luigi Carli of Segni, in response to the one he had sent Paul VI in the name of the Coetus Internationalis Patrum. The then Cardinal Secretary of State, very likely following instructions from Paul VI, advised Bishop Carli to dissolve the Coetus. Its full text can be found in Chap. VI.4 § 99.

We must note that there is no record of any reprimand having been made to the progressivist wing, which was very well organized - as was proven in the well-documented book by Fr. Wiltgen - and counted on the invaluable support of three of the four Cardinal-Moderators, chosen by Paul VI to preside over the Council and who were openly allied with the progressivists (R. Wiltgen, *The Rhine Flows into the Tiber,* pp. 82, 248).

Brazil takes great pride in having the world's largest Catholic population.[17] South America is the continent with the largest Catholic population, estimated at 270 million.[18] In this country and continent was found the world's largest network of influential associations of Catholic laymen that support the traditional doctrine of the Church. These associations – the Societies for the Defense of Tradition, Family and Property – were made up of idealist men who dedicate their lives to defend Christian Civilization in the temporal sphere. Catholics who lead exemplary lives, they were models of honor, uprightness and manliness for the countries that witnessed their action. In their private lives they had always shown an enthusiastic devotion to the Papacy and obedience to the Hierarchy even when, at times, they were victims of misunderstandings and even persecution at the hands of ecclesiastical authorities.

It was in this network of associations that the conflict of conscience reached its highest expression. Indeed, in their struggle for the basic principles of Christian Civilization – Tradition, Family and Property – these associations played a large role in impeding the advance of Communism and the wily penetration of Socialism into their countries. They always founded the argumentation for their fight on the traditional principles of the social doctrine of the Church. Faced with the concessions that Paul VI was making to representatives of Communism all over the world and the futility of their appeals to the Pontiff,[19] and after serious study and mature reflection, these autonomous kindred organizations decided to publicly express their fidelity to the Church and the Papacy, but also their attitude of resistance against the pro-communist Vatican policy.

Written by the founder and president of the Brazilian TFP, Prof. Plinio Corrêa de Oliveira, and signed by all TFPs, the *Declaration of Resistance*[20] was published on April 10, 1974. This was the document that, in our view, represented the crystallization of the wide-

17. 130 million Catholics.

18. In a lecture to the International Policy Forum in Dallas (April 1985), Prof. Plinio Corrêa de Oliveira spoke about "The Importance of the Religious Factor in the Direction of a Key Bloc of Countries: Latin America" *(Catolicismo,* June 1985, pp. 3-8). In it, he characterized the central role of Catholicism in the Latin American continent, destined because of its natural and human resources to become a world power in the dawn of the 21st century.

19. General Introduction, Note 16.

20. *Ibid.;* the English translation of this document can be found online at http://www.traditioninaction.org/bestof/bst004plinio.htm

spread malaise that affected the Catholic world [21] faced with the rising tide of concessions and omissions by personages of the Hierarchy toward international Communism. With respect but firmness, the TFPs proclaimed their position:

"The Church is not, the Church never was, the Church never will be such a prison for consciences. The bond of obedience to the Successor of Peter, which we will never break, which we love in the depth of our souls, to which we give the best of our love, this bond we kiss at the very moment in which, battered by sorrow, we affirm our position. And kneeling, gazing with veneration at the figure of His Holiness Paul VI, we express to him our fidelity.

"In this filial act we say to the Pastor of Pastors: Our soul is yours, our life is yours. Order us to do whatever you wish. Only do not order us to stay idle in face of the assailing red wolf. To this, our conscience is opposed." [22]

Reactions on other continents, telltale signs of the same phenomenon, soon followed.

From this point onward, the tide of Catholic public opinion began to change. Obedience to the Hierarchy and to the Pope could no longer be used as easily as in the past to hinder Catholic reaction. Mistrust legitimately generated a certain critical analysis.

Thus, excessive speed in the application of the Council caused an attitude of perplexity, if not doubt, to rise in conservative circles and in the "silent majority" regarding certain episcopal and even papal documents.

---

21. It is well to remember that this diffused unease with regard to the Vatican *Ostpolitik* was recorded by Plinio Corrêa de Oliveira in a series of articles in the *Folha de S. Paulo,* one of the dailies with largest circulation in Brazil and South America. In them he stated the position of Resistance of the TFPs and reported to the Brazilian public on the widespread rejection, on a world level, of the directions of Paul VI's diplomacy. The articles were entitled: "A indispensável resistência" (4/14/1974); "Resistindo ..." (4/21/1974); "Voz dos que se calam acabrunhados" (4/28/1974); "Mais um Cardeal em resistência" (5/12/1974); "A *Ostpolitik* do Vaticano favorece Moscou" (6/9/1974); "Casaroli: 'incorporação no contexto'" (6/30/1974); "Não conseguimos compreender" (7/7/1974); "1958-1974: Que resultados?" (7/14/1974); "Détente ..." (9/1/1974); "Ternuras que arrancariam lágrimas" (10/13/1974); "Conforme quer Budapest" (10/20/1974); "Détentes' geminadas" (12/8/1974).

22. Plinio Corrêa de Oliveira, "The Vatican Policy of Distention toward the Communist Governments – The Question for the TFP: To Take No Stand? Or to Resist?," in *Crusade for a Christian Civilization,* September 1974, p. 18.

It is therefore explicable that the reactions of the "silent majority" began to embarrass the progressivist current starting in 1975.

§ 9

For its part, the progressivist current was already contesting papal authority since the appearance of the Encyclical *Humanae vitae* on July 25, 1968.[23] As is known, the Encyclical condemned the use of contraceptives. It was the banner the progressivist *arditi* used to indirectly attack papal infallibility by claiming that Paul VI had erred in solving the grave problem of birth control. For them, the use of contraceptives, condemned by *Humanae Vitae,* was obviously licit.[24]

---

23. "Insegnamenti di Paolo VI, 1963 a 1970," *Encicliche,* pp. 165-186.

24. a. Manifestations of non-conformity with *Humanae vitae* by several Bishops' Conferences (in Austria, Belgium, Brazil, Canada, France, Holland, Norway and Scotland), as well as by individual churchmen, theologians and lay people, soon became widespread.

Below are the main positions denying the Encyclical's doctrine to be infallible and attributing to the consciences of spouses the role of supreme judge to decide on the legitimacy of artificial contraception:

b. At the end of their meeting in Konigstein (August 29-30, 1968), the German Episcopate stated that the Encyclical's teaching is "vested with ecclesiastical authority, but is not infallible," and decided that in fulfilling their pastoral ministry and particularly in administering the sacraments, "the shepherds shall respect the decisions taken consciously and responsibly by the faithful" ("Après l'Encyclique Humanae Vitae," *in Informations Catholiques Internationales,* 9/15/1968, p. 19).

c. The Belgian Episcopate, after a special meeting on August 23, 1968, explained: "We are not faced with an infallible declaration." It established the principle that if a person who is "competent in the subject and capable of forming a well-founded personal judgment ...after a serious examination before God, arrives in some points at different conclusions [than the Encyclical's], he has the right to follow his conviction in this matter" *(ibid.,* p. 20).

d. The Dutch Episcopate, in January 1969, manifested its solidarity with the "many Catholics ... who see as unjust the condemnation (of contraceptives) and criticize it with well-founded arguments" (Lucio Brunelli, "A pílula que dividiu a Igreja," in *30 Giorni,* July 1988, pp. 50-51).

e. The French Episcopate made a statement to the same effect: "Contraception can never be a good. It is always a disorder, but not always culpable. It can happen that the spouses are faced with conflicting duties. ... On this matter we shall call to mind the constant teaching of morality: If there is a conflict of duties on account of which an evil cannot be avoided no matter what decision is taken, traditional wisdom says that one should strive to determine, before God, what is the greater duty. The spouses shall decide after common reflection made with all the care required by the grandeur of the married vocation. One can never forget or despise any of the duties in conflict" ("Orientação Pastoral de 12 de November of 1968 sobre a Encíclica *Humanae vitae,*" in Sedoc, vol. I, February 1969, col. 1118, in A. V. Xavier da Silveira, "Pode haver erro em documentos do Magistério?," in *Catolicismo,* July 1969).

f. The CNBB - National Conference of Bishops of Brazil - interpreted the Encyclical in the same way: "Let them [the confessors and spiritual directors] strive in earnest to form in an upright manner the consciences of those who trust them, leading them to conform with the objective truth taught by the authentic Magisterium. Let those who still have not reached a conviction about the expounded truth not be driven away from the sacraments of Confession and Communion so long as they sincerely seek to remain faithful to the love of Christ" ("Declaração da Comissão Pastoral da CNBB sobre a Encíclica *Humanae Vitae,*" October 25, 1968, in Sedoc, col. 1029, *ibid.*).

g. In Brazil, pronouncements to the same effect were made by Bishop Gregorio Warmeling of Joinville, Bishop Marcos Noronha of Itabira, and Bishop Boaventura Kloppenburg of Novo Hamburgo, among others (A. V. Xavier da Silveira, *ibid.*).

h. The Swiss-German theologian Hans Küng was categorical: "Those who, after serious and mature reflection by themselves and their spouses before God, reach the conclusion that in order to protect their mutual love, consolidate their marriage and make it a happy one, they must act other than indicated by the Encyclical are obliged to follow their own consciences as has been taught by the Popes and traditional doctrine" *(Veracidade – O futuro da Igreja,* p. 192).

i. In England, organs of the Catholic press echoed the criticisms and dissensions of members of the clergy. Priests in the Dioceses of Liverpool, Birmingham, Northampton, Southwark, Arundel, Brighton and others made public statements against the Encyclical (*ICI,* "Après l'Encyclique *Humanae Vitae,*" p. 22).

j. Meanwhile, the former Archbishop Thomas Roberts of Bombay, a resident of London, deplored the 'weakness' of the Pope's argumentation (*Ibid.*; L. Brunelli, "A pílula que dividiu a Igreja," p. 51).

k. In the United States, the professors of theology of the Catholic University of Washington wrote a public letter of protest. In a few days, they had collected 645 signatures from theologians, such as the famous moralist Fr. Bernard Häring, CSSR (ICI, "Après l'Encyclique *Humanae Vitae," ibid*).

l. In South Africa, Archbishop Denis Hurley of Durban, stated that the Encyclical *Humanae vitae* "was one of the most arduous experiences" of his life as a Bishop (*Ibid.*, p. 23; L. Brunelli, "A pílula que dividiu a Igreja," *ibid.*).

§ 10   If, among conservatives, it was an excessively fast application of the Council's tenets that generated mistrust of papal authority, among the progressivist *arditi* it was slowness that gave rise to revolt and rejection of pontifical authority.

This constitutes the essence of the so-called crisis of authority.

§ 11   The Council's "opening" toward the other religions and the world, which brought about the relativization of the Faith and the liberalization of customs,[25] was also to cause the crisis of vocations among priests and religious and the crisis of Faith among the laity, as will be shown by some of the texts we present below.

§ 12   Crisis of unity, crisis of authority, crisis of vocations, crisis of Faith: These are the contours of the present crisis in the Church, born of the ambiguity in conciliar documents.

1. Crisis of Unity in the Church

§ 13   To corroborate what we said about the crisis in the Church, we will cite Paul VI, John Paul II and well-known magazines and authors.

§ 14   Let us first look at the eloquent testimony of Paul VI in the Allocution *Resistite fortes in fide,* of June 29, 1972.

Referring to the situation in the Church, **the Pontiff affirms he has the sensation that "through some crack the smoke of Satan has entered the temple of God. There is doubt, uncertainty, a conjunct of problems, disquiet, dissatisfaction, confrontation. One no longer trusts the Church**. ... Doubt has entered our

---

m. In this regard, Fr. Congar comments: "As for *Humanae vitae,* there was a refusal, or rather a failure, to take it into account by the mass of the faithful, who had already taken their liberties. ... A large number of theologians and even episcopates 'welcomed' the doctrine of the Encyclical but interpreted it in such a way that it amounted to saying: You will not sin if you don't obey it by virtue of serious reasons weighed by a ... docile and enlightened conscience" *(Eglise Catholique et France moderne,* p. 199).

n. One sees that, parallel to the question of contraceptives, *Humanae vitae* served as a wick to explode in the Church a crisis of contestation of pontifical authority and papal infallibility.

25. This conciliar "opening," which constituted the basis for ecumenism and secularization, will be analyzed in greater detail in Volume V of this Collection, *Animus Delendi II.*

consciences, and it has entered through windows that should be open to the light. From science, which is made to offer us truths that do not drive us away from God but make us seek Him even more and glorify ever more intensely, has come, instead, criticism, has come doubt.... **This state of uncertainty also reigns in the Church.** It was believed that after the Council a sunny day would come in the History of the Church. On the contrary, **there came a day filled with clouds, tempest, darkness, questions, uncertainty.** We preach ecumenism and remove ourselves ever farther from one another. We seek to dig chasms instead of burying them." [26]

§ 15   Without mentioning the Council, John Paul II nevertheless points out its consequences: "In fact, **one cannot deny that in many Christians the spiritual life is passing through a moment of uncertainty that encompasses not only moral life but also prayer and even the theological integrity of the faith.** Already put to the test by a confrontation with our time, **Faith is at times disoriented by erroneous ideological addresses that are disseminated also as a result of the crisis of obedience in relation to the Magisterium of the Church."** [27]

§ 16   The magazine *La Civiltà Cattolica* dedicates an editorial to analyze the first 20 years of the post-conciliar era. The comment reveals the position of the Jesuit magazine, which, although not the same as this Work's, attests to the crisis we mention.

"At the same time, **there was not – and there is not – any lack of internal confusion and tension, which, added to pressures, ideologies and changes ... aggravated ... a crisis that many today see as having frightened away the great hopes for a 'springtime awakening' of religion nourished by the two Popes who wanted the Council.** We cannot fail to point out this crisis even though we are unable to go into a lengthy, meticulous and exhaustive analysis. **Not only have the conciliar documents been considered obsolete and cast aside by some, but the very 'spirit' of Vatican II was taken over and cast with its 'anti-spirit' by a class of theologians,** not numerous but combative, **who have taken for their parameter of reflection and truth a kind of anthropological immanentism,** accepted *de facto* even when not formally enunciated ...

"Someone pretended ... to speak about going beyond Vatican II, not in the legitimate sense of a gradual maturation ... but in the

---

26. *Insegnamenti di Paolo VI,* vol. X, pp. 707-708.
27. John Paul II, Apostolic Letter "Tertio millennio adveniente," in *L'Osservatore Romano,* 9/14-15/1994, Supplement, n. 36.

unacceptable sense of the manipulation of defenseless Christian masses carried out in various ways ... by some theological pressure groups ... Thus, **there were 'anarchical excesses,'** as Cardinal H. de Lubac justly defined them ... **A distorted reading of the Council was thus proposed ... that consists of seeking contradictions in conciliar texts to tilt their balance in favor of preconceived theses that find no backing in the Council, or stating that the conciliar texts were unable to express,** for various reasons, **that which the Fathers really meant to say."** [28]

The editorialist of *La Civiltà Cattolica* closes: "Concluding this quick overview, we should say that after 20 years of experience, studies and discussions, Vatican II remains little known and little understood by the majority, be it the clergy or laity; in this regard, **people either remain obstinately closed or have indiscriminately forged ahead. On the one hand, the refusal by the integrism of traditionalists, and on the other hand, the 'para-Council' phenomenon with its clamor, have contributed to render inoperative** (when not casting them into discredit) **the seeds sown by the Council in the Church."** [29]

From the editorial of *La Civiltà Cattolica* we have retained primarily the comments confirming the existence of the post-conciliar crisis. Its attempts to attack those who attribute ambiguities and contradictions to Vatican II are without foundation, as we have demonstrated with abundant documentation in the preceding Chapters of this Volume. Such attempts are typical of the "moderate synthesis" line of which we spoke above. [30]

§ 17   The testimony below, by Cardinal Ratzinger, also attests to the existence of the post-conciliar crisis.

"The results [of the Council] appear cruelly opposed to the expectations of everyone, beginning with those of John XXIII and later of Paul VI. A new Catholic unity was expected and, instead, we moved toward a dissension which ... seems to change from self-criticism to self-destruction. A new enthusiasm was expected, but so many people have ended in discouragement and disgust. A leap forward was expected, and instead **we are faced with an increasing process of decadence that has developed,** to a large extent, precisely **under the sign of a movement favoring**

---

28. *La Civiltà Cattolica,* Editorial: "Concilio, post-Concilio, para-Concilio," 1/5/1985, pp. 11-12.

29. *Ibid.,* p. 13.

30. Chap. VI.3.

the Council, but it contributed toward discrediting it among many. The balance appears to be, therefore, negative ... **It is undeniable that this period was decisively unfavorable to the Catholic Church.**"[31]

In an earlier analysis, Ratzinger had said: **"The naive optimism of the Council and the self-exaltation of many** who made and propagate it **justify in a disturbing way the most somber diagnoses of early churchmen about the danger of councils. Not all valid councils**, after being tested by the facts of History, **have shown themselves to be useful councils; in the final analysis, all that was left of some was a great nothing.**"[32]

And he added: **"From a global perspective, one should say that the years of euphoria [of the post-conciliar era] were followed by a phase of disillusionment and crisis.**"[33]

§ 18   Msgr. Luigi Sartori, then president of the Italian Theological Association, remarks: **"We live, in this period of the post-Council, in a grave crisis.** After so much fervor and enthusiasm in which everyone seemed to be in agreement, **ruptures and lacerations now begin. Different, not to say opposed, interpretations of the Council are offered; everyone pulls to his own side. Even worse, no small parcel of responsibility for the mix-ups and confusions is attributed to the Council. Some go as far as to speak with irritation of 'Babel' and the 'confusion of languages;'** they once again dream of the medieval ideal of a unity of language, for only thus – they think – can the Church still accomplish her function as *signum unitatis* amongst the peoples of the earth."[34]

§ 19   Soon after the Council, Fr. Leo A. von Geusau, founder of IDOC, "prophesied" its results:

"To many it will seem that the very supports of Christian action are falling. Many will believe they are faced with or on the eve of a new wide-scale destruction of Jerusalem. It is

---

31. *L'Osservatore Romano:* "Il Cardinale Ratzinger: 'La fede è il bene più alto. Bisogna sempre vigilare perchè non si corrompa,'" 11/9/1984, p. 4; this article is a selection of statements by J. Ratzinger to the Italian magazine *Jesus.*

32. J. Ratzinger, *Zehn Jahre Vaticanum 11,* Regensburg, 1976, in Rosino Gibellini, "Siamo d'accordo sul concilio?" in *Il Regno,* 12/15/1984, p. 545.

33. *Ibid.*

34. L. Sartori, "Il linguaggio del Vaticano II," in V.A., *Il linguaggio teologico oggi,* p. 236.

not exaggerated to say that we are living a moment of rupture and discontinuity in the history of salvation ... Many who think that they are Christians may find themselves in a situation in which they no longer understand what is happening; others whom we would never expect to find in similar conditions will appear to us as true Christians. **The crisis attacking the Church is evident** ... **Some go as far as to speak of 'two Churches' to express the reality of a profound and growing dislocation between the two mentalities.**

"All this may seem terribly sad or pessimistic. But, instead, it could turn out to be the sign of the birth of a renewed Church which, slowly, groaning, is leaving the exceedingly 'stable and safe' land of the old ecclesiastical structures to consciously take the road to the desert. One speaks of 'theology of the Exodus.'... Maybe we will be more tranquil within a few generations, when change will have become a familiar method of advancing."[35]

§ 20   Comments on Vatican II by the former Cardinal-Archbishop of Vienna Franz König are not far removed from those above:

"Every council caused inquietude. It is not by chance that today there is insistence on the acceptance of Vatican II. **The conciliar Fathers spoke with great openness, causing astonishment.** The Church should open herself, *aggiornarsi*. **Have we gone too far? Have we become too liberal? So some may have feared. Many had the impression they no longer found themselves facing the same Church.** Hence the arguments between right and left. So many diverse opinions."[36]

§ 21   Maurice Druon, a man of letters and member of the *Academie Française*, adds his voice to these testimonies. Referring to the bewilderment of a common man watching the radicality and inopportune measures that caused the post-conciliar crisis, he says:

"Nothing, at least from the outside, threatened or attacked the Church any longer. No one ridiculed priests as they passed by; anti-clericalism was relegated to a museum of memories; laicism was no longer a pretext for fights. **Never had the Church,** from the simple village pastor to the Pope ... **benefited from a more secure situation, a more general respect, and a more certain prestige. Suddenly, she cracks, is degraded, loses her roots and – one would**

---

35. L. A. von Geusau, "La Chiesa 'scandalo' del mundo," in V.A., *La fine della Chiesa come "società perfetta,"* pp. 192f.

36. Franz König, "Il Concilio, sorpresa per il mondo," interview with Silvano Stracca, in *Avvenire,* 10/16/1992.

say – is about to come crashing down on herself. Priests turn the altars around, sell church ornaments, take the saints away; Prelates change their language, close the organs, welcome the guitars and bless the demolishers. No rite is maintained, no rule spared. The gothic arch of dogmas is cracked. The house of the Good God opens itself to all storms. Bewildered, we watch this internal quake...

"What is happening to the Catholic Church? Everyone asks with anxiety. ... Because when an institution of this order and this grandeur was for centuries the main spiritual shield of a people and the principal moral power of a nation, she influenced everything, impregnated everything, marked everything, the ways of thinking, the references of memory, living habits, individual and collective behavior, artistic expressions, everything, including the law and the very relationships between the citizen and the State. Therefore, when the Church goes through a crisis of such amplitude, she is not the only one at stake: It is the nation's life as a whole that is affected by this. It is the very personality of a people that can change.

"**Everywhere a great need for spirituality is manifested; everywhere anguished youths are in search of supreme values. And this is the moment the Church chooses,** by means of part of her clergy, **to walk on her lowest level, to lavish smiles on her philosophical adversaries and to behave in everything as though she were the bearer of relative truths.** ... The Church, according to some, could not resist the rise of modernity and must radically transform herself. Attention, my priests! Everything can be modernized, except God.

"**Could it not be that this great agitation is caused simply by a weakening of faith among those who were given the responsibility of communicating it?** I know Prelates of the highest level ... who are openly disturbed about this crisis of faith in the clergy."[37]

§ 22   Speaking about the crisis in the priesthood, Bishop Walter Kasper opines:

"The crisis of the priesthood in the Catholic Church has multiple causes; it is the reflection of profound changes and great subversions in the conscience and practice of the Church ... as well as in Western society seen in its complexity. Therefore, one cannot face this problem by isolating it from its context, let alone search for any

---

37. Maurice Druon, "Une Eglise que se trompe de siècle," in *Le Monde,* 8/7/1971.

solution if it is not defined in its context. **At the depth of this crisis we undoubtedly find the accentuation of the ecclesiology of the people of God, carried out by Council Vatican II itself, which clearly showed the reality of the common priesthood of all the baptized and valued the specific vocation of lay Christians."** [38]

§ 23   Fr. Schillebeeckx points to a specific fruit of the spirit of the Council at the Dominican convent of Nijmegen, where he lives:

"For me, the first evolution in religious life took place in my years of study, but **the greatest one happened after Vatican Council II, not directly under the influx of the Council as such, but of the spirit of the Council. In 1968, there was a veritable hecatomb among religious [men], a terrible decimation. In the Albertinum [monastery] we were then about 110. Half of them left the order, and this fact had an enormous repercussion on those who stayed. Many priests went to live in small communities** of seven or eight, in simple apartments. **Now there are 28 of us in our monastery."** [39]

§ 24   Gabriel Steinschulte, writing for *L'Osservatore Romano,* notes with respect to the liturgy:

"In a global view of the ambience of German culture ... one finds that **the reform [of the Council] gave rise, above all, to misunderstandings, superfluous polarizations, the taking of unilateral stands,** a frequent and ever more evident **dismantling of the liturgy."** [40]

§ 25   In the same sense, Cardinal Virgilio Noé, titular Archbishop of Voncaria, Secretary of the Sacred Congregation for the Sacraments and Divine Worship, consultant to the Special Commission on the Liturgy, writes:

"Also **the liturgical restoration** [in the post-conciliar period] **gave rise to fights, arguments, and divisions between 'progressivists' and 'integralists.' Some left the Church because they could no longer recognize themselves in the new liturgy. Oth-**

---

38. Walter Kasper, "E in questione la Chiesa e l'immagine di Dio," in *Il Regno,* 10/15/1993, p. 567.

39. E. Schillebeeckx, "Dio è un dono, non una garanzia," interview with F. Strazzari, in *Il Regno,* 6/15/1990, p. 332.

40. Gabriel Maria Steinschulte, "Paesi di lingua tedesca – Vent'anni di riforme, prima e dopo," in *L'Osservatore Romano,* 12/14/1983, special supplement on the Constitution *Sacrosanctum concilium,* p. IV.

ers, remaining in the Church, corrupted the liturgy with fantas-
tic creations and many other factors usually qualified as 'abuses.'"[41]

§ 26   Fr. Aloís Müller, professor at the Theological Faculty of
Lucerne, member of the board of directors of the magazine *Concilium,*
also points to the crisis provoked by Vatican II:

"In the countries with a long Christian tradition, **the reforms
of Vatican II did not bring to the Church that vital impulse that
was expected. To the contrary, these reforms ... led to a break-
down of the structures and a disintegration of the ecclesial
community's social fabric. For this reason, the present conscience of the Church is a conscience in crisis.**"[42]

§ 27   Although the crisis in the Church since the Council has been
noted by so many high-ranking personalities, it is nonetheless curious
to note that the lamentations it has caused do not touch the root of the
question. No question is asked about whether or not the conciliar
documents, with their characteristic ambiguity, were what inevitably
caused the crisis. Any analysis that fails to address this question appears to be *ipso facto* inefficacious.

2. Strategic Impasse

§ 28   For Vatican dignitaries who continue trying to impose conciliar doctrine, the crisis in the Church takes on the characteristics of a
grave strategic impasse in directing Catholic public opinion. Excerpts
by Cardinal Julius Döpfner and Fr. Louis Boyer, as well as some
principles of action enunciated by Fr. René Laurentin, are illustrative
of this impasse.

§ 29   Cardinal Döfner, one of the Council's directors, recognizes
this: **"The renewal started by the Council currently finds itself
in the crossfire of criticism. To some, the reform is too hesitant,
to others it is too revolutionary."**[43]

§ 30   Louis Boyer, SJ, a French theologian of considerable renown,
consultant to the Secretariat for Non-Christians, arrives at the same
finding: **"[The Church] has been blocked by the absurd conflict**

41. Virgilio Noé, "Il primo dono al popolo cristiano," in *L'Osservatore Romano,* 12/14/1983, special supplement on the Constitution *Sacrosanctum Concilium,* p. VIII.

42. Aloís Müler, "Chiesa e riforma," in V.A., *Verso la Chiesa del terzo millennio,* pp. 137-138.

43. J. Döpfner, *La Chiesa vivente oggi,* p. 87.

... between integrists and progressivists; her mission has been paralyzed and will continue to be until it steps out of this deadly circle." [44]

§ 31   On the adaptation to modern times suggested by conciliar reforms, Laurentin puts forward general principles that foresee the strategic impasse in which high-ranking ecclesiastical authorities find themselves in this post-conciliar era. He says:

"To 'act precipitously' is not, therefore, a rule of conduct, much less a panacea. Does this mean one should 'march slowly, without raising obstacles'? The answer is also no, because **in matters of reform, compromises, accommodations and half-measures are the worst things. Usually they compute the inconveniences of the *status quo* and of the changes without making the former comfortable or the latter advantageous. Vatican II must conquer not only the dangers of opposition and adventure, but also a more redoubtable one: a certain ecclesiastical prudence that is a caricature of Christian prudence.**

"This false virtue is fecund with sterile but surprisingly popular proverbs: 'Everything excessive is insignificant,' for example. This formula, by Talleyrand, frontally clashes (do people realize this?) with the Gospel, St. Paul and charity itself, whose characteristic law, according to St. Thomas, is not that of a middle ground and does not err by excess. Christ saved us by an excess of love that confounds us." [45]

3. Moderates and *Arditi* Lament the Emergence of the Conservative Reaction

§ 32   Reflecting a general suspicions among the faithful, the conservative reaction appeared around 1975. It is interesting to note the displeasure and concern it caused both among moderate and more fervent progressivists.

§ 33   Cardinal Roger Etchegaray, president of the Pontifical Councils for Justice and Peace and *Cor unum*, although employing an accommodating language, appears displeased with the recalcitrance of innumerable people to follow conciliar reforms. As a matter of fact, on the occasion of the 20th anniversary of Vatican II, he stated:

---

44. Louis Boyer, A *decomposição do Catolicismo,* Sampedro (Lisbon, n.d.), pp. 188-189.

45. R. Laurentin, *Bilan de la première session,* pp. 83-84.

"Twenty years is little to measure the results of the Council. More than 100 years were needed for the Council of Trent (16ᵗʰ century) to implement its decisions everywhere. Certainly, with the acceleration of History, changes now take place more rapidly; but we **realize that it is easier to change structures than mentalities, and religious mentalities are among the most tenacious,** understandably so, **because they touch the most profound fibers of man.**" [46]

§ 34   Bishop Boaventura Kloppenburg, a conciliar *perito* usually presented as a moderate and even a conservative, does not hide his displeasure with the conservative reaction:

"It is certain – and it is necessary to say it to those who, with pharisaic pride, proclaim themselves to be 'traditionalists'– that the Church must adapt, renew and purify herself. ... This is the tension between the dynamics of progress and the constancy of Tradition. The equilibrium is not easy. ... It requires time, serenity, maturity ... **To be hasty, to raise suspicions, to generalize isolated cases, to alarm and disturb the authorities, to create a climate of party or division, none of this will resolve anything in the historical moment we are living and will only serve to waste time and postpone (once again) the process.**" [47]

Kloppenburg now takes to an extreme his aversion to conservatives:

"There already are organized movements who call themselves 'traditionalist' with the end of safeguarding the patrimony of the past and openly fighting what they call 'Progressivism.' **Tempers boil and there appears, more and more clearly, a spirit of fight and crusade,** of a partisan fanaticism **that blinds and deafens to such a point that it prevents sufficient serenity to see, hear and discern what is good and true** on one side and the other. ... This then begins the unfortunate process of generalization by the professional collectors of lamentable isolated facts. **The devil of espionage, denunciations and accusations goes into action.** 'Documents' pile up on the desks of intimidated authorities. **One would say that they are about to start the process of the Inquisition all over again.**" [48]

---

46. Roger Etchegaray, "Le Cardinal Etchegaray, Archevêque de Marseille, se souvient et balise l'avenir," in *Historia* (Paris), October 1982, p. 100.

47. B. Kloppenburg, A *eclesiologia do Vaticano II,* pp. 102-103.

48. *Ibid.,* pp. 94-95.

Karl Rahner

Metz

§ 35

Fr. Johann Baptist Metz, founder of the so-called "Political Theology" and one of Rahner's disciples who became notorious for his radical positions, laments:

"Too quickly the faith of the reformers is cast into doubt. Too quickly the awakening of critical freedom in the Church is denigrated as the apotheosis of incredulity. ... To any reform, to the degree that it is substantial and comes from the faith, **such an imputation certainly is fatal and, in the final analysis, deadly.** For this reason, it is necessary to change this."

Metz goes on: **"Any reform that wants to have a possibility to advance must emerge from this dilemma in which it finds itself. Or will it be necessary to maintain the fatal impression that reactionary mentalities enjoy a privileged right of citizenship in the Church** and that the Christian faith can accommodate them more easily and with fewer problems than the disquiet of reforming positions?"** [49]

Here the *ardito* Metz aligns himself with the fears of the "moderate" Kloppenburg: "Clearly, **groups that are suspicious of Vatican II are established again in the Church, and they want to expel from us the spirit of this Council. Again, there are veiled, very subtle forms of ... inquisition that are not less harmful by being veiled, rather they are a much greater cause for concern."** [50]

§ 36

Fr. Cardonnel, certainly in the *avant garde* of the French clergy, enunciates the conservative reaction as the great danger for the application of the Council:

"The greatest danger is not letting in too much air but, on the contrary, leaving the windows ajar for a few minutes just before shutting them again in a hurry" He adds: **"What is the only threat? It is to stick strictly to the law, to codify the spirit, to return to port, to not turn the [ship's] bow to the future, to fear to become obsolete, to want to preserve oneself. To fear becoming lost."** [51]

---

49. Johann Baptist Metz, *Más allá de la religión burguesa – Sobre el futuro del Cristianismo.* (Salamanca: Síueme, 1982), pp. 105-106.

50. *Ibid.,* pp. 102-103.

51. Jean Cardonnel, "Vatican II," interview with Michel Dubost, in *Historia,* October 1982, p. 96.

4. Non-conformity of the *Arditi* with the Slowness of Moderate Leaders

§ 37   Here also we present confirmation of what was said in this Chapter's introduction on the slow pace of the moderates.

§ 38   Leonardo Boff makes a general lamentation, not exclusive to the Council, about the slowness of the leadership to draw consequences from the principles they profess:

"In this earnest commitment to liberation, **we Christians go through the bitter experience of the slowness of processes and the persistence of oppressions.**" He goes on to ask: "Shouldn't the faithful community, amid the oppressions of our people, plead like the Virgin: '**Lord,** show the power of your arm ... **overthrow the mighty from their thrones** ... fill the hungry with good things?'" [52]

§ 39   In a dialogue with Rahner, Metz analyzes the causes and recognizes the slowness of the institutional Church:

"**There seems to be a secret correspondence between what I would call 'ideological extravagances' of current theology and a certain immobility of the institutional Church to reform herself, a reform that has certainly been proclaimed but which appears to advance very slowly.**" [53]

Metz also analyzes, in his own way, the state of mind of the Catholic "silent majority" and blames the crisis on the moderate leaders, who carried out post-conciliar changes without sufficiently preparing the faithful as a whole. Metz accuses the leadership of a failure to communicate a "love" of the reforms.

"**The problem of the Church of tomorrow,**" he says, "**will not be represented mainly by intellectual critics, but instead by the 'simple people' of the so-called 'flock of Christ,' which already appears to be profoundly disturbed.** It will not issue foremost from a critical theology, but rather from the very institution of the Church itself. **The actual concrete transformations being carried out in the Church are what have provoked dispersion and a crisis of identity. The so-often-deplored confusion among the faithful derives ... from the fact that the faithful were exposed by the**

---

52. Leonardo Boff, *O rosto materno de Deus – Ensaio inter-disciplinar sobre o feminino e suas formas religiosas* (Petrópolis: Vozes, 1979), p. 211.

53. "Karl Rahner em diálogo corn Johann Baptist Metz," in V.A., *Cinco problemas que desafiam a Igreja hoje,* p. 158.

Church to a change without love, without having been given a critical explanation of the reformability of the Church. How could the 'simple faithful' conceive the identity of the critical liberty of the one Church in her mutations? Why should they not feel deceived once they lack an adult behavior? ...

"One of the causes of the ecclesiastical crisis today is not an excess of criticism but a catastrophic failure in exerting the most fundamental critical liberty in the Church. This failure makes the 'flock of Christ' the focus of the crisis in the Church of tomorrow. The 'silent majority' has become a very problematic question also in the Church. Let the crisis of religious identity of our good mothers not be underestimated. Who, after all, will save them from a dangerous indifferentism or a skeptical resignation that causes an ever wider chasm between the ecclesiastical institution and the faithful?" [54]

§ 40   Longings for a Vatican III among many *arditi* stem from their hope to end the slow pace of the leadership.

Prof. Giuseppe Alberigo, a specialist in Church History and author of a well-known book about John XXIII, explains:

"Why have a new Council properly speaking? On the one hand, the answer can be sought in the great impulse Vatican II has given all churches: It had been centuries since Catholicism in particular had seen such an intense springtime. On the other hand, it is useful to recall how **the** actual **plan for the meeting of Notre Dame[55] and its development took place in the final years of the pontificate of Paul VI, when not only the conciliar impulse seemed worn out but also the leadership of the Church suffered an alarming paralysis. In such circumstances, it seemed urgent to stimulate a reflection on the near future of the faith and the Church, placing its realization under the augur and in the framework of a new Council."** [56]

§ 41   In the same sense, Fr. Peter Huizing, SJ, dean of the Gregorian University's Faculty of Canon Law and consultant to the Pontifical Commission for the Revision of the Code of Canon Law, writes:

---

54. J. B. Metz, "Sulla presenza della Chiesa nella società" in V.A., *L'avvenire della Chiesa,* p. 141.

55. The theological meeting promoted in 1977 by the magazine *Concilium* at the American Catholic University of Notre Dame (South Bend, Indiana) under the title "Toward Vatican III."

56. Giuseppe Alberigo, "Editoriale," in V.A., *Verso la Chiesa del terzo millennio,* p. 7.

"Vatican Council II did not translate its doctrine into the institutions of the Church. The statements on the collegiality of Bishops, on the responsibility of the laity, on the nature of Christian marriage and so on, are absolutely useless if they are not anchored in the institutions of the Church. This is the main reason for the collapse of Vatican II. Vatican III should fill this gap." [57]

§ 42   The impatient words of a Spanish missionary, Fr. Benedito Revilla Torices, reported by the press on the day we finished the first draft of this Volume, were quite vivid. In an audience with John Paul II at the Vatican, he asked the latter to convene a new ecumenical council: "Courage, optimism, **out with fears, ease up on the brakes and slam on the accelerator!**" [58]

5. Among Progressivists, Authority Loses Credibility and Is Contested

§ 43   As we said in the introduction to this Chapter, the *arditi* also lost confidence in the authority of the Hierarchy. This weakening was manifested mainly as a loss of credibility and the most expressive fruit it generated was a denial of the authority of Rome and of the Pope. That is what can be found in the texts that follow.

§ 44   Swiss theologian Aloís Müller, a member of the board of directors of *Concilium,* complains about the position of the Hierarchy, whose action, he believes, favors traditional lines and reveals that Rome has lost its authority in progressivist quarters.

"**Soon after the Council, counter-currents were formed in the Roman Curia, in some Conferences of Bishops and also among the grassroots, the people. First of all, they interpreted the Council only in its more traditional lines instead of apprehending by intuition its calls for renewal. Furthermore, in later legislation they sought to moderate the impulses of the Council itself. With this march in reverse, the Curia and the Hierarchy lost their credibility among those who had committed themselves**, soul and body, **to the reform. This was the main reason for the jungle of disorderly and uncontrolled private initiatives.** These initiatives also favored an evolutionary movement in reverse,

---

57. Peter Huizing, "Vaticano III: una costituzione sulla Chiesa," in V.A., *Verso la Chiesa del terzo millennio,* p. 167.

58. Benedito Revilla Torices, Statements to the press, "D. Aloisio quer Igreja em ação político," in *O Estado de São Paulo,* 12/6/1985.

which nourished a desire to return to the old schemas, even among Bishops who used to favor the reform. Furthermore, the speeches of the Pope often put people on guard against 'Progressivism' under the pretext of defending and favoring reform."[59]

§ 45   Hans Küng reflects well the thinking of various currents of *arditi*. He does not hesitate to blame the Pope for the faults that generated the crisis of credibility of the Hierarchy and the Church herself:

> **"Behind all this, as** I see it, **[is] the fundamental shortcoming of the post-conciliar period: a lack of spiritual leadership in Rome and among the Bishops.** Today we need an inspiring intellectual and spiritual authority at all levels. ... **There is a dangerous abyss,** now greater, now smaller, **between the Bishops and a great majority of the priests in regard to the serious problems of the Church today. ... Here you have the result: a most lamentable and well-deserved damage to the credibility of the post-conciliar Church. ...**

> **"In a long interview in New York. ... I said this, and I stand by it: 'The present Pope [Paul VI] started out with the Catholic Church having perhaps the greatest credibility in the last 500 years. We now arrive at the end of this pontificate and I find that the credibility of the Catholic Church is so low that we cannot explain what has happened.'"**[60]

§ 46   This discrediting of the Pope begins the period of "respectful indifference," which the Archbishop Cabral Duarte of Aracaju, with the magazine *Communio,* spoke about in the Synod of 1983. Expounding his ideas on "Liberation Theology," he notes the following:

> **"They no longer contest the Pope: they hear him, are silent, and then continue acting as before. This is the time of 'respectful indifference.' The Synod should, I believe, make a pronouncement on this urgent reconciliation of many Catholic minds with the supreme Magisterium of the Church."** [61]

§ 47   However, this "respectful indifference" apparently supposes that the Pope approves the celebrated theological pluralism. Otherwise, brazen and aggressive contestations will arise.

---

59. Aloís Müller, "Chiesa e riforma," in V.A., *Verso la Chiesa del terzo millennio,* pp. 136-137.

60. Hans Küng, *O que deve permanecer na Igreja* (Petrópolis: Vozes, 1976), pp. 16-17.

61. Lucian Cabral Duarte, "Riconciliare le intelligenze Cattoliche," in *L'Osservatore Romano,* 10/6/1983, Supplement, p. III.

Patrick Jacquemont, a French Dominican, puts forward the principle of defiance as a question:

"Shouldn't the Church be contested when this pluralism in the language of the faith is not accepted, when the confession of Faith is wrapped in the formulation of some catechism or profession of Faith?" [62]

§ 48   Regarding the deposition of Bishop Jacques Gaillot from the Diocese of Evreux because of his stands favoring homosexuals, contraceptives, the abolition of obligatory priestly celibacy and so on, commentator Jacques Duquesne, of the newspaper *La Croix,* offers his opinion on the *arditi*'s distancing from the Vatican's "conservative" attitude:

"Many European Catholics no longer admit the impositions of the Church, there is much resentment against Rome, the Church is losing her social base, **we are currently living in a process I call silent schism."** [63]

§ 49   Finally, Küng also lists "errors of the ecclesiastical Magisterium' regarding conjugal morals as a factor in the credibility crisis. Citing moralists to his liking, Küng sets out the doctrinal position held by those who led the opposition against the Encyclical *Humanae vitae* of Paul VI: [64]

"And we must hold in high esteem the theologians who prepared the moral-theological position paper for the progressivist conciliar majority, [on account of the] fact that they spoke out with extraordinary frankness about the errors of the ecclesiastical Magisterium ... in regard to marital morals. **'Not a few theologians and faithful fear that a change in official doctrine could damage the confidence of Catholics in the Magisterium of the Church. So they ask: how could the assistance of the Holy Spirit have permitted such an error for a series of centuries, errors with so many consequences, above all in the last centuries?**

" But it is almost impossible to determine *a priori* the criteria to establish whether or not the Holy Spirit could allow it. In fact, it is known that there have been errors in the declarations of the Magisterium and in Tradition. As for sexual relations, it should be noted that for

---

62. Patrick Jacquemont, "Igreja e contestação," in V.A., A *Igreja do futuro,* p. 38.

63. Jacques Duquesne, Comments on the deposition of Bishop Gaillot, in Any Bourrier, "Demissão de Bispo revolta os franceses," in *Jornal do Brasil,* 1/17/1995.

64. See Note 24.

long centuries it was taught in the Church in an almost unanimous fashion and in active concordance with the Popes that the married relation is illicit if unaccompanied by an intention to procreate or, at least ... if it does not serve as a relief for [one of] the partners. Nevertheless, **'today this viewpoint is not shared by any theologian, nor does it represent an official opinion.'** [65]

"In any case, one should not deviate from the conclusion that **only a critical reinterpretation of ecclesiastical infallibility could be able to overcome the present difficulties."** [66]

§ 50 Küng's much desired "critical reinterpretation of infallibility" finds echo in an editorial in *La Civiltà Cattolica* published a few days before the beginning of the Synod of Bishops in November 1985.

One could say that in this point the "moderates" of *La Civiltà Cattolica* join the aforementioned *arditi* to make a common front. For even though the editorial theoretically appears to look for doctrinal solutions, in fact, its publication, on the eve of a Synod being prepared to deal with the question of pontifical primacy, took on the character of real defiance. We have chosen a few excerpts:

"One cannot hide the fact that **the definition of Vatican I ... carries the marks of a conception of authority that no longer corresponds to the theological maturity and the cultural level of the Church and society today.** This explains why a re-proposal of the doctrine of the Petrine-Roman Primacy desired by Vatican II was met in the Church herself by an impressive array of difficulties, intolerance and ennui. ... **The doctrinal wrapping with which *Pastor Aeternus* surrounded the truth of the primacy of Peter and of the Bishops of Rome has a different, if not opposed, perspective from the wrapping used by *Lumen gentium*, because Vatican I conceives the Pope as the structural vertex and perfective causality of the Church-visible-society, whereas Vatican II envisages this most high post as a sign and reality of the service of authority placed at the heart of the Church-communion.** ...

"After Vatican I, the aura of transcendence around the Pope was strongly accentuated. The visible Chief of the Church, supreme interpreter of Revelation, then appeared alone, exceedingly alone before God, with the charge committed to his conscience to decide the most serious questions for the Church and the world: a dramatic and

---

65. Küng refers to the conservative minority in the Council's theological commission. The quotation inside the text was published in *Herder-Korrespondenz*, n. 21, 1967, p. 440 (*Veracidade,* pp. 136-138).

66. *Ibid.,* pp. 140-141.

almost insupportable task for a human creature, capable of conferring to the Pope's Magisterium and government an almost divine reverberation as a direct consequence of his psychological isolation with regard to other members of the Church." [67]

The editorial of the well-known Jesuit magazine, then directed by Fr. Gianpaolo Salvini, goes on to introduce a subtle distinction between infallibility and "infallibilism." Such a distinction appears to be made, as we will see, to facilitate criticism of the traditional devotion that the faithful have always had to the sacred person of the Vicar of Christ. According to *La Civiltà Cattolica,* such devotion, which is the honor of every faithful Catholic, would amount to nothing but "servility" and a vile, self-interested "courtier mentality." The magazine goes so far as to call it "exaggerations of papolatry" and "courtly byzantinism."

Eschewing direct attacks on pontifical infallibility by means of this conveniently forged distinction, the editorial nevertheless indirectly criticizes the Pope as Monarch of the Church. These are the words of *La Civiltà Cattolica:*

"In the 'aura' of transcendence and sovereignty that was accentuated after the definition of Vatican I, it is necessary to look at the so-called 'infallibilism,' as many people say, which is something totally different from infallibility. Indeed, as a prerogative intimately connected with the Petrine primacy, the latter is a charism which, under certain conditions, makes the Roman Pontiff immune from errors; ... on the contrary, **infallibilism expresses a maximalist mentality that confounds infallibility with impeccability** or extends the scope of the Petrine charism beyond the confines of Revelation. ...

"Therefore, **infallibilism is a psycho-sociological attitude not always removed from the servility typical, in some way, of the courtier mentality that germinates outside of the** pure doctrine of the Pope's personal infallibility as an excrescence of it; and if, at times, for contingent reasons, it was able to play an apologetic role,** let it be said frankly that **this was the effect and cause of that ecclesiastical pyramidism that saw exaggerations of papolatry and courtly byzantinism proliferate."** [68]

The official magazine of the religious order that St. Ignatius placed especially at the service of the Pope continues:

---

67. *La Civiltà Cattolica,* Editorial: "Il ministero del Papa dopo i due Concili Vaticani," 11/2/1985, pp. 212, 215.

68. *Ibid.,* p. 217.

"The papacy is called to reveal itself increasingly to the Church and the peoples as a humble minister of the sole Savior, the custodian and interpreter of His Gospel, as a humble servant of the human conscience ... rejecting at the same time the human temptations of despotism and paternalism. ...

"The new morphology of the papacy was prepared by Vatican II. This Council did not renege the Gregorian and Tridentine theology but completed it, grafting it on to the doctrine of the Church as people of God and the doctrine of episcopal collegiality. With the first, it annihilated hierocracy, showing the equal baptismal dignity of all Christians in the difference of charisms and offices; with the second it tempered the monistic tendency inherent to the old conception of the Roman primacy. Nonetheless, while laying the foundations for a theology of the primacy purged and freed from pious exaggerations and wordly excesses, the Council also professes, without ambiguity, the primacy and personal infallibility of the Bishop of Rome." [69]

The comments in the editorial of *La Civiltà Cattolica* are such as to "de-mythify" the papal power, undermine monarchy in the Church and favor an ecclesiological conception based on the supremacy of the people, whom the Pope should serve. Despite the subtleties of style, all this creates a propitious climate for the contestation of papal authority. It seems to us that the excerpts presented are a significant example of how "moderates" such as those of *La Civiltà* indirectly help *arditi* like Küng.

*

---

69. *Ibid.,* pp. 218-220.

6. Crisis in the Clergy and in the Religious Orders [70]

§ 51

Ever since the Council, a crisis has ravaged the Catholic clergy, both secular and regular. John Paul II attests to this in his *Closing Speech* to the Synod of 1990. In fact, on delving into the causes of the "identity crisis in the priesthood," he says:

"This crisis arose in the years immediately following the Council. It was founded on an erroneous and sometimes voluntarily tendentious comprehension of the doctrine of the conciliar Magisterium. **Here is, undoubtedly, one of the causes of the great number of losses then suffered by the Church, losses which gravely affected pastoral service and vocations for the priesthood,** particularly missionary vocations." [71]

§ 52

Similarly grave words come from the pen of Cardinal Ratzinger:

"The crisis in today's Church is, first of all, a crisis of the priests and religious orders. This is a tough thesis. It is a very sharp accusation, but it can contain a truth. **During the shock of the post-conciliar period, the great religious orders vacillated ... suffered a heavy hemorrhage, saw the number of new vocations reduced to levels never before found, and even today, they appear shaken by an identity crisis."** [72]

---

70. The last two Items of this Chapter – crisis in the Clergy and crisis of faith among the faithful – might seem out of place in an ensemble dealing primarily with the disciplinary crisis. Indeed, of themselves such topics would better fit a chapter on the doctrinal or institutional reality of the Church. Nevertheless, here they will be dealt with from a specific standpoint. The crisis of adhesion to the Faith and to the institution of the priesthood undoubtedly have multiple causes with varied depths. Here we focus on only one of them, which justifies the inclusion of the said items in the sequence of the disciplinary crisis.

Once the Church's internal unity and cohesion is broken, and the power, prestige and example of the ecclesiastical authority, above all that of the Pope, are brought into question, a huge number of faithful will inevitably become disoriented and discouraged. This easily generates a crisis of faith, customs and vocations. This is how the two following Items harmonize with the remainder of the Chapter.

71. John Paul II, Closing Speech to the Synod of 1990, published under the title: "Grazie al Sinodo sono stati affrontati problemi cruciali che hanno sempre trovato la risposta collegiale della Chiesa," in *L'Osservatore Romano,* 10/28/1990, pp. 4-5.

72. J. Ratzinger, *Rapporto sulla Fede,* p. 55.

What the Pope and the Cardinal from the Congregation for the Doctrine of the Faith authoritatively confirm is public and well-known. Every Catholic could give specific examples and point to this same phenomenon. The media frequently carry news items on the grave symptoms of an evil that contaminates the whole ecclesiastical body.

A. Crisis in the Secular Clergy

§ 53   Here we present an overview of the crisis by means of a collection of facts published over the years that reflect the extent and gravity of the situation generated by the Council.

The main characteristics of this post-conciliar crisis, along whose lines we have ordered the presentation below, are: abandonment of the ministry; drop in the number of vocations and consequent shortage of priests; opposition to priestly celibacy coupled with the phenomenon of married priests; the scandal of ecclesiastical concubinage; the addiction of priests to the vice of alcoholism and the perversion of homosexuality.

a. Abandonment of the Ministry, Drop in the Number of Vocations, Shortage of Priests

§ 54   Assembled in Medellin in 1968, the Latin American Bishops Council (CELAM) made these observations on the crisis of the ministry:

"**Doubts arise also regarding the priestly vocation itself. Doubts caused by factors characteristic of this hour of ecclesial renewal: The growing valorization of the role of laymen** in the development of the world and the Church. ... **The superficiality with which the priesthood presents itself** in routine religious functions and in a bourgeois way of life. A **crisis also is found among the priests who, either because of their age or formation, feel unable to assume the changes promoted by the Council.**" [73]

§ 55   Referring to the first eight years of post-conciliar era (**1965-1973**), Fr. Hans Küng lists some general elements of the crisis:

"In the Catholic Church we are undoubtedly in a very critical phase: **Vatican II has failed in every way to solve some problems that could have been entirely solved** ... **Some phenomena of this crisis,** especially in the Catholic Church, **are:**

---

73. CELAM, *A Igreja na atual transformação da América Latina e à luz do Concílio – Conclusões de Medellin* (Petrópolis: Vozes, 1980), p. 122.

"**a. The mass exodus from the ecclesiastical ministry: 22,000 to 25,000 in the last eight years.**

"**b. In ever more catastrophic proportions, the growing crisis of vocations among the new generation,** from North America to Spain.

"**c. A weakening of discipline among the faithful and churchmen,** above all with respect to Sunday worship." [74]

§ 56   No source could be more reliable regarding the crisis of vocations in the clergy from 1973 onward than the *Church Statistics Yearbook* for 1986, published by the Vatican's organ, *L'Osservatore Romano*. The charts presented cover **1973 to 1986,** years in which the total numbers of priests worldwide were, respectively, 433,089 and 402,886. Summarizing the charts for the period in question, **there were:**

- **27,366 defections;**
- 88,751 ordinations;
- 98,436 deaths. [75]

§ 57   About these data, one can note the following:

- **If we add to the defections mentioned by *L'Osservatore Romano*** **for the period 1973-1986 (27,366) the average estimate presented by Fr. Küng** – whom we suppose to be well informed – **on the period 1962-1973 (23,500 defections), we find that since 1962, a total of 50,866 priests are said to have abandoned their sacred mission.**

§ 58   - Taking into account only the period 1973-1986 (using data provided by *L'Osservatore Romano),* one sees that the difference between deceased and ordained priests is 9,685. If to this difference

---

74. Hans Küng, 0 *que deve permanecer na Igreja,* pp. 15-16.

75. *L'Osservatore Romano,* "Valutazione delle linee di tendenza dell'attività pastorale della Chiesa Cattolica fino al 1986," 5/30-31/1988, Supplement, pp. 11-12.

Curiously, an error appears to have slipped into the statistics that *L'Osservatore Romano* presented in its charts. If the number of priests in 1973 was 433,089 and there was a deficit of 37,051 priests in the period 1973-1986 (27,366 defections + 9,685 representing the difference between the 98,436 deceased priests and the 88,751 ordained priests), the total number in 1986 should be 396,038. But *L'Osservatore* puts the 1986 figure at 402,886 – a surplus of 6,848 priests.

we add the number of defections (27,366), we will have in this period a negative balance of 37,051 priests. [76]

§ 59   We know that in the period 1973-1986 the Catholic population increased by about 200 million people. [77] In order to fulfill her apostolic needs with the same level of service she had formerly provided, the Church, which in 1973 had 433,089 priests, in 1986 should have had roughly 570,000 priests. **Since in 1986 she had only 402,886, proportionally the difference is 167,000 priests.**

§ 60   In the period 1986-1990 the world Catholic population, which numbered 864,379,000 [78] grew to 928,500,000, [79] that is, an increase of just over 64,000,000 faithful. Taking the year 1973 as a point of reference, to maintain the same proportion of the number of priests in relation to that of faithful, there would need to be about 612,000 priests. Now, **in 1990 the official tally of secular and regular priests was 403,173,** [80] **a difference of 208,827 priests. This amounts to a proportional deficit of more than 50%.**

§ 61   More recent data do not essentially change this picture. Indeed, *L'Osservatore Romano* discloses that in the year 1992 the total number of priests was 404,641. Of these, 64.2 % were secular and 35.8 % regular. The paper adds that in relation to the year 1978 there was a drop of 2.8 % resulting from a small increase in the secular clergy (0.6%) and a decrease of 8.3 % in the regular clergy.

---

76. Furthermore, the situation of many of those who remained in the ranks of the clergy is far from auspicious. See, for example, "Les volets du presbytère sont ouverts," a work published by the French Catholic weekly *La Vie* on the responses it received from about 2,000 of the 29,000 priests in France: 31% wish to be called by their names without the title of priest; 21% call themselves favorable to the left; 44% hold reservations regarding Catholic Morals; 29% approve the marriage of priests; 83% wish married men to be ordained; 36% are for the ordination of women, and 50% admit to having or having had doubts about the Faith (in L. Langre, "Francia – el Clero, de derechas, distinto y levemente utopico," in *Vida Nueva,* Madrid, 11/2/1985, pp. 31-32.).

77. René Laurentin, "A retomada existe. Eis a prova," in *30 Dias*, December 1988, p. 52.

78. *Ibid.*

79. Ufficio Centrale di Statistica della Chiesa, "La Chiesa Cattolica alla luce di alcuni fenomeni statistici dal 1978 al 1990," in *L'Osservatore Romano,* 7/15/1992, Supplement, p. IV; *L'Osservatore Romano,* 10/17/1992, Supplement, p. II.

80. *Ibid.*

Drops were registered in Europe (9.9 %), North America (10%), the Middle East (4.1 %) and Oceania (5.6 %), whereas Africa and Southeast Asia saw increases of 29% and 41% respectively.[81]

§ 62   A confirmation or update of this data about the Church as a whole or for any particular country can be found in press reports from the individual countries.

Newsweek magazine comments on the severe scarcity of priests in the United States: **The Church in the United States "is quickly losing its priests.** Since 1962, when Council Vatican II started, more than 12,000 priests have dropped out of the priesthood in the U.S., and comparatively few young men have shown up to replace them. **Two decades ago the American Church had 48,000 seminarians; at present they are less than 12,000, and probably only 60% will persevere until the final vows.** The average age of American priests is now 56; at the end of the century, specialists calculate, it will be 73." **Presently even "homosexuals are more readly admitted in the priesthood,** as long as they are not sexually active. In the United States even **the Bishops recognize that the problem of ordaining women and married men cannot be ruled out forever."** [82]

§ 63   In the same year 1983, *La Croix* published an analogous finding on the scarcity of priests in France: "Twenty years ago priests were still numerous in France and the seminaries teeming. In 1983 there are fewer priests! ... It seems to me that they don't dare tell Catholics the whole truth; that we are poorly prepared for the years 1990-2000 and that, at times, awkward solutions have been improvised. ... Compared with the years 1960-1965, today there are extremely few young men in the seminaries. Nor will ordinations in the next few years be numerous." [83]

§ 64   Articles published in various issues of the magazine *30 Giorni* confirm that the crisis and the consequent shortage of priests are continuing.

In its December 1988 edition, a columnist in the magazine writes: "It will fall to historians to analyze the reasons for the blindness in the post-conciliar period. As far as the Church is concerned, it

81. *L'Osservatore Romano,* "Presentato al Santo Padre l'Annuario pontificio 1994," 2/28-3/1/1994, p. 7

82. Kenneth L. Woodward, "An Acute Shortage of Priests," in *Newsweek,* 4/18/1983, pp. 49-50.

83. Jean Frechet, "Vocations sacerdotales et sacerdoce des baptisés, lettre," in *La Croix,* Paris, 8/31/1983.

seems to me that the disorientation originates mainly from a grave identity crisis in the clergy ... **The uniform having been dropped, commanders saw themselves without troops, and de-Christianization confirmed the preceding secularization. Traumatized by mass desertions ... and the lack of vocations, the clergy let themselves be dragged along."** [84]

§ 65   Fr. René Laurentin, pointing out a relative increase in the number of ordinations, [85] finds that even if such a trend were to continue, it

---

84. Xavier Tilliette, "Começar de novo. Com fé," in *30 Dias,* December 1988, pp. 52-53.

85. a. Many see as a sign of hope a slightly higher number of admissions into secular seminaries and, as a consequence, a relatively higher number of priests ordained. An analogous phenomenon could be pointed out in relation to the regular clergy.

However, what the figures fail to show is the origin of these new vocations. Indeed, the countries that have provided the largest number of seminarians and novices are India, Poland, some African nations (Stefano Paci, "Precisam-se vocações – Pesquisa – A crise das religiosas," in *30 Dias,* April 1990, p. 65) and, more recently, the Philippines, whereas the situation of vocations in Western European countries, which have always set the tone in the Church, remains catastrophic. Hence it could be predicted that the Church – due to the future influence of Indian and African priests – will move away from the Western cultural area, in which most of her faithful are found. Or some of those priests will be sent to Europe and the Americas, with the consequent cultural clashes that this entails. In the case of Polish priests – formed under a Communist regime and usually imbued with a collaborationist mentality – one may fear they will disseminate a doctrine opposed to the regime of private property and free initiative, and favorable to Socialism and Communism.

Optimists about the "recovery" in the number of vocations are silent about such data.

b. In this sense, the words of a woman religious speaking about the difficulties experienced by novices from mission regions seem more realistic than Fr. Laurentin's optimism. Certainly the problems she raises also apply *mutatis mutandis* to the recruiting of male novitiates and seminarians: "Sister Vittorina, of the Sisters of St. Dorothea (an order which opened up to the missions only after the Council), faced the problem of forming novices from mission lands, a road that often requires a long time and the understanding of diverse cultural roots. But, in fact, it brings the congregation out of 'a period of stagnation, opens new horizons and obliges one to assume change as a criterion of life'" (Miela d'Attilia, "Donne sulle vie della missione," in *Avvenire,* Milan, 6/16/1991).

c. This perspective is emphasized by statements of Cardinal Jaime Sin. Indeed, the Archbishop of Manila, talking about a certain prose-

would take until the year 2000 to replenish the ranks of the clergy to the level of 1971. Meanwhile, the Catholic population grew by 200 million new faithful in 15 years (1971-1986), a figure likely to double by the turn of the millennium.

---

lytism without adequate criteria that some religious congregations have been carrying out in the Philippines, expounds reasons that may perhaps be valid for other countries as well: "These are the principal arguments against indiscriminate recruiting: 1. While we are pleased with the generous response of Philippine male and female vocations from the provinces, we must continue to be particularly sensitive about their true motivation. 2. In any case, the **'recruiting' of vocations, especially abroad, causes serious concerns, above all when certain 'favors' appear to become an exchange currency for those recruited**. Vocations are gratuitous gifts, they have no price. 3. The mystery and beauty of a religious vocation have been stained by various incidents over the last few years. On the one hand, we are happy with the quantitative growth, but, on the other hand, **we suffer due to the costly loss in vocation quality**. 4. **The urgency and aggressiveness that can characterize our zeal** for the Kingdom **can become real obstacles** instead of steps toward a gradual coming of the Kingdom to us. Prudence suggests that sometimes we must respect times that are not our own" ("Por algumas túnicas a mais," interview with Lucio Brunelli, in *30 Dias,* October 1994, p. 26).

d. The Italian press transcribes excerpts from a document that the Philippine Episcopate delivered to the Synod of 1994 denouncing the "enticement of [female] novices" by Italian religious orders (Orazio la Rocca, "Dalle Filippine arriva la 'tralta delle novizie,'" in *La Repubblica,* 10/3/1994).

According to the document, "in Manila alone, 87 feminine and 32 masculine congregations have been established in a few years' time. **To try to remedy their vocational crisis, such congregations are allegedly luring young people into the convent, to the point of using as bait the idea of a possible transfer to Italy with better paying jobs**" *(ibid.).*

"What we must safeguard," the Philippine Bishops write, "is the holiness of one's own vocation. **We are not recruiting for the army, nor are we advertising a new brand of soap**" *(ibid.).* They continue: "**We must prevent a vocational problem from becoming a recruitment of ... domestic employees**" *(ibid.).*

e. On vocations in Africa, the Bishop of Bulawayo (Zimbabwe) warned at the Synod of 1994 that "**religious vocations should not be seen as a means to gain social status and an education**" (Henry Ernest Karlen, "Dimensione umana della formazione religiosa," in *L'Osservatore Romano,* 11/23/1994, Supplement, pp. 51-52). The Bishop of Maken (Sierra Leone) points to the same problem: "Great discernment is needed

"The number of priests continues to drop," says Laurentin. "It went from 420,429 in 1971 to 402,886 in 1986. ... Today, however, while the overall number of priests continues to diminish, the number of seminarians and ordinations is recovering some ground. The current deficit in the number of priests (obtained by comparing deaths and desertions with the number of ordinations) was 3,870. It dropped to less than 3,000 in 1978 and less than 2,000 in 1984. ...

"The number of desertions of priests entering the lay state (3,690 to 1,057) weighed less than deaths, since the clergy 'aged' during the years of crisis. A country such as France, where a large part of the clergy is over 60, had 761 deaths to 200 ordinations, a negative balance of almost 600, a factor that weighs on world statistics. But the general tendency has changed once again. ... It is necessary for this expansion to continue, since to return to the number of 1971 (420,000 priests), which has been forecast for the year 2000, would not be a satisfactory goal. The number of Catholic faithful has increased by more than 200 million since 1970 (from 653,532,000 to 864,379,000 in 1986)." [86]

§ 66   The Eighth Synod of Bishops, held in Rome in October 1990, dealt with *The Formation of Priests in the Present Circumstances*. In regard to the topics that the issue suggests, a writer in *30 Dias* stated:

"The Synod will also discuss the crisis of vocations that has dramatically reduced the ranks of diocesan and regular clergy in the

in recruiting candidates for the religious life. **Because of the poverty in our countries, many can be attracted to religious life in order to improve their living standards**" (George Biguzzi, "Tenere alta la faiccola dell'evangelizzazione, della giustizia e della pace," *ibid.,* p. 43). The Bishop of Ndalatando (Angola) concluded his words at the same Synod by stating that "**in Angola**, the number of religious being formed is increasing, but **one senses a lack of serious educators**" (Pedro Luís Guido Scarpa, "Formazione 'inculturata' ma esigente," *ibid.,* p. 46).

f. Cardinal Silvio Oddi has this to say about the Eastern European clergy: "With some exceptions of noble figures victimized by persecution, **Christians in the East are ignorant in religious matters. They did not have the support of the clergy, in large part intimidated and inert, when not servants to the Communist police**" ("Confissões de um Cardeal," interview with Tommaso Ricci, in *30 Dias,* November 1990, p. 65).

These statements add serious qualifications to the statements of the apologists about a "new springtime" in religious vocations.

86. R. Laurentin, "A retomada existe. Eis a prova," in *30 Dias*, December 1988, pp. 51-52.

last few years. **In 1978 there were 258,541 diocesan priests and 157,878 regular priests all over the world. In 1987, according to data from the statistics department of the Roman Curia, there were 254,281 diocesan priests and 147,962 regular priests. In less than 10 years there was a drop of over 14,000 priests.** There is little reason for rejoicing." [87]

§ 67   The crisis is reaching such a point that the shortage of priests is felt even in the Diocese of Rome, the capital of Christianity. This finding was related by the then Vicar of Rome, **Cardinal Ugo Poletti, in a report presented at the annual meeting of Rome's priests.** According to him, **the number of priests is "diminishing at a terrifying pace."** [88]

b. Controversy about Priestly Celibacy and the Phenomenon of Married Priests [89]

§ 68   While the number of priests drops at a "terrifying pace," a growing number of them marry, with or without Rome's permission.

In 1968, CELAM described in general terms the situation in Latin America: "In relation to priestly celibacy, a laudable deepening of the emotional value of the human person and an exacerbated eroticism in the environment, along with frequent negligences in spiritual life and other causes, have opened the way to a new and varied set of problems." [90]

§ 69   In 1985, 400,000 priests carried out their ministry worldwide, while about 70,000 had left the priesthood to get married. In 1994 this latter figure had reached almost 100,000. [91]

---

87. Lucio Brunelli, "Colegialidade, quanto trabalho!," in *30 Dias,* June 1989, p. 39.

88. Ugo Poletti, Statements to the press, in 0 *Estado de S. Paulo,* "Faltam padres em Roma, diz Cardeal," 6/14/1989.

89. "It is still to this same end [of combating the Catholic Religion, the divine authority of the Church and her no less venerable laws] that tends this shameful conspiracy recently formed against the sacred celibacy of the members of the clergy. A conspiracy which counts, oh sorrow! among its promoters, some members of the ecclesiastical order who, miserably forgetting their own dignity, let themselves be vanquished and seduced by the shameful illusions and fateful attractions of voluptuousness" (Pius IX, *Qui pluribus,* November 9, 1846, in V.A., *Recueil des allocutions,* p. 183).

90. CELAM, *Conclusões de Medellin,* p. 122.

91. Marisa Fumagalli, "Anatema del vescovo di Rimini – 'No' al raduno dei preti sposati," in *Corriere della Sera,* 8/27/1994.

§ 70
In various countries, some of them have been founding very active associations to have the Vatican reinstate them into the priestly ministry.

In 1985 the "universal synod of married Catholic priests and their wives" assembled in Aricia on the outskirts of Rome. There were 150 participants coming from 15 countries: Argentina, Austria, Belgium, Brazil, Canada, Czechoslovakia, England, France, Germany, Haiti, Spain, Switzerland and the United States.

The "synod" featured three discussion panels, followed by lectures and testimonies. The meeting concluded that obligatory celibacy is "illegitimate from the dogmatic and juridical standpoints" and could not be imposed by a general law. The married priests also alleged that both priesthood and marriage are Sacraments and, therefore, cannot be incompatible. Addressing the problem constituted by the grave shortage of priests, they made an appeal to the Bishops who were to meet at an extraordinary Synod a few months later:

"We are at our posts, we are married priests. Send for us and the scarcity of priests will be resolved."[92]

The daily *La Repubblica* reported that the second meeting of married priests was organized by about 20 associations from around the world. The "synod's" secretary-general, Paolo Camellini, was reduced to the lay state during the pontificate of Paul VI "to be able to dedicate himself to married priests." He communicated to the Sacred Congregation for the Clergy that the "synod" was being held. Their informal answer was, "You may not claim that we are officially present, but we are pleased that you can express your faith and assemble like any other Christian."[93]

It is noteworthy that, according to the same Italian daily, the conference chairman, Giovanni Gennari, a former priest who directs Vocatio, Italy's association of married priests, is a sympathizer of the Italian Communist Party. Gennari says:

"Some years ago Cardinal Evaristo Arns wrote the Pope a letter in the name of other Bishops asking for a reform of celibacy." **Gennari goes on to add that the 70,000 married priests were "only the tip of a much larger iceberg."**[94]

---

92. Georges Mattia, "70,000 prêtres mariés en quête de légitimité," in *La Croix*, 8/27/1985.

93. Domenico del Rio, "Sono settanta mile i sacerdoti sposati," in *La Repubblica*, 8/25/1985

94. *Ibid.*

In the following year, 1986, Vocatio organized its third national conference. In an interview with the press, Gennari said there were 8,000 married priests in Italy and a total of 50,000 in the world. He also revealed that in April of the same year the International Federation of Married Priests had been founded. This is an organization that brings together 22 groups from 16 countries. [95]

§ 71   Movements advocating the ordination of married laymen also join forces with associations of married priests to combat priestly celibacy. They enjoy important support even from members of the ecclesiastical Hierarchy. **In 1987, when American Jesuit Terence Sweeney took a poll asking 312 American Bishops and 122 Cardinals from around the world what they thought of priestly celibacy and the ordination of women, he received 144 replies from the Bishops and 10 from the Cardinals. Fifty percent of the respondents favored revising the Church's attitude regarding the two issues.** [96]

§ 72   The same article reports there were then about 80,000 married priests, with 17,000 in the United States, 7,000 in Spain and 6,000 in Brazil.

§ 73   In Brazil there are several organizations of married priests. One of them, called Rumos, also admits former seminarians. This group coordinated its members' participation in the First Latin-American Encounter of Married Priests, held in Curitiba in 1990. [97]

Another association that brings together a good number of former clergymen is the Movement of Married Priests of Brazil, created in 1972. It has 2,500 registered members. Aristides Pimentel, secretary of the movement's São Paulo Section, states that "for the most part, our associates are canonically ordained former priests who carried out the ministry for periods ranging from 5 to 25 years." [98]

§ 74   Many more examples could be cited to illustrate the growing pressures brought to bear on the Holy See to have it modify its millenary discipline on priestly celibacy.

---

95. Giovanni Gennari, Statements to the press, in *O Globo,* "Padres casados abrem em Roma seu congresso," 8/29/1986.

96. Dermi Azevedo, "Oposição ao celibato obrigatório ganha força dentro da Igreja," in *Folha de S. Paulo,* 1 1/7/1988.

97. *Ibid.*

98. Aristides Pimentel, Statements to the press, in *0 Estado de S. Paulo,* "Ex-padres estão organizados," 6/15/1989.

In October 1989, the Third National Encounter of Priests, promoted by the National Commission of the Clergy, an organization of the National Conference of Brazilian Bishops (CNBB), was held at Itaici with the participation of 18 Bishops and 434 priests. The meeting issued a document sent to Cardinal Silvio Oddi, Prefect of the Congregation for the Clergy, asking for the ordination of married men as a "first step toward the abolition of obligatory priestly celibacy." [99]

§ 75   One year later, the Eighth Synod of Bishops was convened in Rome to study problems related to the priestly ministry. At the Synod, the president of the International Federation of Married Priests (which claims a membership of 90,000 former priests) accused the Vatican in a press interview of preventing a debate on obligatory priestly celibacy. At the same time, the Federation presented for the Synod's consideration a proposal that "celibacy should not be obligatory, but the fruit of personal choice." [100]

§ 76   In 1994, as Vocatio assembled in the town of Riccione, its director, Guido D'Altri, provided a more updated figure of their membership: Vocatio represents 1,000 married priests out of the 10,000 in Italy and 100,000 in the whole world. He also says there are 40 associations of married priests around the world. D'Altri claims that such figures are only the tip of the iceberg: For if that many priests have openly married, how many more are clandestinely living in irregular situations? [101]

§ 77   The movement for abolishing priestly celibacy received important support at the Synod of 1990. In one of its sessions, Bishop Valfredo Tepe of Ilheus (Brazil), looking at the question of celibacy, stated:

"The possibility of ordaining presidents of the Eucharist for the numerous communities without a pastor should be studied with neither fear nor taboo." He added there was no certainty that "authentically celibate vocations" would appear in the coming generations and that the faithful left without a pastor risked "falling into the hands of the sects." [102]

---

99. Celso Falashi, "Ordenação de casados é defendida por padres," in 0 *Estado de S. Paulo,* 10/14/1989.

100. "Celibato é discutido no Sínodo," in 0 *Estado de S. Paulo,* 10/3/1990.

101. Guido d'Altri, Statements to the press, in M. Fumagalli, "Anatema del vescovo di Rimini *";* "Preti sposati in cerca di diritto," *La Repubblica,* 8/29/1994.

102. "Celibato é discutido no Sínodo," in 0 *Estado de S. Paulo.*

§ 78   At the opening of the Synod, Archbishop Aloisio Lorscheider of Fortaleza (Brazil), spoke in name of the American and Canadian Bishops. He proposed to upgrade the Synod from a merely consultative body to a deliberative one. Such a proposal, clearly intended to democratize the government of the Church, was interpreted as a strong encouragement for the movement seeking the abolition of priestly celibacy.

Italian journalist Rocco Morabito gives more details about the intervention of the Bishops who favored ending priestly celibacy:

"There are persons in the Vatican who see the idea of a deliberative synod as a decisive step toward approving the abolition of priestly celibacy. For some, this would be the goal of the Bishops from the United States and Canada, on whose behalf the Brazilian Cardinal spoke at the opening of the meeting. Another important moment of the synod was the speech on Tuesday of Bishop Valfredo Bernardo Tepe of Ilheus. When he said he was not afraid of taboos and defended the ordination of *viri probati* [experienced men] as priests, he had in mind the abolition of obligatory celibacy ...

"Repercussions from the speech by the Bishop of Ilheus were not slow in coming. **Cardinal Joseph Louis Bernardin, Archbishop of Chicago, spoke of 'a celibacy that oftentimes appears irrational.' Bishop Herbertus Brandenburg of Stockholm asked for the ordination of Anglican pastors, even married ones, who have converted to Catholicism.** ... Yesterday afternoon, the auxiliary Bishop of London (Canada), Frederick Bernard Henry, recalled recent cases of sexual abuse by some priests in his country. For the Canadian Bishop, 'the sacrifice of celibacy demands a high degree of psycho-social development' that requires a 'very efficacious' formation. Bishop Frederick Henry stated that seminaries should have a program of 'psychosexual' development for future priests.

"Archbishop Aloisio, speaking in the name of the Brazilian Bishops' Conference and not of the American Bishops ... said that a priest cannot be separated from the church community in which he lives and whose primacy he must recognize. ... The priest's mission does not consist of carrying out actions different from those of the other faithful, but in doing the same things 'with sacrifice and sacramental grace.'"[103]

§ 79   According to the German weekly *Quick* of April 28, 1992, **20% of the world's priests married during the period 1964-1992. In Germany, half of the priests oppose ecclesiastical celibacy.**[104]

---

103. Rocco Morabito, "Discussão do celibate domina Sínodo," in 0 *Estado de S. Paulo,* 10/4/1990.

104. "Un prete cattolico su cinque si sposa," *Adista,* 5/16/1992, p. 2.

c. The Scandal of Ecclesiastical Concubinage

§ 80   Amid the whirlpool of the current crisis in the Clergy, innumerable priests scandalously resort to concubinage. The publication in 1983 of a book by Fr. Guus van Hemmert, SJ, who wrote the final version of the famous *Dutch Catechism*, brought this subject to public attention. In his work, Fr. Hemmert tells about his "experiences" during an immoral and sacrilegious relationship. In an interview with the newspaper *Eindhovens Dagblad*, he explained the goal of his book. *Confrontatie*, a magazine of Haerlem, Holland, reproduced his statements with an explanatory introduction:

"After the scandal that Fr. W. Berger, a well-known professor at the Catholic University of Nijmegen, caused last year by stating that he had been living in concubinage for 25 years, an even more serious case has now taken place. Fr. Guus van Hemmert has just written a book on the practice of concubinage by priests. In the work, entitled *A Way of Being Christian*, he narrates his experiences and observations. A Jesuit for over 35 years, Fr. Hemmert wrote the final version of the [Dutch] ***New Catechism*** and regularly writes articles on catechesis for dailies, weeklies and magazines. He also makes television and radio programs (including for Catholic stations) on faith and religious movements. If Hemmert's superiors fail to punish him, the number of priests 'living with a [female partner]' will continue to increase, especially among young priests.

"We reproduce here what Fr. Hemmert told the daily *Eindhovens Dagblad* on March 5 of this year: **'I find it normal for secular priests to be able to marry**. ... At times I am astonished to see people so busy with Church matters adhere to concubinage with such great ease. It is possible they do so to make life a little easier. By the way, I judged this in a different light when I saw it happen with other priests. With regard to what some of them were doing, I used to think: I must not do this now. As for others, [I thought]: it is all right for them. ... On some occasions (when I was with the woman) I thought: I am a Jesuit, I am free regarding you! But after five years of living together, I could no longer think that way. In fact, this is a marriage and it has lasted longer than many [official] marriages. ... **In my book, I tried to show how eroticism and sexuality can be reintegrated as values.** And I am convinced that, by doing this, I am not that much out of line with ecclesiastical tradition." [105]

---

105. Guus van Hemmert, Statements to the daily *Eindhovens Dagblad*, in *Confrontatie* (Haerlem), May 1983.

§ 81

A study carried out in Sardinia in 1987 shows that 70 % of Italian priests live in concubinage. Italian journalist Monica Falcone reports:

"**A courageous study** undertaken with modern methods and a representative poll **has proven** what popular hearsay has always taken for granted: **70% of priests have lovers**. ... One hundred priests, chosen from all regions of the Island of Sardinia, agreed to undergo extensive questioning in exchange for anonymity and probably, a certain relief to be able to reveal their situations and perhaps principally to be able to reveal their situation. In fact, the person charged with the study, which took four years, is a former priest who recently received a dispensation to get married. He is psychoanalyst Paolo Follesa, president of Cagliari's Neo-Freudian Institute. ...

"Follesa was able to demonstrate what some scholars had only proposed. **In 1979, a poll taken by Catholic sociologist Silvano Burgalassi caused a veritable scandal when he revealed that one-third of Italian male religious wanted the vow of chastity to be revoked. In 1984, Fr. Luigi Fischela consulted Italian priests and found that 53% of his colleagues opposed sexual abstinence.**"[106]

§ 82

The magazine *30 Dias* reports on statistical data provided by German theologian and psychotherapist Eugene Drewermann, professor of Systematic Theology at the Faculty of Theology of Pederborn, Germany. According to him, **6,000 out of the 18,000 Catholic priests in Germany have marital relations with a woman.**[107]

§ 83

In 1992, Bishop Eamonn Casey of Galway, regarded by some as the most popular Prelate in Ireland since the time of St. Patrick, resigned his post "for personal reasons." Such reasons had to do with a report in *The Irish Times* disclosing that over the last 15 years, Bishop Casey had made regular payments to Annie Murphy. By 1990, such payments reportedly totaled $115,000. Miss Murphy, an Irish-American residing in Connecticut, told a nationwide U.S. radio station that the Bishop is the father of her son Peter, age 17. The money to maintain her and her son was taken from Church funds. Since the scandal broke, private donors have been covering the $120,000 defi-

---

106. Monica Falcone, "Pesquisa: 70% dos padres na Itália têm mulher," in 0 *Globo* (Rio de Janeiro), 3/22/1987.

107. Tommaso Ricci, "Engrenagem quase perfeita," in *30 Dias,* December 1989, p. 33.

cit, plus interest. Casey was also president of the Church-run organization Third World Development Agency. [108]

d. Priests Succumb to the Vice of Alcoholism

§ 84   Another disastrous characteristic of the crisis affecting the
Clergy is the spread of alcoholism in their ranks. A report in *Folha de
São Paulo* gives a wealth of data on this topic in Brazil and other
countries. The report says this vice also lures Bishops and nuns:

"**Alcoholics make up about 10%** (**1,200**) **of a total of
12,000 Brazilian Catholic priests,** and also affects Bishops and
women religious. These data are furnished by the Vida Nova community, founded in Curitiba eight years ago ... which brings together
60 alcoholic priests and nuns from around the country. Its director is
the American priest, William Tracy. Having managed to control his
own alcoholism, he sees himself as a 'hunter' of alcoholic men and
women religious, whom he directs to specialized clinics. ...

"**The files of *Vida Nova* show the cases of two Catholic
Bishops from Brazil ... who died recently from alcohol-related
illnesses. In the United States, where alcoholic priests number
about 3,500, a Bishop was recently arrested** (and forcibly interned in a specialized clinic) **after he was caught driving while
intoxicated. The problem of alcoholism in the Clergy** (which also
**affects about 10% of European priests, mainly in Ireland, Great
Britain and the Scandinavian countries**) has grown to such proportions that the *Code of Canon Law* ... in canon 924, allows alcoholic priests to celebrate Mass with grape juice instead of wine." [109]

§ 85   The magazine *30 Dias* describes a similar situation in Germany: "Alcoholism among priests: The curtain of silence that has long
covered this taboo becomes ever more permeable. **The priest drunk-
ard, who in the past was a figure in literature ... is today a cause**

---

108. Richard Ernsberger Jr. and Lucy Howard, "Ireland is Talking ..." in
Newsweek, 5/18/1992, p. 3; "Fallen from Grace," in *Time,* 5/25/1992, p.
14; "Scandalo sessuale nella Cattolica Irlanda – Vescovo progressista
aveva amante e figlio," in *Corriere della Sera* (Milan), 5/9/1992; "L'amica
del Vescovo si confessa," 5/10/1992; "Sesso, bugie e videotapes: sotto
choc la Cattolica Irlanda," 5/12/1992; "Il Vescovo confessa la paternitè e
i furti," 5/13/1992; "L'amante del Vescovo Casey ringrazia per la
solidarietà," 5/7/1992; "Dopo lo scandalo it pentimento – Il Vescovo diventa
missionario," 10/19/1992.

109. D. Azevedo, "Clero brasileiro tem 10% de alcoólatras," in *Folha de
S. Paulo,* 8/14/1988

of serious concern for diocesan curias and religious orders in Germany. The fact is no longer hidden or disguised as atypical. Diocesan personnel departments have been forced to come to grips with the fact that **in the last few years the number of alcoholic priests has increased significantly**. ...

"A drunken priest causes scandal in the community, the schools and among the people he meets. This was demonstrated recently by Gottfried Wiesbeck, the parish priest of Dorfen, a province in northern Bavaria. ... To the bewilderment of his faithful, Wiesbeck revealed [in a sermon] that only a small part of his colleagues have no problem with the priestly way of life. **'In no profession are there so many alcoholics as among us priests. One out of every three sporadically faces problems of this kind. One out of 10 priests is an alcoholic and needs a long treatment.'**...

"The Catholic Diocese of Rottenburg-Stuttgart, one of the largest in Germany, disclosed that in 1988 it was found that 5 % of its Clergy were affected by problems of this type. Doctors specialized in this field put the actual percentage of affected Catholic priests at around 10%. **In Germany about 2,000 priests are reportedly alcohol-dependent. A study by Hannover University estimated that one out of 10 patients interned in detoxification clinics is a priest or theologian.**" [110]

e. Homosexuality in the Clergy

§ 86   Given the gravity of the subject matter dealt under this title, we believe it more appropriate to analyze it in greater detail in a work that became a special edition to this Collection. This work was titled *The Catholic Church and Homosexuality* and was published in the first two editions of *In the Murky Waters of Vatican II* as an appendix. However, given the extent that the phenomena of homosexual and pedophile priests assumed in the Catholic Church, many friends asked us to update that work in order to cover those scandals mainly in the United States. So, responding to those requests, in 2004 we published a much expanded work which now is titled *Vatican II, Homosexuality & Pedophilia*.

We direct our Reader to it. This has the twofold advantage: it does not lengthen this Chapter and gives the Reader a more complete view of one of the Items concerning the moral crisis in the Catholic Clergy as a consequence of Vatican II.

---

110. Guido Horst, "0 álcool como antidoto," in *30 Dias,* April 1989, pp. 78-79.

B. Crisis of Religious Orders

§ 87   Concerning the crisis that affects the Regular Clergy, we found it more adequate to present a paradigmatic example rather than make a general analysis. The example we chose is the Society of Jesus, the Church's largest Order in terms of membership and certainly one of the most powerful and, in the past, brilliant and prestigious Orders.

a. A Paradigmatic Example: The Society of Jesus

On analyzing the internal situation in the Society of Jesus, we find it shaken by multiple crises. In addition to internal rivalries, one can detect a crisis of vocations, of ideas, of faith, a crisis in its relations with the Vatican, the death of its militant characteristics and a bleak future looming on the horizon.

Three articles published by the magazine *30 Dias* reveal significant indications of the Society's internal situation. [111]

Crisis of Vocations

I was 8 yrs old!

§ 88   The articles present 1965, the year that saw the closure of the Council, as the point of reference to analyze the situation that followed. On that occasion, the Superior General of the Society was Fr. Pedro Arrupe, elected to that post during the Council.

The orientation Fr. Arrupe gave the Society, consonant with conciliar reforms, caused the number of its members to drop from 36,038 in 1965 [112] to about 26,500 in 1982 [113] when he resigned.

---

111. The three-part series, to which *30 Dias* gave great prominence, includes these articles:

• Lucio Brunelli, "O balanço de Kolvenbach: Os cinco anos do Papa Negro" (November 1988, pp. 54-59);

• L. Brunelli, "Kolvenbach: o Papa pode contar conosco – Em primeiro plano, os jesuítas" (February 1989, pp. 6-16);

• Gerard Leclerc, "Depressão jesuítica – Europa, França" (May 1989, pp. 22-25).

Future bibliographical references to this trio of articles will be designated simply by *30 Giorni* or its Portuguese edition *30 Dias*.

112. *30 Dias*, November 1988, p. 58.

113. *Ibid.*, February 1989, p. 16. The article includes a chart from which we have taken this approximate figure.

After that, under the direction of the new superior Fr. Peter-Hans Kolvenbach, elected in 1983, that number continuously decreased. On January 1, 1988, the Society had 24,924 members, that is, 11,414 less than in 1965, which amounts to a reduction of about one-third of its contingent. [114] In a press conference held on March 22, 1995 during the 34th General Congregation of the Jesuits, Fr. Kolvenbach stated that the Society then had 23,000 members. [115]

Crisis of Ideas

§ 89   The cause of such a loss was the crisis of ideas: "Shortly before May 1968, an intellectual agitation took hold in the Jesuit formation center at Fourviere, the famous school of Lyon. ... The directors tried to control the revolt by allowing it the right to exist. But the crisis was so profound that it ended up by causing a real hemorrhage. Many years of study were sacrificed as young men dropped out *en masse,* intensely contesting society and the Church. The whole structure of the Society was affected by this phenomenon, which was not restricted to France.

"The Society's Superior General, Fr. Arrupe, convened the 32nd General Congregation ... to lay down the points of reference for an evangelizing action. ... The goal of establishing social justice in the structures imposed itself as an absolute rule. Paul VI began to become concerned about the climate of doubt spreading among Jesuits and threatening their identity. Solicitude for the poor, indisputably inspired by the Gospel, has not always been free from ideological equivocations." [116]

Crisis of Faith

§ 90   Nevertheless, even more than the crisis of ideas, the Jesuits' situation stems above all from a crisis of faith.

Vatican II concepts to the effect that "sanctity" and "elements of salvation" supposedly exist in the other religions and in all men are indirectly targeted as having caused the Society's demise. Such notions are moderate expressions of the theory of Fr. Karl Rahner's

---

114. *Ibid.,* November 1988, p. 59.

115. Peter-Hans Kolvenbach, "Conferencia de prensa," 3/22/1995, in *Oficina de Prensa e Información,* 34th General Congregation.

116. *30 Dias,* May 1989, p. 22.

"anonymous Christianity," according to which every man who believes in being is already a Christian, even if unknowingly. [117]

The magazine *30 Dias* reported this testimony of a young theologian who did not identify himself: **"Our Order, understood as an official establishment, is already dead. From this standpoint, all there is to do is to wait for its physical disappearance.** It was killed by a diluted Rahnerism that in the last few years has spread theories on 'anonymous Christianity.' From this have come all the errors on how social and political compromise, as well as ecumenism and inculturation, should be understood." [118]

Crisis in the Society's Relationship with the Vatican

§ 91   Fr. Arrupe was preparing an American priest, Fr. Vincent O'Keefe, to be his successor: "After the election of John Paul I, [O'Keefe] deemed it well to make three requests: to abolish the condemnation of artificial means of contraception, to allow the ordination of women to the priesthood, and to permit priests to marry."[119]

In 1981, Fr. Arrupe resigned as Superior General and designated Fr. O'Keefe as Vicar General of the Society, "indirectly provoking the Vatican's intervention." There is little information on the manner or the content of such intervention . All that is known is that Karl Rahner, "the Society's most important theologian," defined it as "an obscure administrative maneuver." The report continues: "On September 1, 1983, the Superiors of the Society of Jesus gathered in Rome to elect their new Superior General after the two years administration of the 'delegate.'"

The Vatican suggested three candidates. A long and agitated election was expected. To everyone's great surprise, the 220 delegates elected St. Ignatius' 29th successor in the first round, which lasted less than one hour. They chose Fr. Kolvenbach, who "was neither linked to the previous directives nor did his name come from the Vatican." [120]

---

117. On the "anonymous Christianity" theory, see Vol. V, *Animus Delendi II*, Part II, Chap. III.

118. *30 Dias,* November 1988, p. 59.

119. *Ibid.,* p. 54.

120. *Ibid.,* p. 55.

Fundamental Changes in the Society's Profile

§ 92   Fr. Kolvenbach's own words on several topics permit us to infer the orientation he is giving his Order.

As is well known, St. Ignatius of Loyola conceived the work he founded as a military corps. Hence he gave it a military structure, established the rigorous Jesuit obedience and imparted the spirit of conquest that characterizes the Order's members. Its very name, Company of Jesus is a military term, which in English we translate simply as "Society of Jesus," stripping it of its military character.

In relation to this military character, Fr. Kolvenbach asserts: **"Any military connotation in relation to the Society and its [Superior] General must be eliminated. ... In this process of renewal [proposed by Vatican II], a certain way of being of the Society of Jesus has died.** This explains why a theologian said in this magazine that the Society 'was dead.'"[121]

§ 93   Other characteristics clearly establish the orientation of Fr. Kolvenbach. According to his own words, a rich understanding of Our Lord Jesus Christ could be expressed by the image of a "guru:" "We all use images to find Christ. In the *Spiritual Exercises,* St. Ignatius explicitly resorts to the image of a medieval king in order to understand better the Eternal Father. **Even the 'guru' could be on the long list of images that Christians use to try to understand some aspect of the mysterious richness of Christ,** so long as the integrity of the Lord not be reduced to this single aspect."[122]

§ 94   On the collaboration of Jesuits with the Chinese Communist regime, the Society's General explains: "As they left jail, some Jesuits reflected for a long time about China's situation and ... decided to collaborate in some sectors with this organization [The Patriotic Association, made up of collaborationist Catholics] approved by the Communist regime."[123]

The Future that Looms on the Horizon

§ 95   Proselytism by the Society of Jesus is carried out today primarily in Asia, to such a point that Indian priests have become the second largest number of vocations after the Americans.[124]

---

121. *30 Dias*, February 1989, pp. 14-15.

122. *Ibid.*, p. 8.

123. *Ibid.*, p. 9.

124. *30 Dias*, November 1988, p. 57.

In Europe, the situation is catastrophic. Only one young man entered the Society's novitiate in France in 1987. In Italy, 10 joined, but the average death rate among the Jesuits in that country is 30 per year. [125] "If this pace continues," says the writer about the situation in France, "superiors will be obliged to close two houses per year." [126]

Other reports add these facts: "The only exception to the aridity of vocations in Europe comes from the East ... particularly Poland and Yugoslavia." [127]

"In the United States the Society lost 195 members through death or resignation. The numbers are not very encouraging, to the point that an important American Jesuit, Fr. Robert Drinan, professor of Law at Georgetown University, said this to the magazine *The Tablet* last month [October 1988]: 'What will become of the 28 faculties and universities and 42 colleges directed by Jesuits in the United States when membership drops even further? Today, these institutions have 1,300,000 students. Will they be forced to secularize, as happened with the 110 American faculties founded by the Methodist church?'"[128]

In 1995, during the 34th General Congregation of the Jesuits, Fr. Kolvenbach addressed the internal situation of the Society without sparing words: "The General Congregation has fully taken into account the reality of the numeric diminution and the increasing age of available forces with the inevitable consequences of fatigue, loss of stability and a fatal drop in the quality of the apostolic service to be carried out. This is the price we must pay for working in demanding conditions in order to continue in vanguard apostolates and act entirely within [the guidelines of] pluralism and secularism." [129]

§ 96   As for the intellectual formation of its priests, a Jesuit linked with *30 Dias* comments: "If we observe the present situation attentively, we are impressed with the relative intellectual sterility and theological ignorance. ... In fact, there is an emptiness." [130]

§ 97   Despite the moral crises similar to those of the secular Clergy, which certainly have not spared members of the Society as well, this is the panorama that emerges regarding its internal situation since Vatican II.

---

125. *Ibid.*, p. 59.

126. *30 Dias,* May 1989, p. 23.

127. *30 Dias*, November 1988, p. 59.

128. Robert Drinan, Statements on the Society of Jesus in the United States, in L. Brunelli, "0 balanço de Kolvenbach: os cinco anos do Papa Negro," p. 59.

129. P. H. Kolvenbach, "Conferencia de prensa."

130. *30 Dias,* May 1989, p. 25.

§ 98   Analogous considerations could be made, in general, about the Benedictine, Carmelite, Dominican and Franciscan Orders, as well as the innumerable Religious Congregations that make up the bulk of men and women religious in Holy Church.

During the Synod of 1994, expressive data came to light on the drop in the numbers of vocations for the state of perfection. In fact, the magazine *30 Dias* **published comparative charts revealing among the regular Clergy a figure of 167,208 in 1970 compared to 139,258 in 1992. Among non-ordained religious, the number went from 79,408 in 1970 to 54,793 in 1992.**" [131]

§ 99   About the crisis in the regular Clergy as a whole, here is what Cardinal Ratzinger has to say:

"The Orders and Congregations of an active life are in a grave crisis; the discovery of professionalism, the concept of 'social assistance' that has replaced that of 'charity,' **the often indiscriminate and even enthused adaptation to new and hitherto unknown values of modern secular society, the introduction,** sometimes without a critical sense, **of psychologies and psychoanalyses of all types into the convents: All this brought excruciating problems of identity and has led to the loss of sufficient motivation to justify religious life for many women** ... The spiritual treatises of old have been replaced with manuals of psychoanalysis; theology has given its place to psychology, even the cheapest ones.

"Nearly irresistible, furthermore, is the fascination for what is Eastern or presumed such. In many religious houses, both masculine and feminine, the Cross has often given its place to symbols of Asian religious traditions. In several places the devotions of old have disappeared to be replaced with the techniques of *yoga* or *zen*." [132]

§ 100   To have an overview of the situation in the religious Orders as an immediate consequence of the crisis in the regular Clergy, it would be well to say a word about women religious *in genere,* whether they belong to feminine branches of religious Orders or Congregations.

---

131. Andrea Tornielli, "O outono quente dos religiosos," in *30 Dias,* September 1994, p. 26.

132. J. Ratzinger, *Rapporto sulla Fede,* p. 100.

b. Crisis Among Women Religious

§ 101

The data on the crisis in religious Orders deals mainly with men religious. But there are data also on women religious. We divide it here as follows: crisis of vocations, moral crisis, and feminism.

We believe the words of the Mother Superior of the Daughters of Charity, Sister Guillemin, present at the Council as an observer, serve well to explain certain causes of the crisis we are now seeing. In October 1965, speaking about "the woman religious today," she told how conciliar reforms placed her Congregation at a radical impasse:

"The woman religious is led to change from a situation of insertion, from a position of authority to a position of collaboration, from a religious superiority to a sentiment of fraternity, from a human inferiority complex to an open participation in life, from a preoccupation with moral conversion to a missionary preoccupation. One must admit that this represents a real reversal in relation to our traditional positions and means [requires] a long and persevering preparation of mentalities. One must also be aware that this will lead us to make some very serious decisions; finally, one must be convinced that not to accept this re-conversion is to move in the opposite direction of the march of the world and the Church and condemn oneself to suffer the consequences." [133]

Her words reflect well the pressure undergone by women religious to accept Vatican II's *aggiornamento*.

Crisis of Vocations

§ 102

On this matter, Cardinal Ratzinger gives us a symptomatic and terrifying example: **"There is an updated and detailed report on the women religious of Quebec. ... As far back as 20 years ago, in the beginning of the '60s, Quebec had the world's highest number of women religious *per capita* in a population totaling six million. Between 1961 and 1981, counting departures, deaths and losses in recruitment, the number of women religious fell from 46,933 to 26,294. This was a drop, therefore, of 44%, and [this trend] seems unstoppable. In the same period, new vocations diminished by 98.5%.** Furthermore, a large part of the remaining 1.5% is made up not of young people, but of 'late vocations.'" [134]

133. Guillemin de la Charité, "La religieuse contemporaine," in H. Fesquet, *Le journal du Concile,* p. 1000.

134. J. Ratzinger, *Rapporto sulla Fede,* pp. 101-102.

§ 103   The magazine *Il Regno* reports a drop of more than 25% in the number of women religious in Italy in the period 1988-1993 alone: **"Women religious were 150,174 in 1974, 121,183 in 1988 and 111,490 in 1993. ... [This is] a massive drop which does not show signs of abating** ... add to this numerical drop, an increase in the average age. **Only 3.3% of the sisters are less than 29 years old ... while 59.2% of the sisters are over 60."** [135]

However, if we take as reference the year 1966, when there were 160,000 women religious in Italy, [136] the deficit increases to more than 30%.

§ 104   A reliable survey on the situation of man and women religious Orders and Congregations in the United States says: "The 30 years that followed Vatican Council II were turbulent for Catholic religious Orders in the United States. **The average age of members of many Congregations rose to about 67 years, while the number of men and women religious dropped by about 45% among brothers and sisters, and** 27% **among regular priests."** [137]

§ 105   The data depicting the particular situations presented above are far from reassuring: "The crisis of female vocations was denounced in many reports by Bishops' Conferences around the world. While avoiding 'irrational alarmism,' the Vatican Congregation for Catholic Education recently said that the situation is very grave: There are religious families without any [new] vocation on record for the last 10 years."[138]

§ 106   The year 1994 saw the publication of impressive comparative figures on the number of women religious in the whole world: **In 1970 there were 1,003,670 women religious with perpetual or provisional vows; in 1992 that number was down to 655,031."** [139]

---

135. Lorenzo Prezzi, "Vescovi e religiosi, profile modesto," in *Il Regno*, 11/15/1993, p. 589.

136. Giancarlo Rocca, "Modelli in crisi e nuove vie," *ibid.*, p. 12. In fact this journalist points out a total of 103,000 women religious in Italy in 1992. That would mean a drop of more than 35% in relation to 1966. However, the figure quoted for 1992 is smaller than the one for 1993, referred to in the news item by L. Prezzi above. So we do not know if there was an increase in vocations between 1992 and 1993, which would seem unlikely, or whether the information from the two journalists of *Il Regno* was contradictory.

137. David Nygren and Miriam Ukeritis, "USA: Il futuro dei religiosi," in *Il Regno*, 4/1/1993, p. 242.

138. Bruno Bartoloni, "La rivolta silenziosa delle suore," in *Corriere della Sera*, 6/4/1993.

139. A. Tornielli, "O outono quente dos religiosos," p. 26.

Moral Crisis

§ 107   In 1985 a great scandal was caused in the United States by the publication of a book by two lesbian former nuns. The work brought to light a reality much more painful than the perversion of two sisters. Indeed, if the authors' statements are to be taken at face value, 9,000 of the 120,000 women religious in the United States are lesbian, in addition to the 51 nuns who give their testimonies in the book. If 9,000 are lesbians, how many others would have abandoned purity of customs without falling into this perversion against nature?

Here is the news on the launching of the book: "There can be no greater success for a book than selling out before publication. That is what happened with *Lesbian Nuns: Breaking Silence,* published this year by Naiad Press in Florida. ... **Written by two teachers, Nancy Manahan and Rosemary Curb, lesbians and former nuns, it includes the testimonies of 51 Catholic nuns (nine of whom still keep their vows) telling about their experiences with lesbianism.** Naiad Press printed 125,000 copies....

"The New York Times dedicated a large article to the book, reporting that several of the ex-nuns who testify in it have stood out in the struggle for the rights of homosexuals. One of the authors says that a goal of the book is to break the taboo of lesbianism and to show that it is everywhere. ... **With solemn sociological airs, Nancy Manahan says that 9,000 of the 120,000 American nuns are lesbians."** [140]

§ 108   The year before, 24 American nuns had signed an advertisement published in *The New York Times* in support of abortion. According to *The Washington Times,* none of the nuns attended to the Vatican demand that they recant. The paper also reported that their superiors supported their rebellious attitude, saying that they respected their consciences. [141]

§ 109   In May 1992, the Gallup Institute conducted a survey – published around the middle of June – whose results showed that 45% of American Catholics deem homosexual relationships morally acceptable, while only 48% agree with traditional Catholic doctrine on the matter.

Sister Jeannine Gramick, one of the Sisters of Notre Dame and a member of the National Coalition of American Women Reli-

---

140. Paulo Sérgio Pinheiro, "A transa das freiras e outran transas," in *Folha de S. Paulo,* 6/18/1985.

141. William F. Willoughby, "Superiors 'Honor the Conscience' of Nuns Who Signed Pro-choice ad," in *The Washington Times,* 1/11/1985.

gious, analyzes the results of the survey in a letter to *The New York Times* and appears to be satisfied with the erosion of morality among Catholics. She writes:

"Only five years ago, when Pope John Paul II visited the United States, *Time* magazine and *The Los Angeles Times* reported that 66% to 68% of Catholics agreed with Catholic teaching on homosexual behavior. This 20% decrease in five years is as significant as the 20% change in favor of women's ordination in the last seven years. Most likely, the trend to accept lesbian and gay relationships will continue because 57% of those younger than 35 accept it." [142]

§ 110   In Bogota, Colombia, the women Religious of the Adoration – a Congregation that assists women of bad lives – walked in a parade alongside prostitutes to protest police repression of illegal brothels. [143]

Best Little Convent in Bogota

Feminism

§ 111   Also growing is the number of "feminist women religious" who advocate the ordination of women. Such is the case of 120 sisters of the Daughters of Mary, Help of Christians, a Congregation founded by St. John Bosco:

"Feminist ideas have influenced the 120 sisters gathered at a conference in this capital [Rome]. They have advocated a new theology to overthrow sexual barriers in the Church and permit women to enter the priesthood. Promoted by the College of Educational Sciences, the conference, entitled 'Woman and Church,' was the scene of heated discussions among the Daughters of Mary, Help of Christians. The women religious of this order founded by St. John Bosco claim that feminist theology must overthrow the 'macho' understanding of God based on traditional 'macho' models.

"In summary, the women religious are convinced that 'the primitive Church patriarchalized the word of God with all the consequences that followed,' including the traditional subordination of organizations of women religious to a male authority and the refusal to ordain women. According ... to the newspaper *La Repubblica,* which gave prominent coverage to the conference, the women religious insist that the priesthood 'is not a right to be claimed but a vocation that must be valued individually, without distinction of sex.'" [144]

142. Jeannine Gramick, "Homosexuality To Be a Burning Catholic Issue" (letter of 6/24/1992), in *The New York Times,* 7/11/1992.

143. Steve Gutkin, "Best Little Convent in Bogota," in *Newsweek,* 10/19/1992, p. 37.

144. *O Globo,* "Religiosas feministas lutam pelo sacerdocio," 8/7/1988.

§ 112   A demand by female Superior Generals to be represented by their own sisters at the Synod of Bishops is telltale of the trend to abolish the mediation of male Superiors. A Vatican watcher from *Corriere della Sera* reports:

"Without raising their voices, but with much determination, **the sisters asked to be heard at the Bishops' Synod that will address the topic of religious life next year. The International Union of [female] Superior Generals recently sent the Pope a document to request that a significant number of its delegates be present at the assembly. Soon the Union of Italian Superior Generals will make the same type of request.** ... Fifteen men religious and 15 women religious were invited to the Italian Bishops' assembly to be held in Collevalenza from October 25 to 28 [1993]."[145]

§ 113   An expressive manifestation of "religious feminism" took place on the eve of the Synod of 1994, which was discussing the institutes of religious perfection. Referring to the preparations for the meeting, a columnist of *30 Dias* says: "The most debated ... topic is certainly the one related to the role of women. In fact, **a document drafted by female religious Superiors of the United States in preparation for the Synod advances a proposal that women be given more relevance in Vatican congregations so that a woman religious might also climb to the top of organizations of the Holy See.**" [146]

These words by an Italian journalist demonstrate the feminist impact caused by the demands of women religious:

"**Salaries, powers and posts of responsibility in the Vatican Curia. This is the surprising request that a group of sister delegates officially presented yesterday to the** ongoing **Vatican Synod on religious life.** Without beating around the bush, the women religious surprised the roughly 250 Synod Bishops by **presenting a 'contractual' platform that would raise the envy of the most demanding union activist** of the CGIL.

"**This is the first time that expressions such as 'we ask to be admitted to decision-making posts in the congregations,' 'we want to enter the pontifical Curia with positions of responsibility,' or 'we call for adequate stipends'** have been heard at the Vatican in the presence of the Pope and a ponderous array of Cardinals, Bishops and high-ranking pontifical Prelates. **Never have sim-**

---

145. B. Bartoloni, *ibid.*

146. A. Tornielli, "O outono quente dos religiosos," p. 24.

ilar requests been made by the silent world of women religious in the 2,000 years of the History of Christianity." [147]

Even seasoned analysts were somewhat disconcerted at the Holy See's unrestricted acceptance of the participation of women in the Synod's debates of 1994. In fact, *L'Osservatore Romano,* which publishes the minutes of the meeting, noted that women religious spoke no less than 44 times, and in some instances with far from modest considerations and requests, especially if one keeps in mind that, as far as we know, this is the first time that women religious were heard openly in a synod. The following statements, presented in chronological order, seem worthy of note:

Sister Baril, of the Dominican Missionaries of the Adoration (Canada), claims that the Church has a "feminine personification:"

"The expression 'femininity of the people of God' reveals the appropriate sense of two biblical images: that of a conjugal union symbolizing the Covenant of God with his people, and that of the maternity of this people which collaborates with God to accomplish his design of salvation. ...

I stress, among others, three major meanings that derive from this symbology. First, it shows us the Church who receives her being and fecundity through Christ the Redeemer. This meaning makes one understand the priority in Church life of a behavior of active welcoming, which constitutes the living faith. ... Finally, speaking of ecclesial collaboration in terms of maternity, we better understand that what must be emphasized in all Church activities is, above all, the full life offered by God to persons and communities." [148]

Sister Sumah, of the Missionaries of Our Lady of the Apostles (Ghana), asks that religious work receive financial remuneration:

"**Women religious who work in the pastoral sector are often inadequately remunerated and in some places are not paid at all. Nevertheless, the pastoral 'worker' needs to survive. A worker, independent of the ambit in which she works, deserves to be paid.**" [149]

---

147. Orazio la Rocca, "Le suore a Wojtyla: 'Più soldi e potere'– Ecco le 'sindacaliste di Dio,'" in *La Repubblica,* 10/8/1994; "'Dimenticate i beni terreni' – Il Papa contro le 'sindacaliste di Dio,'" in *La Repubblica,* 10/13/1994; Marco Politi, "Eva sull'altare," in *La Repubblica,*10/12/1994.

148. Gilberte Baril, "La femminilità del popolo di Dio e la vita consacrata femminile," in *L'Osservatore Romano,* 11/23/1994, Supplement, p. 38.

149. Rose Sumah, "Le religiose nelle giovani chiese," in *ibid.,* p. 54.

Mother Sietmann, Superior General of the Missionary Sisters of the Sacred Heart of Jesus (Peru), president of the International Union of Superior Generals, emphatically advocates a determinant role for women in "spirituality and in theology" and calls for equality with men with respect to "planning and decision-making" in all levels of the Church, including the organs of the Curia:

"We find there is an urgent need for the consecrated woman to proclaim the riches of God from her feminine perception, and to participate more amply and efficaciously in the sphere of spirituality and theology, in which she still has not been given due consideration nor an adequate and equivalent possibility of integration. What must be created and promoted are an attitude of discernment and a permanent dialogue between the Hierarchy and the people of God, which will favor the balanced and effective presence of consecrated women in pastoral functions, works and tasks inside the Church on planning and decision-making levels, both at the local and universal levels, as well as in the official organs of the Roman Curia."[150]

Mother Boullanger, Superior General of the Canons of St. Augustine of the Congregation of Our Lady (Canada) and vice-president of the International Union of Superior Generals, presents a whole platform of feminist demands:

"Very often women have the image of themselves that men have of women. It is, therefore, an image imposed from the outside, an image that does not entirely reflect the qualities that, though not exclusively feminine, distinguish women in an outstanding way.

"Their sensibility facing the realities of creation, their innate sense of life, their capacity to listen, their respect for the person, their willingness to dialogue, allow them to establish authentic human relationships and be instruments of communion. This sensibility makes them more vulnerable to the suffering of the small and the poor. They strive to protect life, above all when it is weak and fragile. Their tenacity stands out in their quest for an organization of the world in which the poor, whoever they may be, can find their just place. Their capacity to adapt to situations and to diverse lifestyles makes them able to understand and individualize differences so that they can become instruments of evangelization according to the reality in which they find themselves. ... **All this gives their thinking a specific hue that stems from life, instead of abstract concepts. For this reason the voice of women is not always heard. ... We wish,** furthermore, **that on the various levels – parochial, diocesan, national**

---

150. Klara Sietmann, "Rendere visibili i trati del volto di *Dio,*" *in ibid.,* p. 56.

and even Vatican – a real place be given to women in the ambit of reflection and decision-making, and not only in the executive ambit, with the aim being a participation and a real collaboration [sic]."[151]

§ 114   Mother Rochette, Superior General of the Sisters of Notre Dame (Canada), calls for religious Institutes to be given the faculty of changing their own structures as needed:

"In order to favor this prophetic action, **the Institutes must enjoy the freedom to make adequate changes to their structures;** they have the means to discern which structures favor [people's] insertion and creativity in apostolic choices to fulfill the needs of today's world." [152]

Mother Kanongata'a, Superior General of the Sisters of Nazareth (Fuji Islands), calls for **"women to have the same opportunity as men to pursue theological studies."** [153]

Mother Bassil, Superior General of the Congregation of the Sacred Hearts of Jesus and Mary (Lebanon) makes this request of the Synod: "That Islam become better known by men and women religious and that Islamic fundamentalism be understood as a sign of the times and an invitation to dialogue; that **Christians and Muslims build tomorrow's society together."** [154]

Mother Choi, Superior General of the Olivetan Benedictine Sisters (Korea) presents this "inter-religious argument:" **"Can we learn any valid methods from the monastic discipline of Buddhism? Some sisters who practice *zen* find it very useful for profound prayer."** [155]

Mother Carpetti, Superior General of the Sisters of Catholic Apostolate and president of the Union of Italian Superior Generals, appears to adopt feminism with no embarrassment and apply it to religious life:

151. Stéphanie-Marie Boullanger, "La vita apostolica e la condizione fernminile," *in ibid.,* p. 103

152. Madeleine Rochette, "Il ruolo profetico della vita religiosa," *in ibid.,* 106.

153. Keiti Ann Kanongata'a, "La 'passione' per il Regno di Dio," *in ibid.,* p. 123.

154. Antoinette Bassil, "La vita religiosa femminile in Libano," *in ibid.,* p. 124.

155. Angela Choi, "Profonda conversione e solida formazione," *in ibid.,* p. 147.

"The response given by the [women] religious to the *Lineamenta* and, even more, their daily life, **make it evident that in Italy there is a feminism that entails a growing maturation capable of acting generously in the construction of the new civilization of love. The emerging leaders of the feminine world are also prepared to reinterpret [religious] consecration, evangelical counsels, community life and the missions.**" [156]

§ 115   One becomes perplexed upon learning that such opinions, some of them openly revolutionary, were pronounced in the presence of the Pope and about 250 Synod Fathers, who gave their seal of approval, either by tacit acquiescence or explicit support to the rise of women in the Church. [157]

Furthermore, the Synod's final statement, supported by all those present, declares that **"consecrated women must participate more in consultations and decision-making in the Church in situations that require it."** [158]

§ 116   These are some of the major features of the crisis that rages in the secular and regular Clergy, as well as among women religious.

---

156. Lilia Capretti, "La vita consacrata femminilee ripensata ed elaborata in Italia con riferimento alla comunione ecclesiale," *in ibid.,* p. 151.

157. a. The most significant of the various remarks of the Synod Fathers about the role of women in the Church was that of the Bishop of Owando (Congo), Ernest Kombo, who said: "May He [God] inspire the prophetic behavior that would lead to designating women, an important part of those who are consecrated, both on the numeric and qualitative planes, to posts of responsibility, even to the highest posts in the Hierarchy, such as lay cardinals, if possible" ("Dopo aver gratuitamente ricevuto bisogna saper gratuitamente dare," *in ibid.,* p. 86).

b. With regard to this possibility, "some vaticanologists commented that the proposal was not absurd" ("Bispo propõe mulheres como Cardeais," in *O Globo,* 10/11/1994).

Not only vaticanologists think this. In a report at the end of the Synod of one of the circles of French-speaking Bishops, Bishop Pierre Raffin of Metz concluded with words that appear to assume the elevation of women to the lay cardinalship. Indeed, he said: "The principle that should guide Church action in this field [the condition of consecrated women] is as follows: All lay people, men and women, whether consecrated or not, should have access to all the offices and leadership levels in the Church that do not require ordination" ("I beni dei religiozi al servizio della missione," in *L'Osservatore Romano,* 11/23/1994, Supplement, p. 158).

158. Bishops' Synod of 1994, *Message to the People of God,* p. 163.

7. Crisis of Faith among the Faithful

§ 117   It does not seem superfluous to recall here the wise consider-ations of Pius IX in the Encyclical *Qui pluribus,* of November 9, 1846, pointing out the cause of religious crises among the faithful. Certainly the law enunciated by the Pontiff in the 19th century applies as well to the present case. Addressing the Patriarchs, Primates, Arch-bishops and Bishops at the beginning of his pontificate, Pius IX said:

> "When ministers are ignorant or neglectful of their duty, then the morals of the people also immediately decline, Christian discipline grows slack, the practice of religion is dislodged and cast aside, and every vice and corruption is easily introduced into the Church." [159]

If it is a proven law in the History of the Church that the deca-dence of the faithful results from bad Shepherds, what should one say of a Council that so "revolutionized" Church life?

As we said above, the opening of the Council to the world was bound to bring about a crisis of Faith among the faithful.

§ 118   On February 6, 1981, in an Allocution to the priests and reli-gious participating in Italy's First National Conference on the topic "Missions to the People in the 1980s," John Paul II recognized:

> **"We must realistically** and with profound sensibility **admit that Christians today in large part feel lost, confused, perplexed and even disillusioned:** ideas strongly contrasting with revealed Truth, which had always been taught, have been spread; **real heresies in the dogmatic and moral fields have also spread and have cre-ated doubts, confusions and rebellions; even the liturgy has been altered; immersed in intellectual and moral 'relativism' and, thereby, in permissiveness. Christians are tempted by Athe-ism, Agnosticism,** a vaguely moralistic Illuminism, **a sociological Christianity without defined dogmas and objective morals.**" [160]

§ 119   The final document of Medellin points to the crisis of Faith currently spreading so insidiously among the faithful:

> **"This religiosity ... which holds God's answer to all ques-tions and needs of man, can enter into a crisis and, indeed, has begun to enter one** based upon the scientific knowledge of the world

---

159. Pius IX, Encyclical *Qui pluribus,* November 9, 1846, in V.A., *Recueil des allocutions,* p. 189.

160. John Paul II, Allocution to the First Italian National Convention for religious men and priests, February 6, 1981, in *Insegnamenti di Giovanni Paolo II,* vol. IV/1, p. 235.

that surrounds us. This religiosity places the Church before the dilemma of continuing to be the universal Church or converting herself into a sect and, therefore, no longer incorporating the men who express themselves under this type of religiosity. Because she is a Church and not a sect, she must offer her message of salvation to all men, even if she runs the risk that not all will accept her in the same way and with the same intensity." [161]

§ 120   The Jesuits of *La Civiltà Cattolica* say this: **"It is enough to read a certain Catholic literature today to feel the great bitterness and disillusionment of some Catholics, even priests, in relation to the Church, the Pope and the Bishops, and to sense their dismal previsions about the future of the Church and of Christianity: It seems to them that the crisis which the Church is now going through is a mortal one!** From this standpoint, there is no difference between the so-called 'progressivists,' for whom the Church has already missed the train of History and has nothing more to say to the world, and the so-called 'conservatives,' for whom the Church pushed herself forward to the point of losing her own identity, almost ceasing to be the Church of Christ." [162]

§ 121   On the crisis of faith, Cardinal Thiandoum, Archbishop of Dakar, offers this opinion:

"The years that followed the Council were very difficult. ... The crisis of faith was evident. It resulted not only from social transformations, but primarily from erroneous interpretations of the Council. **Some people thought that Vatican II had changed the Church and the faith. Confusion became generalized.** In 1967, ... Paul VI decreed that this year would be the 'year of faith.' He saw that the application of Vatican II would bring problems. Two years later, he pronounced his famous 'Creed.' **People's faith was disturbed."** [163]

§ 122   In the 1994 Synod, Bishop Foley noted this about the Institutes of consecrated life:

"Unfortunately, but understandably, non-fidelity to freely assumed commitments is very communicative. And **the scandal caused by dissolute acts on the part of some consecrated persons and**

---

161. CELAM, A *Igreja na atual transformação da América Latina à luz do Concílio – Conclusões de Medellin,* p. 90.

162. *La Civiltà* Cattolica – Editorial, "Testimoniare la 'gioia nella speranza," 4/17/1971, p. 109.

163. Hyacinthe Thiandoum, "Paulo VI? Um Papa fiel," interview with Stefano Paci, in *30 Dias,* August/September 1992, p. 18.

by the abandonment of their vows, made many people blind
and deaf to the message of the Gospel and shook the faith and
fervor of many who had found in persons dedicated to a consecrated life a source of inspiration and example according to the model
of Christ." [164]

§ 123   On the post-conciliar crisis, Bishop Graber issues this grave
general assessment: "**Over the last 25 years we have been crossing through the second Protestant and Enlightenment period,
accompanied by a Neo-Modernism.**" [165]

§ 124   The diminution of the sense of God and of sin is also recorded
in passing by the Synod of 1983. Summarizing its conclusions, the
secretary general of the Synod, Archbishop Jozef Tomko, later Cardinal, said:

"The Fathers of the Synod have indicated the causes that provoked the diminution of the sense of sin and, consequently, of moral
responsibility, above all . **a diminution of the sense of God that
necessarily leads to indifferentism, permissiveness and practical materialism.**" [166]

§ 125   Bishop Tshibangu Thsishiku of Kinshasa and member of the
Secretariat for Non-Christians, noted at the same Synod of 1983 "a
strong diminution in the practice of the Sacrament of Reconciliation in
its traditional form." As a reason for the crisis, he pointed to the
"relativization of the sense of sin owed to, among other things,
the insufficient explanation of **the spirit of some reforms coming
out of the principles of the Council.**" [167]

§ 126   Ecumenism has also caused the crisis in the Faith. This becomes clear as one considers another statement by Hans Küng. It is
especially meaningful testimony if one bears in mind that the professor
of Tübingen is an ecumenist *à outrance*. "**That feeling of insecu-
rity,**" says Küng, "**which emotionally insinuated itself in many
Christians after the reforms put into practice by the Church
herself, was later aggravated by even more intense contacts**

---

164. John Patrick Foley, "Formazione di base per l'uso dei mass-media
nella diffusione del Vangelo," in *L'Osservatore Romano*, 11/23/1994,
Supplement, pp. 24-25.

165. Rudolf Graber, "Como no tempo de Atanásio," interview with Tommaso Ricci, in *30 Dias*, September 1990, p. 46.

166. J. Tomko, "Riconciliazione e penitenza," in *L'Osservatore Romano*,
12/1/1983, Supplement, p. III.

167. Tharcisse Tshibangu Thsishiku, "Crisi dei confessori," in *L'Osservatore Romano*, 10/5/1983, Supplement, p. II.

with the doctrine and spirituality of other churches. In many places, therefore, ecumenism *(oecumene)* acts as a catalyst for existing tensions." [168]

§ 127   For all these reasons the situation has reached such an extreme that the people of Rome no longer identify themselves with the Catholic Church. Indeed, in May 1995, the Vicariate of the Holy See was presented with a survey carried out by sociologist Franco Garelli. In various matters of Faith – resurrection, the existence of Heaven and Hell, the divine origin of the Church – and of Morals – homosexuality, divorce, abortion, pre-marital relations, masturbation – most Romans have abandoned Catholic doctrine. [169]

"To explain this situation," a journalist notes, "the Cardinal Vicar [of Rome] based himself on the words of the Pope: 'One speaks of countries in which whole groups of the baptized have lost the living sense of the faith or no longer see themselves as members of the Church.' But these regions mentioned by *Redemptoris Missio*, Cardinal Camillo Ruini points out, are no longer distant ones: 'This is also, to a large extent, the situation of Rome.' The capital of Catholicism has become 'mission territory.'" [170]

*

§ 128   A crisis of priests and religious. A crisis of the faithful. Would it be an exaggeration or a lack of objectivity to attribute them to conciliar ambiguity?

Fr. Chenu himself, interviewed by Jacques Duquesne, responds:

Question: "In your opinion, **how should one see this whole upheaval? Is it the fault of the priests, the theologians, the faithful?**

Answer: "**I see its cause in the Council itself, in the logic of its march and its dynamism.**" [171]

---

168. Hans Küng, "Vatican III: problemi e prospettive per il futuro," in V.A., *Verso la Chiesa del terzo millennia*, p. 88.

169. "Roma: Cidade Católica mas nem tanto," in *O Estado de S. Paulo,* 5/11/1995; Marco Politi, "Sesso, preghiere & aldilà," in *La Repubblica,* 5/9/1995.

170. Roberto Zuccolini, "Ruini: Vero, la cittá è ormai diventata una terra di missione," in *Corriere delta Sera,* 5/12/1995.

171. *Jacques Duquesne interroge le Père Chenu,* p. 191.

why ambiguous language destroys unity of thought & in practice: chaos ≠ not of God order not of chaos

About this, Chenu is entirely right. All the crises are, in our view, necessary consequences of the ambiguity of Vatican II's documents and, afterward, the different interpretations they were given. [172] How would it be possible to avoid a laceration in the unity of thinking in the Church when the conciliar texts were written so as to please two opposing currents? How could divergence in the moral and disciplinary ambits be prevented when they rise from such a conflict of beliefs? Finally, how can the increase of an atmosphere of chaos be prevented? How to avert this chaos from disorienting the faithful and causing them to doubt the Church and the Faith?

§ 129

*New World Order - freemasonic Goal**

Here we close Chapter X, considering that its thesis title has been fully demonstrated. As a result of conciliar ambiguity, a great crisis of unity and internal cohesion erupted in the Church, discrediting ecclesiastical authority, including that of the Pope. This shook the faith of priests, religious and laity in God and in the Church.

*   *   *

VII is responsible for crisis

172. We often find mention of the crisis that was established in the Church since Vatican II (Item 1 of this Chapter). Less often, however, do we find in print that which a huge number of people think but few have the courage to write, that is, that the Council holds primary responsibility for the crisis that followed it. As an example of the latter, we quote below the words of a Brazilian journalist with whom we do not always agree, but who has the merit of fearlessness and clarity:

"The Council [Vatican II] – and this can hardly be denied – profoundly changed the spiritual, religious and moral life of the West and produced equally profound reverberations in the cultural sphere. What is in question is whether the changes came for the better or for the worse, both for the Church and society. Part of the answer can be anticipated by an obvious fact: Vatican II plunged Western spirituality and morality into an unprecedented crisis – a 'crisis' that contradicts its own definition, since the term means a violent, sudden and fleeting rupture of equilibrium. But in the post-conciliar Church, the crisis never ends; on the contrary, it becomes more serious every year that goes by. ... 'Many Catholics over age 30 remember living in that Church as if in a spiritual fortress – comforting at times, inhibiting and even frightening at others. But it was a secure and orderly universe with guarantees of eternity for those who lived according to its rules. Now this fortress has fallen,' wrote *Time* magazine one decade after the Council.

"Thirty years after the beginning of the conciliar revolution, in the 'world's largest Catholic country,' Brazil, there are more evangelical ministers than Catholic priests. Every year the Church in Brazil loses more than half a million faithful who no longer identify with her, according to data provided by the CNBB [National Conference of Brazilian Bishops]. To realize how unusual and grave the situation is, all one has to do is compare the documents of Popes such as Pius IX (1846-1878), St. Pius X (1903-1914), Pius XI (1922-1939) and Pius XII (1939-1958) with the conciliar and post-conciliar texts. There is an abyss between the theses defended by the former and the latter. Heterodoxy was raised to the position of orthodoxy. 'The promoters of error should no longer be sought among declared enemies, for they are hidden in the very bosom of the Church, thereby becoming all the more harmful to the extent they are less noticed. ... The enemies pose as reformers. ... It is in the very veins and entrails of the Church that the danger is found.' Prophetic words spoken by St. Pius X in the encyclical *Pascendi,* written in 1907, but in their essence as current as if they had been written today.

"Chaos is not limited to the interior of the Church; it spreads. For the Council not only turned inside out what people believe in (doctrine) and practice (liturgy and morality) in the Catholic sphere, but also what people believed and practiced in all of Western society, of which the Church was the spiritual center. All that was said and done until 1960 was said and done with her as reference, be it for or against her. Even so, in less than three decades, this point of reference was almost totally obliterated by the turbulent waves of *aggiornamento.* Had it been attacked by its worst, declared secular enemies, religion would not have suffered so many losses as it has suffered from the action of its own representatives, which undermined it from within.

"The Council closed in 1965, with the Church abdicating her responsibilities as one who guides and orients consciences. ... Without the conciliar abdication, how could one imagine the explosion that took place at end of the '60s (May of '68, the revolution in customs, the increased use of drugs, homosexuality, violence against women and children, satanic sects, etc.)? It is no wonder that Cardinal Suenens compared Vatican II to '1789 in the Church,' and the theologian Yves Congar, to 'October 1917.' ... Thus, with the conciliar revolution, the leaders of the new Church brought down its own walls. Afterward it took only one more step for the walls of society also to crumble" (Mattos Soares de Azevedo, "O Concílio que não terminou," in *Jornal da Tarde,* 10/24/1992).

CONCLUSION

§ 1   As this Volume, which sought to be an objective and serene analysis, comes to a close, it has demonstrated that the Ecumenical Council Vatican II was ambiguous in the official texts of its documents.

Three types of questions inevitably arise from this fact:

§ 2   *First*: Whereas the Council's texts are written in a deliberately imprecise, hesitant and provisional language that generates disparate and many times contradictory interpretations;

Whereas the doctrine that often reveals itself behind the ambiguity leads, or may lead, to a visualization that differs from traditional Catholic doctrine;

Whereas as a consequence of these two facts, the official line of application of the Council has produced in the Church the greatest crisis in her History, one asks:

What value should one attribute to Vatican Council II?

Are precision, clarity and orthodoxy not characteristic of the ecclesiastical Magisterium? Are the applications of its teachings not conducive to a more fervent faith, adhesion to moral norms and disciplinary submission?

Therefore, given the fundamental ambiguity of Vatican II, its variance on certain points with the earlier Magisterium of the Church, and the crisis it has generated, could one not advocate that it is null?

This Volume offers multiple elements for reflection about these questions. We hope that the whole Collection *Eli, Eli, Lamma Sabacthani?* will further contribute to their clarification. It will do this not so much through a canonical discussion on the possibility of a Council being considered null – we believe that in this regard the masters are clear and History is rich in teachings – but by presenting the facts and doctrines that characterize the Council of John XXIII and Paul VI.

§ 3   *Second*: Since the Council's texts lend themselves to disparate interpretations by conflicting currents, it becomes impossible, based directly on them, to know their exact meaning. Faced with this impossibility, how can one understand the thinking and the intentions of the Council?

We see no other way but an indirect one, much longer and more arduous. It is to study the spirit of the Council, the thinking of the men who designed, wrote and applied it, as well as the fruits it has generated. By seeking in these various realms the underlying unity that defines the whole "Vatican II phenomenon," an interpretation that clarifies such texts becomes possible.

Grandis enim tibi restat via – "For thou hast yet a great way to go" (3 Kgs. 19:7) said the Angel to the Prophet Elias, giving him strength to continue his arduous pilgrimage through the desert.

Encouraged by this august example and under the patronage of the Prophet Elias, who will re-enter History for the final combats of Holy Church, a simple layman could attempt to tread this road, the only one left open to him. That is what we intend to do in the next Volumes of this Collection.

§ 4   *Third*: upon closing this Volume, notwithstanding the apocalyptic character of innumerable aspects of the conciliar and post-conciliar crisis, we would like to express our unshakable belief in the promise of Our Lord Jesus Christ regarding the Catholic Church: *Et portae Inferi non praevalebunt adversus eam* – "And the gates of Hell shall not prevail against her" (Matt 16:18). This certainty is fortified by the prophetic words of the Blessed Virgin Mary at Fatima: "In the end my Immaculate Heart will triumph."

Therefore, it is with an approach of vigilance before the enemies of the Church, of compassion in face of her sufferings and of interior peace in the certainty of victory, that we invite the Reader to accompany us in the analysis of the spirit of Vatican II, of the thinking that inspired it and of the fruits that it generated.

*   *   *

BIBLIOGRAPHY

ABBOT, Alter M. – *The Documents of Vatican II,* Herder and Herder: 1962. **ACERBI, Antonio** – *Due ecclesiologie - Ecclesiologia giuridica ed ecclesiologia di communione nella 'Lumen gentium,'* Bologna: Dehoniane, 1975. **ADAM, K.** – "Die Katholische Tubingen Schule," in *Gesammelte Aufsätze,* Augsburg, 1936. **ADISTA** (Rome) – "Un prete cattolico su cinque si sposa," 5/ 16/1992. **d'AGOSTINO, Biagio** – Comments on Hell in the conciliar assembly, *apud* B. KLOPPENBURG; *Concílio Vaticano II,* vol. IV. **AHLBRECHT, Ansgar** – *Dialogo con los protestantes,* in V.A., *La reforma que llega de Roma.* **ALBERIGO, Giuseppe** – Editorial, in V.A., *Verso la Chiesa del terzo millennio*; *Per un Concílio ecumenico cristiano nella prospettiva dell'unità della Chiesa,* in V.A., *Verso la Chiesa del terzo millennio*; See V.A., *Conciliorum oecumenicorum decreta.* **ALSZEGHY, Zoltan** – *Sens de la Foi,* in V.A., *Vatican II: Bilan et perspectives,* vol. I; see M. FLICK. **d'ALTRI, Guido** – Press statement, *apud* M. FUMAGALLI. **AMANN, Emile** – *L'époque carol-ingienne,* in V.A., *Histoire de l'Église,* vol. VI.

AMELUNXEN, Remi and Paul TRINCHARD – "Historical Prelude: A Brief History of the Holy Mass from the Canonized Liturgy to the *Novus Ordus* English Liturgy," in P. TRINCHARD, *New Mass in Light of the Old.* **AMERIO, Romano** – "Sob a cúpula, o vazio," in *30 Dias* (São Paulo), January 1991. **ANTÓN, Angel** – *L'ecclésiologie post-conciliaire - Les attentes, les résultats et les perspectives pour l'avenir,* in V.A., *Vatican II: Bilan et perspectives,* vol. I. **ARAÚJO OLIVEIRA, Hermes de** – *Guerra revolucionária,* Rio de Janeiro: Biblieux, 1965. **ASSOCIAZIONE TEOLOGICA ITALIANA** – See V.A., *Il linguaggio teologico oggi.* **d'ATTILIA, Miela** – "Donne sulle vie della missione," in *Avvenire,* 6/16/1991. **AUBERT, Roger** – *La géographie ecclésiologique au XIXe. siècle,* in V.A., *L'ecclésiologie au XIXe. siècle; La théologie catholique au milieu du XXe. siècle,* Tournai/Paris: Casterman, 1954; *La théologie catholique durant la première moitié du XXe. siècle,* Tournai/Paris: Casterman, 1970, in V.A., *Bilan de la théologie du XXe. siècle,* vol. I; See V.A., *Nouvelle Histoire de l'Église* .

AUGUSTINE, St. – *De baptismo contra Donatistas,* in PL 43, 135, *apud* V. PROAÑO GIL; *Contra Julianum,* in PL 662, *apud* C. GARCIA EXTREMEÑO; *De dono perseverantiae,* in PL 1031, *apud* V. PROAÑO GIL; *De duabus animabus contra manichaeos,* in PL 42, 105; *Epistula 19, apud* C. a LAPIDE, *Ad Galatas,* vol. XVIII; *Epistula 19 ad Hieronymum, apud ibidem*; *Epistula 82,* in PL 33, 285-286; *De gratia Christi et peccato originali, apud* G. de PLINVAL; *Sermo 294,* in PL 38, 1346, *apud* V. PROAÑO GIL; *Ad Galatas, apud* St. THOMAS AQUINAS; *Summa theologiae.* Regula, *apud* St. THOMAS AQUINAS, *IV Sententiarum.* **AZEVEDO, Dermi** – "Clero brasileiro tem

10% de alcoólatras," in *Folha de São Paulo*, 8/14/1988; "Oposição ao celibato obrigatário ganha força dentro da Igreja," in *Folha de São Paulo*, 11/7/1988.

BACHELET, Xavier-Marie le – *Benoit XII,* in DTC, vol. XII, *apud* C. GARCIA EXTREMEÑO. **BALLERINI, Antonius** – See J. P. GURY. **BALTHASAR, Hans Urs von** – *Abbatere i bastioni,* Turin: Borla, 1966; *El complejo antirromano* – *Integración del papado en la Iglesia universal,* Madrid: BAC, 1981; *De l'intégration* – *Aspects d'une theólogie de l'Histoire,* Bruges: Desclée de Brouwer, 1970; *Love alone: The way of Revelation,* London/ Dublin: Sheed & Ward, 1982; "Von Balthasar: La mia opera è abbozzata più che terminate, in *L'Osservatore Romano*, 6/24/1984. **BANWART, Clemens** – See H. DENZINGER (1). **BARAÚNA, Guilherme** – See V.A., *A Igreja do Vaticano II.* **BARBIER, Enunanuel** – *Histoire du Catholicisme liberal et du Catholicisme social en France* – *Du Concile du Vatican á l'avènement de S.S. Benoit XV (1870 - 1914),* Bordeaux: Imprimerie Y. Cadoret, 1924, 5 vols. *Les infiltrations maçoniques dans l'Église,* Paris/Brussells: Desclée de Brouwer, 1910. **BARBIERI, Raffaele** – Comments on the Schema XIII in the conciliar assembly, *apud* L. CARLI. **BARIL, Gilberte** – "La femminilità del Popolo di Dio e la vita consacrata femminile," in *L'Osservatore Romano*, 11/ 23/1994, supplement.

BARTOLONI, Bruno – "La rivolta silenziosa delle suore," in *Corriere della Sera*, 6/4/1993. **BARTZ, Wilhelm** – *Le Magistère de l'Église d'après Scheeben,* in V.A., *L'ecclésiologie au XIXe. siècle.* **BASIL, St.** – *Adversus Eunomium,* in PG 29, 654, *apud* C. GARCIA EXTREMEÑO. **BASSIL, Antoinette** – "La vita religiosa femminile in Libano," in *L'Osservatore Romano*, 11/23/ 1994, supplement. **BEA, Augustin** – Comments on the Schema XIII in the conciliar assembly, *apud* G. CAPRILE, *Il Concilio Vaticano II,* vol. V. **BEAUVAIS, Vincent de** – *Speculum quadruplex sive speculum maius,* Akadem- ische Druck-Verlagsanstalt, Graz, 1964. **BELGIAN EPISCOPATE** – Declara- tion against the Encyclical *Humanae vitae, apud* ICI, 11/15/1968. **BELLARMINE, St. Robert** – See ROBERT BELLARMINE, St. **BENEDICT XII** – Constitution *Benedictus Deus,* January 29, 1336, *apud* X. M. le BACHELET and H. KÜNG, *Vida Eterna?* **BENEDICT XV** – Encyclical *Ad beatissime,* of November 1, 1914, in V.A., *Les enseignements pontificaux*; Encyclical *Soliti nos,* of March 11, 1920, *in ibidem.*

BETTI, Umberto – *Qualification théologique de la Constitution,* in V.A., *L'Église de Vatican II,* vol. II. **BEUMER, Johannes** – *Histoire de la théologie et des dogmes,* in V.A., *Bilan de la théologie du XXe. siècle,* vol. II. **BIGUZZI, George** – "Tenere alta la fiaccola dell'evangelizzazione, della giustizia e della pace," in *L'Osservatore Romano*, 11/23/1994, supplement. **BILLOT, Louis** – *De Ecclesia Christi,* Rome: Aedes Universitatis Gregorianae, 1921. **BOFF, Leonardo** – *Igreja: Carisma e poder - Ensaio de eclesiologia militante,* Petrópolis: Vozes, 1982; *Le Ministère dans l'Église,* Paris: Cerf, 1981; *O rosto* *materno de Deus - Ensaio inter-disciplinar sobre o feminino e suas formas religiosas,* Petrópolis: Vozes, 1979. **BONNET, Piero Antonio** – *Le "fidèle" récupéré comme protagoniste humain dans l'Église,* in V.A., *Vatican II: Bilan et perspectives,* vol. I. **BOULLANGER, Stéphanie-Marie** – "La vita apostolica e la condizione femminile," in *L'Osservatore Romano,* 11/23/1994, supplement. **BOURRIER, Any** – "Demissão de bispo revolta os franceses," in *Jornal do Brasil,* 1/17/1995. **BOUYER, Louis** – *A decomposição do Catolicismo,* Lisbon: Sampedro, n.d. **BOWMAN, Jim** – "The Bishops with the gays," in *Commonweal,* 4/24/1992. **BRAGA, C.** – See BUGNINI, A. **BRAZILIAN EPISCOPATE** – See CNBB PASTORAL COMMISSION.

BRUNELLI (1), Lucio – "O balanço de Kolvenbach: os cinco anos do Papa Negro," in *30 Dias,* November 1989; "Colegialidade, quanto trabalho!" in *30 Dias,* June 1989; "Kolvenbach: o Papa pode contar conosco - Em primeiro plano, os jesuítas," in *30 Dias,* February 1989; "1994 - Ao som de Bill e da família",* in *30 Dias,* December 1993; "A pílula que dividiu a Igreja," in *30 Dias,* July 1988. See J. SIN. **BRUNELLI (2), Lucio and Alfred LABHART** – See CULLMANN, O. **BUGNINI, A. and C. BRAGA** – *Ordo Hedomadae Sanctae instauratus,* Rome, 1956, in P. ROMANO ROCHA. **BULGANIN, Nikolay** – "Citação sobre guerra revolucionária," *apud* H. de ARAUJO OLIVEIRA. **BUONAIUTI, Ernesto** – *Le modernisme catholique,* Paris: Ed. Rieder, 1927. **BUTLER, Christopher Basil** – *The Theology of Vatican II,* London, 1967, *apud* Y. CONGAR, *Le Concile Vatican II.* **BUTTIGLIONE, Rocco** – *Il pensiero di Karol Wojtyla,* Milan: Jaca Book, 1982.

CABRAL DUARTE, Luciano – "Riconciliare le intelligenze cattoliche," in *L'Osservatore Romano,* 10/6/1983, supplement. **CAMPO, Carlos del** – See CORRÊA DE OLIVEIRA, P., *A propriedade privada e a livre iniciativa no tufão agro-reformista* and *Sou católico: posso ser contra a reforma agraria?* **CANO, Melchor** – *De locis theologicis,* Rome, 1890, *apud* C. GARCIA EXTREMEÑO. **CAPRETTI, Lilia** – "La vita consacrata femminile ripensata ed elaborata in Italia con riferimento alla comunione ecclesiale,"* in *L'Osservatore Romano,* 11/23/1994, supplement. **CAPRILE, Giovanni** – *Il Concílio Vaticano II,* Rome: La Civiltá Cattolica, 1965-1969, 5 vols; Interview granted to A. SINKE GUIMARÃES, Rome, Februrary 3, 1983. **CARDONNEL, Jean** – *Vatican II,* interview with Michel DUBOST, in *Historia* (Paris), October 1982. **CARLI, Luigi** – *Il comunismo e il Concílio Vaticano II,* in G. SCANTAMBURLO. See CICOGNANI, A.

CARTECHINI, Sisto – *Dall'opinione al domma,* Rome: La Civiltà Cattolica, 1953, *apud* A. V. XAVIER DA SILVEIRA, *Qual a autoridade doutrinária dos documentos pontifícios e conciliares?* **CASSIANO** – *De Incarnatione Christi contra Nestorium haericutum,* in PL 50, 30, *apud* C. GARCIA EXTREMEÑO. **CASTRO MAYER, Antonio de** – "Petição a Paulo VI, subscrita por 213 Padres conciliares, para que fizesse a condenação do marxismo e do comunismo," in

Catolicismo, January 1964; See CORRÊA DE OLIVEIRA, P., *Reforma agrária, questão de consciência,* and *Declaração do Morro Alto.* **CATOLICISMO** (Campos/São Paulo) – "Grupos ocultos tramam a subversão na Igreja," April-May 1969; "TFP: Em 58 dias, 1 milhão e meio de assinaturas," August-October 1968.

CELAM – See LATIN AMERICAN EPISCOPAL CONFERENCE. **CERTEAU, M. de** – "La parole du croyant dans le language de l'homme," in *Esprit,* 55, 1967. **CHAVASSE, A.** – *L'ecclésiologie au Concile du Vatican- L'infalibilité de l'Église,* in V.A., *L'ecclésiologie au XIXe. siècle.* **CHAVES, Henrique** – "Desfazendo manobras astuciosas de Moscou, duzentos Padres conciliares pedem nova condenação do comunismo e do socialismo," in *Catolicismo,* January 1964. **CHENU, Marie-Dominique** – *La Chiesa e il mondo,* in V.A., *I grandi temi del Concílio;* Interview granted to A. SINKE GUIMARÃES, Paris, February 20, 1983; *The history of salvation and the historicity of man in the renewal of theology,* in V.A., *Theology of renewal,* vol. I; "A Igreja dos pobres no Vaticano II," in *Concilium* (Petrópolis), 1977; *Jacques Duquesne interroge le Père Chenu- Un théologien en liberté,* Paris: Centurion, 1975; *Omelia tenuta nel corso della celebrazione eucaristica,* in V.A., *L'avvenire della Chiesa; Les signes des temps - Reflexions théologiques,* in V.A., *L'Église dans le monde de ce temps. 'Vox populi, vox Dei' - L'opinione pubblica nell'ambito del popolo di Dio,* in V.A., *La fine della Chiesa come società perfetta.* **CHOI, Angela** – "Profonda converzione e solida formazione," in *L'Osservatore Romano,* 11/23/1994, supplement. **CICOGNANI, Amleto** – "Carta a Luigi Carli proibindo a ação do Coetus Internationalis Patris," *apud Corrispondenza Romana* (Rome), 3/28/1990. **LA CIVILTÀ CATTOLICA** (Rome) – Editorial: "Concílio, post-Concílio, para-Concílio," 1/5/1985; Editorial: "Il ministero del Papa dopo i due Concili vaticani," 11/2/1985; Editorial: "Dalla 'società perfetta' alla Chiesa 'mistero,'" 1/19/1985; Editorial, "Testimoniare la 'gioia nella speranza,'" 4/17/1971.

CLEMENT of ALEXANDRIA – *Stromatum,* lib. VII, *c.* 17, *apud* LEO XIII, Encyclical *Satis cognitum.* **CLOUGH, Joy** – "Forum: Letter in defense of Cardinal Joseph Louis Bernardin," in *The Wanderer,* 5/14/1992. **COLAIANNI, Nicola** – "Crítica ao Vaticano II na literatura atual," in *Concilium,* July 1983. **COLOMBO, Giuseppe** – *La création,* in V.A., *Bilan de la théologie du XXe. siècle,* vol. II. **COLUNGA, Alberto** – See V.A., *Biblia Sacra juxta Vulgatam clementinam.* **COMBLIN, Joseph** – *La théologie catholique depuis la fin du pontificat de Pie XII,* in V.A., *Bilan de la théologie au XXe. siècle,* vol. I. **COMMISSION OF STUDIES OF THE TFPs (Hispanic-American)** – *Tradicíon, Familia, Propiedad - Un ideal, un lema, una gesta - La Cruzada del siglo XX,* São Paulo: Artpress, 1990. **COMMISSION OF STUDIES OF THE TFP (Brazilian)** – *Meio século de epopéia anticomunista,* São Paulo: Vera Cruz, 1980; *Um homem, uma obra, uma gesta - Homenagem das TFPs a Plinio Corrêa de Oliveira,* São Paulo: Ed. Brasil de Amanha, 1989.

CONCETTI, Gino – See PARENTE, P. **COUNCIL OF TRENT** – *Canons and Decrees of the Council of Trent,* trans. by H. J. Schroeder, Rockford, Ill.: Tan Publishers, 1941; *Catechism of the Council of Trent,* trans. by John A. McHugh and Charles J. Callan, South Bend, Ind.: Marian Publications, 1923. **CONGAR, Yves** – *Le Concile de Vatican II- Son Église, peuple de Dieu et Corps du Christ,* Paris: Beau-chesne,1984; *La crisi nella Chiesa e Mons. Lefêbvre,* Brescia: Queriniana, 1976; *L'ecclésiologie, de la Révolution Française au Concile du Vatican, sous le sine de l'affirmation de 1'autorité,* in V.A., *L'ecclésiologie au XIXe. siècle. Église Catholique et France moderne,* Paris: Hachette, 1978; Interviews granted to A. SINKE GUIMARÃES, Paris, February 16 and 19, 1983; *À guisa de conclusão,* in V.A., *A Igreja do Vaticano II. Jean Puyo interroge le Père Congar - Une vie pour la verité,* Paris: Centurion, 1975; *Ministeri e communione ecclesiale,* Bologna 1973, *apud* P. A. BONNET. *Un peuple messianique,* Paris: Cerf, 1975; *Le rôle de l'Église dans le monde de ce temps,* in V.A., *L'Église dans le monde de ce temps,* vol. II; *Salvation y liberación,* in V.A., *Conversaciónes de Toledo*; See V.A., *L'Église dans le monde de ce temps.*

CONGREGATION FOR DIVINE WORSHIP – *Epistula - De usu Missalis romani iuxta editionem typicam anni MCMLXII,* October 3, 1984, in ACTA APOSTOLICAE SEDIS, Ed. Typis Polyglottis Vaticanis, vol. LXXVI, 12/1/ 1984. **CONGREGATION FOR THE DOCTRINE OF THE FAITH** – "Lettera della Congregazione per la Dottrina della Fede a P. Schillebeeckx," June 13, 1984, in *L'Osservatore Romano,* 1/11/1985; "Notification de la Congrégation pour la Doctrine de la Foi à propos du livre de L. Boff: '*Église: Charisme et pouvoir,*' in *La Documentation Catholique,* 5/5/1985. See RATZINGER, J. *Instrução sobre a vocação eclesial do teólogo.* **CONGREGATION OF THE HOLY OFFICE** – *Decreto contra o comunismo,* June 1, 1949. **CONGREGA- TION OF SEMINARIES AND UNIVERSITIES, Sacred** – Letter to Plinio Corrêa de Oliveira about *The Freedom of the Church in the Communist State.* September 2, 1964. Signed by Cardinal G. PIZZARDO and Msgr. D. STAFFA, Prefect and Secretary of the Congregation respectively; a facsimile of the letter is found in the various editions of the work. **CONWAY, Willian** – *Comments on the Schema XIII in the conciliar assembly, apud* CARLI, L.

CORRÊA DE OLIVEIRA, Plinio – *Acordo com o regime com-unista: para a Igreja esperança ou autodemolição?,* São Paulo: Vera Cruz, 1967; first published with the title "A liberdade da Igreja no Estado comunista," in *Catolicismo,* August 1963. See Chapter VI, Note 83, for a list of some newspapers that published news items on the launching of this work during the Council. See also CONGREGATION OF SEMINARIES AND UNIVERSITIES, Sacred; "Artigo - bomba explode em Madrid," in *Folha de S Paulo,* 5/7/1969. *Baldeação ideológica inadvertida e diálogo,* São Paulo: Vera Cruz, 1966; *No Brasil: A reforma agrária leva a miséria ao campo e à cidade - A TFP* *informa, analisa, alerta,* São Paulo: Vera Cruz, 1986; "Comunismo e anticomunismo na orla da última década deste milênio, in *Folha de S. Paulo,* 2/14/1990; "Casaroli: 'incorporação no contexto,'" in *Folha de S Paulo,* 6/30/ 1974; "As CEBs... das quais muito se fala, pouco se conhece - A TFP as descreve como são" (in collaboration with G. A. SOLIMEO and L. S. SOLIMEO), São Paulo: Vera Cruz, 1982; "Conforme quer Budapeste," in *Folha de S. Paulo,* 10/29/1974; *Declaração do Morro Alto* (in collaboration with A. CASTRO MAYER, G. P. SIGAUD, and L. M. FREITAS), São Paulo: Vera Cruz, 1964; *Em defesa da Ação Catolica,* São Paulo: Ed. Ave Maria, 1943; São Paulo: Artpress, 1983; see MONTINI, G. B., Letter to Plinio Corrêa de Oliveira; See MASELLA, B.A. "Détente...," in *Folha de S Paulo,* 11/1/1974; "Détentes geminadas," in *Folha de S Paulo,* 12/8/1974; "Os 'grupos profeticos' a serviço da Igreja - Nova e do comunismo," in *Folha de S Paulo,* 5/21/1969; "Guerreiros da Virgem - A réplica da autenticidade - A TFP sem segredos," São Paulo: Vera Cruz, 1985; *A Igreja ante a escalada da ameaça comunista - Apelo aos Bispos silenciosos,* São Paulo: Vera Cruz, 1976.

CORRÊA DE OLIVEIRA, Plinio (continued) – "A Igreja Catolica infiltrada por adversários velados," in *Catolicismo,* April-May 1969; "A importância do fator religioso nos rumos de um bloco-chave de países: a America Latina," in *Catolicismo,* June 1985. "A indispensável resistência," in *Folha de S Paulo,* 4/14/1974; "Da infiltração à subversão," in *Folha de S Paulo,* 5/14/1969; "A liberdade da Igreja no Estado Comunista, see Acordo com o regime comunista - Para a Igreja esperança ou autodemolição?; Mais um Cardeal em resistência," in *Folha de S. Paulo,* 5/12/1974; "1958-1974: que resultados?" in *Folha de S. Paulo,* 7/14/1974; "Morreu o comunismo? E o anticomunismo também?" in *Correio Brasiliense,* 10/18/1989; "Não conseguimos compreender, in *Folha de S. Paulo,* 7/7/1974; *Nobility and Analogous Traditional Elites in the Allocutions of Pius XII.* York, PA: The American Society for the Defense of Tradition, Family and Property, 1993; "Na 'noite Sandinista': o incitamento à guerrilha dirigido por sandinistas "cristãos" à esquerda católica no Brasil e na América espanhola," in *Catolicismo,* July-August 1980; "A Ostpolitik do Vatican favorece Moscou," in *Folha de S Paulo,* 6/9/1974; "Das páginas da imprensa para as da História - I," in *Folha de S Paulo,* 8/17/1968; "A política de distensão do Vaticano com os governos comunistas- Para a TFP: omitir-se ou resistir?," in *Folha de S Paulo,* 4/10/1974; *Catolicismo,* April 1974. See *General Introduction,* Note 16b for an extensive list of newspapers and magazines that published this manifesto. "Projeto de Constituição angustia o País, in *Catolicismo,* October 1987, extra edition; "A propaganda progressista: um dinossauro discreto," in *Folha de S Paulo,* 3/26/1969; *A propriedade privada e a livre iniciativa no tufão agro-reformista* (in collaboration with C. del CAMPO), São Paulo: Vera Cruz, 1985; *Reforma agraria - Questão de consciencia* (in collaboration with A. CASTRO MAYER, G. P. SIGAUD, and L. M. FREITAS), São Paulo: Vera Cruz, 1960; "Resistindo...," in *Folha de S*

Paulo, 4/21/1974; *Revolution and Counter-Revolution*, 3rd ed., York, PA: The American Society for the Defense of Tradition, Family and Property, 1993. Originally published as *Revolução e Contra-Revolução*, in *Catolicismo*, April 1959; Updated in *Catolicismo*, January, 1977, and later in *Catolicismo*, August 1992; "O socialismo autogestionário: em vista do comunismo barreira ou cabeça - de ponte?*, in Folha de S Paulo*, 12/17/1981; "SOS de milhões - A mala pequena - Tudo normal," in *Folha de S Paulo*, 11/30/1969; *Sou católico: posso ser contra a reforma agrária?* (in collaboration with C. del CAMPO), São Paulo: Vera Cruz, 1981; "Ternuras que arrancariam lágrimas," in *Folha de S Paulo*, 10/13/1974. *Tribalismo indígena: ideal comuno-missionario para o Brasil no século XI*, São Paulo: Vera Cruz, 1977; "Voz dos que se calam acabrunhados," in *Folha de S Paulo*, 4/28/1974.

CORRIERE DELLA SERA (Milan) – "L'amante del vescovo Casey ringrazia per la solidarietà," 7/5/1992; "L'amica del vescovo si confessa," 5/10/1992; "Dopo lo scandalo it pentimento - Il vescovo diventa missionario," 10/19/ 1992; "Scandalo sessuale nella cattolica Irlanda -Vescovo progressista aveva amante e figlio," 5/9/1992; "Sesso, bugie e videotapes: sotto choc la cattolica Irlanda," 5/12/1992; "Il vescovo confessa la paternità e i furti," 5/13/1992. **CNBB PASTORAL COMMISSION** – Declaration about the Encyclical *Humane vitae*," October 25, 1968, in SEDOC (Petrópolis), February 1969, col. 1029, *apud* A. V. XAVIER DA SILVEIRA, "Pode haver erro em documentos do Magistério? Orientação pastoral sobre a Enciclica *Humanae vitae*," November 12, 1968, in SEDOC, February 1969, col. 1118, *apud ibidem.* **CULLMANN, Oscar** – "O filho de Lutero e Ratzinger," interview with L. BRUNELLI and A. LABHART, in *30 Dias*, March 1993. **CURB, Rosemary** – See MANAHAN, N.

DANIELOU, Jean – *Relacões entre Igreja e civilizacão*, in V.A., *Cinco problemas que desafiam a Igreja hoje.* **DAVIS, H. F.** – *Le rôle et l'apostolat de la Hierarchie et du laicat dans la théologie de l'Église chez Newman*, in V.A., *L'ecclésiologie au XIXe. siècle.* **DELHAYE, Philippe** – *In caritate non ficta*, Louvain-la-Neuve: Centre Cerfaux-Lefort, *apud* E. MARIANI, *Vatican II: Autorité des textes conciliaires*, in DTC, Tables, vol. III. **DELMONT, Th.** – *Modernisme et modernistes*, Paris: P. Lethielleux, 1909. **DENIFLE-CHATELAIN** – *Chartularium Universitatis Parisiensis*, Paris: 1851, II, *apud* C. GARCIA EXTREMEÑO.

DENZINGER (1), **Henricus and Clemens BANWART** (DB) – *Enchiridion Symbolorum definitionum declarationum*, Friburgi-Brisgoviae: Herder, 1955. Collection of the most important excerpts from documents of the Magisterium compiled by the German priest Heinrich Joseph Denzinger (1819-1883) and first published in 1854. Updated by C. BANWART between 1908 and 1921. **DENZINGER** (2), **Enrique and Carlos RAHNER** (DR) – *El Magisterio de la Iglesia*, Barcelona: Herder, 1963. This is the same *Enchiridion Symbolorum definitionum declarationum* published in Spanish under another title. Updated by K. RAHNER between 1946 and 1954. **DENZINGER** (3), **Henricus and Adolfus SCHÖNMETZER** (DS) – *Enchiridion Symbolorum definitionum declarationum,* Friburgi-Brisgoviae: Herder, 1965. Updated by A. SCHONMETZER, between 1955 and 1965. **DÖPFNER, Julius** – *La Chiesa vivente oggi,* Bari: Paoline, 1972; Comments on the Schema XIII in the conciliar assembly, *apud* G. CAPRILE, *Il Concílio Vaticano II,* vol. V. **DOSSETTI, Giuseppe** – "Vaticano II: Quale recezione," in *Il Regno* (Bologna), 12/1/1991.

(LA) DOCUMENTATION CATHOLIQUE (Paris) – *Bilan du dialogue judeo-chretien,* 1/19/1986. **DRINAN, Robert** – Comments about the state of the Society of Jesus in the USA, apud L. BRUNELLI, "O balanço de Kolvenbach." **DRUON, Maurice** – "Une Église que se trompe de siècle," in *Le Monde,* 8/7/1971. **DUBOST, Michel** – See J. CARDONNEL. **DULLES, Avery** – "The Church, the churches and the Catholic Church," in *T.S. 33,* 1972, *apud* F. A. SULLIVAN; *Ecumenismo: problemi e possibitá per il futuro,* in V.A., *Verso la Chiesa del terzo millennio.* **DUMONT, Fernand** – *Pour la conversion de la pensée chrètienne,* 1964, *apud* The sociology of Religion and the renewal of theology, in V.A., *Theology of renewal,* vol. II. **DUPUY, B.D.** – *Schisme et primauté chez J.A. Möhler,* in V.A., *L'ecclésiologie au XIXe. siècle.* **DUQUESNE, Jacques** – Comments on the deposition of Bishop Gaillot, *apud* A. BOURRIER. See CHENU, M. D., *Jacques Duquesne interroge le Père Chenu.* **DUQUOC, Christian** – "Il popolo di Dio, soggetto attivo della fede nella Chiesa," in *Concilium,* April 1985. **DUTCH EPISCOPATE** – Statement. See BRUNELLI, L., *A pílula que dividiu a Igreja.*

ERNSBERGER Jr., Richard and Lucy HOWARD – "Ireland is talking..." in *Newsweek,* 5/18/1992. **O ESTADO DE S. PAULO,** (São Paulo) – "D. Aloísio quer Igreja em ação política," 7/6/1985; "Celibato é discutido no Sínodo," 10/3/1990; "Ex-padres estão organizados," 6/15/1989; "Faltam padres em Roma, diz Cardeal," 6/14/1989; "Roma: Cidade católica, mas nem tanto," 5/11/1995. **ETCHEGARAY, Roger** – "Le cardinal Etchegaray, archevêque de Marseille, se souvient et balise l'avenir," in *Historia,* October 1982. **EUSEBIUS OF CESAREA** – *História eclesiástica,* Buenos Aires: Ed. Nova, 1950. **EYT, Pierre** – *Igreja e mutações sócio-culturais,* in V.A., *A Igreja do futuro.*

FACUNDUS Hermianense – *Liber VII,* in PL 45, 1723. *Pro defensione trium capitulorum,* in PL 67, 687. **FALASHI, Celso** – "Ordenação de casados e defendida por padres," in *O Estado de S. Paulo,* 10/24/1989. **FALCONE, Monica** – "Pesquisa: 70% dos padres na Italia têm mulher," in *O Globo,* 3/22/1987. **FEINER, Johannes** – Untitled, in V.A., *Commentary on the documents of Vatican II.* **FELICI, Pericle** – *Notificações,* November 16, 1964, in V.A., *Atas do Concílio Ecumenico Vaticano II.* **FESQUET, Henri** – *Le journal du Concile,* Forcalquier: Robert Morel, 1966. **FISCHER, E.** – *Kirche and Kirchen nach dem Vatikanum II,* Munich, 1967, *apud* F. A. SULLIVAN. **FLICHE, Augustin** – See V.A., *Histoire de l'Église.* **FLICK, Maurizio and**

Zoltan ALSZEGHY – *Il mistero della croce - Saggio di teologia sistematica,* Brescia: Queriniana, 1978. **FOGAZZARO, Antonio** – *Il santo,* Milan: n.p., 1970. **FOLEY, John Patrick** – "Formazione di base per l'uso dei mass-media nella diffusion del Vangelo," in *L'Osservatore Romano,* 11/23/ 1994, supplement. **FOLHA DE S. PAULO** (São Paulo) – "AIDS-1," 1/15/ 1989. **FONCK, A.** Nicolas – *Möehler,* in *DTC,* vol. X. **FORCELLA, Enzo** – "Papa Wojtyla e i farinacisti," in *La Repubblica,* Rome, 11/5/1990. **FRADE, Christina** – "El sexo de los Obispos," in *El Mundo* (Madrid), 3/19/1995.

FRANZINI, Alberto – *Tradizione e Scrittura - Il contributo del Concílio Vaticano II,* Brescia: Morcelliana, 1978. **FRECHET, Jean** – "Vocations sacerdotales et sacerdoce des baptisés, lettre," in *La Croix,* 8/31/1983. **FREITAS, Luis Mendonca de** – See P. CORRÊA DE OLIVEIRA, *Reforma agrária, questão de consciência* and *Declaração do Morro Alto.* **FRENCH EPISCOPATE** – "Declaration against the Encyclical *Humanae vitae,*" in SEDOC, February 1969, col. 1118, *apud* A. V. XAVIER DA SILVEIRA, "Pode haver erro em documentos do Magistério?" **FRIES, Heinrich** – "C'è un magistero dei fedeli?" in *Concilium,* April 1986; *Église et églises,* in V.A., *Problèmes et perspectives de théologie fondamentale, apud* F. A. SULLI-VAN. **FRISQUE, Jean** – *L'ecclésiologie au XXe, siècle,* in V.A., *Bilan de la théologie du XXe. siècle,* vol. II. **FUMAGALLI, Marisa** – "Anatema del vescovo di Rimini – 'No' al raduno dei preti sposati," in *Corriere della Sera,* 8/27/1994. **FURET, François and Mona OZOUF** – *Dictionnaire critique de la Révolution Française,* Paris: Flammarion, 1988, *apud* P. CORRÊA DE OLIVEIRA, *Nobility and Analogous Traditional Elites.*

GALLI, Mario von – *La nueva liturgia,* in V.A., *La reforma que llega de Roma.* **GARCIA EXTREMEÑO, Claudio** – "El sentido de la Fe, criterio de la Tradición," in *La Ciencia Tomista* (Salamanca), July-December 1960. **GARCIA DE SIERRA Y MÉNDEZ, Secundo** – Comments on Hell in the conciliar assembly, *apud* B. KLOPPENBURG, *Concílio Vaticano II,* vol. IV. **GEISELMANN, J. R.** – *Les variations de la définition de l'Église chez J. A. Möehler,* in V.A., *L'ecclésiologie au XIXe. siècle*; Introduction to the critical edition of *Die Einheit,* Kölh-Olten, 1956; *Der Wandel des Kirchenbewusstseins and der Kirchlichkeit in der Théologie J. A. Möhlers,* Freiburg, 1961. **GENNARI, Giovanni** – Statement to the press, *apud* "Padres casados abrem em Roma seu congresso," *O Globo,* 8/29/1986. **GERMAN EPISCOPATE** – Declaration against the Encyclical *Humanae vitae, apud* ICI (Paris), 9/15/ 1968. **GEUSAU, Leo Alting von** – *La Chiesa, 'scandalo' del mondo,* in V.A., *La fine della Chiesa come società perfetta.* **GIBELLINI, Rosino** – "Siamo d'acordo sul Concílio?," in *Il Regno,* 8/15/1984.

(O) GLOBO (Rio de Janeiro) – "Bispo propõe mulheres como cardeais," 10/ 11/1994; "Padres casados abrem em Roma seu congresso," 8/29/1986; "Religiosas feministas lutam pelo sacerdócio," 8/7/1988. **GONZALEZ RUIZ,**

Jose M. – "Lettera aperta al Cardinal Ratzinger - Le 'verità' del Cardinale prima e dopo it S. Ufficio," in *Adista*, 1/19-21/1987. **GORI, Alberto** – Comments on Hell in the conciliar assembly, *apud* B. KLOPPENBURG, *Concílio Vaticano II*, vol. IV. **GRABER, Rudolf** – *Athanasius and die Kirche unserer Zeit*, Abensberg: Josef Kral, 1973; "Como no tempo de Atanásio," interview with T. RICCI, in *30 Dias*, December 1990; *Por que a Igreja está em crise*, Rio de Janeiro, Grifo, 1971. **GRAMICK, Jeannine** – "Homosexuality to be a burning Catholic issue" (letter of 6/24/1992), in *The New York Times*, 7/11/ 1992. **GREGORY XVI** – Encyclical *Mirari vos*, of August 15, 1832, in V.A., *Les enseignements pontificaux*. **GREGORY THE GREAT, St.** – *Homilia 18 in Ezechielem, apud* C. a LAPIDE, *Ad Galatas*, vol. XVIII.

GREGORY NAZIANZENE, St. – *Epistula 102, 2 ad Cledon*, in PG 37, 200, *apud* V. PROAÑO GIL. **GRILLMEIER, A.** – Untitled, in V.A., *Commentary on the documents of Vatican II*. LThK, K1, 189, *apud* H. WALDENFELS. **GUCHT, Robert van der** – See V.A., *Bilan de la théologie au Xxe. siècle*. **GUERANGER, Prosper** – *L'année liturgique - Le temps de la septuagesime*, Tours: Maison Mame, 1932. **GUILLEMIN de la Charité** – *La religieuse contemporaine, apud* H. FESQUET, *Le journal du Concile*. **GUIMARAES, Atila Sinke** – Interview with G. CAPRILE, Rome, February 3, 1983; Interview with M. D. CHENU, Paris, February 20, 1983; Interview with Y. CONGAR, Paris, February 16 and 19, 1983; Interview with R. SCHWAGER, Innsbruck, February 11, 1983. **GURY, Joannes Petrus and Antonius BALLERINI** – *Compendium Theologiae Moralis*, Turin: Marietti, 1866, 2 vols., *apud* A. V. XAVIER DA SILVEIRA, *La nouvelle Messe*. **GUTIÉRREZ, Gustavo** – "Os pobres na Igreja," in *Concilium*, April 1977. **GUTKIN, Steven** – "Best little convent in Bogota," in *Newsweek*, 10/19/1992.

HALLEUX, A. de – "Les principes catholiques de l'oecumenisme," *Revue Theologique de Louvain*, n.16, 1985, *apud* F. A. SULLIVAN. **HAMER, Jérôme Clemente RIVA** – *La libertà religiosa nel Vatican II*, Turin: Elle Di Ci, 1967. **HÄRING, Bernard** – Public letter in opposition to the Encyclical *Humanae vitae, apud* ICI, 9/15/1968. Statement, *apud* T. RICCI, "O mistério do pacto Roma-Moscou," in *30 Dias*, October 1989; "Minha participação no Concílio Vaticano II," in *Revista Eclesiastica Brasileira*, June 1994. **HARRISON, Brian** – "Se a trompa emite urn som confuso," in *30 Dias*, July 1989. **HEMMERT, Guus van** – Statements to the daily *Eindhovens Dagblad, apud Confrontatie*, Haarlem, May 1983. **HENRY, Frederick Bernard** – *Discurso no Sfndo '90, apud* R. MORA-BITO. **HERMANIUK, Maxim** – Comments on the Schema XIII in the conciliar assembly, *apud* L. CARLI. **HIANDOUM, Hyacinthe** – "Paulo VI? Um Papa fiel?," interview with S. PACI, in *30 Dias*, August/September 1992. **HILDEBRAND, Dietrich von and John McMANEMIN** – "Why the Tridentine Mass?," in *Una Voce pamphlets on the Liturgy*, St. Paul: Remnant Press, n.d.

HOLZER, Anton – *Vatikanum II - Reformkonzil oder Konstituante einer neuen Kirche,* Saka, Basel, 1977. **HOPE, David** – Letter of March 3, 1995, *apud* R. GLEDHILL. **HORST, Guido** – "O álcool como antídoto," in *30 Dias,* April 1989. **HORTAL, Jesus S.** – *Comentários ao Código de Direito Canonico,* in JOHN PAUL II, *Code of Canon Law.* **HOUTART, Francois** – *Les religions comme réalités sociales,* in V.A., *Bilan de la théologie du XXe. siècle,* vol. I. **HOWARD, Lucy** – See ERNSBERGER, R. **HUGUES, William A.** – Statements to the press about the homosexual conference in Chicago, *apud* K. PICHER. **HUIZING, Peter** – *Vaticano III: una costituzione sulla Chiesa,* in V.A., *Verso la Chiesa del terzo millennio.* **HURLEY, Denis** – Declarations against the Encyclical *Humanae vitae, apud* ICI, 9/15/1968. **HURTER, H.** – *Theologiae Dogmaticae compendium,* Innsbruck/Paris: Lib. Academica Wagneriana, 1883, 3 vols.

IGNATIUS DE LOYOLA, St. – Letter to D. João III, of March 15, 1545, in *Obras completas,* Madrid: BAC, 1952; *Exercícios espirituais, apud* P. H. KOLVENBACH. **INFORMATIONS CATHOLIQUES INTERNATIONALES** (Paris) – *Après l'Encyclique Humane vitae,* 9/15/1968. **ITALIAN COMMUNIST PARTY** – Arguments in *Propaganda,* apud R. GRABER, *Athanasius and die Kirche unserer Zeit. Declarações sobre o diálogo com os católicos,* in *Propaganda, apud ibidem.*

JACQUEMONT, Patrick – *Igreja e contestação,* in V.A., *A Igreja do futuro.* **JAFFE-WATTENBACH** – *Regesta Pontificum Romanorum,* Leipzig, 1885, *apud* G. de PLINVAL. **JAKI, S.** – *Les tendances nouvelles de l'ecclésiologie,* Rome: Herder, 1957. **JEROME, St.** – *Contra Vigilantium,* in PL 23, 343, *apud* C. GARCIA EXTREMEÑO; *De viris illustribus XXXVI, apud* J. LEBRETON. **JOANNOU, Peride** – See V.A., *Conciliorum oecumenicorum decreta.* **JOHN XXIII** – Pontifical communication extracted from conciliar debates on the Schema *De fontibus revelationis,* in B. KLOPPENBURG, *Concilio Vaticano II,* vol. II; Opening Speech of Vatican Council II of October 11, 1962, *apud* B. KLOPPENBURG, *Concilio Vatican II,* vol. II; *L'Osservatore Romano,* 10/12/1962; *Discorsi, messaggi, colloqui del Santo Padre Giovanni XXIII,* Tipografia Poliglota Vaticana, 1963, vol. IV; Encyclical *Pacem in terris,* of April 11, 1963, *apud* K. RAHNER, *Theological reflections on the problem of secularization;* Encyclical *Mater et Magistra,* of May 15, 1961, *apud ibidem;* "Resposta aos votos do Cardeal Eugene Tisserant," of December 23, 1962, in *L'Osservatore Romano,* 12/24-25/1962, *apud* A. WENGER, *Chronique de la première session.*

JOHN PAUL II – Allocution to priests and men religious participating in the First Italian National Conference on the topic *"Missions to the People in the '80s,"* of February 6, 1981, in *Insegnamenti di Giovanni Paolo II,* vol. IV/1; Apostolic Letter *Ecclesia Dei,* of July 2, 1988, in *Insegnamenti di Giovanni*

Paolo II, vol. XI/3; Apostolic Letter *Tertio millennio adveniente,* in *L'Osservatore Romano,* 11/14-15/1994, supplement; *Codigo de Direito Canonico,* São Paulo: Loyola, 1983; Apostolic Constitution *Pastor bonus,* de June 28, 1988, in *Insegnamenti di Giovanni Paolo II,* vol. XI/2; Closing Speech of the Synod '90, published under the title "Grazie al Sinodo sono stati affrontati problemi cruciali che hanno sempre trovato la risposta collegiale della Chiesa," in *L'Osservatore Romano,* 10/28/1990; "Homilia na concelebração final da Assembléia sinodal," in *L'Osservatore Romano,* (Portuguese edition), 10/30/1987; Homily for the Mass at the conclusion of the Synod, published under the title "Solene encerramento do Sinodo extraordinario dos Bispos," in *L'Osservatore Romano,* 12/15/1985; "Giovanni Paolo II alla consegna del Premio Internazionale Paolo VI - Hans Urs von Balthasar ha messo la sua conoscenza al servizio del vero che promana da Cristo," in *L'Osservatore Romano,* 6/24/1984; See WOJTYLA, K.

KANONGATA'A, Keiti Ann – "La 'passion' per ilt regno di Dio," in *L'Osservatore Romano,* 11/23/1994, supplement. **KARLEN, Henry Ernest** – "Dimensione umana della formazione religiosa," in *L'Osservatore Romano,* 11/23/1994, supplement. **KASPER, Walter** – "É in questione la Chiesa e l'immagine di Dio," in *Espirito-Cristo- Igreja, Il Regno,* 10/15/1993, in V.A., *A experência do Espírito Santo.* **KLOPPENBURG, Carlos Boaventura** – *Concilio Vaticano II,* Petrópolis: Vozes, 1962-1966, 5 vols. *A eclesiologia do Vaticano II,* Petrópolis: Vozes, 1971. See V.A., *Documentos do Vaticano II.* **KNOWLES, M. D.** – See V.A., *Nouvelle Histoire de l'Église.*

KOLVENBACH, Peter-Hans – Press conference of 3/22/1995, in *Oficina de Prensa Información,* Congregación General 34; Statements about the internal situation in the Society of Jesus, in L. BRUNELLI, *Kolvenbach: o Papa pode contar conosco.* **KOMBO, Ernest** – "Dopo aver gratuitamente ricevuto bisogna saper gratuitamente dare," in *L'Osservatore Romano,* 11/23/1994, supplement. **KÖNIG, Franz** – "Il Concílio, sorpresa per il mondo," interview with S. STRACCA, in *Avvenire,* 10/16/1992. **KÜNG, Hans** – *A Igreja,* Lisbon: Moraes, 1969-1970, 2 vols.; *Prêtre, pour quoi faire?* Paris: Cerf, 1971; *O que deve permanecer na Igreja,* Petrópolis: Vozes, 1976; *Vaticano III: problemi e prospettive per il futuro,* in V.A., *Verso la Chiesa del terzo millennio; Veracidade - O futuro da Igreja,* São Paulo: Herder, 1969; *Vida eterna?* Madrid: Cristiandad, 1983.

LABHART, Alfred – See L. BRUNELLI (2). **LACTANCIO** – *Lactantii divinarum institutionum libri septem IV, apud* PIUS XI, Encyclical *Mortalium animos.* **LANDAZURI RICKETTS, Juan** – *Comments on the Schema XIII in the conciliar assembly, apud* G. CAPRILE, *Il Concílio Vaticano II,* vol. V. **LANGRE, L.** – "Francia- El Clero, de derechas, distinto y levemente utopico," in *Vida Nueva,* Madrid, 11/2/1985. **LANNE, Emmanuel** – "L'Église locale at l'Église universelle," in *Irenikon,* Chevetogne/Belgique, 43, 1970, *apud* Y.

CONGAR, *Le Concile de Vatican II.* **LAPIDE, Cornelius a** – *Commentaria in Scripturam Sacram,* Paris: Ludovicum Vivès Ed., 1874-1877, 24 vols. **LATIN AMERICAN EPISCOPAL CONFERENCE** – *A Igreja na atual transformação da América Latina à luz do Concílio - Conclusões de Medellin,* Petrópolis: Vozes, 1980. **LATOURELLE, Rene** – Introduction, in V.A., *Vatican II: Bilan et perspectives,* vol. I. See V.A., *Problèmes at perspectives de théologie fondamentale.*

LAURENTIN, Rene – *L'enjeu et le bilan du Concile,* Paris: Seuil, 1962-1966, 5 vols. "A retomada existe. Eis a prova," in *30 Dias,* December 1988. **LEO XIII** – *Motu proprio* about Popular Catholic Action, of December 18, 1903; Encyclical *Aeterni patris,* of August 4, 1879, Petrópolis: Vozes, 1960; Encyclical *Auspicatum concessum,* September 17, 1882, Petrópolis: Vozes, 1953; Encyclical *Diuturnum illud,* June 28, 1881, in V.A., *Les enseignements pontificaux;* Encyclical *Graves de communi,* January 18, 1901, Petrópolis: Vozes, 1956; Encyclical *Humanum genus,* April 20, 1884, Petrópolis: Vozes, 1960; Encyclical *Immortale Dei,* November 1, 1885, Petrópolis: Vozes, 1954; Encyclical *Laetitiae sanctae,* September 8, 1893, Petrópolis: Vozes, 1953; Encyclical *Libertas praestantissimum,* of June 20, 1888, in V.A., *Les enseignements pontificaux.* Encyclical *Parvenu,* of March 19, 1902, Petrópolis: Vozes, 1960; Encyclical *Quod apostolici muneris,* of December 28, 1878, in V.A., *Les enseignements pontificaux;* Encyclical *Rerum novarum,* of May 15, 1891, Petrópolis: Vozes, 1954; Encyclical *Satis cognitum,* of June 29, 1896, Petrópolis: Vozes, 1960; Encyclical *Ubi primum,* May 5, 1824, in DS 2720. **LEBRETON, Jules** – *L'École chrètienne d'Alexandrie avant Origène,* in V.A., *Histoire de l'Église ,* vol. II. L **LECLERC, Gerard** – "Depressão jesuítica- Europa, Franca," in *30 Dias,* May 1989.

LEFÈBVRE, Marcel – *Ils l'ont decouronné - Du libéralisme à l'apostasie - La tragédie conciliaire,* Escurolles: Fideliter, 1987. See SIGAUD, G. P., *Aditamento ao Esquema XIII.* **LEONARDI, Claudio** – See V.A., *Conciliorum oecumenicorum decreta.* **LERINS, St. Vincent de** – See VINCENT DE LERINS. **LONERGAN, Bernard** – *Theology in its new context,* in V.A., *Theology of renewal,* vol. I. **LOPES, Gregório** – "Plinio Corrêa de Oliveira, um cruzado do seculo XX," in *Catolicismo,* September 1985. **LÓPEZ TRUJILLO, Alfonso** – *A los veinte años del Concílio,* Departamento de Publicaciones de la Arquidiócesis de Medellin, 1985. **LORSCHEIDER, Aloisio** – Pronouncement at the Synod '90, *apud* R. MORABITO. **LOSADA, Joaquin** – *El pos-Concílio: el problema de la transformación de la Iglesia,* in V.A., *Desafios cristianos.* **LOYOLA, St. Ignatius de** – See IGNATIUS DE LOYOLA. **LUBAC, Henri de** – *Athéisme et sens de l'homme - Une double requête de 'Gaudium et spes,'* Paris: Cerf, 1968; *Catholicisme - Les aspects sociaux du dogme,* Paris: Cerf, 1947; *Entretien autour de Vatican II,* Paris: Cerf, 1985; "Irrequieto ma ubbidiente - La Chiesa e i suoi protagonisti - Henri de Lubac," interview with M. POLITI, in *Il Messaggero* (Rome), 2/2/1983;

Paradoxe et mystère de l'Église, Paris: Aubier & Montaigne, 1967. **LUGO, J. de** – *De Fide, apud* C. GARCIA EXTREMEÑO.

MADIRAN, Jean – "Autour du Concile," in *Itinéraires* (Paris), December 1962; February 1963, *apud* A. WENGER. **MALINSKI, Mieczslaw** – *Mon ami Karol Wojtyla*, Paris: Centurion, 1980. **MANAHAN, Nancy and Rosemary CURB** – *Breaking silence: Lesbian nuns on convent sexuality*, Naiad Press, 1985, *apud* P. S. PINHEIRO. **MANGENOT, Eugène** – See V.A., *Dictionnaire de Théologie Catholique*. **MANSI, Joannes Dominicus** – *Sacrorum Conciliorum nova et amplissima collectio*, Venice, 1759, 31 vols., *apud* G. de PLINVAL. **MARIANI, Eliodoro** – *La morale cristiana di fronte ai problemi degli uomini d'oggi*, in *L'Osservatore Romano*, 1/5/1984. **MARLÉ, René** – *Méthodes historiques et problèmes theologiques*, in V.A., *Bilan de la théologie du XXe. siècle*, vol. II. **MARRANZINI, Alfredo** – *Introduzione*, in V.A., *Il linguaggio teologico oggi*. **MARTELET, Gustave** – *Deux mille ans d'Église en question* – *Crise de la foi, crise du prêtre*, Paris: Cerf, 1984. **MARTIN, Victor** – See V.A., *Histoire de l'Église*. **MASELLA, Bento Aloisi** – Preface to *Em defesa da Ação Católica*, see CORRÊA DE OLIVEIRA, P. **MATOS SOARES** – See V.A., *Bíblia Sagrada*. **MATTIA, Georges** – "70.000 prêtres mariés en quête de légitimité," in *La Croix*, 8/27/1985. **MAYER, Antonio de Castro** – See A. CASTRO MAYER. **MAYER, Paul Augustin** – "Cardeal anti-cisma," interview with S. M. PACI, in 30 Dias, June 1991. **MAZZELLA, Camillus** – *De Religione et Ecclesia, apud* A. V. XAVIER DA SILVEIRA, *La nouvelle Messe*. **MÉGRET, Maurice** – *La guerra psicologica*, Buenos Aires: Paides, 1959. **MESSORI, Vittorio** – See RATZINGER, J., *Rapporto sulla Fede*.

METZ, Johann Baptist – *Diálogo com Karl Rahner*, in V.A., *Cinco problemas que desafiam a Igreja hoje*. *Más allá de la religión burguesa - Sobre el futuro del Cristianismo*, Salamanca: Sigueme, 1982; *Sulla presenza della Chiesa nella società*, in V.A., *L'avvenire della Chiesa*. **MIGNE, J. P.** – See V.A., *Patrologie Grecque-Latine;* See V.A., *Patrologie Latine*. **MINDSZENTY, Jozsef** – *Erinnerungen*, Frankfurt: Ullstein, 1974. **MOCELLIN, G.** – "IV Istruzione liturgica - 30 anni dopo pensando all'Africa," in *Il Regno*, 4/15/1994. **MÖHLER, Johann Adan** – *Unidade na Igreja ou Die Einheit in der Kirche oder das Prinzip des Katholezismus dargestellt im Geiste der Kirchenväter der drei ersten Jahrhunderte*, Tübingen, 1825, *apud* A. N. FONCK; *Simbólica ou Symbolik, oder Darstellung der dogmatischen Gegensätze der Katholiken and Protestanten nach ihren offentlichen Bekenntnisschriften*, Mainz, 1832, *apud* A. N. FONCK; *La Civiltà Cattolica*, 1/19/1985. **MOLARI, Carlo** – *La problematica del linguaggio teologico*, in V.A., *Il linguaggio teologico oggi*. **MONDIN, Battista** – *Introduzione alla teologia*, Milan: Massimo, 1983. *Os grandes teólogos do século vinte*, São Paulo: Paulinas, 1979, 2 vols. **MONKS OF SOLESMES** – See V.A., *Les enseignements pontificaux*.

MONTINI, Giovanni Baptista – Letter to Plinio Corrêa de Oliveira, of February 26, 1949, in P. CORRÊA DE OLIVEIRA, *Em defesa da Ação Católica* (1983 edition). See PAUL VI. **MORABITO, Rocco** – "Discussão do celibato domina Sínodo," in *O Estado de S. Paulo*, 10/4/1990. **MOTOLESE, Guglielmo** – "La Chiesa, compagna di viaggio dell'uomo - I grandi testimoni del Vaticano 11/7," interview with S. STRACCA, in *Avvenire*, 9/27/1992. **MOUROUX, Jacques** – *Situation et signification du chapitre I (de la Gaudium et spes): Sur la dignité de la personne humaine*, in V.A., *L'Église dans le monde de ce temps*, vol. II. **MOYNIHAN, Robert** – "A Aids cria problemas," in *30 Dias*, Februrary 1980. **MUCCHIELI, Roger** – *La subversión*, Paris: Bordas, 1972. **MUGGERIDGE, Anne Roche** – *The Desolate City - Revolution in the Catholic Church*, San Francisco: Harper & Row, 1990. **MÜLLER, Alois** – *Chiesa e riforma*, in V.A., *Verso la Chiesa del terzo millennio*.

NATIONAL CONFERENCE OF BRAZILIAN BISHOPS (CNBB) – *Roma locuta - Documentário sobre o livro 'Igreja: Carisma e poder- Ensaios de eclesiolgia militante' de Frei Leonardo Boff, OFM*, Petrópolis: Vozes, 1985. See CNBB PASTORAL COMMISSIONS. **NEWMAN, John Henry** – "On consulting the faithful in matters of doctrine," in *The Rambler*, 1859, *apud* C. GARCIA EXTREMEÑO. **NICODEMO, Enrico** – Comments on Hell in the conciliar assembly, *apud* B. KLOPPENBURG, *Concílio Vaticano II*, vol. IV. **NOÉ, Vigilio** – "Il primo dono al popolo cristiano," in *L'Osservatore Romano*, 12/14/1983, special supplement on the Constitution *Sacrosanctum Concilium*. **NUBIUS** – "Secret instructions about the conquest of the Church," *apud* E. BARBIER, *Les infiltrations maçoniques dans l'Église*, Paris/Brussells: Desclée de Brouwer, 1910. **NYGREN, David and Miriam UKERITIS** – "USA: il futuro dei religiose," in *Il Regno*, 4/1/1993.

ODDI, Silvio – "Confissões de um Cardeal," interview with T. RICCI, in *30 Dias*, November 1990; *Il tenero mastino di Dio*, Rome: Progetti Museali Editore, 1995. **OPTATUS OF MILEVIS, St.** – *Libri septem de schismate Donatistarum*, apud LEO XIII, Encyclical *Satis cognitum*. **L'OSSERVATORE ROMANO (Vatican City)** – "Il Cardinale Ratzinger: 'La fede è il bene più alto. Bisogna sempre vigilare perchè non si corrompa,'" 11/9/1984; "O Concílio é dom de Deus à Igreja e ao mundo," 12/15/1985; "Presentato al Santo Padre l'Annuario Pontificio 1994," 2/28/1994 - 3/1/1994; "Solene encerramento do Sinodo extraordinário dos Bispos - O Sinodo projecta o Concílio para o terceiro milênio," 12/15/1985; "Valutazione delle linee di tendenza dell'attività pastorale della Chiesa cattolica fino al 1986," 5/30-31/1988, supplement. **OTTAVIANI, Alfredo** – Interview with *Corriere della Sera*, 10/28/1965, apud H. FESQUET, *Le journal du Concile*. **OZOUF, Mona** – See FURET, F.

PACI, Stefano – "Precisam-se vocações - Pesquisa - A crise das religiosas," in *30 Dias*, April 1990; See P. A. MAYER, *Cardeal anti-cisma*, F. SCHMIDBERGER and H. THIANDOUM. **PARENTE, Pietro** – "Cristo,

Maria, la Chiesa: i punti nevralgici della mia ricerca teologica," interview with G. CONCETTI, in *L'Osservatore Romano*, 12/29/1985. **PAUL VI** – Allocution to the students of the Lombard Seminary of December 7, 1968, in *Insegnamenti di Paolo VI*, Tipografia Poliglotta Vaticana, vol. VI; Allocution *Resistite fortes in fide*, of June 29, 1972, in *Insegnamenti di Paolo VI*, vol. X; Allocution to the Sacred College, of May 18, 1970, in *Insegnamenti di Paolo VI*, vol. VIII. Apostolic Constitution *Missale romanum*, of March 4, 1969, in *Ordo Missae*, Typis Polyglottis Vaticanis, 1970; General Audience, of January 12, 1966, in *Insegnamenti di Paolo VI*, vol. IV; Audience to the participants of the 13th Week of Pastoral Updating, of September 6, 1963, in B. KLOPPENBURG, *Concílio Vaticano II*, vol. III; Audience to the participants of the International Thomist Congress of September 12, 1970, in *Insegnamenti di Paolo VI*, vol. VIII; Brief *In Spiritu Sancto*, of December 7, 1965, in B. KLOPPENBURG, *Concílio Vaticano II*, vol. V; Opening Speech of the Second Conciliar Session, of September 29, 1963, in B. KLOPPENBURG, Concílio Vaticano II, vol. VIII; Encyclical *Ecclesiam suam*, of August 6, 1964, in *Insegnamenti di Paolo VI*, 1963 - 1970; Encyclical *Humanae vitae*, of July 25, 1968, in *Insegnamenti di Paolo VI*, 1963 - 1970: Encicliche; "Formulas of Promulgation of the Sixteen Conciliar Documents," in V.A., *Documentos do Vaticano II*; Encyclical *Populorum progressio*, of March 26, 1967, *apud* K. RAHNER, *Theological reflections on the problem of secularization. Novus ordo Missae ou Nuevas normas de la Misa - Ordenación general del Missal Romano*, Madrid: BAC, 1969; *Ordo Missae*, Rome: Typis Polyglottis Vaticanis, 1969; See MONTINI, G. B.

PEINADOR, Antonio – *Cursus brevior Theologiae Moralis*, Madrid: Coculsa, 1946-1956, 4 vols. **PELLAND, Gilles** – *À propos de triomphalisme*, in V.A., *Vatican II: Bilan et perspectives*, vol. I. **PELÂTRE, Louis** – "Islam: la paura ingiustificata," interview with F. STRALIARI, in *Il Regno*, 3/15/1993. **PEUCHMAURD, Maurice** – See V.A., *L'Église dans le monde de ce temps.* **PHILIPS, Gérard** – *La Chiesa e il suo mistero nel Concilio Vaticano II - Storia, testo e commento della Costituzione Lumen gentium*, Milan: Jaca Books, 1975; *L'Église et son mystère au deuxième concile du Vatican, apud* F. A. SULLIVAN. **PIGHI, J. Baptista** – *Institutions Historiae ecclesiasticae*, Verona: Bibliopolae Editoris Pontificii, 1922, 3 vols. **PIMENTEL, Aristides** – Press statement, *apud O Estado de S. Paulo*, "Ex padres estão organizados," 6/15/1989. **PINHEIRO, Paulo Sergio** – "A transa das freiras e outras transas," in *Folha de S Paulo*, 6/18/1985. **PINSK, J.** – *La situation actuelle de la théologie catholique en Allemagne*, in V.A., *Catholicisme allemand.*

PIUS V, St. – Bull *Quo primum tempore*, of 1570. **PIUS VI** – Allocution at the Secret Consistory, of June 17, 1793, in *Pii VI Pontificis Maximi Acta*, Rome: Typis S. Congreg. de Propaganda Fide, 1871, vol. II; Bull *Auctorem Fidei*, of August 28, 1794; Letter-Decree to the Cardinal de La Rochefoucauld and the Archbishop of Aixen-Provence, of March 10, 1791, in *Pii VI Pontificis Maximi Acta*, vol. I; Encyclical *Inscrutabile divinae sapientiae*, of December 25, 1775. **PIUS IX** – Allocution *Acerbissimum,* of September 27, 1852, in V.A., *Recueil des allocutions*; Allocution *Iamdudum cernimus,* of March 18, 1861, in idem; Allocution *Maxima quidem,* of June 9, 1862, in idem; Allocution *Nemo vestrum* of July 26, 1855, in idem; Allocution *Nunquam fore,* of December 15, 1856, in idem; Allocution *Singulari quadam,* of December 9, 1852, in D 1642; Allocution *Ubi primum,* of December 17, 1848, in V.A., *Recueil des allocutions*; Letter *Gravissimas inter,* of December 22, 1862, in DS 2850-2861; Letter *Multiplices inter,* of June 10, 1851, in V.A., *Recueil des allocutions*; Letter *Tuas libenter,* of December 21, 1863, in DS 2875; Encyclical *Nostis et nobiscum,* of December 8, 1849, in V.A., *Les enseignements pontificaux*; Encyclical *Quanta cura,* of December 8, 1864, in DS 2890, Petrópolis: Vozes, 1951; Encyclical *Quanto conficiamur,* of August 10, 1863, in DS 2865ff., V.A., *Recueil des allocutions*; Encyclical *Qui pluribus,* of November 9, 1846, in DS 2785; V.A., *Recueil des allocutions,* Petrópolis: Vozes, 1960; Encyclical *Singulari quidem,* of March 17, 1856, in V.A., *Recueil des allocutions*; *Syllabus*, of December 8, 1864, in DS 2902, 2915-2918, 2977-2980, Petrópolis: Vozes, 1951.

PIUS X, St. – Apostolic Letter *Notre charge apostolique,* of August 25, 1910, Petrópolis: Vozes, 1953; *Catecismo maior*, São Paulo: Vera Cruz, 1976; Encyclical *Pascendi Dominici gregis*, of September 8, 1907, Petrópolis: Vozes, 1959; *Motu proprio* about Catholic Action, in *Lettres apostoliques de S. Pie X*, Paris: Bonne Presse, 1926. **PIUS XI** – Encyclical *Divini Redemptoris,* of March 19, 1937, in DS 3773, Buenos Aires: Ed. Rome, n.d.; Encyclical *Quadragesimo anno,* of March 15, 1931, in DS 3742-3744, Paris: Ed. Spes, 1954. Encyclical *Mortalium animos,* of January 6, 1928, in *Actes de S.S. Pie XI*, Paris: Bonne Presse, Paris, vol. IV. **PIUS XII** – Letter to the 41st Social Week of France, of July 14, 1954, in *Discorsi e radiomessaggi,* vol. XVI; Decree of the Supreme Congregation of the Holy Office Against Communism, of June 1, 1943; Speech to the 1st International Congress of Social Studies and the International Christian Association, of June 3, 1950, in *Discorsi e radiomessaggi*, vol. XII; Speech to the International Congress on Problems of Rural Life, of July 2, 1951, in *Discorsi e radiomessaggi,* vol. XIII; Speech to the IX International Conference of Catholic Associations, of May 7, 1949, in *Discorsi e radiomessaggi*, vol. XI; Speech to the VII Congress of the Christian Union of Corporate Heads and Managers of Italy, of March 7, 1957, in *Discorsi e radiomessaggi,* vol. XIX; Encyclical *Humani generis,* of August 12, 1950, Petrópolis: Vozes, 1961; Encyclical *Mystici Corporis Christi*, of June 29, 1943, Petrópolis: Vozes, 1960; Radiomessage of Christmas of 1944, Petrópolis: Vozes, 1951; Radiomessage to the *Katholikentag* of Vienna, of September 14, 1952, in *Discorsi e radiomessaggi*, vol. XIV.

PIZZARDO, Giuseppe – See SACRED CONGREGATION OF SEMINARIES AND UNIVERSITIES. **PLINVAL, G. de** – *Les luttes pélagiennes*, in V.A., *Histoire de l'Église*, vol. IV. **PLOEG, J. van der** – "Pesquisa entre párocos de Utrecht," in *Katholieke Stemmen* (Tilburg), June-July 1983. **POLETTI, Ugo** – Press statements, *apud O Estado de S. Paulo*, "Faltam padres em Roma, diz Cardeal," 6/14/1989. **POLITI, Marco** – "Eva sull'altare," in *La Repubblica*, 10/12/1994; "Sesso, preghiere & aldità," in *La Repubblica*, 5/9/1995; See LUBAC, H. de, *Irrequieto ma ubbidiente - La Chiesa e i suoi protagonisti - Henri de Lubac*. **PREZZI, Lorenzo** – "Vescovi e religiosi, profilo modesto," in *Il Regno*, 9/15/1993. **PROAÑO GIL, Vicente** – Infallibility, in V.A., *Gran enciclopedia*, vol. XII. **PRODI, Paolo** – See V.A., *Conciliorum oecumenicorum decreta*. **PROENÇA SIGAUD, Geraldo de** – See G. P. SIGAUD. **PROSPER OF AQUITAINE, St.** – *Liber contra Collatorem*, in PL 45, 1808. **PRZYWARA, Erich** – *Corpus Christi mysticum. Eine Bilanz*, in *Zeitschrift für Aszese und mystik*, 15, 1940, apud A. ACERBI. **PUYO, Jean** – See CONGAR, Y., *Jean Puyo interroge le Père Congar.*

QUALTER, Terence H. – *Propaganda and psychological warfare*, New York: Random House, 1965.

RAFFIN, Pierre – "I beni dei religiosi al servizio della missione," in *L'Osservatore Romano*, 11/23/1994, supplement. **RAHNER, Karl** – *Karl Rahner em diálogo com Johann Baptist Metz*, in V.A., *Cinco problemas que desafiam a Igreja hoje; La Chiesa peccatrice nei decreti del Concilio Vatican II*, Rome, 1968, apud M. FLICK and Z. ALSZEGHY; *Magistero e teologia dopo il Concilio*, Brescia: Queriniana, 1967; *Théologie et anthropologie*, in V.A., *Théologie d'aujourd'hui et de demain; Theological reflections on the problem of secularization*, in V.A., *Theology of renewal*, vol. I; *Vaticano II: Um começo de renovação*, São Paulo: Herder, 1966; See DENZINGER (2). **RATZINGER, Joseph** – "La eclesiología del Vaticano," in *Iglesia-Mundo* (Madrid), October 1986; "Ecco perché la fede è in crisi," interview with V. MESSORI, in *Jesus* (Milan), November 1984; Instruction on the ecclesial vocation of theology, published under the title: "Rinnovato dialogo fra Magistero e Teologia," in *L'Osservatore Romano*, 6/27/1990; "La fede è il bene più alto. Bisogna sempre vigilare perchè non si corrompa," in *L'Osservatore Romano*, 11/9/1984; *Il nuovo popolo di Dio*, Brescia: Queriniana, 1971, apud J. M. GONZALEZ RUIZ; "Um passado que não lhes diz respeito," in *30 Dias*, January 1994; *Les principes de la Théologie Catholique - Esquisse et materiaux*, Paris: Tequi, 1985; *Problemi e risultati del Concilio Vaticano II*, Brescia: Queriniana, 1967; *Rapporto sulla Fede - Vittorio Messori a colloquio con Joseph Ratzinger*, Rome: Paoline, 1985; "Ratzinger reafirma identidade católica," interview with W. FALCETA, in *O Estado de S. Paulo*, 8/29/1990; *Der Weltdienst der Kirche: Zehn Jahre nach Vaticanum II*, Eds. A. Bauch, A. Glasser, and M. Seybold , 1976; *Zehn Jahre Vaticanum II*, Regensburg, 1976, apud R. GIBELLINI.

(LA) REPUBBLICA – "Preti sposati in cerca di diritto," 8/29/1994. REED, Luther – *The Lutheran Liturgy,* Philadelphia: Fortress Press, 1959, in A. V. XAVIER DA SILVEIRA, *La nouvelle Messe.* REIFFENSTUEL, Anacletus – *Theologia Moralis,* Venice: Bortoli, 1704, in A. V. XAVIER DA SILVEIRA, *La nouvelle Messe.* REVILLA TORICES, Benedito – Statements to the press, *apud O Estado de S. Paulo,* 7/6/1985. RICCI, Tommaso – "A distração do Concílio," in *30 Dias,* August/September 1989; "Engrenagem quase perfeita," in *30 Dias,* December 1989; "O mistério do pacto Roma-Moscou," in *30 Dias,* October 1989; See S. ODDI and R. GRABER. RIO, Domenico del – "Sono settanta mile i sacerdoti sposati," in *La Repubblica,* 8/25/1985. RIPALDA, J. M. de – *De Fide, apud* C. GARCIA EXTREMEÑO. RIVA, Clemente – See HAMER, J. ROBERT BELLARMINE, St. – *Disputationes de controversiis christianae Fidei adversus huius temporis haereticos* (1586-1593), Venice, 1721, *apud La Civiltà Cattolica,* Editoriale: "Dalla 'società perfetta' alla Chiesa 'mistero,' 1/19/1985. *De Romano Pontifice,* in *Opera omnia,* Neapoli/Panormi/ Paris: Pedone Lauriel, 1871, vol. I. *De Verbo Dei, apud* C. GARCIA EXTREMEÑO. ROBERTS, Thomas – Press statement in opposition to the Encyclical *Humanae vitae,* apud ICI, 9/15/1968.

ROCCA, Giancarlo – "Modelli in crisi e nuove vie," in *Il Regno,* 1/15/1993. ROCCA, Orazio la – "Dalle Filippine arriva la 'tralta delle novizie,'" in *La Repubblica,* 10/3/1994; "Le suore a Wojtyla: 'Più soldi e potere' - Ecco le 'sindacaliste di Dio,'" in *La Repubblica,* 10/8/1994; "'Dimenticate i beni terrani' - Il Papa contro le 'sindicaliste di Dio,'" in *La Repubblica,* 10/13/1994. ROCHETTE, Madeleine – "Il ruolo profetico della vita religiosa," in *L'Osservatore Romano,* 11/23/1994, supplement. ROGIER, L. J. – See V.A., *Nouvelle Histoire de l'Église.* ROMANO ROCHA, Pedro – "La principale manifestation de l'Église," in V.A., *Vatican II - Bilan et perspectives,* vol. II. ROUSSEAU, Olivier – "A Constituição no quadro dos movimentos renovadores de teologia e de pastoral das últimas décadas," in V.A., *A Igreja do Vaticano II;* "Les attitudes de pensée concernant l'únite chrétienne au XIXe. siècle," in V.A., *L'ecclésiologie au XIXe. siècle.* RUFFINI, Ernesto – Comments on the Schema XIII in the conciliar assembly, *apud* G. CAPRILE, *Il Concilio Vaticano II,* vol. V; *Comments on Hell in the conciliar assembly,* apud B. KLOPPENBURG, *Concílio Vaticano II,* vol. IV.

SARTORI, Luigi – *Il linguaggio del Vaticano II,* in V.A., *Il linguaggio teologico oggi. Spirito Santo e storia-Testimonianza cattolica,* in V.A., *Lo Spirito Santo pegno e primizia del regno.* SCANTAMBURLO, Giovanni – *Perché il Concílio non ha condannato il comunismo,* Rome: Ed. L'Appennino, 1967. SCARPA, Pedro Luis Guido – "Formazione 'inculturata' ma esigente," in *L'Osservatore Romano,* 11/23/1994, supplement. SCHILLEBEECKX, Edward – Statement, *apud* R. AMERIO. "Dio è un dono non una garanzia," interview with F. STRAZZARI, in *Il Regno,* 6/15/1990; *Fundamento da autoridade na Igreja,* in V.A., *Cinco problemas que desafiam a Igreja de hoje*; *Gott ist jeden Tag neu - Ein Gespräch*, Mainz: Matthias Grunwald, 1984, *apud Orientierung* (Zurich), 1/31/1985; *I laici nel popolo di Dio,* in V.A., *La fine della Chiesa come società perfetta, Le ministère dans l'Église,* Paris: Cerf, 1981; *The real achievement of Vatican II,* New York: Herder & Herder, 1967, *apud* A. R. MUGGERIDGE. *Igreja ou igrejas?,* in V.A., *Cinco problemas que desafiam a Igreja hoje*; "Wij denken gepassioneerd en in cliche's," in *De Bazuin,* January 1965, *apud* A. ACERBI. **SCHMIDBERGER, Franz** – "Mas eu respondo a König," interview with S. PACCI, in *30 Dias,* November 1992. **SCHÖNMETZER, Adolfus** – See DENZINGER (3). **SCHOUPPE, F. X.** – *Curso abreviado de Religião ou verdade e beleza da Religião Cristã,* Porto: Liv. Chardron, 1875. **SCHWAGER, Raymund** – Interview granted to A. SINKE GUIMARÃES, Innsbruck, February 11, 1983. **SESBOÜÉ, Bernard** – *O Evangelho na Igreja – A tradição viva da fé,* São Paulo: Paulinas, 1977. **SIETMANN, Klara** – "Rendere visibili i trati del volto di Dio," in *L'Osservatore Romano,* 11/23/1994, supplement.

SIGAUD, Geraldo de Proença – Correction to the Schema XIII, delivered jointly with M. LEFÈBVRE, and signed by 435 conciliar Fathers, *apud* L. CARLI, "Il comunismo e it Concilio Vaticano II," in *30 Dias,* August-September 1989; See P. CORRÊA DE OLIVEIRA, *Declaração do Morro Alto* and *Reforma agrária, questão de consciência.* **SILVA, José Ariovaldo da** – *O movimento litúrgico no Brasil - Estudo histórico,* Petrópolis: Voces, 1983. **SILVA HENRÍQUEZ, Raid** – Comments on the Schema XIII in the conciliar assembly, *apud* G. CAPRILE, *Il Concilio Vaticano II,* vol. V. **SIN, Jaime** – "Por algumas túnicas a mais," interview with L. BRUNELLI, in *30 Dias,* October 1994. **SINKE GUIMARÃES, Atila** – See GUIMARÃES, Atila Sinke. **SIPE, Richard** – "A Secret World: Sexuality and the Search of Celibacy," *apud The Economist,* 6/18/1992. **SIXTUS V** – Bull *Triumphantis,* 1588, *apud* LEO XIII, Encyclical *Aeterni Patris.*

SOARES DE AZEVEDO, Mateus – "O Concílio que não terminou," in *Jornal da Tarde,* 10/24/1992. **SOLIMEO, Gustavo Antonio** – See CORRÊA DE OLIVEIRA, P., *As CEBs ... dos quais muito se fala, pouco se conhece.* **SOLIMEO, Luís Sergio** – See P. CORRÊA DE OLIVEIRA, *As CEBs... das quais muito se fala, pouco se conhece.* **SORGE, Bartolomeo** – "I cristiani nel mondo postmoderno - Presenza, assenza, mediazione?," in *La Civiltà Cattolica,* 5/7/1983. **SORRENTINO, Aurelio** – La Chiesa, compagna di viaggio dell'uomo - Il grandi testimoni del Vaticano 11/7," interview with S. STRACCA, in *Avvenire,* 11/27/1992. **SOUZA LIMA, Lizânias de** – *Plinio Corrêa de Oliveira, um cruzado do século XX,* University of São Paulo, Ph.D. dissertation, 1985. **SPIRAGO, Francisco** – *Catecismo católico popular,* Lisbon: Uniao Grafica Ed., 1951, vol. II. **STAFFA, Dino** – See SACRED CONGREGATION OF SEMINARIES AND UNIVERSITIES. **STEINSCHULTE, Gabriel Maria** – "Paesi di lingua tedesca -Vent'anni di riforme, prima e dopo," in *L'Osservatore Romano,* 12/14/1983, special supplement on the Constitution *Sacrosanctum Concilium.* **STIMPFLE, Joseph** – Comments on the Schema XIII in the conciliar assembly, apud L. CARLI.

STRACCA, Silvano – See KÖNIG, F.; MOTOLESE.; G., SORRENTINO, A.; , SUENENS L.J., *Un nuovo battesimo per la cristinianitâ.* **STRAZZARI, Francesco** – See L. PELATRE; See E. SCHILLEBEECKX, *Dio è un dono non una garanzia.* **SUAREZ, Francisco** – *Defensio Fidei catholicae,* apud A. V. XAVIER DA SILVEIRA, *La nouvelle Messe; apud* F. X. WERNZ and P. VIDAL. *De Christo, apud* C. GARCIA EXTREMEÑO; *De Fide,* in *Opera omnia,* Paris: Vives, 1958, vol. XII, *apud* A. V. XAVIER DA SILVEIRA, *La nouvelle Messe. De legibus,* in *Opera omnia,* 1956, vol. V, *apud ibidem.* **SUENENS, Leo Józef** – *Co-Responsibility: Dominating Idea of the Council and its Pastoral Consequences,* in V.A., *Theology of renewal,* vol. II. Statement to Vatican Radio, of November 7, 1985; *Discorso ufficiale d'apertura - Alcuni compite della teologia oggi,* in V.A., *L'avvenire della Chiesa; Souvenirs et esperances,* Paris: Fayard, 1991; "Un nuovo battesimo per la Cristianitá - I grandi testimoni del Vaticano 11/2," interview with S. STRACCA, in *Avvenire,* 10/23/1992.

SULLIVAN, Francis A. – *Le sens et l'importance de la décision de Vatican II de dire, à propos de l'Église du Christ, non pas qu'elle 'est' mais qu'elle 'subsiste dans' l'Église Catholique Romaine,* in V.A., *Vatican II: Bilan et perspectives,* vol. II. **SUMAH, Rose** – "Le religiose nelle Giovani Chiese," in *L'Osservatore Romano,* 11/23/1994, supplement. **SYNOD OF BISHOPS - 1994** – "Message to the People of God," in *L'Osservatore Romano,* 9/23/ 1994, supplement. **SYNOD OF BISHOPS, EXTRAORDINARY - 1995** – "Message to the People of God," in *L'Osservatore Romano,* (Portuguese edition), 12/15/1985; "Relatio finalis," in *Enchiridion Vaticanum,* 9/1798, *apud* G. DOSSETTI.

TANQUEREY, Adolphus – *Synopsis theologiae dogmaticae,* Tournai: Desclée, 1937, vol. I. **TEPE, Valfredo** – "Celibato a discutido no Sinodo," in *O Estado de S. Paulo,* 10/3/1990; Speech in the Synod '90, *apud* R. MORABITO. **TERTULLIAN** – *De praescriptionibus adversus haereticos,* in PL 2, 40, *apud* V. PROAÑO GIL. **THOMAS AQUINAS, St.** – *Commentaria super libros sententiarum,* L. Lethielleux, Parisiis, 1929-1947, 5 vols.; *Super Epistulas S. Pauli, Ad Galatas,* Turin/Rome: Marietti, 1953; *Summa theologiae,* Turin/ Rome: Marietti, 1948, 4 vols.; *Summa teologica,* Madrid: BAC, 1947-1960, 16 vols. **TILLIETTE, Xavier** – "Começar de novo. Com fé," in *30 Dias,* December 1988. **TODARO, Margaret Patrice** – *Pastors, prophets and politicians: A study of the Brazilian Catholic Church, 1916-1945,* University of Columbia, 1971.

TOMKO, Jozef – "Riconciliazione e penitenza," in *L'Osservatore Romano,* 12/1/1983, supplement. **TORNIELLI, Andrea** – "O outono quente dos religiosos," in *30 Dias*, September 1994; "O timoneiro do Concílio," in *30 Dias*, July 1992. **TRINCHARD, Paul** – *New Mass in Light of the Old*, Monrovia, CA: Marian Publications, 1995; See AMELUNXEN, R. **TSHIBANGU TSHISHIKU, Tharcisse** – "Crisi dei confessori," in *L'Osservatore Romano*, 10/5/1983, supplement. **TUCCI, Roberto** – *Introduzione storico-dottrinale alla costituzione pastorale Gaudium et spes*, in *La Costituzione pastorale sulla Chiesa nel mondo contemporaneo*, Turin, 1966, *apud* G. CAPRILE, *Il Concilio Vaticano II*, vol. V. **TURRADO, Laurentio** – See V.A., *Biblia Sacra juxta Vulgatam clementinam.*

UFFICIO CENTRALE DI STATISTICA DELLA CHIESA – "La Chiesa cattolica alla luce di alcuni fenomeni statistici dal 1978 al 1990," in *L'Osservatore Romano*, 7/15/.1992, supplement; *L'Osservatore Romano*, 10/17/1992, supplement. **UKERITIS, Miriam** – See NYGREN, D. **UNION OF PASTORAL AGENTS** (Utrecht) – "Párocos rejeitam doutrina da Igreja sobre homo-sexualismo," apud J. van der PLOEG. **URDANOZ, Teofilo** – "Commentaire sur les `Relecciones teologicas de Francisco Vitoria,'" *apud* A. V. XAVIER DA SILVEIRA, *La nouvelle Messe.*

V.A. (Various Authors) – *Atas do Concílio Ecumênico Vaticano II, apud* V.A., *Documentos do Vaticano II. L'avvenire della Chiesa - Il libro del Congresso* (from the magazine *Concilium*), Brescia: Queriniana, 1970; *Biblia Sacra juxta Vulgatam clementinam*, Madrid: BAC, 1965; *Bíblia Sagrada* (translated from the Vulgate and annotated by MATOS SOARES), São Paulo: Paulinas, 1964; *Bilan de la théologie au XXe. siècle* (eds. R. VANDER GUCHT and H. VORGRIMLER), Tournai/Paris: Casterman, 1970, 2 vols.; *Catholicisme allemand*, Paris: Cerf, 1956; *Cinco problemas que desafiam a Igreja hoje*, São Paulo: Herder, 1970; *Commentary on the documents of Vatican II*, Herder, 2 vols., apud F. A. SULLIVAN; *Conciliorum oecumenicorum decreta* (ed. G. ALBERIGO, P. JOANNOU, C. LEONARDI and P. PRODI), Freiburg im Breisgau: Herder, 1962; *Conversaciones de Toledo - Teología de la liberación*, Bruges: Aldecoa, 1973; *Desafios cristianos*, Madrid: Loguez Ed., 1990; *Dictionnaire de Théologie Catholique - DTC* (eds. A. VACANT and E. MANGENOT), Paris: E. Librairie Letouzey & Ané, 1927-1972, 18 vols.; *Documentos do Vaticano II - Constituições, decretos e declarações* (eds. B. KLOPPENBURG and F. VIER; Portuguese edition reviewed by the undersecretaries of the National Conference of Brazilian Bishops) Petrópolis: Vozes, 1966; *L'ecclésiologie au XIXe. siècle*, Paris: Cerf, 1960.

V.A. (Various Authors - continued) – *L'Église dans le monde de ce temps - Constitution pastorale Gaudium et spes* (eds. Y. CONGAR and M. PEUCHMAURD), Paris: Cerf, 1967, 3 vols; *Les enseignements pontificaux - La paix interiéure des nations* (ed. MONKS DE SOLESMES), Tournai: Desclée & Cie, 1952; *A experiência do Espirito Santo*, Petrópolis: Vozes, 1979; *La fine della Chiesa come società perfetta*, Verona: Mondadori, 1968; *Gran encic-*

lopedia, Madrid: Ed. Rialp S/A, 1971-1976, 24 vols.; *Enciclopedia universal ilustrada europeo-americana,* Madrid/Barcelona: Espasa Calpe, 1930-1956, 70 vols., 10 appendices and 3 supplements; *Histoire de l'Église depuis les origins jusqu'à nos jours* (eds. A. FLICHE and V. MARTIN), Paris: Bloud & Gay, 1946-1952, 21 vols.; *I grandi temi del Concilio,* Rome: Paoline, 1965; *A Igreja do futuro,* Petrópolis: Vozes, 1973; *A Igreja do Vaticano II* (ed. G. BARAUNA), Petrópolis: Vozes, 1965; *Il linguaggio teologico oggi* (ed. ASSOCIAZIONE TEOLOGICA ITALIANA,) Milan: Ancora, 1970; *Nouvelle Histoire de l'Église* (eds. R. AUBERT, M. D. KNOWLES and L. J. ROGIER), Paris: Seuill, 1975, 5 vols.; *Patrologiae Grecquae-Latinae cursus completus ... Series Graeca* (PG), (ed. J. P. MIGNE), Paris: Migne, 1857-76, 217 vols., 4 indices; *Patrologiae Latinae cursus completus ... Series Latina* (PL), (ed. J. P. MIGNE), Paris: Migne. 1841-64, 161 vols., 1 index.

V.A. (Various Authors - continued) – *Problèmes et perspectives de théologie fondamentale* (ed. R. LATOURELLE), Paris/Toumai/Montreal: G. O'Collins Ed., 1982; *Recueil des allocutions consistoriales, encycliques et autres lettres apostoliques des Souverains Pontifes Clément XII, Benoît XIV, Pie VI, Pie VII, Léon XII, Grégoire XVI et Pie IX. Citées dans l'Encyclique et le Syllabus du 8 décembre 1864, suivi du Concordat de 1801 et de divers autres documents,* Paris: Adrien le Clere, 1865; *La reforma que llega de Roma,* Barcelona: Plaza & Janes, 1970; *Lo Spirito Santo pegno e primizia del regno - Atti della XIX session di formazione ecumenica organizzata dal Segretariato Attività Ecumeniche,* Trento, Turin: Elle Di Ci, 1982; *Théologie d'aujourd'hui et de demain,* Paris: Cerf, 1967; *Theology of renewal - Renewal of religious thought,* Montreal: Palm Publishers, 1968, 2 vols; *Vatican II: Bilan et perspectives, vingt-cinq ans après (1962-1987)* (ed. R. LATOURELLE), Montreal/Paris: Bellarmin-Cerf, 1988, 3 vols.; *Verso la Chiesa del terzo millennio,* Brescia: Queriniana, 1979. **VACANT, Alfred** – See V.A., *Dictionnaire de Théologie Catholique.*

VAGAGGINI, Cipriano – *Presentazione,* in A. ACERBI. **VANCOURT, Raymond** – *Patriarchates,* in DTC, vol. XI. **VANDER GUCHT, Robert** – See V.A., *Bilan de la théologie du XXe. siècle.* **VATICAN COUNCIL I** – *Constitutio Dogmatica de Fide catholica, apud* PIUS XII, Encyclical *Mystici Corporis Christi.* **VERGOTE, Antoine** – *La presenza della Chiesa nella società di domani - Riflessioni bibliche,* in V.A., *L'avvenire della Chiesa.* **VERMEIL, Edmond** – *Jean-Adam Möhler et l'École Catholique de Tubingue,* Paris: Armand Colin, 1913. **VINCENT OF LÉRINS, St.** – *Commonitorium,* in PL 50, 670. **VIDAL, Pedro** – See WERNZ, F. X. **LA VIE (Paris)** – "Les volets du presbytère sont ouverts," *apud* L. LANGRE. **VIER, Frederico** – See V.A., *Documentos do Vaticano II.* **VITORIA, Francisco de** – *Obras de Francisco de Vitoria,* Madrid: BAC, 1960. **VORGRIMLER, Herbert** – "Dal 'sensus fidei' al 'consensus fidelium,'" in *Concilium,* April 1986. See V.A., *Bilan de la théologie au XXe. siècle.*

WALDENFELDS, Hans – "Autorità e conoscenza," in *Concilium*, April 1985. THE WANDERER (St. Paul, Minnesota) – "The Forum - Journalistic Ethics," 5/14/1992. WERNER-KÜMMEL – *Les recherches exégétiques sur le Nouveau Testament*, in V.A., *Bilan de la théologie au XXe. siècle*, vol. II. WENGER, Antoine – *L'Église en son temps - Vatican II - Chronique*, Paris: Centurion, 1963-1966, 4 vols. WERNZ, Francisco Xavier and Pedro VIDAL – *Ius Canonicum*, Rome: Aedes Universitatis Gregorianae, 1927, 2 vols. WHITE, John – Statements, *apud* "Aids é debatida no Vaticano," in *O Estado de S. Paulo*, 6/14/1989. WILLEBRANDS, Jan – Allocution au Comité international de liaison du dialogue judéo-chrétien, in *La Documentation Catholique, Bilan du dialogue judéo-chrétien*, 1/19/1986.

WILLOUGHBY, Willian – "Superiors 'honor the conscience' of nuns who signed pro-choice ad," in *The Washington Times*, 1/11/1985. WILTGEN, Ralph – *The Rhine Flows into the Tiber*, Devon (England): Augustine, 1978. WOJTYLA, Karol – *Alle fonti del rinnovamento - Studio sull'attuazione del Concílio Vaticano Secondo*, Città del Vaticano: Libreria Editrice Vaticana, 1981; See JOHN PAUL II. WOODROW, Alain – *A Rome: Trente théologiens du monde entier pour accomplir le Concile*, in ICI, 5/15/1969. WOODWARD, Kenneth L. – "An acute shortage of priests," in *Newsweek*, 4/18/1983.

XAVIER DA SILVEIRA, Arnaldo Vidigal – *Na nouvelle Messe de Paul VI: Qu'en penser?* Chiré-en-Montreuil: Diffusion de la Pensée Francaise, 1975; "Pode haver erro em documentos do Magistério?" in *Catolicismo*, July 1969; "Qual a autoridade doutrinária dos documentos pontificios e conciliares?" in *Catolicismo*, October 1967.

YU PIN – Comments on Schema XIII in the conciliar assembly, *apud* L. CARLI.

ZEILLER, Jacques – *La propagation du Christianisme*, in V.A., *Histoire de l'Église*, vol. I. ZOZIMO, St. – *Letter Magnus pondus, apud* G. de PLINVAL; Letter *Postquam nobis*, of September 21, 417, *apud ibidem; Tractatoria, apud ibidem*. ZUCCOLINI, Roberto – Ruini: "È vero, la città é ormai diventata una terra di missione," in *Corriere della Sera*, 5/12/1995.

* * *

SUBJECT INDEX

ADAM – Seen as a Species and Cosmic Reality: Chap. VIII § 6.

ADMONISHMENTS – What led the Holy See to admonish the excesses of certain theologians? Chap. I § 3, Notes 11, 12.

ADAPTATION OF THE CHURCH TO THE WORLD, AGGIORNAMENTO – **Ambiguity** and *aggiornamento*: Chap. IX §§ 57-98. End of **Christendom** and *aggiornamento*: Chap. IX §§ 85-93. **Elimination** of the boundaries between the spiritual and temporal orders: Chap. IX §§ 75, 85, 94, 98. **Fruits** of *aggiornamento*: Chap. IX §§ 98f.; Chap. X § 11. **Homosexuality** and *aggiornamento*: § 86. **Influence** of the Church on the temporal order should end: Chap. IX §§ 67-73. New concept of **"Revelation"** and of the theology subjacent to *aggiornamento*: Chap. IX §§ 75-78, 84. **Spirit of the Council** and *aggiornamento*: General Introduction §§ 5, 20-26. **Socialization,** consequence of *aggiornamento*: Chap. IX §§ 94-98.

ALCOHOLISM AMONG THE CLERGY – Chap. X §§ 84f.

AMBIGUITY (A) – General Introduction, §§ 19, 21. **Abandonment** of scholastic language: Chap. III §§ 1, 3. **Clash** between the two currents of thought forms base of A: Chap. II § 3; Chap. IV § 7; Chap. VI §§ 1-14, 16-25. **Concept of the Church and Faith** in relation to conciliar A: Chap. VII §§ 20-31. **Concept** of A: Chap. II § 1. **Concept of world** and A: Chap. IX § 62. **Council as dogmatic** and ambiguous: Chap. VI §§ 60, 65, 120 ff. **Council as pastoral** and ambiguous: Chap. VI §§ 49ff., 60ff., 65, 120-124. **Defining council** and the use of A: Chap. VI §§ 65-133. **Difficulty in harmonizing** conciliar texts: General Introduction §§ 19f., Chap. VI §§ 16-25. **Doctrine** justifying A: Chap. VII §§ 1, 10-19, 32. **Deliberate use** of A: Chap. III §§ 5-14, 21-24, Chap. V §§ 22f. Universal **evolution** latent in the A of conciliar texts: Chap. VII §§ 10-19. **Excerpts** illustrating A: Chap. I §§ 1-5. **Futility** of discussion based on ambiguous texts: General Introduction § 19. A of **History**: Chap. VII §§ 6f. **Metaphysical principle** behind A: Chap. II § 4. **Modernism** and A: Chap. II § 6. **Nullity** of the Council because of A: Conclusion § 2. **Omissions** in the Council texts: Chap. VIII, *passim.* **Radical pretexts** underlying A: Chap. V § 1-23. **Relativism** in theology and A: Chap. VII §§ 2-9. **Risk** in using A: Chap. III §§ 15-20. **Strategies and tactics** that employ A: Chap. II §§ 2-7; Chap. IV §§ 1-16; Chap. V §§ 23; Chap. VI §§ 67. **Synthesis** of opposing positions: Chap. VI §§ 26-32. **Tendencies** and doctrines defeated in Vatican I were protected in the A of Vatican II: Chap. IV §§ 3f., notes, 6, 7a, b, c; Chap. VI §§ 2, 7, 10, 15; Chap. X § 1. **Testimonies** about A: Chap. III §§ 1-25. **Theological qualification** of Vatican II and A: Chap. VI §§ 34-64, 68-134. **Thinking and intention** of the Council with regard to A: Conclusion § 3. **Transitory phase** in the process of A: Chap. II § 5. **Types** of A: Chap. II §§ 1-5. **Various ways** that A can be employed: Chap. II §§ 2-5. **View** of the ensemble of the study of A: Introduction to Volume I, §§ 1-6.

ANTHROPOLOGY, CHRISTIAN – Main ideas: Chap. VII § 15.

ARIANISM – History of: General Introduction, Note lg.

AUTO-DEMOLITION OF THE CHURCH – General Introduction, § 7, Note 2; Chap. X, Note 7, §§ 13-27, 43-50.

BASIC CHRISTIAN COMMUNITIES – Egalitarian inspiration: Chap. I, Note 7, d.

BIBLE – Biblical School of Jerusalem: Chap. IV, Note 3. Movement for Biblical Renewal: Chap. IV, Note 3.

CATHOLIC ACTION – Chap. 1 § 2.

CELIBACY, PRIESTLY – Negation of: Chap. X §§ 68-79; see *CLERICAL CONCUBINAGE.*

CELEBRET – See *MASS.*

CHAOS, CRITERIOLOGICAL – as a factor in accepting the "conciliar revolution": Chap. X, Note 11.

CHRIST, COSMIC – Chap. VIII § 6; Chap. IX § 75, Note 72.

CHRIST, VIRGINAL BIRTH – Progressivist concept of: Chap. VIII § 3.

CHRISTENDOM – The conciliar doctrine of adapting to the world implies the destruction of Christendom: Chap. IX §§ 85-93.

CHRISTIAN CIVILIZATION – And grace: Chap. IX § 64. Genesis of: Chap. IX, Note 58.

CHURCH, CONCEPTS OF – **Church of Christ** and ambiguity: Chap. I § 1. *According to the past Popes* the Catholic Church is the Church of Christ: Chap. I, Note 2; *According to the progressivists* she is not the Church of Christ: Chap. IX §§ 52f., 56. **Church Militant**: Chap. VI § 9; Elimination of the *distinction between Church Militant and Church Triumphant*: Chap. VIII § 15; *Society of Jesus* eliminates its militant character: Chap. X § 92. **Church as Mystery or Sacrament**: General Introduction § 26; Chap. VI §§ 11f., 14. **Church as ongoing Incarnation**: Chap. VI §§ 11f. **Church of the Spirit**: Chap. VI § 11. **Church as Spouse**: General Introduction § 26. *Ecclesia semper reformanda:* Chap. VII §§ 20-31, Chap. IX § 1. **Mystical Body**: Chap. VI §§ 8-11, 27f., Note 28. **People of God**: General Introduction § 26; Chap. I §§ 2, 4. **Pilgrim Church:** Chap. VI § 132. **Pneumatic Church** – concept of Möhler: Chap. VI §§ 2, 4-7. **Sinning Church:** General Introduction § 26; Chap. VII §§ 27f., Chap. IX § 1. *Societas perfecta* – concept of St. Robert Bellarmine: Chap. VI §§ 2-5, 9, 13, 15.

Church, Hierarchical Character of – **Aversion** to: Chap. I §§ 2f. **Tendentious omissions** regarding the Western Patriarchates: Chap. VIII §§ 19f.

Church, Militant Character of – **Adaptation** of the Church to the errors of the Enlightenment and the French Revolution: Chap. I § 4. **Aversion** to: General Introduction § 24; Chap. VIII § 15. **Decline** of: General Introduction § 22. See *Church, Concepts.*

Church, Missionary Character of – Negation of: Chap. IX § 1, 50-56.

Church, Roman Character of – Omissions in the conciliar texts: Chap. VIII §§ 16-18.

Church-State Relations – **Adaptation** of the Church to the temporal order: Chap. IX §§ 67-73. See *Adaptation to the World.* **Ambiguity** regarding the concept of the world: Chap. IX §§ 58-66, Note 57. **Distinction** between spiritual and temporal spheres disappears; Chap. IX § 74. **Negation** of the ideal of Christendom: Chap. IX §§ 85-93. See *Christendom.*

Cognition – Knowledge through co-naturality: General Introduction, Note li.

Collection: Eli, Eli, Lamma Sabacthani? – **Audience** to whom this work is directed (Pope, bishops, theologians, laymen): General Introduction § 16. **Brief history**: General Introduction, § 14, §§ 19-32. **Citations**: General Information §§ 1f., 5; Notes on Style §§ 1-4. **Credentials** of the author: General Introduction §§ 7-13. **Criteria** for analysis: General Introduction § 2. **Disposition** of the author: General Introduction § 117; Clarifications: §§ 1, 4. **Duty and right** to analyze the Council: General Introduction, §§ 7-12, Notes 3, 4. **Inspiration** and orientation given by Plinio Corrêa de Oliveira: Homage and Gratitude; General Introduction §§ 13, 19, 25, 27. **Limits in responsibility** of the author: General Information § 9; General Introduction § 14. **Limits of the work**: General Introduction § 6. **Method** used: General Introduction § 4. **Official documents** authorizing a layman to analyze the Council: General Introduction §§ 8-11. **Persons who aided** in preparing and publishing the work: Homage and Gratitude. **Objectives**: General Introduction §§ 1, 31ff. **Plan** adopted: General Introduction § 5. **Prism of analysis**: General Introduction § 3. **Publications and interviews**: General Information §§ 3f, Bibliography, *passim*. **Reason for the title**: General Introduction § 14. **Style and language**: General Introduction § 18. **Updating credentials** of the cited authors: General Information § 7.

Collegiality – Chap. IV. § 11; Chap. VI §§ 22, 61ff., 100ff.; Chap. X, Note 15.

Communism (C) – **Adaptation** of the Church to C: Chap. I, Note 13c. **Jesuits** who collaborate with the Chinese regime: Chap. X § 94. *Ostpolitik:* General Introduction, Note 16b, Chap. X § 8, Notes 21, 22. **Papal documents** condemning C: Chap. I, Note 14c. **Petition asking for condemnation** of C:

Chap. VI §§ 85-98. **People of God** and C: Chap. I §§ 2, 4. **Pressure** on Vatican leaders to avoid condemnation of C: Chap. VI §§ 85-98. **Satisfaction** of Italian Communist Party with the direction taken by Vatican II: Chap. I, Note 13c.

Concessions to the False Religions – As **fruits of the Council**: Chap. IX §§ 1-57, 99; Chap. X § 11. **Judaism**: Chap. VI § 119; Chap. IX § 50. Related to the **spirit of the Council**: General Introduction, § 22, 24. **Protestantism**: Chap. VII § 26; Chap. IX §§ 6, 10, 12, 22. 32, 34, 37-40. 46-50. **Rationale for concessions**: hierarchy of truths: Chap. IX § 51. **Schismatics**: Chap. VIII, Note 33.

Concubinage, Clerical – Chap. X §§ 80-83.

Conflicting tendencies in the Post-Conciliar phase: Clarification § 3, Chap. X §§ 1-5.

Consecration – See Mass.

Conservatives – **Conservative leaders** adhere to the theses that they previously fought: Chap. VI §§ 104-107. **Unprepared** for the Council: Chap. VI §§ 76f. See *Council: Currents of thought.*

Contestation – Vatican directives for the Episcopates and radical progressivists: Chap. X §§ 9, 43-50, Note 24.

Contradictions – In texts of conciliar documents: Chap. I § 5.

Copernican, Revolution – Chap. VII § 28; Chap. IX § 84, Note 91. See *Conciliar Revolution.*

Council, Jerusalem II – Chap. V §§ 11, 19.

Council of Trent – Chap. IV § 2; Chap. VI § 2, 31.

Council, Vatican I – Chap. IV §2, Note 7a, b; Chap. VI § 7; Chap. VI §§ 16, 31.

Council, Vatican II (C) – **Babel** and the confusion of tongues: Chap. III § 5. **Background** thought: General Introduction §§ 21, 23, 25-28; Conclusion § 3. **Criteriological chaos** as a factor in accepting the C: Chap. X, Note 11. **Conservative current**: Chap. IV § 2. Presented as **continuation of traditional doctrine**: Chap. X § 2, Note 6. **Crisis**: see Conciliar Crisis. **Currents of thought** that clashed in the C: Chap. IV §§ 1-7; Chap. VI §§ 2-15, 68-133; Chap. X § 4. **Definitions** of pastoral and dogmatic: Chap. VI, Note 40. **Difficulty in harmonizing** its texts: General Introduction § 19; Chap. VI §§ 16-25. **Emphasis** given to its dogmatic aspect: Chap. VI §§ 60, 65. **Emphasis** given to its pastoral aspect: Chap. VI §§ 49-59, 61ff., 65, 120ff. **Confusion** as fruit of C: Chap. III § 10. **Failure** of the C: Chap. V § 21. **Fruits**: see *Fruits of the Council*. **Genesis** of the C: Chap. IV § 3, Notes

3, 6, 7; Chap VI §§ 2, 8-15. Its **importance** in the History of the Church: Chap. X. Note 7. Presented as **infallible**: Chap. VI §§ 108f, 117ff., 125ff. **Key concepts** of its documents: General Introduction § 25. Inadequate **Latin**: Chap. III § 18. **Language** intentionally equivocal: Chap. III §§ 4-25; Chap. VI § 18. Its **legacy**: Introductory words by Paul VI, p. III. **Objectives** according to John XXIII: Chap. VI §§ 52-56. Had as an **objective** to stop half-way: Chap. V §§ 1-17. **Oscillation** of the theological qualifications in view of strategic interests: Chap. VI §§ 65-133. **Papal Policy** (John XXIII and Paul VI) in the C in dealing with the conservative current: Chap IV § 2, Note 2; Chap VI §§ 50, 78f, 84, 87, 92-96, 99-102; Chap. X §§ 4, 7. **Policy of compromise** as characteristic of the C: Chap. III §§ 8f. **Present-day situation:** the C is outdated: Chap. V §§ 19ff. **Progressivist current**: Chap. IV §§ 3-6. **Rejection** of preparatory schemas: Chap. IV §§ 2, Note 2; Chap. VI §§ 50, 83f. **Represents end** of an era: Chap. VI § 31. **Spirit** of the C: General Introduction §§ 20-24; Conclusion § 3. **Tactics**: General information § 4; see *AMBIGUITY.* **Themes** of conciliar preparatory schemas: Chap. VI, Note 47. **Theological qualifications** of the C: Chap. VI §§ 33-64, 65-134. **Theological qualifications** of other councils in History: Chap. VI §§ 35f, Notes 42, 44. **Subjects** dealt with: Chap. VI §§ 37-48. **Titles** of the authors who wrote about the C: General Information § 7.

COUNCIL, VATICAN III – Chap. V §§ 11, 19, 21; Chap. VI §§ 16, 131f.; Chap. X § 40.

COUNCILS, HISTORY OF – Chap. VI § 35, Notes 42-45.

CRISIS, CONCILIAR – Strategic impasse in the **application** of Council directives: Chap. X §§ 28-31, 32-36, 37-42. The **authority** loses credibility and is contested: Chap X, §§ 43-50. **Cause** of conciliar crisis is the Council itself: Chap. X § 128, Note 172. Crisis in the **clergy and religious orders**: Chap. X §§ 51-116. Crisis in the **Faith**: Chap. X §§117-128. Crisis of **unity**: Chap. X §§ 13-27.

CURIA, ROMAN – Reforms made by John XXIII, Paul VI, and John Paul II: General Information § 6.

DEMOCRATIZATION OF CHURCH – Inter-relationship with the notion of the People of God: General Introduction § 26; Chap. 1 § 2, Notes 6, 7.

DIALECTICS, HEGELIAN – General Introduction § 25.

DIALOGUE – As a talismanic word: General Introduction § 25.

DOCTRINAL – Ways in which it can be understood: Chap. VI, Note 40b, c.

DOGMATIC – **Concept**, according to Möhler: Chap. IV, Note 5d. **Dogmatic formulations** must change according to the evolution of things: Chap. VII §§ 10-14, 17.

DUTY, MORAL – That a Catholic has in relation to his Faith: General Introduction § 7; Notes 3, 4.

ECUMENISM – See *CONCESSIONS TO FALSE RELIGIONS.*

ELI, ELI, LAMINA SABACTHANI? – See *COLLECTION.*

ELIAS, PROPHET – Conclusion § 3.

ENLIGHTENMENT – **Errors** of the Enlightenment and the People of God: Chap. I §§ 2, 4. Inspirer of the **modern world** Chap IX § 65.

ESCHATOLOGY – Doctrine of evolution as a basis for conciliar eschatology: Chap. VII §§ 17, 19.

EVOLUTION – **Essence of**, and the Spirit of God: Chap. VII § 13. **Man** and evolution: Chap. VII § 15. **Natural and supernatural**: Chap. IV, Note 5f. **Objective** toward which the Church should tend: Chap. VII § 12. **Progressivism** and evolution: General Introduction, Note 23. **Signs of the times** and evolution: Chap. VII § 14. Evolution **underlies** conciliar ambiguity : Chap. VII §§ 10-19. **Word** evolution in conciliar texts: Chap. VII § 11.

EXISTENTIALISM – General Introduction § 26; Chap. VII § 5.

EXTRA ECCLESIAM NULLA SALUS – Chap. I § 5.

FAITH – **According to Möhler**: Chap. IV, Note 5c. **Vatican II denied the exclusivity of the Catholic Faith**: Chap. IX §§ 52f., 56.

FEMINISM – Among women religious: Chap. X §§ 111-115.

FRUITS OF THE COUNCIL – **Alcoholism** among the clergy: Chap. X § 84. **Ambiguity:** General Introduction §§ 19ff. **Celibacy contested** and demand for married priests: Chap. X §§ 68-79. **Concessions** to the modern world: Chap. IX §§ 57-98. **Concessions** to other religions: Chap. IX §§ 2, 6, 10, 12, 24, 32, 34, 37f., 40f., 46-49, 50-56, Note 10. **Concubinage**: Chap. X §§ 80-83. How the **conservative and progressivist faithful** faced the conciliar crisis: Chap. X §§ 1-10; 13-49, 128. **Crisis in the faith among the faithful**: Chap. X §§ 117-128. **Crisis in the regular clergy**: Chap. X §§ 87, 98f. Crisis in the regular clergy exemplified in the *Society of Jesus*: Chap. X §§ 87-98; *Crisis in ideas*: Chap. X § 89; *Crisis in the Faith*: Chap. X § 90; *Crisis regarding the future*: Chap. X §§ 95f. **Crisis in the secular and regular clergy**: Chap. X §§ 5If., 128f. **Crisis in vocations**: Chap. X §§ 54-67. **Crisis among women religious**: *In general*: Chap. X §§ 101; *Feminism*: Chap. X §§ 111-115; *Regarding moral teachings*: Chap. X §§ 107-110; *Regarding vocations*: Chap. X § 88; §§ 102-106. **Homosexuality** in the clergy: Chap. X §§ 86, 107-110.

HELL – Tendentious omissions about Hell in conciliar texts: Chap. VIII §§ 7-14.

participate in its elaboration: Chap. IX, Note 10. **Publication dates**, promulgation, and reforms: Chap. IX § 4, 22.

Modernism (M) – **Ambiguity**, tactic of M: Chap. II §§ 6f. **Concept** of the Church: Chap. IV, Note 5g. **Dogmatic teachings**, concept of: Chap. IV, Note 5d. **Encyclical** *Pascendi* gives blow to M: Chap. II § 6. **Evolution** of the natural to the supernatural: Chap. IV, Note 5f. **Faith**, concept of: Chap. IV, Note 5c. **Goal**: Desire for the reforms that were realized in the Council: Chap. IV, Note 7d-g. **Influence of Möhler** on French and English M: Chap. IV, Note 5a; Chap. VI § 6. **Neo-modernism**: General Introduction § 19. **Other influences**: Chap IV, Note 3. **Progressivism** and M: General Introduction, Note 23; Chap. IV, Notes 5b, 7c, d; Chap. VI §§ 2, 67. Modernist **pneumatology**: General Introduction § 26. Concept of interior **Revelation**: General Introduction, Note 1k. Concept of **Tradition**: Chap. IV, Note 5e.

Moral Teaching of Church – Criticisms of traditional moral teachings of the Church: Chap. X § 49, Note 24.

Natural Law – General Introduction § 7; Note 3. Example given by St. Ignatius: General Introduction § 12; Note 10.

Naturalism – Pontifical documents condemning naturalism: Chap. I, Note 14b.

Nullity of Vatican II – Conclusions § 2.

Obstestatio (oath taken with God as witness) – Texts of the *obstestatio* of St. Augustine, St. Aurelius, and the African Bishops to Pope Zozimus: General Introduction, Note 20.

Offertory – See *Mass*.

Original Sin – Omissions in conciliar texts: Chap. VIII §§ 4ff.

Our Lady's Virginity – Tendentious omissions in conciliar texts: Chap. VIII §§ 2f.

Papacy – Criticisms of papal primacy: Chap. X § 50. See *Infallibility*.

Pastoral – **Ambiguity** in the concept of: Chap. III §§ 7, 19. **Doctrinal** grounds: Chap. VI § 111-115. **Psy war tactic:** General Introduction §§ 25f. **Significance** of: Chap. VI, Note 40a. See *Council; Theological Qualifications*.

Patriarchates, Western – Conciliar tendency to diminish their importance: Chap. VIII § 19f.

Patristic – Movement toward Patristic renovation: Chap. IV, Note 3.

Peccatum Taciturnitatis (sin of being silent) – General Introduction, Note 4, 5b.

Phenomenology – Chap. VII § 5.

mention of the Protestant theory of the **two tables:** Chap. IX § 12. Promoting **social equality**: Chap. IX § 10. **Tendencies** that open the doors for abuses: Chap. IX § 20. Encouraging use of the **vernacular**: Chap. IX § 18.

SCHOLASTICISM – **Benefit** to Church: Chap. III § 2. **Praise** of Scholasticism by Pope Sixtus V: Chap III § 2. Not used in the language of **Vatican II**: Chap. III § 3. See *THOMISM.*

SENSUS FIDEI – **Link to the *sensus fidelium*:** General Introduction, Note 1c. Its **significance**: General Introduction, § 13,Note 1c, e, f.

SENSUS FIDELIUM – **Amplitude** and profundity according to progressivist authors: General Introduction, Note 1k, I. **Application** and limits: General Introduction, Note Id. **Assistance of the Holy Ghost**: General Introduction, Note If. **Authority:** General Introduction, Note 1b, f. **Concept**: General Introduction § 2; Note la-c. **Contemporary authors** who deal with the subject: General Introduction, Note 1g, k. **Criterion** for analysis of the Council: General Introduction § 2. **Example in our days**: movement and school of thought of Plinio Corrêa de Oliveira: General Introduction § 13; Notes 13, 14, 15. **Historical examples**: General Introduction, Note 1f, g, h. Importance as a testimony of the **indefectible Faith** of the Church: General Introduction, Note 1b, j. **Intellectuals who deal with the subject**: General Introduction, Note lb, d, i, j, k. Link with the **sense of the Faith**: General Introduction, Note 1c, e, f. **Similar expressions**: General Introduction, Note la-c, I, k.

SILENT MAJORITY – As a segment of public opinion: General Introduction, Note 23; Chap. X §1-8. See PUBLIC OPINION.

SMOKE OF SATAN – Metaphor used by Paul VI describing the crisis in the Church: Introduction to Volume I § 6; Chap. X § 14.

SOCIALISM – See *COMMUNISM; POLITICAL THEOLOGY.*

SOCIETY OF JESUS – Crisis in: Chap. X §§ 87-97. See *AMBIGUITY: Consequences.*

SUBSISTIT IN – Theory according to which the Church of Christ is not the Catholic Church – Chap. I § 1; Notes 1, 2, 3.

SYNTHESIS – Supposed position of impartial equilibrium between the traditional and progressivist doctrines: Chap. VI §§ 26-32.

TEMPORAL ORDER – **Reflected** in laws, customs and institutions: Chap. IX §§ 64f. As synonymous of **world**: Chap. IX § 60

THEOLOGY – **Liberation Theology**: Chap. V, Note 21, Chap. IX § 92; Chap. X §§ 38, 46. **Pastoral Theology**: Chap. VI § 115. **Political Theology**: Chap. V § 20, Note 21b; *Socialism* as sign of the times: Chap. IX §§ 94-98, Chap. X §§ 35, 39. **Scholastic Theology**: Its language: Chap. III §§ 1-3; Attacks

*   *   *

WORD INDEX

Acerbi, Antonio: 131, 137-138, 140
Ad gentes, Decree: 145
Adjubei, Alexis: 50 (n. 16b)
Aggiornamento: 117, 122, 175, 197, 200, 201, 253, 282, 295, 333, 347 (n. 172)
Agostino, Biagio d': 215
Ahlbrecht, Ansgar: 204
Alberigo, Giuseppe: 251-252, 303
Alfrink, Bernard: 111, 163, 261 (n. 66)
Allocution *Ubi primum* (Pius IX): 76
Alszeghy, Zoltán: 204
Altri, Guido d': 321
Amelunxen, Remi: 20, 229 (n. 15)
Ambiguity [in Vatican II documents]: 13, 56-58, 71-73, 75, 79, 83, 87, 89; testimonies 93-102; strategies leading to 103-104; to achieve unanimity 112-114; radical consequences of 115-122; causes clash in thought 122-126; 135, 138; in theological qualification 141-157; 151, 157; serves Progressivism 157-158; 188; underlying doctrine 191-195; 202, 206-207, 208; tendentious omissions 209-219; 217, 221; example in liturgy 229-237; generates crisis of Faith and Morals 279-280, 291, 309, 345-346, 349-350
Amerio, Romano: 13
Ancien Regime: 64 (n. 29)
Anonymous Christian: 329
Announcement to LG: 155-157
Anthropology (Christian): 198, 201
Antón, Angel: 96-97, 98, 107 (n. 7ba), 132, 254 (n. 57)
Apostolicam actuositatem, Decree: 145
Ardite, arditi: 280, 283, 284, 289, 291, 299, 302-306, 307, 309.
Arian heresy: p. 31 (n. 1g),
Arns, Evaristo: 319
Arrupe, Pedro: 327-328, 329
Augustine, St.: 29 (n. 1b), 36 (n. 2b), 37 (n. 3c), 38 (n. 3g), 53-54, 219
Aurelius, St.: 54
Author (Atila S. Guimarães): 13, 15-17, credentials 35-36, 41-48; state of mind

in writing 53, 55, 57; interview with Y. Congar 55 (n. 23), 121 (n. 20); interview with G. Caprile 115 (n. 10); interview with R. Schwager 130 (n. 18), 180; interview with M.D. Chenu 164, 196.
Auto-demolition (Church): 36 (n. 2), 73

Babeuf: 64-65 (n. 29)
Balthasar, Hans Urs von: 111, 259, 264, 265 (n. 75)
Barbier, Emmanuel: 108 (n. 7g)
Barbieri, Raffaele: 167 (n. 86e)
Basel, Council of: 142 (n. 44)
Basic Christian Communities (BBCs): 80-83 (n. 7)
Baum, Gregory: 261 (n. 66)
Bea, Augustin: 99, 111
Bellarmine, St. Robert: 38 (n. 3f), 107 (n. 7a), 123-124, 125, 126
Benedict XII: 32 (n. 1h), 212
Benedict XV: 279
Benedict XVI: *see* Ratzinger, Joseph
Benedictus Deus (Constitution): 212
Berger, W.: 323
Bergson, Henri: 104 (n. 3b)
Bernadin, Joseph: 322
Betti, Umberto: 177
Biblical Commission: 271
Bishops' Synods: 43-44, 50, 116, 117, 154, 163, 186 (n. 141b), 305, 307, 310, 316 (n. 85d), 317, 319, 321, 322, 332, 337, 338, 340, 341, 341 (n. 157b), 343, 344, see also Council of Bishops, collegiality
Blondel, Maurice: 104 (n. 3b)
Boaventure, St.: 93
Boff, Leonardo: 81-82 (n. 7d), 83 (n. 12), 302
Bolatti, G. (Argentine): 1687 (n. 86g)
Boyer, Louis: 298-299
Brandenburg, Herbertus: 322
Bugnini, Annibale: 228, 228 (n. 9)
Buonaiuti, Ernesto: 90, 91, 108 (n. 7e)
Burgalassi, Silvano: 324

*   *   *

THE COLLECTION ELI, ELI, LAMMA SABACTHANI?
by Atila Sinke Guimarães

Volume 4 - Animus Delendi I (Desire to Desrroy I)

Presents the plan of self-destruction of Holy Mother Church as designed and executed by progressivist theologians and high-ranking ecclesiastics. The authors shows that hidden behind the spirit of the Council lies a desire to destroy. *Powerful!* 502 pp. $20

Volume 5 - Animus Delendi II (Desire to Destroy II)

Know about these two important maneuvers coming from Vatican II that are misleading well-intentioned Catholics: Secularization and Ecumenism. Secularization moves toward a trans-Socialist structure to replace the State. Ecumenism heads toward a Pan-Religion. *An eye-opener!* 384 pp. $20

Volume 6 - Will He Find Faith? (Inveniet Fidem?)

Shows the systematic attack against the Catholic Faith as a fruit of the Council. Before, the Faith was objective, absolute, universal, and expressed in immutable dogmas. Now, after the Council, it has become subjective, relative, valid only for particular situations, and adaptable to history. A total inversion made in our Holy Faith. *A must read!* 384 pp. $20

SPECIAL EDITIONS TO THE COLLECTION

Quo Vadis, Petre?
(Where are you going, Peter?)

Analyzes the events of the Millennium under the light of perennial Catholic Doctrine. A clear and lucid refutation of Ecumenism. *Crucial.* 108 pp. $8

Previews of the New Papacy

More than 500 photos present an objective overview of the changes being made to transform the Papacy and the Church. *A blockbuster!* 285 pp. $15

Vatican II, Homosexuality & Pedophilia
(former Appendix to *In the Murky Waters of Vatican II*)

Denounces the present-day Vatican as an accomplice in the scandal of homosexuality and pedophilia in the Church, and raises serious suspicions about Paul VI. Also shows how Vatican II opened the doors to this immorality flooding the Church. *Courageous, frank, thorough.* 315 pp. $18

TRADITION IN ACTION, INC.
PO Box 23135 * Los Angeles, CA 90023
Phone: 323-725-0219 Fax: 323-725-0019
Order online at www.TraditionInAction.org